DAVID'S MIGHTY MEN

DAVID'S MIGHTY MEN

A Portrait of the Christ

Barry Blackstone

RESOURCE *Publications* · Eugene, Oregon

DAVID'S MIGHTY MEN
A Portrait of the Christ

Copyright © 2026 Barry Blackstone. All rights reserved. Except for brief quotations in critical publications or reviews, no part of this book may be reproduced in any manner without prior written permission from the publisher. Write: Permissions, Wipf and Stock Publishers, 199 W. 8th Ave., Suite 3, Eugene, OR 97401.

Resource Publications
An Imprint of Wipf and Stock Publishers
199 W. 8th Ave., Suite 3
Eugene, OR 97401

www.wipfandstock.com

PAPERBACK ISBN: 979-8-3852-6084-3
HARDCOVER ISBN: 979-8-3852-6085-0
EBOOK ISBN: 979-8-3852-6086-7

OTHER BOOKS BY THE AUTHOR:

Though None Go With Me
Rendezvous In Paris
Though One Go With Me
Scotland Journey
The Region Beyond
Enlarge My Coast
From Dan to Beersheba and Beyond
The Uttermost Part
Homestead Homilies
Rover: A Boy's Best Friend
North to Alaska and Back
Another Day in Nazareth
Sermonettes from the Seashore
Earth's Farthest Bounds
Angling Admonitions
Beyond the Bend
Expendable
Meows from the Manse
At a Moment's Notice
Reaching the Unreached
Satan's Super Soldiers
Threescore and Ten
Won by One

I dedicate this book to the "mighty men" who helped me reach the position I did as a soldier of Jesus Christ. I will only mention a few here: Carroll, Wendell, and Bob Blackstone, Tony Miller, Ken Robbins, Mike Hangge, Shibu and Shagu Simon, and Calvin Greenlaw.

Contents

Acknowledgement xiii

Prelude: The Mighty Man of the Mighty Men xv

1. Joab: Jehovah is Father (I Chronicles 11:6) 1
2. Adino: Ornament (II Samuel 23:8) 5
3. Eleazar: God has Aided (I Chronicles 11:13) 9
4. Shammah: Renown (II Samuel 23:12) 13
5. Abishai: Source of Wealth (I Chronicles 18:12) 17
6. Benaiah: Whom Jehovah has Built Up (II Samuel 23:20) 21
7. Asahel: God has Made (I Chronicles 11:26) 25
8. Elhanan: God is Gracious (II Samuel 23:24) 29
9. Shammoth: Fame (I Chronicles 11:27) 33
10. Helez: Strength (I Chronicles 11:27) 37
11. Elika: God is Rejecter (II Samuel 23:25) 41
12. Ira: Watcher (II Samuel 23:26) 45
13. Abiezer: Father of Help (I Chronicles 27:12) 49
14. Mebunnai: Built Up (II Samuel 23:27) 53
15. Zalmon: Ascent (II Samuel 27:28) 57
16. Maharai: Swift (I Chronicles 27:13) 61
17. Heldai: Enduring (I Chronicles 27:15) 65
18. Jonathan: The Lord has Given (II Samuel 21:21) 69
19. Elhanan: God is Gracious (II Samuel 21:19) 73
20. Ittai: Existing (II Samuel 18:2) 77

CONTENTS

21. Ithai: Living (I Chronicles 11:31) 81
22. Benaiah: Whom Jehovah has Built Up (I Chronicles 27:14) 85
23. Hiddai: Mighty, Chief (II Samuel 23:30) 89
24. Abiel: My Father is God (I Chronicles 11:32) 93
25. Azmaveth: Counsel (II Samuel 23:31) 97
26. Eliahba: Hidden of God (I Chronicles 11:33) 101
27. Jonathan: Jehovah is Given (II Samuel 23:32) 105
28. Sons of Hashem: Shining (I Chronicles 11:34) 109
29. Shammah: Renown (II Samuel 23:33) 113
30. Ahiam: A Mother's Brother (I Chronicles 11:35) 117
31. Eliphal: God is Judge (I Chronicles 11:35) 121
32. Eliphelet: God is Deliverance (II Samuel 23:34) 125
33. Eliam: People's God (II Samuel 23:34) 129
34. Hepher: A Well (I Chronicles 11:36) 133
35. Ahijah: The Lord is Brother (I Chronicles 11:36) 137
36. Hezrai: Beautiful (II Samuel 23:35) 141
37. Naarai: Pleasantness of Jehovah (I Chronicles 11:37) 145
38. Joel: Jehovah is God (I Chronicles 11:38) 149
39. Mibhar: Choice, Youth (I Chronicles 11:38) 153
40. Bani: Posterity (II Samuel 23:36) 157
41. Zelek: Split, or Rent (I Chronicles 11:39) 161
42. Naharai: Snorting One (II Samuel 23:37) 165
43. Ira: Watcher (I Chronicles 11:40) 169
44. Gareb: Despiser (II Samuel 23:38) 173
45. Uriah: Jehovah is Light (II Samuel 23:39) 177
46. Zabad: Endower (I Chronicles 11:41) 181
47. Adina: The Ornament of God (I Chronicles 11:42) 185
48. Hanan: Merciful (I Chronicles 11:43) 189
49. Joshaphat: God has Judged (I Chronicles 11:43) 193
50. Uzzia: Jehovah is Strong (I Chronicles 11:44) 197

CONTENTS

51. Shama: Obedient (I Chronicles 11:44) 201

52. Jehiel: God is Living (I Chronicles 11:44) 205

53. Jediael: God Knows (I Chronicles 11:45) 209

54. Joha: Jehovah is Living (I Chronicles 11:45) 213

55. Eliel: My God is God (I Chronicles 11:46) 217

56. Jeribai: Jehovah Contends (I Chronicles 11:46) 221

57. Joshaviah: Jehovah is Equality (I Chronicles 11:46) 225

58. Ithman: Purity (I Chronicles 11:46) 229

59. Eliel: My God is God (I Chronicles 11:47) 233

60. Obed: Servant (I Chronicles 11:47) 237

61. Jasiel: God is Maker (I Chronicles 11:47) 241

62. Ahiezer: Helping Brother (I Chronicles 12:3) 245

63. Joash: Jehovah Supports (I Chronicles 12:3) 249

64. Jeziel: God Gathers (I Chronicles 12:3) 253

65. Pelet: Escape (I Chronicles 12:3) 257

66. Berachah: Blessing (I Chronicles 12:3) 261

67. Jehu: The Lord is He (I Chronicles 12:3) 265

68. Ismaiah: The Lord Hears (I Chronicles 12:4) 269

69. Jeremiah: Jehovah is High (I Chronicles 12:4) 273

70. Jahaziel: God Reveals (I Chronicles 12:4) 277

71. Johanan: The Lord is Gracious (I Chronicles 12:4) 281

72. Josabad: The Lord has Bestowed (I Chronicles 12:4) 285

73. Eluzai: God is My Strength (I Chronicles 12:5) 288

74. Jerimoth: Elevation (I Chronicles 12:5) 292

75. Bealiah: The Lord is Lord (I Chronicles 12:5) 296

76. Shemariah: Jehovah Guards (I Chronicles 12:5) 300

77. Shephatiah: The Lord is Judge (I Chronicles 12:5) 304

78. Elkanah: God is Possessing (I Chronicles 12:6) 308

79. Jesiah: Jehovah Exists (Chronicles 12:6) 312

80. Azareel: God is Helper (I Chronicles 12:6) 316

CONTENTS

81. Joezer: Jehovah is Help (I Chronicles 12:6) 320

82. Jashobeam: To Whom the People Turn (I Chronicles 12:6) 324

83. Joelah: God is Snatching (I Chronicles 12:7) 328

84. Zebadiah: Jehovah is Endower (I Chronicles 12:7) 332

85. Ezer: Help (I Chronicles 12:9) 336

86. Obadiah: Servant of God (I Chronicles 12:9) 340

87. Eliab: God is Father (I Chronicles 12:10) 344

88. Mishmannah: Fatness (I Chronicles 12:10) 348

89. Jeremiah: The Lord is Exalted (I Chronicles 12:10) 352

90. Attai: Timely (I Chronicles 12:11) 356

91. Eliel: My God is God (I Chronicles 12:11) 360

92. Johanan: Jehovah is Gracious (I Chronicles 12:12) 364

93. Elzabad: God has Given (I Chronicles 12:12) 368

94. Jeremiah: The Lord Establishes (I Chronicles 12:13) 372

95. Machbanai: Clad with a Cloak (I Chronicles 12:13) 376

96. Amasai: Burden-Bearer (I Chronicles 12:18) 380

97. Adnah: Pleasure (I Chronicles 12:20) 384

98. Jozabad: Jehovah Endows (I Chronicles 12:20) 388

99. Jediael: God Knows (I Chronicles 12:20) 392

100. Michael: Who is like God? (I Chronicles 12:20) 396

101. Jozabad: The Lord has Bestowed (I Chronicles 12:20) 400

102. Elihu: God Himself (I Chronicles 12:20) 404

103. Zilthai: Shadow (I Chronicles 12:20) 408

104. Jehoiada: The Lord Knows (I Chronicles 12:27) 412

105. Zadok: Righteous (I Chronicles 12:28) 416

POSTLUDE: The Mighty Men of the Mighty Man 421

Acknowledgement

I WOULD NOT HAVE gotten this book project finished if not for the editing and compiling by my friend and sister-in-Christ, Rosemary Campbell. I would like to thank her for the numerous hours and many days she spent reading and correcting the errors in the original script. Thanks again Rosemary for all your work; may you share in the eternal rewards of this book.

PRELUDE:
The Mighty Man of the Mighty Men

FOR YEARS (1998–2017), I have been anticipating writing this devotional book on the subject of David's mighty men (II Samuel 23:8). The reason I delayed its construction was a scriptural answer to my prayer to the Lord as to when I should compile my research. While studying for a series of messages on the famous Hebrew King David, the Lord spoke to me through this verse in the First Book of the Chronicles: ***"Among the Hebronites was Jerijah the chief, even among the Hebronites, according to the generations of his fathers. In the fortieth year of the reign of David they were sought for, and there were found among them mighty men of valour at Jazer of Gilead."*** (I Chronicles 26:31) To most this is an isolated verse from a meaningless text, but for me it spoke volumes of God's will for me in connection to the collecting and writing of this book. Little did I know that it would take so long to finish the book for publishing?

The verse not only spoke of David's mighty men, my subject matter, but it gave a chronological time, the 40th year of David's rule. Interestingly, this was also David's last year ruling and reigning over Israel (II Samuel 5:4). Once again meaningless to most, but to me, as I was nearing the fortieth year of my faith (I was born again in 1958); I felt the Lord was saying to me: **"In your fortieth year you will write of David's mighty men!"** I don't know if this is the first day of my last year or not (it wasn't as I am re-editing this book for publication in 2025), but on the first day of the year 1998 I began sharing what and who I have discovered to be David's mighty men by sharing "the man behind the men" (I Chronicles 10:11) before I share with you "the men behind the man" (I Chronicles 11:10). It is only fitting that we would introduce this series of devotionals by giving a short account of the mighty man who made these mighty men mighty.

PRELUDE: THE MIGHTY MAN OF THE MIGHTY MEN

For your own study of the personality behind the man David, I would share with you an outline of David's life gleaned from the Biblical chapters concerning David. (Did you know that there are at 59 chapters in the Holy Word that speak about David and that doesn't include the numerous psalms from David's own hand? Over the years I have compiled a series of handouts and PowerPoint's on each of those chapters, and have corresponded them with one of David's psalms). This is my broad outline of David:

1. The Character of David (Ruth 4:22) Jesse's Son; Jesus' Similitude.
2. The Call of David (I Samuel 16:1–13) Man Appoints; God Anoints.
3. The Choosing of David (I Samuel 16:14–23) Saul's Mood; David's Music.
4. The Courage of David (I Samuel 17:1–58) Goliath's Sword. David's Sling.
5. The Change of David (I Samuel 18:1–16) David's Fame; Saul's Fury.
6. The Contempt of David (I Samuel 18:17–19, 24) Saul's Fear; David's Flight.
7. The Covenant of David (I Samuel 20:1–42) Jonathan's Covenant; David's Course.
8. The Companions of David (I Samuel 21, 22, 23) David's Soldiers. God's Seers.
9. The Conquests of David (I Samuel 23:1; I Chronicles 19:17) David's Battlefields; God's Battles.
10. The Chasing of David (I Samuel 23:7–29) Saul's Pursuits; David's Protection.
11. The Compassion of David (I Samuel 24:1–22) Saul's Vulnerability; David's Virtue.
12. The Concubine of David (I Samuel 25:1–44) Abigail's Wisdom; David's Wife.
13. The Crisis of David (I Samuel 26:1–18, 25) David's Depression; God's Deliverance.
14. The Correction of David (I Samuel 29:1–30; 31) David's Sin; God's Sovereignty.

PRELUDE: THE MIGHTY MAN OF THE MIGHTY MEN

15. The Crying of David (II Samuel 1:1–27) Saul's Slaying; David's Song.
16. The Crowning of David (II Samuel 2:1–5; 25) Saul's Thorn; David's Throne.
17. The Cart of David (II Samuel 6:1–23) God's Way; David's Will.
18. The Compact of David (II Samuel 7:1–8; 18) God's Promises; David's Posterity.
19. The Courtesy of David (II Samuel 9:1–10; 19) David's Love; Mephibosheth's Lameness.
20. The Craving of David (II Samuel 11:1–26) David's Lies; Uriah's Loyalty.
21. The Confession of David (II Samuel 11:27–12:14) David's Problem; Nathan's Parable.
22. The Consequences of David (II Samuel 12:15–15:12) David's Faults; David's Family.
23. The Cursing of David (II Samuel 15:13–19; 43) David's Character; Shimei's Curse.
24. The Cost of David (II Samuel 20:1–21; 22) David's Troubles; God's Test.
25. The Chorus of David (II Samuel 22:1–23:7; Psalms 1–72) David's Sorrows; David's Songs.
26. The Champions of David (II Samuel 23:8–39) David's Champions; God's Conquests.
27. The Catching of David (II Samuel 24:1–25) Satan's Thoughts; David's Temptation.
28. The Concluding of David (I Kings 1:1–10) David's Ending; Solomon's Exalted.
29. The Christ-likeness of David (Acts 13:22 and Revelation 22:16) Jesus' Body; David's Bio.

David was not only God's man, but a man's man as well. David had CHARISMA. A charismatic individual is "one who has a special divine endowment, an attractive personality with power." David had charisma physically (I Samuel 16:12). He was a "hunk," a "babe," a "ten," handsome and physically attractive. His outward appearance automatically drew

PRELUDE: THE MIGHTY MAN OF THE MIGHTY MEN

people to him. David also had a charismatic personally (I Samuel 18:1). People of all ranks and nationalities were drawn to his character, and he got instant loyalty from those who became his companions, friend or foe. David also had charisma publically (I Samuel 18:6). Not just individuals but groups of people and nations were drawn to him. He filled a void in the heart of the leaderless multitudes. Masses flocked to his side. He was a teenage star, a young folk hero, a middle-aged idol, and a legend in his own time. Is it any wonder that he drew around him a group called *"the mighty men?"*

David had COURAGE. It is one thing to have charisma, but add bravery and daring, and you now have a real hero. Though David wasn't a giant physically, he was a giant on the battlefield and in just about any other arena where courage was needed. Like Lord Nelson, the great English admiral, David brought the best out in his soldiers. His men would follow him into the heat of battle without a thought. David gained this respect by fighting side by side with his men, and they knew he would not ask them to go anywhere he himself would not go. They also knew that David would lead them to victory (Did you know David never lost a battle?). Whether alone with the bear and the lion (I Samuel 17:34–35), in the eye of the storm fighting the local bully (I Samuel 17:45–46), or fighting countless battles with his mighty men (I Chronicles 19:17), David always showed himself to be a courageously brave leader, and so did his men!

David was CREATIVE. A saying goes: *"In a group of giants, only a titan stands out!"* David was one of those rare men in history that seemed to have everything going for him; a multi-talented individual that had the touch of gold in his fingers. David wasn't just good at one job, in one area of life; he was good at everything he touched. As we study David's mighty men, we will discover that David gathered around him an exceptional group of highly skilled and talented men, yet he excelled above them all. David was a faithful shepherd (I Samuel 16:11). David was a fabulous soldier (I Samuel 17:49). David was famous on a stringed instrument (I Samuel 16:18). David was a fantastic song writer (II Samuel 23:1). David was a fine sovereign (II Samuel 2:4). David was creative with his harp, when in the heat of battle, with words and music, and in government. It is not surprising his mighty men would show sure creative style.

There will always be a debate which is more important, the leader or those he leads. Could David have gained the kingdom without them? Would these men have become mighty men without him? I will let Holy

PRELUDE: THE MIGHTY MAN OF THE MIGHTY MEN

Writ settle these questions: *"These also are the chief of the mighty men whom David had, who strengthened themselves with him in the kingdom, and with all Israel, to make him king, according to the Word of the Lord concerning Israel."* (I Chronicles 10:10) David was famous before the advent of the mighty men, but to become the next king of Israel David needed some broad shoulders to ride on. Even *"the best of men are men at best,"* and David was one of the best, yet even the best need someone, or a group of some ones, to help them to their final goal. David was known for his integrity (Psalm 78:72), and it took that integrity to bring the best out of the worst (I Samuel 22:2). Let us just say, it took the man of the mighty men and the men of the mighty man to accomplish God's mission; they needed each other.

It is not my purpose to make this tracing of David's mighty men just a historical exercise because in my study of David's amazing men I discovered a wonderful parallel between David's mighty men and Christ's mighty men and women. As David was the captain of these mighty men (I Samuel 22:2), Jesus Christ is our Captain (Hebrews 2:10), and we are His soldiers (II Timothy 2:3–4). Spiritual warfare is clearly taught in Scripture (Ephesians 6:10–18), and we are challenged to fight a good fight (I Timothy 6:12) and war a good warfare (I Timothy 1:18). The only question is whether or not we are one of Christ's mighty men. Another great hymn writer, Isaac Watts, once asked an interesting question in his classic hymn, Am I A Soldier Of The Cross?

> Am I a soldier of the Cross?
> A follower of the Lamb?
> And shall I fear to own His cause?
> Or blush to speak His name?
>
> Must I be carried to the skies?
> On flowery beds of ease?
> While others fought to win the prize
> And sail through bloody seas?
>
> Are there no foes for me to face?
> Must I not stem the flood?
> Is this vile world a friend to grace?
> To help me on to God?

In answer to his own questions, Isaac Watts gives the answer, not only for himself but for every believer:

PRELUDE: THE MIGHTY MAN OF THE MIGHTY MEN

Sure I must fight if I would reign,
Increase my courage Lord!
I'll bare the toll; endure the pain,
Supported by Thy Word.

As David and his mighty men fought to gain the Israeli kingdom, so we must fight to rule and reign with Christ (Revelation 1:6, 20:4). The making of a mighty man doesn't happen overnight as we will see, but for those who follow after a mighty man, a mighty man they will eventually become (Romans 8:29). I like the way the Apostle Paul put it to the Corinthians: *"Be ye followers of me, even as I am of Christ."* (I Corinthians 11:1) David was a mighty man after God's own heart (Acts 13:22) and, as we will see, so were his "mighty men," and what was true of David and his mighty men ought to be true of Christ and his Christians (I John 2:6). My prayer is that this Old Testament journey will bring you to a place where you, too, will be known as a mighty man or woman for Christ in a New Testament context and will bravely wage a mighty fight against God's enemies, your adversaries, and the Church's foes!

Barry Blackstone
January 1, 1998

1.

JOAB: JEHOVAH IS FATHER

I Chronicles 11:6: *"And David said, Whosoever smiteth the Jebusites first shall be chief and captain. So **JOAB** the son of Zeruiah went up first, and was chief."*

When you begin a study of David's Mighty Men, you have to start with Joab. Joab attained this lofty position as number one on David's list of "the elite of the elite" by his extraordinary bravery and ingenuity at the Battle of Jebus, better known as Jerusalem (I Chronicles 11:4). The Jebusites had turned Jerusalem into what they thought was an impregnable fortress, an invincible city. They were so confident that David and his men couldn't capture the bastion, they taunted them from the battlements and bulwarks that the blind of the city and the lame of the town could resist any assault they threw at them (II Samuel 5:6) so David challenged his soldiers with the instruction printed above. This is what the chronicler records next: *"So Joab the son of Zeruiah* (David's sister) *went up first, and was chief and David dwelt in the castle; therefore they called it the city of David."* (I Chronicles 11:7) Joab captured Jerusalem with a daring strike through what has become known as Warren's Shaft (named after the explorer that first discovered it in the modern world and I got to see in 2010). David knew of the strength of the walls and the difficulty of the terrain surrounding the city, but seemingly David also knew of its "Achilles' heel." On that day David said, *"Anyone who conquers the Jebusites will have to use the water shaft to reach those lame and blind"* (II Samuel 5:8 NIV). The water shaft was a tunnel through which water entered the city.

Perhaps, the Jebusites didn't know that David knew of it, but certainly it was through that tunnel Joab gained entrance into the city, surprising the inhabitants and capturing their impregnable fortress and the top job in David's ever expanding army.

"And the general of the king's army was Joab." (I Chronicles 27:34) This would be equal to the post of Commander of the Joint Chief of Staff in our American army today, a position highly sought after in military circles and very difficult to attain. Few men are successful at such a level, but Joab was and would attain that position until after David's death. He might have been the nephew of the King (I Chronicles 2:15-16), but Joab had earned the job on the battlefield, not in the board room. Joab would become a ruthless leader and a man who coveted his position above anything else. Loyal and professional, Joab, however, overstepped his authority on a number of occasions ending his brilliant career in disgrace and dishonor. There were many signs throughout Job's life that warned of such an end and God's universal precept of *"be not deceived: God is not mocked, for whatsoever a man soweth that shall he also reaps"* (Galatians 6:7) is clearly illustrated in the life of Joab. We will discover in our study of David's Mighty men that they are shared in the Bible with us as good examples, but also as sobering warnings. Joab is a warning!!

The first seed planted by Joab was the murder of Abner, the general of Saul's defeated army after King Saul's death at the Battle of Gilboa (I Samuel 31). Abner had come to surrender after a long civil war, but because Abner had killed Joab's brother in one of those battles in that long civil war (II Samuel 3:1), Joab sought revenge instead of leaving it with God (Romans 12:19). *"And afterward when David heard it he said, I and my kingdom are guiltless before the Lord forever from the blood of Abner..."* (II Samuel 3:28). Personal vengeance is a bitter seed that can only reap misery to the sower. I have come to believe that the murder of Abner was not only for revenge, but to eliminate a possible rival to his position in David's army. Selfishness is sometimes disguised as revenge. Read the story in II Samuel 3:12-39 and decide for yourself.

The second seed planted by Joab was his assisting David in the murder of Uriah, the husband of Bathsheba. Joab arranged to have Uriah killed in battle so David could cover up his adultery (II Samuel 11:14-17). Loyalty must stop when it oversteps its bounds into a transgression. If a man knowingly is ordered to commit a gross sin, like murder, he must obey the higher command, even if that command comes from a King David. When Peter and John were ordered not to preach the Gospel by the

Sanhedrin, they replied: *"We ought to obey God rather than man."* (Acts 5:19) This should have been Joab's reply to David because Exodus 20:13 was a higher command than David's order. But once again in allowing his personal ambition to get in the way of what was morally right, it might have even cost him his job, he went along in the murder of an innocent man; interestingly enough, one of David's Mighty Men (II Samuel 23:39). Personal ambition is another dangerous seed to sow. It will often reap disaster as we will see in the life of Joab.

The third seed planted by Joab was the murder of Absalom. Absalom was the charismatic son of David who had led a very successful revolt against his father. Despite David's order not to kill the rebellious prince, Joab murdered him as he hung helplessly from the branches of an oak tree (II Samuel 18:9–17). What is interesting about this story is that Joab had once been the ally of Absalom (II Samuel 14:28–33). Wrong alliances are often responsible for the sowing of seeds in darkness (remember, only the devil and those who follow him do that, Matthew 13:25, 39) that when reaped in the light bring great embarrassment to the planter. I believe that was Joab's fate when in the end what he had done in secret would be revealed in the open. So with him, so with us!

The fourth seed planted by Joab was the murder of Amasa. By this time in Joab's career, he had slipped from the favor of David because of his former atrocities. Joab was being replaced as David's top general with a man that was *"...more righteous and better than he."* (I Kings 2:32) However, during the revolt of Sheba, Joab was asked to return and help Amasa put down the rebellion. Joab instead used the opportunity to murder his rival. In cold blood Joab killed Amasa (II Samuel 20:13) and then went on to crush the Sheba uprising. (Nobody ever said that Joab was not good at his job.) The seed of jealousy should never be sown because it produces a very bitter fruit.

Seed produces in kind so there was only one way Joab could meet his end. When David was on his death bed and his sons were jockeying to replace him, Joab backed the wrong son, Adonijah. So Solomon, the new king, took no chances lest this powerful man became a thorn in his side as he had been in his father's side and had Joab murdered under the advice of his father (I Kings 2:5–6). The murderer was murdered (I Kings 2:28–35). The tragedy of Joab's story is he never lived up to his name, Jehovah is Father. He lived his life for Joab and not for Jehovah. He might have been David No. 1 Mighty Man, but he wasn't even on God's honorable mention list because of his behavior. Joab is an example of what not to be even if you are number one. I am convinced Joab was playing for the other side. Joab's father gave him a good name, but Joab seemingly switched teams, and somewhere along the line Joab changed "gods" and instead of Jehovah being his Father, Satan became his father!

John 8:44: *"Ye are of your father the devil, and the lust of your father ye will do. He was a murderer from the beginning…"*

2.

ADINO: ORNAMENT

II Samuel 23:8: "These be the names of the mighty men whom David had: the Tachmonite that sat in the seat, chief among the captains; the same was **ADINO** *the Eznite: he lifted up his spear against eight hundred, whom he slew at one time."*

The exploits of Adino are only recorded in two similar Bible verses: Second Samuel 23:8 and First Chronicles 11:11. Each of these verses record basically the same event but with different details. Both verses are also in the context of David's numbering his greatest soldiers, his amazing warriors, his "mighty men." It would be like the honor roll of our nation's Congressional Medal of Honor winners, our country's highest award for bravery on the battlefield. In the Samuel account the first name after Joab on that list of 37 names was Adino, or Jashobeam. I have come to believe that placement on any Biblical list reveals importance, even if we don't know what importance. Twice in Second Samuel 23 it says: *"He was more honorable than the thirty, but he attained not to the first three,"* speaking of Abishai in verse 19 and Benaiah in verse 23. The three spoken of in these verses were Adino, Eleazar, and Shammah, yet the greatest of these was Adino. Like when Paul wrote: *"And now abideth faith, hope, and charity, these three; but the greatest of these is charity."* (I Corinthians 13:13) Adino attained in David's mind the greatest recognition in a standing army of 1,300,000 (II Samuel 24:9)!

All we know about Adino is that he was first the son of a man named Zabdiel, a Harchmonite, and that he would eventually command David's leading division of warriors (I Chronicles 27:2). He seemingly attained this honorable position because of all the acts of bravery performed while under David's direct control and the times his King saw his courage. Adino's mightiest deed was judged by David as the greatest single feat accomplished by any of his faithful soldiers. I believe David himself witnessed this extraordinary event on an unnamed battlefield during one of the countless wars David and his men fought in over forty years. And what a feat it was! It is described through the pen of David with these simple words: *"He raised his spear against* **eight hundred men**, *whom he killed in one encounter."* (II Samuel 23:8) No other soldier in David's massive army ever came close to this unbelievable exploit. For this act Adino was made chief of the mighty three. Next to Samson's killing one thousand Philistines with a jawbone of an ass in a single battle (Judges 15:15), Adino's slaughter of 800 enemy soldiers with his spear goes down as the second greatest military act of heroism recorded in the Bible.

There are those who would refute the numbers, as they do the story of Jonah, but *"with God all things are possible."* (Luke 1:37) Even though it isn't mentioned in direct context with Adino, it is mentioned in the postscripts of the other two mighty men and their amazing victories, *"And the Lord wrought a great victory."* (II Samuel 23:10, 23) What was true of the others was true with Adino, and as Paul asked: *"If God be for us, who can be against us?"* (Romans 8:31) Through Joshua God had promised the children of Israel that if they remained faithful to Him, *"One man of you shall chase a thousand, for the Lord your God He it is that fighteth for you as He hath promised you."* (Joshua 23:10) Moses would write in the 91st Psalm: *"A thousand shall fall at thy side…I will be with him in trouble, I will deliver him and honor him."* (Psalm 91:7, 15) When it is 800 to 1 you are in trouble, but you are well within the limits prescribed by God's promise. I believe Adino was victorious because He had God on his side, and so will we. As David wrote of these men and their extraordinary exploits, he always made sure his God got the ultimate credit, as should we, because without Him we can do nothing (John 15:5).

Military history is full of heroes like Adino. Some of my favorites are King Leonidas and his bodyguard of 300 Spartans who refused to surrender and died to the man at the Thermopylae Pass in 480 BC resisting the invasion of the Persians. Then there was Major General James Wolfe of the British Army who died bravely while winning Quebec for the English on the Plains of Abraham in 1759. Our own American heroes could be mentioned like Lt. Col. William B. Travis, James Bowie, and Colonel David Crockett as they defended the Alamo against Santa Anna's thousands in 1836. What about my own Joshua Chamberlain from Maine who at the Battle of the Little Round Top secured the Union right in 1863? Or what of George Custer at the Little Big Horn, and so many more! Heroes all, but what of other heroes, the heroes of faith, who fought not on a military battlefield but on countless spiritual battlefields around the world; ornaments of bravery every one. Bravery comes in many forms and courage in many ways.

    I speak of the heroic soul of a personal favorite, Hudson Taylor, who took on China's inland millions almost singlehandedly. I speak of another favorite, Mary Slessor, and her mighty victories for God in Calabar, West Africa. Or what of Amy Carmichael and her exploits on the battlefields of India. Then in my own time I could speak of Jim Elliot, Pete Fleming, Rogar Youderian, Ed McCully, and Nate Saint and their fight to the death in the jungles of Ecuador against the stone-age Auca warriors. I speak of Corrie Ten Boom, my daughter Marine's favorite hero, and her family and their willingness to fight a fight that was not their own. I speak of Livingstone and Studd in the historic wars of darkest Africa. I speak of Moody and Spurgeon and the great warfare in England and Scotland in the 19th century. Time would fail me to mention Luther, Wesley, Finney, Sunday, and Jones. These were the great heroes who fought bravely in many a battle and came out like Adino, a victor, a winner, a hero of the faith.

    How are you in battle? Will it be said of you, *"He was mighty in battle?"* Paul said to the young preacher Timothy that he *"...mightest wage a good warfare..."* (I Timothy 1:18), and that he would *"...fight a good fight of faith..."* (I Timothy 6:12,) and that he would *"...endure hardness as a good soldier of Jesus Christ."* (II Timothy 2:3) I know at times it seems that we are outmatched, outnumbered, or outclassed, yet it might be at just such a time we are called on to accomplish the impossible, the one memorable act of our lives, the only victory we will be remembered for. Maybe it will be this week or this day. Are we ready to let God use us to win a great fight? Perhaps the words of John Monsell might inspire us: "Fight the good fight with all thy might. Christ is thy strength and Christ thy right. Lay hold on life and it shall be, thy joy and crown eternally." Let us get back into the fight; let us become an ornament of bravery around the neck of our Champion, the Lord Jesus Christ. We are living in a day when we need again a spiritual hero; someone that is brave in the fight even if he must take on the 800 skeptics, the 800 critics, the 800 atheists that confront him. God never promised us that we would be in the majority, but He did promise us that we could take on the majority and win. I don't know when Adino joined David's band, but I do know when David was writing his memoirs of his mighty men he remembered a time when he watched one of his men win over 800!

II Timothy 2:4: *"No man that warreth entangled himself with the affairs of this life; that he may please him who hath chosen him to be a soldier."*

3.

ELEAZAR: GOD HAS AIDED

I Chronicles 11:13: *"He (ELEAZAR) was with David at Pas-Dammam, and there the Philistines were gathered together to battle, where was a parcel of ground full of barley; and the people fled from before the Philistines."*

PAUL WROTE YEARS AFTER Eleazar this inspiring instruction: *"And take… the sword of the Spirit which is the Word of God."* (Ephesians 6:17) David only records one feat of Eleazar, but what an exploit. It was a day of battle and the archenemies of the Jews, the Philistines, were pressing hard the army of David to the point they were in retreat or in full flight (II Samuel 23:9). As the rest of David's men scurried for safety, David and Eleazar stood together to fight on. How many Eleazar and David fought, how long they fought, is not recorded, but what David remembered best was as the struggle dragged on and they grew tired the sword of Eleazar never left his hand *"…till his hand grew tired and froze to the sword."* (I Samuel 23:10) A saying I heard many years ago has helped me understand this fight: **"Weary in the battle, but never weary of the battle!"** It is never wrong to get weary or tired in the spiritual struggle of the Christian life because even our Lord got weary. But like Eleazar, we must never let down our sword. In the great wilderness battle between the Lord and the devil, Jesus was hungry but the sword was unsheathed and ready to strike (Matthew 4:4). Jesus was taken to the temple and then to a mountain, but in both cases the sword was in Christ's hand, and He used it affectively against Satan's attacks (Matthew 4:7, 10). Like Eleazar, Jesus never let go of the sword, and I believe the promise is clear that God will aid those who hold the sword of the Word of God.

This is the danger of Biblical illiteracy. A dull sword, a drooping sword, or a dropped sword will never defend you properly. Eleazar knew the minute he let go of the sword on the Battlefield of Pas-Dammim, he was finished and so was his king. Like Eleazar, we, too, must wheel the sword until it becomes an extension of our lives. The Psalmist asks: *"How can a young man keep his way pure?"* (Psalm 119:9 NIV) The Psalmist's answer: *"By living according to your Word. I have hidden your Word in my heart that I might not sin against you."* (Psalm 119:9, 11 NIV) The sword is no use in battle in the sheath or on the shelf. It must be in the hand or in the heart. It will do you no good until it is "cleaved" to. Are you ready at a moment's notice to use the "Sword of the Word of God?" Or do you stumble and search for the right verse or the right illustration to share and, before you finally find it your enemy has already defeated your argument. Eleazar was a "cleaver." When he needed to defend his king and his own life in the most important battle of his career, he was ready to hang on, hold on, until the battle was won, and his king never forgot what he did that day in the barley field. Note the doctrine of "**cleaving:**"

1. **Eleazar first clave to his savior, David.** He was with David at Pas-Dammim in a time of battle. We don't know exactly when Eleazar joined David army, but when David needed him most, when all others had forsaken him, Eleazar was there. David's fights were Eleazar's fights. Bible scholars tell me that Pas-Dammim is the same as Ephesdammim (I Samuel 17:1), the place where David first fought the Philistines and their champion, Goliath. As with Eleazar, we, too, must march with our Savior, the Lord Jesus Christ and fight in His battles (I Timothy 6:12). Too many Christians today are not cleaving to their Commander (Hebrews 2:10) as Eleazar did. I love the words of this grand old Church hymn: "Down in the valley with my Saviour I would go where the storms are sweeping and the dark waters flow. With His hand to lead me I will never, never fear. Danger cannot fright me if my Lord is near." One of the first doctrines Barnabas taught the young saints at Antioch was **"...that with purpose of heart they would cleave unto the Lord."** (Acts 11:23) This Greek word for "cleave" is "abide." Jesus taught: *"Abide in me, and I in you, as the branch cannot bear fruit of itself, except it abide in the vine, no more can ye, except ye abide in me."* (John 15:4–5) Are you

still cleaving to your Commander like Eleazar cleaved to David in the midst of a tough battle?

2. **Eleazar clave to his stand, the barley field in Pas-Dammim.** Everybody else fled, but Eleazar stood his ground (I picture Eleazar back to back with David as Jonathan and his armor bearer did at the Battle of Bozez Ridge in I Samuel 14:4–14). One of the most famous battles in US history was not one of our bloodiest, or biggest, but it would become one of the best known because it was a "last stand." General George Custer and his men took a stand on a small ridge in Sioux Country on the banks of the Little Big Horn River. Like Eleazar's field of barley, this, too, was a simple field with little protection against the onslaught of a gathering of a number of Indian nations. Custer and his men all died in their stand, but David and Eleazar survived to tell how they did it. The bean (II Samuel 23:9) or barley field (I Chronicles 11:13) was unimportant. It was the courageous stand, the defiant resistance, the brave defense that counted. Paul would challenge the saints at Ephesus with these words: *"Wherefore take unto you the whole amour of God that ye may be able to WITHSTAND in the evil day, and having done all to STAND. STAND therefore…"* (Ephesians 6:13–14). We, too, at times need to take a stand against the armies of the aliens (Hebrews 11:34) that are marching across the land. **Ours is not to choose the battlefield, but to battle on any field of their choosing!**

3. **Eleazar clave to his sword on the day of battle.** The struggle was so intense that the muscles and the tendons of Eleazar's hand literally froze in the grip of his sword. His hand and his sword had become one. So, too, should the Word of God become one with us. We should not be known aside from the Word of God. When we talk or act, the people that hear us and see us should see and hear the Word of God. It was this aspect of this battle that David admired. For Adino it was the 800, but for Eleazar it was the position of the sword after the battle. Will we be recognized at the end of our warfare for the placement of the Spirit's sword?

Notice again: *"And the Lord wrought a great victory that day."* (II Samuel 23:10) I believe that it takes this combination to win any battle over the invaders: the Lord, the Word, and a pair of undaunted warriors. Isaiah tells us that God works through His Word (Isaiah 55:11). It was not Eleazar, or Eleazar's sword, but the Lord working through Eleazar and Eleazar's sword that won the victory. Whether Moses' rod, Samson's jawbone, Adino's spear, or Eleazar's sword, the principle is the same. Whether the army of Pharaoh (Exodus 14:13) or the army of the Philistines (I Chronicles 11:14), none can stand against God! Isn't it time for you to sharpen "the Sword" and get ready for battle?

Revelation 1:16: *"And He had in his right hand seven stars: and out of His mouth went a sharp two edged sword…"*

4.

SHAMMAH: RENOWN

> II Samuel 23:12: *"But he (**SHAMMAH**) stood in the midst of the ground, and defended it, and slew the Philistines: and the Lord wrought a great victory."*

THE CONTEXT AND THE circumstance of this Biblical battle are not very clear in Scripture, but what is clear to me is the fact that David's mighty man Shammah was a man not afraid to stand alone in the midst of a battlefield. His fame and renown as a warrior centers around the word "middle," and it is important that we, too, learn the doctrine of the **"midst,"** a very misunderstood teaching today.

One never knows on a given day where or whom he might have to confront. That is why we need each day the admonition of Paul: *"Wherefore take unto you the whole armour of God that ye may be able to withstand in the evil day, and having done all to stand. Stand therefore..."* (Ephesians 6:13–14). This precept was dramatically demonstrated one day by Shammah: *"And the Philistines were gathered together into a troop, where was a piece of ground full of lentils: and the people fled from the Philistines. But..."* (II Samuel 23:11). David seemed to have a problem with the bulk of his army. This is the second story he shares of how his army ran away, but his mighty men stood (II Samuel 23:9). Praise the Lord for men and women like Shammah that when everybody else runs, they stand. When everybody flees, they resist. When everybody takes flight, they fight!

DAVID'S MIGHTY MEN

I am of the persuasion that Shammah started life as a bean (lentil) farmer, and only after his exploit against the Philistines did this Hararite become a part of David's army. You find a similar story told in the history of the judges in Judges 3:31. We are not told by David what Shammah fought with (Shamgar used what was in his hand-an ox goad). Maybe Shammah used a hoe? We are not told by David how many Shammah fought (Shamgar fought at least 600, the third greatest slaughter by one man on a battlefield after Samson's 1000 and Adino's 800), it all depends on your definition of "a troop." We are not told by David where the field of battle was, like Shamgar, but like Shamgar I believe it was in Shammah's own field. What we do know is that *"the Lord wrought a great victory!"* What we have learned and will continue to learn in our study of David's mighty men is this classic principle from the pen of Zechariah: **"Not by might, nor by power, but by my Spirit saith the Lord of Host"** (Zechariah 4:6) and **"the battle is the Lord's"** (I Samuel 17:47). When we take a stand for the Lord, He can use us to win a great victory no matter the field of battle. We need not know the time, the place, or the opponent. All we need to decide is will we stand and defend against the invader. Maybe it is an invasion of our mind, our beliefs, or our convictions. We must defend each as valiantly as Shammah defended that field of lentils. The wicked one is out to retake what we have worked so hard for. Will we back down, run away, or will we think so little of the sweat and the time we have put into the development of our character that we will flee in the face of the first foe that attacks? It takes courage to stand on our convictions alone. It takes bravery to defend our beliefs when no one else will stand with us. It takes valor to live virtuously when nobody else is, but if we don't stand against the "armies of the aliens" (Hebrews 11:34), who will? If we don't stop them in our field, they will soon be in somebody else's field, and they will run rough shod over us, then them. If we don't defeat them today, we will have to face them tomorrow; sooner or later we must stand.

I see Shammah and Shamgar in the same set of circumstances with these exceptions. On the day the Philistines came to Shamgar's field, Shamgar was alone. On the day the Philistines came to Shammah's field of lentils Shammah was working with others, but he, too, was soon alone. Shamgar was plowing. Shammah was gathering. It takes more to harvest than to sow! As Shammah and his companions brought in their labor, a band of Philistines suddenly approached (like the Midianites and Amalekites-Judges 6:3-before them, the Philistines were raiders and just loved to show up at harvest time). Being farmers and not fighters, the rest fled.

If David had been there, he wouldn't have fled (I Chronicles 11:12–15) so David must have heard this story later. On this field of lentils was Shammah's baptism of fire, his first fight (David knew all too well the first fight-I Samuel 17), and, like Shamgar and David, Shammah faced his first battlefield alone with only God to help.

It says that Shammah *"...stood in the midst of the ground..."* Not on a corner so that he could easily retreat if the battle went wrong. Not in the back so it would take the enemy awhile to get to him, and not in the front so that the aliens might slip in behind him, but in the middle. Shammah was determined to defend the entire field. We are living in a day of extremes. Not only those who live in excess, but that live so *"...that every imagination of the thought of his heart is only evil continually"* (Genesis 6:5), but extremes in Christian beliefs as well. Some fighting fundamentalists have become ultra-fundamentalists breaking fellowship over trivial truth. Truly, we must stand and fight against all attacks upon our Lord and our faith, but when we get so Pharisaical to think we are the only ones that have all the answers, we become like Elijah who thought he was the only one that hadn't bowed the knee to Baal. We need to be reminded *"that no prophecy of the scripture is of any private interpretation."* (II Peter 1:20) One of the most ignored Scriptures today is this admonition from Paul: **"Let your moderation be known unto all men."** (Philippians 4:5) Let us like Shammah take a stand in the midst of Biblical truth; let us neither go to the liberal left or the self-righteous right; let us like Shammah take a stand in the midst; and let us not go to the "love" left only or the rigid right only. **Remember, legalism is just as dangerous as liberalism!**

Today on the battlefield for truth, we have so many on the right or the left of issues, but few standing and defending the middle ground. Any general will tell you that the middle ground is the most important ground on any battlefield. We need the bravest soldiers on the middle ground. Extremists today seemingly have planted their flag on the high ground, but the true soldier of Christ is in the midst *"...earnestly contending for the faith which was once delivered unto the saints."* (Jude 3) Granted, the liberals have the low ground in everything from theology to compromise and co-existing with the world, but the fundamentalists are just extreme in their own way. The high ground of ultra-Calvinism and Roman Catholicism is heavily defended by their sides, but who is defending the middle ground of simple, Christ-taught Christianity. Jesus warned: *"...for ye pay tithe of mint and anise and cumin and have omitted the weightier matters of the law, judgment, mercy, and faith: these ought ye to have done, and not to leave the other undone."* (Matthew 23:23) One of the dangers of the middle ground is we must be ready for an assault from any side. We must be ready to defend what Christ has given.

Hebrews 2:12: *"...I will declare thy name unto my brethren; in the midst of the Church will I sing praise unto thee."*

5.

ABISHAI: SOURCE OF WEALTH

I Chronicles 18:12: *"Moreover **ABISHAI** the son of Zeruiah slew of the Edomites in the valley of salt eighteen thousand."*

WHEN DAVID NUMBERED HIS "mighty men," (I Chronicles 11:10) Abishai was fifth on that impressive list of warriors. His citation for bravery reads like this: *"And Abishai the brother of Joab, he was chief of the three: for lifting up his spear against three hundred, he slew them, and had a name among the three."* (I Chronicles 11:20 and II Samuel 23:18–19) What I find interesting in this record of bravery is that David leaves out the fact that Abishai singlehandedly killed a giant by the name of Ishbibenob and in the process also saved David's life: *"And Ishbibenob, which was one of the sons of the giant, the weight of whose spear weighted three hundred shekels of brass in weight, he being girded with a new sword, thought to have slain David. But Abishai, the son of Zeruiah, succoured him, and smote the Philistine and killed him."* (II Samuel 21:16–17) As amazing as that seems, David's mind drifted back to a battle in which Abishai stood in the gap and killed 300 soldiers, not one giant soldier, even if that death resulted in saving the king's life. Could that stand and memorable act of courage have taken place in a war against Edom and its most famous Battle in the Valley of Salt?

Abishai was the second of three sons born to David's sister, Zeruiah (I Chronicles 2:15–16). All of Zeruiah's boys would eventually become part of David's grand army, and all of them would excel in daring and boldness and be numbered among David's elite, his "mighty men." Joab, the oldest, would become chief of staff and run David's army (I

Chronicles 11:6), and Asahel, the youngest, would give his life in pursuit of the mighty warrior Abner (II Samuel 2:18-23), but Abishai was the man, the cousin, the soldier that was always there at David's side when he needed someone. In the early days when David was still being hunted down by King Saul's forces, it was Abishai who went with David one night into the camp of the enemy and pulled off a daring raid to prove to King Saul that David was no threat to him (I Samuel 26:6-9). Later, during the rebellion of Absalom, it was Abishai who came to David's defense in David's ignoble retreat from Jerusalem (II Samuel 16:9), and it was Abishai who commanded a third of David's army in the Battle of the Ephraim Woods that won the kingdom back for David (II Samuel 18:2). He was also there at the First Battle of Gob to save David's life from a giant (II Samuel 21:15-18) as we have mentioned before. Seemingly, at least in David's eyes, his crowning achievement on the battlefield and in the service of his king was his contribution in a war against Edom later in David's kingship. Was it here that Abishai lifted up his spear against 300 and won? No doubt many soldiers took part in the Battle of the Valley of Salt, but David mentions Abishai as being primarily responsible for the ultimate destruction of the Edomite army and the death of 18,000 warriors. Why? If David would have given out medals, like The Congressional Medal of Honor, I believe he would have given it to Abishai after this famous battle: **"...for gallantry above and beyond the call of duty!"**

What is most interesting to me about this battle is the fact that it is mentioned in three Biblical places, and in each case a different person is given credit for the victory, Abishai in I Chronicles 18:12, Joab in Psalm 60, and David in II Samuel 8:13-14. One of the great abilities of talented military captains is the skill of leading men in a cooperative endeavor. Read carefully how David's three mightiest men, Adino, Eleazar, and Shammah, cooperated to get a cup of cold water from the well at the gate of Bethlehem (II Samuel 23:13-17). There are those that interpreted this story as not being David's first three, but David's second three, Abishai, Benaiah, and Asahel (II Samuel 23:18-24). Whichever the case, it was David that taught his soldier's team work. Team work wins battles that individuals can't win on their own. Like in basketball, five average players can win against a superstar any time, even if you are LeBron James! I like the definition of George M. Verity on cooperation: **"Cooperation is really spelled with two letters-WE!"** I have come to believe that Abishai was a "we" person. Whenever you read about Abishai in the Bible it is Abishai and somebody else, like his brother Joab or his king David.

Abishai was a team player, and he didn't care if he got the glory or not or where he played. He was ready and willing to do whatever it took for the team to win. Whether with others or alone, it was always "we" not "me" when it came to the warrior Abishai.

Abishai's philosophy in battle was much like what J. Dabney Day once said: **"We would rather have one man or one woman working with us than three merely working for us."** There seems to be a lot of Christians today working for the Lord rather than working with the Lord. Paul taught the Church: *"For we are labourers together with the Lord."* (I Corinthians 3:9) Take time this week to read the context of that precept (I Corinthians 3:4–8 and I Corinthians 12:12–27). Harry C. Mabry tells a fable that illustrates wonderfully this great truth about spiritual warfare:

> A man had just arrived in Heaven and told Saint Peter how grateful he was to be in such a glorious place. He asked Saint Peter to give him one glimpse into Hades in order that he might appreciate his good fortune even more. This Saint Peter did. In Hades he saw a long table extending as far as the eye could see laden down with the most delicious foods, but everybody was starving to death. When asked for an explanation, Saint Peter answered, "Everybody is required to take food from the table only with four-foot long chopsticks. The chopsticks are too long to use for one's self, but in Hades nobody helps or cooperates. That is why they are all starving." Quickly Saint Peter and the man returned to Heaven, and, behold, the new arrival saw an identical table laden with the same delicious food, but everyone around the heavenly table was happy and well-fed. Then the man asked Saint Peter, "With what do they take food from the table?" Saint Peter replied, "Four-foot chopsticks." At that the newest resident of Heaven asked, "Then why are those in Hades starving while all those in Heaven are healthy and full?" Whereupon Saint Peter answered, **"In Heaven, we feed each other."**

Two of the verses that has help me the most in understanding the success of David and his mighty men are I Chronicles 11:9–10: *"So David waxed greater and greater: for the Lord of Hosts was with him. There also* (including Abishai) *are the chief of the mighty men whom David had, who strengthened themselves with him in his kingdom, and with all Israel, to make him king, according to the word of the Lord concerning Israel."* It wasn't just God, or just David, or just the mighty men. It was like Paul taught, it was a planting Paul, a watering Apollos, and the Lord that gives the increase. Whether the war of Edom or the battle we wage everyday against the forces of sin, self, and Satan, cooperation is a source of wealth we have that should never be overlooked.

Philippians 2:2: *"Fulfill ye my joy, that ye be likeminded, having the same love, being of one accord, of one mind."*

6.

BENAIAH: WHOM JEHOVAH HAS BUILT UP

*II Samuel 23:20–21: "And **BENAIAH** the son of Jehoiaha, the son of a valiant man of Kabzeel, who had done many acts, he slew two lion-like men of Moab: he went down also and slew a lion in the midst of a pit in a time of snow. And he slew an Egyptian, a goodly man: and the Egyptian had a spear in his hand; but he went down to him with a staff, and plucked the spear out of the Egyptian's hand, and slew him with his own spear."*

WITHIN THE LISTING OF David's mighty men are sometimes descriptions of their heroic acts of bravery performed on the field of battle, as we have seen, whether singularly or in a group. As I have studied this special group of warriors, I have come to a personal favorite, Benaiah, our sixth soldier on David's list. I like Benaiah, but not because he is the most recognized, that would be Joab or Adino or Eleazar; not because he accomplished the most memorable act of courage on the battlefield, that would be Shammah or Abishai. For me, he is my favorite because he wasn't ashamed to fight the little battle or the simple battle. If it weren't for David, his three recognized fights would have probably been overlooked in the shadow of the other victories of his comrades. Interestingly, David only puts this postscript on Benaiah's amazing feats: *"He was more honorable then the thirty, but he attained not to the first three. And David set him over his guard."* (II Samuel 23:23) Benaiah might not have been David's best warrior, but Benaiah was David's most trusted soldier because David set Benaiah over the king's bodyguard. Why?

Benaiah knew how to win, how to finish a fight, and he wasn't afraid to kill any of the King's enemies. Benaiah was a victor, not a victim. Benaiah was a man that went through battlefields, not around them. Benaiah didn't avoid a fight no matter the danger. Benaiah was the kind of soldier you would want at your side, in your corner, at your back. Benaiah would without question lay down his life for David. Who better to be in charge of your security! Benaiah knew how to fight tough opponents (lion-like men). Benaiah knew how to fight in difficult conditions (a lion in a hole in winter), and Benaiah knew how to improvise when the situation warranted it (having no spear). I have been moved recently by the exploits of the great Confederate, Christian soldier, Lieutenant-General Thomas "Stonewall" Jackson. This famous warrior got his unique nickname at the First Battle of Bull Run in 1861. The battle was going poorly for the Confederates as Brigadier-General Barnard E. Bee rode to the rear of the front for help. Coming upon Jackson and his men, Bee waved his sword in the air and said, "General they are beating us back!" To which Jackson replied, "Sir, we'll give them the bayonet!" As Bee rallied his troops behind Jackson's rapidly forming lines, he saw that his soldiers were nervous and unsteady. Pointing to Jackson and his soldiers, it was then that Bee shouted his immortal battle cry, "There is Jackson standing like a 'stone wall.' Let us determine to die here, and we will conquer. Follow me!" Like Jackson, Benaiah was a man you could stand behind, rally behind. David knew it of Benaiah just like Bee knew it of Jackson.

Who are you rallying behind today? It is a tragic age when the heroes of the world are broken walls, empty cisterns, and uninspiring cowards. It is time to rally behind our Benaiah or Jackson, the Lord Jesus Christ. Men loved to fight with Benaiah because he always left the battlefield victorious, as did Jackson, as will Christ. *"But thanks be to God which giveth us the victory through our Lord Jesus Christ."* (I Corinthians 15:57) It is not by chance that Benaiah means "whom Jehovah has built up." As with the other men in David's command, Benaiah's victories were of the Lord (II Samuel 23:10, 12).

A trilogy of spectacular deeds is recorded of Benaiah by David, more than any other warrior on David's Mighty Men list. Though some of Benaiah's fellow soldiers killed more in battle, David seemed to be impressed with Benaiah's courage against "two lion-like men from Moab," "a lion in a pit on a snowy day," and "a giant Egyptian," all whom Benaiah "slew." Though none seem to compare to the size of Adino's slaying 800 in one battle, David saw the value and the importance of Benaiah's small victories as well as the grander and grandiose victories of Eleazar and Shammah and Abishai. Benaiah wasn't one to look at the size of the fight to determine whether or not to fight. Whether big or small, Benaiah saw the danger and was determine to slay the foe.

For me, the three "acts" of heroism are but three illustrations of the same quality David respected and honored in Benaiah. These were not mighty armies invading David's land, but small irritations that were causing a problem in a particular section of the countryside. Often we have more trouble with the small troubles that invade our space than with the big trials that only come on occasion. Sometimes, we are very quick to tackle the big issues, but we make the mistake of thinking the little things of life can be left to another day. Most of us stand up to the big temptations, but we often see the little temptations as harmless. We should never forget this classic proverb by Solomon: *"Take us the foxes, the little foxes, that spoil the vines: for our vines have tender grapes."* (Song of Solomon 2:15) Sometimes we have more problems with the little "foxes" in our life than the big "foxes" in life. I have come to believe that Benaiah was David's problem solver, and whenever he needed somebody to deal with something, Benaiah was the someone.

Another precept that I have discovered in the Bible is the fact that little victories here on earth are seen as big victories in heaven (Luke 15: 4–10), the singlehanded victories that only God's eyes see. How did David know of Benaiah's wins? Who saw and reported Benaiah's victory over the "two lion-like men," "the battle with the lion in a pit," or the fight with an "Egyptian Goliath?" Who witnesses your resistance of the devil (James 4:7) and his flight? Who watches as you fight off the "roaring lion" that seeks to devour you (I Peter 5:8)? Who records those times that, like the Lord, you simply say "no" to the wicked one and his diabolical devices of deception (Matthew 4:1–10)? I love the words of this old hymn:

> Yield not to temptation for yielding is sin,
> Each victory will help you some other to win.
> Fight manfully onward dark passions subdue,
> Look ever to Jesus He will carry you through.
>
> Ask the Saviour to help you,
> Comfort, strengthen, and keep you.
> He is willing to aid you,
> He will carry you through.

With a name like Benaiah, it was the Lord God Jehovah Himself that watched and witnessed and recorded Benaiah's secret wins over the wicked one. It is my opinion, not by chance, that they were "lion-like" men (the devil's demons), "a lion" (The Devil Himself), and "a giant." (Tracing through the Bible to write a book I have called <u>Satan's Super Soldiers,</u> I am convinced that all "giants" in the Bible were Satan's men!) Satan is still our archenemy.

Benaiah's faithfulness in the small battles ought to be an inspiration to us. Resolve today that if called on to fight an insignificant battle, you will resist not fighting. Whether small or great, your reward and honor will be the same. Remember the result of Jesus' parable of the talents and the pounds. (Matthew 25:14–30; Luke 19:13–27)

> Luke 16:10: *"He that is faithful in that which is least is faithful also in much!"*

7.

ASAHEL: GOD HAS MADE

I Chronicles 11:26: *"Also the valiant men of the armies were,* **ASAHEL** *the brother of Joab, Elhanan the son of Dodo of Bethlehem."*

"Now there was long war between the house of Saul and the house of David: but David waxed stronger and stronger, and the house of Saul waxed weaker and weaker." (II Samuel 3:1) We often forget that there was a king of Israel after Saul, his son Ishbosheth. For two years (II Samuel 2:10), Ishbosheth tried to hold onto his father's kingdom. Through the help and support of one of Saul's ablest commanders, a man named Abner (II Samuel 2:8), he managed to keep David's increasing army at bay and hold off David from taking complete control of the country. Eventually, Abner lost the upper hand, but during that time of civil war a very interesting battle was fought between the forces of Ishbosheth under the command of Abner and the forces of David under the command of Joab. The encounter has become known as the Battle of Gibeon, named for the place the conflict took place. Asahel, considered one of David's top warriors (II Samuel 23:24) was one of the heroes of that battle. Asahel was also David's sister's son (I Chronicles 2:15–16). In David's chain of command Asahel would eventually rise in rank to #4 (I Chronicles 27:7). No doubt Asahel would fight in many battles, but his Biblical call to fame would happen at the Battle of Gibeon, a battle God allowed to test his warrior.

The final action in this Biblical battle (after a confrontation between 12 of David's best against 12 of Abner's best, a general fight took place in which Joab's men got the upper hand and Abner and his surviving soldiers fled-II Samuel 2:12-17) is best described in my opinion in these notes found in the commentary by Jamieson, Fausset, and Brown:

> To gain a general's armor was deemed the grandest trophy. Asahel, ambitious of securing Abner's armor, had outstripped all the other pursuers and was fast gaining on the retreating commander. Abner, conscious of possessing more physical power and unwilling that there should be "blood" between himself and Joab, Asahel's brother twice urged him to desist (II Samuel 2:18-22). The impetuous young soldier being deaf to the generous remonstrance, the veteran raised the pointed butt of his lance, as the modern Arabs do when pursued, and, with a sudden back thrust, transfixed him on the spot (II Samuel 2:23) so that he fell and lay weltering in his blood. But Joab and Abishai continued the pursuit by another route till sunset. On reaching a rising ground and receiving a fresh reinforcement of some Benjamites, Abner rallied his scattered troops and earnestly appealed to Joab's better feelings to stop further effusion of blood, which, if continued, would lead to more serious consequences, a destructive civil war. Joab, which upbraiding his opponent as the sole cause of the fray, felt the force of the appeal and led off his men, while Abner, probably dreading a renewal of the attack when Joab learned of his brother's fate and vow fierce revenge, endeavored, by a force march, to cross the Jordan that night (II Samuel 2:24-39). On David's side the loss was only 19 men, besides Asahel. But of Ishbosheth's party there fell 360 (II Samuel 2:30-31). This skirmish is exactly similar to the battles of the Homeric warriors, among whom, in the fight of one, the pursuit of another, and the dialogue held between them, there is vividly represented the style of ancient warfare."

For me the lesson of Asahel at the Battle of Gibeon is a warning against carelessness in the spiritual struggle. How important it is for us to keep vigilant and alert at all times because we, too, have a crafty foe (I Peter 5:8).

Asahel was a veteran soldier despite his age, and he should have known better than to corner a retreating general of the status of Abner. Asahel let the glory of the fight at the pool of Gibeon (II Samuel 2:13) cloud his judgment at a critical point in his pursuit of Abner. Instead of being careful, alert to a possible counterattack, Asahel became careless to the sudden reverse thrust of Abner's spear. The hunter suddenly became the hunter, and before Asahel realized he was in a very dangerous situation, he was dying on the ground with no help in sight. So it is with us according to the Apostle Paul when he warned the Church at Corinth and us: *"Lest Satan should get an advantage of us: for we are not ignorant of his devices."* (II Corinthians 2:11) Asahel must have known of this tactic of defense. He had probably used it himself. Yet, in the heat of the chase he let down his guard opening up his chest to Abner's thrust. So it is with us. God has armed us with a means to protect us from every assault of the wicked one (Ephesians 6:10–18), but it is up to us to keep our shield up or Satan's fiery darts will get through. Satan's thrusts of temptation will find a weak place, and we will go down in sin. Why are so many believers falling in battle today? Is the armor weak? Are we too old to resist Satan's modern techniques? Are there flaws in the weapons God has provided His warriors? No! No! A resounding no! The problem is not with what God has provided. The problem can be traced back to the carelessness of the soldier: *"But put ye on the Lord Jesus Christ, and make no provision for the flesh, to fulfill the lusts thereof."* (Romans 13:14)

Too many Christian soldiers aren't even wearing their armor most of the time. Too many fail to even raise the shield of faith, and most have the sword of the Spirit still in the sheath. Too many Christian warriors are so focused on the goal, of running right, that they fail to keep a sober vigilance in the face of a determined foe. Take the time to read I Kings 13 and the story of the prophet of God who committed a similar error as Asahel, a man of God who got careless in the last mile of his mission. Despite Asahel's distinct advantages (II Samuel 2:18), instead of using those advantages to his advantage, he ran straight into Abner's spear butt. So often the Christian soldier, believing he is in no danger, lets down his guard only to run straight into a temptation he is unprepared to resist or defeat. Instead of seeing a way of escape (I Corinthians 10:13) and coming out of the conflict victorious, he ends the battle wallowing in defeat. God has prepared us to be winners (I Corinthians 15:57), victors (II Corinthians 2:14), conquerors (Romans 8:37), not losers or victims of a surprise attack by our archenemy.

We, too, are fighting in enemy territory. We, too, have to set *"to flight the armies of the aliens."* (Hebrews 11:34) We, too, have to resist the devil, and he will flee from us (James 4:7). Sound familiar? It is time we recognize that Satan is most dangerous when we have him on the run, and it is at those times we need to set a double guard on our battlefield. One battle doesn't mean the war is over as Asahel thought. One victory doesn't mean our foe has been weakened or has lost his will to fight. Asahel forgot the danger in fighting a retreating enemy and paid dearly for that oversight. Jesus taught us in his wilderness battle with the devil (Luke 4:1–12) that *"he [Satan] departed from Him [Jesus] for a season."* (Luke 4:13) The devil returned, and Jesus was always ready for his thrusts. We, too, must remember our adversary will be back, especially after we said no to him. Asahel thought that he had Abner on the run, and that it would only be a matter of time before he would strike the fatal blow, but he was the one receiving that blow. A warning to us all!

II Corinthians 7:11: *"…what carefulness is wrought in you…"*

8.

ELHANAN: GOD IS GRACIOUS

II Samuel 23:24: *"Asahel the brother of Joab was one of the thirty;* **EL-HANAN** *the son of Dodo of Bethlehem."*

NOT TO BE MIXED up with another soldier in David's army, Elhanan the son of Jair of Bethlehem (I Chronicles 20:5 and II Samuel 21:19), a warrior in David's mighty man list that slew Lahmi the giant, the brother of Goliath, at the Second Battle of Gob. (We will see this mighty man later on in this study of David's Mighty Men.)

All we know about this mighty man is what is recorded about him in the listings of David's mighty men (II Samuel 23:24 and I Chronicles 11:26): (1) His father's name was Dodo, which means beloved. (Was Elhanan a beloved son of this father as most sons are including God's own Son-Matthew 3:17?) (2) His hometown was Bethlehem, the same as David (I Samuel 16:18), and with such a small town were Elhanan and David friends in childhood? (3) And his name means, **God is gracious**. As with so many of the men on David's list, this is all we have to go on to study, but what wonderful trails this meaning can take us on as we come to be challenged by the eighth name on David's Mighty Men list.

We have no record of battles fought by this mighty man like with the others before him, nor do we have any acts of bravery recorded as we have come to expect in the soldiers listed before Elhanan. But as David pondered a list of his most famous and most courageous warriors, Elhanan came to mind after his cousin Asahel. They were listed on the same line. On this distinguished list and coming from Bethlehem, Elhanan might have been one of the very first to follow David: *"David therefore departed thence, and escaped to the cave Adullam: and when his brethren and all his father's house* [from Bethlehem] *heard it, they went down thither to him. And every one that was in distress, and every one that was in debt, and very one that was discontented, gathered themselves unto him; and he became a captain over them: and there were with him about four hundred men."* (I Samuel 22:1-2) Whether a childhood friend or a childhood acquaintance, Elhanan was recognized by David for his outstanding contributions to his rise to the kingship of Israel. But because we know nothing else for sure, we will focus on what we do know from the Bible and that being the meaning of his name which is God is Gracious. What an honorable name and as the wise man Solomon once wrote in his proverbs: *"A good name is rather to be chosen than great riches, and loving favour* (grace) *rather than silver and gold."* (Proverbs 22:1) What can we learn from this name?

Someone has defined grace as **"that action of God by which He withholds a deserved penalty and alleviates suffering and distress** (note, the characteristics of the men who came to David at first-I Samuel 22:2)." The Psalmist wrote this of God: *"The Lord is merciful and GRACIOUS, slow to anger, and plenteous in mercy."* (Psalm 103:8) Moses wrote this of God: *"And the Lord God, merciful, and GRACIOUS, longsuffering, and abundant in goodness and truth."* (Exodus 34:6) Why Dodo named his son Elhanan is not explained in Scripture, but the meaning of Elhanan was certainly meant to exalt the attribute of the Almighty we call "graciousness." Have you experienced this yet?

Moses might have been the first Biblical writer to proclaim this divine characteristic of the Godhead, but he was not the last. King Hezekiah, a great, great, great…grandson of David, had these words printed and published and passed on and proclaimed to every Jew throughout the land as he called all Hebrews to Jerusalem to observe the forgotten Passover: *"For the Lord your God is GRACIOUS and merciful, and will not turn away His face from you, if you return unto Him."* (II Chronicles 30:9) In Nehemiah's rehearsal of the history of the Jews, twice he speaks of the "gracious God" (Nehemiah 9:17, 31). Six times the Psalmist refers to the "gracious God" in the Psalms (86:15, 103:8, 111:4, 112:4, 116:5 and 145:8). The prophet Joel concludes the Old Testament chorus with *"…thou art a GRACIOUS God."* (Joel 2:13) Who says grace is a New Testament doctrine?

As it was in those days, so it is today. The graciousness of God should be a source of wonder and awe to every human being on this planet. Despite our rebellious and ungratefulness, God has not abandoned His principles of graciousness. What love and what patience He shows (II Peter 3:9) towards us in the conditions of our wicked age. We speak of Israel, but the same "gracious God" is forbearing and forgiving still to all who will return back to Him. **We should never forget that God's anger and wrath comes by measure, but God's graciousness and mercy without measure. Amen and Amen!**

It was the Psalmist that said: *"Then called I upon the name of the Lord; O Lord, I beseech Thee, deliver my soul. GRACIOUS is the Lord."* (Psalm 116:4–5) If we call upon the Lord, we, too, will find a GRACIOUS Savior ready to forgive and meet our needs, but like all gifts of God we must receive that grace. Peter wrote: *"If so be ye have tasted that the Lord is GRACIOUS."* (I Peter 2:3) I like what the great British pastor, Charles Spurgeon wrote on the word "if" of this verse:

> If-then, this is not a matter to be taken for granted concerning every one of the human race. If -then there is a possibility and a probability that some may not have tasted that the lord is GRACIOUS. If-then this is not a general but a special mercy; and it is needful to enquire whether we know the grace of God by inward experience. There is no spiritual favour which may not be a matter of earnest and prayerful inquiry, no one ought to be content whilst there is any such thing as an "if" about His having tasted that the Lord is GRACIOUS. Advance beyond these dreary "ifs" abide no more in the wilderness of doubts and fears; cross the Jordan of distrust, and enter the Canaan of peace.

Have you done this yet?

To which I will only add, Amen and Amen. Get rid of the "ifs" of your life by laying claim to the grace of God supplied by the GRACIOUS Jesus. Remember, the law came by Moses, but grace came by Christ (John 1:17). How often people fail to get God's "amazing grace" simply because they have not come to a genuine faith in Christ. Grace is a valuable virtue that Christ gives out to those who sincerely want it (Ephesians 2:8). So whether we are exposed to this grace through a psalm or a person, we are blessed when we come under the influence of the "gracious God" through His son Jesus Christ.

Elhanan was named **"God is gracious,"** and his relationship with David (I Samuel 22:2) must have proved the meaning of his name again and again. Our relationship to our Captain (Hebrews 2:10), the Lord Jesus Christ, ought to have the same effect on others. As God showed grace to Paul's traveling companions during the Euroclydon of Acts 27, God showed grace to David's mighty men, of which Elhanan was one of the best, during their stormy journeys and difficult battles together. Paul tells us: *"For the grace of God that bringeth salvation hath appeared to all men, teaching us that, denying ungodliness and worldly lusts, we should live soberly, righteously, and godly, in this present world."* (Titus 2:11–12) I believe just like a man like Elhanan lived during the days of David.

Joel 2:13: *"And rend your hearts, and not your garments, and turn unto the Lord your God: for He is GRACIOUS…"*

9.

SHAMMOTH: FAME

I Chronicles 11:27: "**SHAMMOTH** *the Harorite, Helez the Pelonite.*"

I WILL WARN YOU now that from now on the real research begins as we try to figure out David's list of "mighty men." It has been a very easy exercise up until now, but from now on we must invoke that classic concept of Biblical interpretation found in II Peter 1:20: ***"Knowing this first, that no prophecy of the scripture is of any private interpretation."*** So from now on this is my opinion on the "who's who" of David's elite men. After much comparison, I have concluded that Shammoth the Harorite of I Chronicles 11:27 and Shammah the Harodite of II Samuel 23:25 are one in the same warrior. My reasoning has four points:

1. They both come ninth on David's two recorded lists.
2. Shammah and Shammoth mean the same thing: fame.
3. Harodite means "belonging to Harod." This is probably the name of the town or place Shammoth was from. The well of Harod (a place I got to visit on my 2010 trip to Israel) (Judges 7:1) was a fountain by which Gideon and his army encamped before the rout of the Midianites. Harod was located in the tribal territory of Manasseh west of the Jordan River in the plain of Jezreel near Gilboa.
4. Harorite means "belonging to Haror." This was probably the name of Shammoth's father or an ancestral name.

My biographical sketch of Shammoth is that he was a "mighty man" of valor from an area near the well of Harod, and he was the son of Haror from the tribe of Manasseh. Could he have been one of the soldiers that followed David from the tribe of Manasseh? The Chronicles makes this description: *"And there fell some of Manasseh to David, when he came with the Philistines against Saul to battle: but they helped them not: for the lords of the Philistines upon advisement sent him away, saying, He will fall to his master Saul to jeopardy of our heads. As he went to Ziklag, there fell to him of Manasseh, and Adnah, and Jozabad, and Jediael, captains of the thousands that were of Manasseh. And they **helped** David against the band of rovers: for they were mighty men of valour, and were captains in the host. For at that time day by day there came to David to **help** him, until it was a great host, like the host of God."* (I Chronicles 12:19–22) Was Shammoth numbered among that host of Manassehites?

The historical context described above is fully developed in the Biblical text in I Samuel 29–30. The battle with the Philistines was the infamous Battle of Gilboa in which King Saul and most of his sons (including my favorite, Jonathan) were slain. Gilboa was near Harod. (In 2010, I was able to drink from the brook flowing from Harod Spring, and from that creek bed I can see the summit of Mount Gilboa.) The battle with the "rovers" is no doubt a reference to the raid by the Amalekite raiders that completely destroyed David's town of Ziklag and took captive the families of David's men. If the Manassehites were there, then Shammoth must have been there. I believe Shammoth's fame began in that encounter against the Amalekite raiders. As with so many of David's "mighty men," this is about all we can glean from Scripture about the warrior called Shammoth. But his true call to "fame" is the simple mention of his name on one of the most famous lists recorded in the Bible, and Shammoth reminds me of another famous man. Today, thanks to newsprint and television, people who become famous for something are recognized immediately. Their image has been shown on the front page of the important newspapers of the land and in the opening story of the evening news until they are known far and wide, and their fame follows them wherever they go. In the cases of Shammoth and Jesus, there were no reporters, no media, no <u>60 Minutes</u>, no headlines, and, yet, Shammoth's name speaks of his fame, and the Gospels speak of Jesus' fame.

Today, a person's fame follows them, but in Jesus' case it went before Him. Jesus' character and customs and charisma caught the attention of the masses (Matthew 4:24–25). These people didn't come for a glimpse of a super star or a famous politician; they didn't come for an autograph, a snapshot, or a selfie; they came to Jesus for help. I find it interesting that the characteristic of the Manassehites, like Shammoth, was help (note again I Chronicles 12:19–22). Jesus didn't charge them so much per head, an entrance fee, or an admission price. Jesus didn't use his fame to make money as so many famous people do today. His notoriety resulted in His help of the helpless, *"and the fame hereof went abroad unto all that land."* (Matthew 9:26) As Jesus had come to help so had Shammoth and his fellow Manassehites come to help David into the kingship.

It seemed that every time Jesus would do something miraculous, His fame would only increase among the common people while at the same time He became infamous among the spiritual elite. There is a story of Jesus that comes out of the town of Capernaum where He made the blind to see. In this specific case there were actually two blind men who came to Him, and, after he simply touched them, they could see again. The aftermath of this event is recorded in Matthew: *"But they, when they were departed, spread abroad His fame in all that country."* (Matthew 9:31) Whereas today most famous people promote their own fame, this is a case where Jesus did just the opposite. Jesus had not come into the world to be famous, and I believe Shammoth didn't join David's army to be famous. In the story of the blind men Jesus actually tells them: *"…see that no man know it."* (Matthew 9:30) On other occasions Jesus tells the people He helped to do the same: a man full of leprosy, **"…He charged him to tell no man…"** (Luke 5:14). Jesus tried to stop the spread of his fame, and maybe that is why we know so little of Shammoth. But like Jesus (Matthew 5:15–16), Shammoth's fame was spread by his commander in recognition of Shammoth's faithful and courageous service. So the people of Galilee and beyond would not stop talking about the wonderful miracles of Jesus and His marvelous help to those in real need.

Jesus became famous for His healings and his homiletics, yet, when it came to the real reason He had come to this earth, He became infamous. The people wanted a physician for their bodies (blind men, lepers, palsy, deaf), not a Savior for their souls. They wanted a provider that would meet their physical needs (feeding of the 5,000 and the 4,000), not a propitiation (I John 2:2) to meet their spiritual needs. They wanted a teacher that would tell them of the wrongs of the Pharisees and Sadducees, but they didn't want the truth about their own sins. The tragedy today is that despite being famous (perhaps the most recognized name in the entire world), Jesus is still rejected by the vast majority as Lord and

Savior of the world. Despite being recognized in images only portraying what we think He might have looked like, Jesus is still ignored. Fame is not the key to believing, but faith! We must look beyond fame, and see the face of the Savior and put our faith in Him. I have come to believe that Shammoth, too, followed faith and not fame.

Matthew 14:1: *"At that time Herod the tetrarch heard of the fame of Jesus."*

10.

HELEZ: STRENGTH

I Chronicles 11:27: *"Shammoth the Harorite, **HELEZ** the Pelonite."*

No doubt the same warrior David mentions in II Samuel 23:26, Helez the Pelonite, is number ten on David's list of "mighty men." Once again, we haven't much to go on Biblically speaking to investigate the history of this special soldier that David thought as worthy as with his companion Shammoth so we will simply develop what we know.

First, we have the appellation of Pelonite. This is no doubt making reference to Helez's hometown of Pelon, and, even though we know of no such town in the Bible, it doesn't mean that there wasn't such a town. I have come to believe it was a small village in the territory allotted to the tribe of Ephraim (I Chronicles 27:10). The only other man mentioned in Scripture having come from this town is another one of David's mighty men, Ahijah (I Chronicles 11:36). Maybe they joined David's elite force together? Hometown boys who enlisted together? Unknown lads from an unknown hamlet that would find fame together in the Army of David?

Second, we have the details described about Helez in this verse: *"The seventh captain for the seventh month was Helez the Pelonite, of the children of Ephraim: and in his course were twenty and four thousand."* (I Chronicles 27:10) The 27th chapter of I Chronicles tells how David marshaled his army. To keep his vast army together would have been a hardship on the land as well as in the country. At the same time it would have been dangerous to disband and disperse them because of the many enemies that surrounded Israel at that time so David kept 24,000 constantly under arms. However, David changed them every month. His total militia amounted to 288,000 soldiers. By being distributed into 12 courses, these soldiers were trained and ready for action at any time and in any crisis. Something like our National Guard system in the United States, each group had a commander, and each commander was responsible for a given month of the year. We know that this would have made Helez eventually one of David's top dozen generals. To Helez fell the seventh month of the military year. It is here we learn that Helez was also from the tribe of Ephraim, Joseph's tribe (Genesis 48:1) and Joshua's tribe (Numbers 13:8), another one of Israel's great soldiers.

Third, we know the meaning of Helez's name. As you have noticed, I have come to put great stock in the importance of the meaning of the names of David's "mighty men," and Helez is no exception. Helez can be defined as **"strength"** or **"strong."** The psalmist writes in Psalm 27:1: *"The Lord is the **strength** of my life; of whom shall I be afraid?"* The Gospel according to John is known for its "I Am's" of Christ, but I have come to believe the psalms are noted for their "My's" of God. Helez no doubt got his great soldiering strength from the Lord, and it was through the strength of God Helez become strong, helping David to bring in the Messianic Kingdom.

This morning as I arose, I asked the Lord, as I always do, for strength claiming the promise given by Moses to the children of Israel, including Helez, but I also believe to any believer: *"And as thy days are, so shall thy **strength** be."* (Deuteronomy 33:25) But through the years in my study of the Psalms (at the writing of this devotional I have started a restudy of Psalms and its classic 150 psalms), I have discovered that strength is not a power, but a Person. *"I will love thee, O Lord, my **strength**."* (Psalm 18:1) As with most of David's warriors, I believe they like David came to an understanding of the strength of the Lord in their lives, as we need to, because we need to realize that strength is not found in exercise (I Timothy 4:8), but in a relationship with Jesus Christ.

Jesus has become many things to me over the years as I have followed him (58 at this writing). First, Jesus became my Savior. As the old hymn writer proclaims: "O happy day that fixed my choice on thee, my Saviour and my God." Second, Jesus became my Supplier. Paul wrote of this relationship with these profound words: *"But my God shall supply all your needs according to His riches in glory by Christ Jesus."* (Philippians 4:19) Third, Jesus became my Supplicator. Once again Paul describes this best when he wrote to the Romans: *"Who is he that condemneth? It is Christ that died, yea rather, that is risen again, who is even at the right hand of God, who also maketh intercession for us."* (Romans 8:34) However, today, as I think about David's "mighty man" Helez, I rejoice in Jesus because He is my Strength. Thanks, Helez.

It is Christ who sustains us when our physical strength is gone. It is Christ who preserves us when our will power runs out. It is Christ that empowers us when we have tapped into the final resources in our reserve. Where would we be, what would we do, if we didn't have the strength of Christ to sustain us, preserve us, and empower us? I, like you, sometimes wake in the morning and wonder if I will have the strength needed to get through the day, yet, as it happens so often, I never fail to see or feel the renewed strength of the Lord throughout the day. Before I know it the day has ended, I have done what I needed to do, and I "lay me down to sleep" thankful that my God has strengthened me for another day. How did I accomplish what I did, and what was it that got me through the trial, the test, and the temptations? David wrote often that it was his God that strengthened him, and I wonder when David saw men like Helez if he was reminded again of the daily strengthening of his God. Day after day like David we face unknown challenges, obstacles that demand extra strength, a strength beyond our capacity. Yet, like David and his mighty men, he and they managed to overcome. I have found the same result in my own life over and over again through the years.

The Apostle Paul drew a similar conclusion when he asked these thought provoking questions: *"What shall we say of these things? If God be for us, who can be against us?"* (Romans 8:31) David's question *"Of whom shall I be afraid?"* (Psalm 27:1) links the two together in my opinion, and when you add them to this statement of Jesus, we have a perfect picture of our need for added strength: *"Fear them not therefore…fear ye not therefore."* (Matthew 10:26, 31) Because the Almighty was David's and David's men strength, David was able to write with confidence: *"Though a host should encamp against me, my heart shall not fear: though war should rise against me, in this will I be confident."* (Psalm 27:3) Could this be the reason David finished his psalm with this challenge for his men and us: *"Wait on the Lord: be of good courage, and he shall* **strengthen** *thine heart: wait I say on the Lord."* (Psalm 27:14) We are not sure when Helez joined David's troop, but we can be confident when we say he no doubt saw many times the deliverance of God through supernatural strength.

Have you for too long been trying to survive in your own strength alone? Have you wondered why you constantly fall short of the goal you are seeking for lack of strength? Recall, *"I can do all things through Christ which **strengtheneth** me."* (Philippians 4:13)

Habakkuk 3:19: *"The Lord God is my **strength**, and he will make my feet like hind's feet, and he will make me to walk upon mine high places."*

11.

ELIKA: GOD IS REJECTER

II Samuel 23:25: *"Shammah the Harodite, **ELIKA** the Harodite."*

ELIKA CAME FROM THE same town as another one of David's mighty men, Shammah (I Chronicles 11:27). Harod was located in the territorial area allotted to the tribe of Manasseh. We need to remember that Manasseh was given land both on the east and west banks of the Jordan River. Harod was situated in the western territory given to Joseph's tribe in the plains of Jezreel near Gilboa (Judges 7:1). Interestingly, Elika's name is omitted in the I Chronicles account of David's mighty men. Why? We are not told, but men from the tribe of Manasseh were well represented in David's grand army (I Chronicles 12:19–22). And that is all we know of the historical Elika, biblically speaking.

As with most of David's mighty men, Elika is only a name on a list. We didn't know of his time of enlistment, the battles he fought, or how he came to his end, in battle or in bed. But we honor him with this devotional because he was one of David's best and is worth our time and consideration. We know of the meaning of his name, and, as you have noticed and will notice in future articles, this becomes the theme of our devotional. **"God is rejecter,"** an odd combination of terms when we are taught in Scripture that God is a receiver, not a rejecter: *"All that the Father giveth me shall come to me; and him that cometh to me I will in no wise cast out."* (John 6:37) Elika caused us to dig a bit deeper into the Holy Writ to discover what has been overlooked by many. I have come to the believe that all Scripture (II Timothy 3:16), including names, are written for our inspiration and can be profitable if we would but take the time to ponder and meditate on them.

John the apostle wrote in his gospel: *"He [Jesus] came unto His own [Jews] and His own received Him not."* (John 1:11) Despite Jesus' holy, honest, and hallowed life, the prophet Isaiah knew through the Holy Spirit (II Peter 1:21) that the Messiah would still be rejected by the very people He came to save (Isaiah 53:3). The tragedy of this doctrine is that after all these years, Jesus is still being rejected by the ones He came to save, Jews and Gentiles alike. Without a doubt mankind is a rejecter, but not God. Or does Elika's name have a meaning of God we need to understand, even in relationship to Jesus?

The King's Business magazine once carried a story of a Christian fisherman who heard a loud splash one night as he lay in his boat. He knew that the man in the yacht nearby was a heavy drinker so without hesitation he jumped into the cold water and with great effort succeeded in pulling the half-drowned victim back on board. He gave him artificial respiration and then put him in his berth. Having done everything to make him comfortable, he swam back to his own boat. The next morning he returned to the yacht to see how he was doing. **"It's none of your business!"** said the man defensively. The fisherman reminded him that he had risked his life to save him. But instead of showing gratitude, the other fellow openly cursed him. As the Christian rowed away, tears filled his eyes. Looking to heaven, he prayed, "When I think of how men have treated you, dear Lord, I'm filled with sorrow. Now I can begin to understand just a little how you must feel." We might think such a story only deals with man rejecting man even when one of these men did a good deed for the other man. I have come to believe that this simple story is a good illustration of just how most of mankind has dealt with Christ over the years. Remember the story told in the Gospel according to Luke about the ten lepers who were healed by Jesus on their way to the priest to verify their healing. In the end only one in ten returned to thank Jesus (Luke 17:11–19). **Ingratitude might be the greatest rejection!**

Rejection hurts no matter who you are, God or man. This next saying came out of the 1952 Presidential election in the United States. Adlai Stevenson had just lost the election to Dwight Eisenhower, and in his concession speech he said, **"It hurts too much to laugh, but I'm too old to cry!"** Those who have gone through painful rejections know of this concept. I still remember in 1986 when I felt called to pastor my home church in Perham, Maine. The church was dying after a series of short-term pastorates and troubling problems as a result of those four pastorates. They were my family and my friends and my church family for most of my life at that time, and I wanted to help, bear their burdens, and share their troubles. I wanted to give back to the church that had nurtured me, guided me, and helped me in my spiritual growth. However, when the final vote was taken, I had been rejected. For the next two years that rejection bothered me terribly, that is, until I realized that now I could better understand, sympathize, and explain the precept of rejection, what Jesus went through (remember, Jesus had been rejected by his home synagogue and town as well-Luke 4:16-30) and what others go through. As I look on that rejection years ago, it was one of the most valuable lessons I have ever learned in my Christian walk.

Also I learned that in the wise providence of God that He, too, had rejected my move to Perham. He had a better path for me, but He knew I had to settle once and for all my desire to return to my hometown to minister. God's rejection of the desire of my heart was an act of love, not hatred; an act of kindness, not disappointment. I began to see just as the Father rejected Christ, His Son's, appeal in the Garden of Gethsemane to let the cup of suffering pass Him by (Matthew 26:39-42). Sometimes, God has to be seen as the rejecter in order to fulfill His perfect will, whether in the life of His Son or His son (John 1:12). I like the analogy of this story told by Dennis DeHaan in an <u>Our Daily Bread</u> article: "Hal Olsen, a veteran missionary in Kenya, told of a doctor who had come to the field to use his skills to relieve suffering and pain. On one occasion he performed a delicate operation that saved a woman's life. As the patient recovered, she didn't express even one word of appreciation, and the doctor was hurt. Olsen commented, 'One of the first lessons a new missionary must learn is that the people to whom he's been called aren't waiting with open arms to applaud his coming. **Some tribal languages have no words to express the idea of thank you.**'" We must learn that rejection comes in many forms, but we can't take it personally because there is a **"well done"** coming someday.

We have many expressions in our language to express gratitude, but do we use them as often as we should? Have you thanked Christ lately for coming to die, to be rejected by both His people (Matthew 27:15-22) and His Father (Matthew 27:46; Isaiah 53:10)? Jesus' "own" turned their back on Him, rejection. God the Father rejected the plea of His Son even on the cross. **He was rejected that we might be received** (Romans 10:13). Thanks, Elika, for provoking in us a look into this title for Jehovah we haven't noticed before. Even in the negative aspect of this term we have discovered an attribute about God that helps us understand to what extent He was willing to go to get the human race back.

Matthew 21:42: *"Jesus saith unto them, did you never read in the Scriptures, the stone which the builders **rejected**, the same is become the head of the corner: this is the Lord's doing, and it is marvelous in our eyes?"*

12.

IRA: WATCHER

II Samuel 23:26: *"Helez the Paltite, IRA the son of Ikkesh the Tekoite."*

There are two other IRAs mentioned in the Scriptures: (1) a chief ruler, a Jairite, of David's kingdom and named among David's top political officials (II Samuel 20:26); and (2) another mighty man of David's "mighty men," but an Ithrite named in II Samuel 23:38. As for this Ira, this is basically all we know about him from the Bible: (1) He was the son of a man by the name of Ikkesh, which means "sutile" (I Chronicles 11:28); (2) He was from the town of Tekoah, a city of Judah, located about six miles southeast of Bethlehem and 12 miles south of Jerusalem (the prophet Amos was from this same town Amos 1:1); (3) He was *"the sixth captain of the sixth month…and in his course were twenty and four thousand…"* (I Chronicles 27:9) making Ira one of David's top dozen generals; and (4) His name means **"watcher."** One of the greatest abilities of any soldier is to have the instinct to be vigilant, alert, and a watcher. One of the first jobs a soldier learns in the army is the duty of sentry. It is around this duty, that no doubt Ira did fulfill, I will focus this devotional in our ongoing search for David's Mighty Men and the lessons they teach us.

The sentry, the watcher, is one of the most important positions in any man's army, David's Army, or the Lord's army. He is the warrior that watches and guards while the rest of the army is at rest, sleeping, or doing other things in preparation for a battle. He is the one that protects his fellow soldier from a surprise attack or sudden assault by their enemy. It is his job to warn if danger is near, to shout out an alarm when something suspicious is happening near the camp. The Biblical word for sentry is **"watchman,"** and the Bible speaks often of the importance of the watchman's responsibilities. Did Ira start his military career as a sentry? Chances are he did so the name fits. This warrior reminds me of a poem that was read at my Grandfather Barton's brother's funeral. Many, many years after my Grandmother Barton's passing and my inheritance of his Bible, I found this poem and learned a bit about my great uncle, Benjamin Stanley Barton. Uncle Ben had been a pioneer missionary to the country of Peru in the 1920s. He had become a missionary after fighting in the First World War. The seeming tragedy of his story is that after only a year and a half of service in that far off and distant land from Maine, he contacted tuberculosis and died before he could return to his native land. My grandfather fell heir to Benjamin's Bible in 1926, as I had in 1991. In the front of this time eaten Bible was a brief history of Uncle Ben's service for God and his faithful life wrapped up in a simple poem entitled <u>The Faithful Sentinel</u>, and I quote:

> Away from his home and the friends of his youth,
> He hastened, the herald of mercy and truth;
> For the love of his Lord, and to seek for the lost;
> Soon, alas! Was his fall, but he died at his post.
>
> The stranger's eye wept; that in life's brightest bloom,
> One gifted so highly should sink to the tomb;
> For in ardor he led in the van of the host,
> And he fell like a soldier, he died at his post.
>
> We wept not for him that his warfare is done;
> The battle was fought, and the victory was won;
> But he whispered for those who his heart loved the most,
> "Tell my brethren for me that I died at my post!"
>
> He asked not for a stone to be sculptured with verse;
> He asked not that fame should his merits rehearse;
> But he asked as a boon, when he gave up the ghost,
> That his brethren might know that he died at his post.
>
> Victorious his fall, for he rose as he fell,
> With Jesus, his Master, in glory to dwell;
> He passed over the sea; he has reached the bright coast,
> For he fell like a martyr, he fell at his post.

And can we the words of our brother forget?
Oh, no, they are fresh in our memory yet;
An example so sacred shall never be lost,
We will fall in the work; we will die at our post!

That brings us to our responsibility to our own generation. Let me give to you what I believe are the three characteristics needed to be a faithful sentinel, a responsible sentry, a successful watcher. <u>First, the watcher must have good eyes.</u> *"If when he seeth the sword come upon the land, he blow trumpet, and warn the people."* (Ezekiel 33:3) The faithful sentry must be at the right place at the right time to sound the right warning. We can't be asleep (Romans 13:11), but alert, eyes open, vigilantly watching for any enemy or foe that might be about like *"the roaring lion"* (I Peter 5:8). <u>Second, the watcher must have good ears.</u> *"So thou, O son of man, I have set thee a watchman unto the house of Israel, therefore thou shalt hear the words of my mouth, and warn them for me."* (Ezekiel 33:7) The sentinel not only watches but listens, and we need not just listen for the approaching enemy, but we also need to be listening for the instruction of the Lord found in the Word of God because this precept still applies today: *"…except the Lord keep the city, the watchman waketh but in vain."* (Psalm 127:1) <u>Third, the watcher must have a good echo.</u> *"Warn the people…warn them for me."* (Ezekiel 35:3, 7) If you have good eyes and good ears, but you do not have a voice to warn, how can you be a good sentinel? We have a lot of Christians today with the head knowledge of the coming judgment, but they still remain silent, no voice, and no warning. Noah set the example we all need to follow as God's watchman just before the flood. For 120 years this preacher of righteousness (II Peter 2:5) warned about God's impending destruction of the world by water. He shouted until the day the door of the ark was shut. Whether people listen or not is not our concern. Our job is to watch as a sentinel and warn as a preacher. (Romans 10:14–15)

It is time we open our eyes and unstop our ears and let the echo of our shout resound around our neighborhood and warn this world. The enemy is at the gate, the foe is near, the city is sleeping, and its citizens are slumbering (I Thessalonians 5:1–7). The enemy is strong, the time is short, and we might be overrun at any moment. Are you at your post?

Ezekiel 3:17–21: *"Son of man, I have made thee a watchman unto the house of Israel: therefore hear the word at my mouth, and give them warning from me. When I say unto the wicked, Thou shalt surely died; and thou giveth him not warning, nor speakest to warn the wicked from his wicked way, to save his life; the same wicked man shall die in his iniquity; but his blood will I require at thine hand. Yet if thou warn the wicked and he turn not from his wickedness, nor from his wicked ways, he shall die in his iniquity; but thou hast delivered thy soul."*

13.

ABIEZER: FATHER OF HELP

> I Chronicles 27:12: *"The ninth captain for the ninth month was **ABIEZER** the Anetothite, of the Benjamites: and in his course were twenty and four thousand."*

ABIEZER'S NAME ONLY APPEARS three times in the Bible, but each time it is listed among David "mighty men." From these three references, we are able to glean this information about this "mighty man":

1. Abiezer eventually became one of David's top dozen generals being put in charge of the national defense of Israel for the ninth month of the year (I Chronicles 27:12). We have mentioned this before, but it is worth repeating that once David gained control of the region, he put his armed forces into a kind of National Guard, dividing his army into twelve divisions and giving each division the responsibility of being on guard a certain month of the year. Each division had a commander and Abiezer was one of those commanders.

2. Abiezer was a Benjamite and according to I Chronicles 12:2: *"They were armed with bows, and could use both the right hand and the left in hurling stones and shooting arrows out of a bow, even of Saul's brethren of Benjamin."* This puts Abiezer in a unique position in that he chose David over his own kinsman, King Saul. It also tells us of the skill of this warrior, and though we don't know of any battles, there is certainly an advantage being an amadexrious soldier.

3. I Chronicles 27:12 has Abiezer an Anetothite; I Chronicles 11:28 has Abiezer an Anthothite; and II Samuel 23:27 has Abiezer an Anethothite. So either we are dealing with three different soldiers or one soldier with different spellings of his hometown. Which is it? All the above in my opinion. Despite the various spellings, we are talking about a man from the town of Anathoth. David had another mighty man from the same town, a man called Jehu, another Benjamite (I Chronicles 12:3). Anathoth was a Levitical city in the territory of Benjamin (Joshua 21:18 and I Chronicles 6:60). David's faithful priest Abiathar was exiled to Anathoth by Solomon because he stood against Solomon's kingship (I Kings 2:26). Ezra and Nehemiah recorded that 120 men from Anathoth came out of the Babylonian Captivity (Ezra 2:23 and Nehemiah 7:27) to resettle Anathoth (Nehemiah 11:32). Anathoth was located only three miles north of Jerusalem. Anathoth was also the birthplace of the famous Hebrew prophet, the weeping prophet, Jeremiah (Jeremiah 1:1).

4. Abiezer's name means "Father of Help." Psalm 70:5: *"But I am poor and needy: make haste unto me, O God: thou art my help and my deliverer; O Lord, make no tarrying."* As with many of David's mighty men, we must focus on the definition of their names to get any spiritual blessing, and we have a great one in Abiezer!

I feel the root of this word and its connection to Abiezer goes back to the days of Moses. Moses had fled Egypt and found sanctuary in the tents of Jethro, his future father-in-law. In time Moses and Zipporah, Jethro's oldest daughter, got married and had two sons. The first they called Gershom, but the second they called Eliezer, *"For the God of my fathers, said he, was mine help, and delivered me from the sword of Pharaoh."* (Exodus 18:4) Eliezer means "My God is my help." So another name for Abiezer could be Eliezer because they are similar in spelling and meaning.

In Moses' last blessing to the tribes of Israel, he shows he had never forgotten God's help in his escape from Egypt the first time because he asked the Lord to help Judah, *"be thou an help to him from his enemies,"* (Deuteronomy 33:7) and *"there is none like unto the God of Jeshurun* (Israel), *who rideth upon the heaven in thy help, and in His excellency on the sky,"* (Deuteronomy 33:29) and *"happy art thou, O Israel: who is like unto thee, O people saved by the Lord, the shield of thy help..."* (Deuteronomy 33:29). No doubt David picked up on this great truth reading the writings of Moses because he used the same Hebrew word, *ERER*, or **"help,"** in relationship to God. He writes: *"Our soul waiteth for the Lord: He is our help and our shield."* (Psalm 33:20) When David met Abiezer, did this man remind him of the help the Lord gave him and was giving him?

    I read recently a story about how President Theodore Roosevelt was saved from an assassin's bullet because the steel case that held his spectacles deflected the bullet from hitting his heart. When he realized what had happened, he said, "I've always considered it a nuisance to carry two pairs of glasses, especially those thick heavy ones I kept in that metal case. Yet tonight, God used it to save my life." Our late president realized that the Lord was his "help and shield." We all know or I would hope we would know that, *"The angel of the Lord encampeth round about those that fear Him."* (Psalm 34:7) An unnamed poet once wrote: "O let thy great Almighty care through all this day attend; from every danger, every snare, me helpless, should defend." When will we realize that day in and day out the Lord takes personally the responsibility for our help because He is our help!

    So when it comes to help, God has thousands of keys to open the doors of deliverance. Whether a metal case for a president, or a jaw bone of a donkey for a judge (Judges 15:15), or an ox goad for a farmer (Judges 3:31), or a walking stick for a mighty man (II Samuel 23:21), or a man by the name of Abiezer. God's help often comes from the strangest of places, but ultimately it will be traced back to the hand of God. Whether a person or a prop, God is not limited by what He uses to administer help. We should never forget that the Benjamites were first united against the kingship of David (II Samuel 3:1). Eventually, Abiezer and many others switched sides. We don't know why or when, but he did and became one that helped David secure the Kingship of all Israel. Again, the Psalmist put it this way: *"I will lift up mine eyes unto the hills, from whence cometh my help. My help cometh from the Lord..."* (Psalm 121:1-2). If hills can help, then so can a traitor help. Didn't a man by the name of Saul, later to be called Paul, switch sides in the early days of the church, and didn't he become a great help to Christ's infant church?

    As I write this article, I sit at my desk in the middle of the coastal city of Ellsworth, Maine. I am being drained here because I see no hills. I am a country boy from northern Maine. I was born and raised among rolling hills of fir and spruce and potatoes and oats. I use to walk in open fields of clover and grain that rose and fell to the will of the hill. It was there I learned that Christ was my help. Though He is in the city, I thought I felt

His help more in the hills. So it is no great surprise that it is through men like Abiezer that I found out that the Lord's help does come from hills, but it also comes from hillbillies that have settled in the city. Truly, the Father of Help is the Lord God, but His help often times comes through a human agent, as it did on the day He sent His only begotten Son into the world to help mankind back to Him. The greatest single act of help that ever took place, took place on a hill outside Jerusalem when that man of helpfulness died.

Psalm 124:8: *"Our help is in the name of the Lord…"*

14.

MEBUNNAI: BUILT UP

II Samuel 23:27: *"Abiezer the Anethothite,*
***MEBUNNAI** the Hushathite."*

COMPARING DAVID'S LISTINGS OF his "mighty men" in II Samuel 23 and I Chronicles 11, the next warrior in order would be a man by the name of Mebunnai or Sibbecai. I have come to believe these two names are for the same soldier because they fall in the same slot or the same order David gave them in II Samuel 23 and the same order recorded in I Chronicles 11. They both are called Hushathites, the patronymic of the family of Hushah of the tribe of Judah (I Chronicles 4:4), and this is all we know for sure about this mighty man of David:

1. Mebunnai: *"the eighth captain for the eighth month was Sibbecai the Hushathites of the Zarhites* [from Zarah or Zerah, the son of Judah- Numbers 26:20] *and in his course were twenty and four thousand."* (I Chronicles 27:11) This would have made Mebunnai one of David's top dozen generals, responsible for a month of the years in the protection of the borders of Israel.

2. Mebunnai is also recorded as the man who killed a "giant:" *"And it came to pass after this, that there was again a battle with the Philistines at Gob: then Sibbechai* (Sibbecai) *the Hushathite slew Saph* [possibly a brother to Goliath], *which was one of the sons of the giant."* (II Samuel 21:18 and I Chronicles 20:4) Mebunnai's only call to Biblical fame was at the first Battle at Gob when he took on the giant Saph and killed him, but that event was enough to immortalize

Mebunnai in the Word of God. We know very little of this battle; we don't even know how Mebunnai slew Saph, but perhaps that is the way the Lord wanted us to remember Mebunnai. I believe Mebunnai was just one of David's ordinary soldiers at the Battle of Gob, but before the battle was over Mebunnai would go down in Jewish history as a "giant-killer!" Will we stand in this evil day against the giants that still stalk the land? These giants might not be gigantic in size, but in intellect, in position, in power whose *"every imagination of the thoughts of the heart was* (is) *only evil continually."* (Genesis 6:5) In the days of Noah they were called "men of renown," and Jesus warned us that, *"as the days of Noah so would the coming of the Son of God be."* (Matthew 24:37) For me, this includes "giants." We, too, must develop our fighting skills so like Mebunnai we might take on the "giants."

3. Sibbecai means "Jehovah is intervening," but Mebunnai means "built up," and it is around that name and meaning I would like to challenge you from this verse in Colossians 2:7: *"Rooted and BUILT UP in Him, and stablished in the faith, as ye have been taught, abounding with thanksgiving."* As Mebunnai helped David build up the nation of Israel after the civil war with the family of Saul and the countless wars with the enemies that surrounded Israel, so, too, must we learn to "build-up?"

Dave Egner, writing in an <u>Our Daily Bread</u> article, once recorded this:

> Scripture portrays the Christian life as a process of growth in which we advance from one stage to the next: from spiritual infancy to maturity, from milk to strong meat, from being rotted in Christ to being firmly established. We may want to be grown up all at once, but we must learn to take one step at a time. I realized this anew as my 16-month-old granddaughter and I were walking along the channel in Muskegon, Michigan. I was in somewhat of a hurry, but Kelsey was not. From her toddler perspective, she had seen a 6-inch-ledge that ran the length of the walkway. Slowly and carefully she climbed on top of the ledge. After standing there triumphantly for a moment, she cautiously stepped back down. It was quite an accomplishment for the little tyke. Then she wanted to make sure she mastered it well. So she a few feet farther down the walk climbed onto the ledge again. I patiently waited for her because I knew this was

> an important phase of her learning. And I thought, I can learn from her. I need to be sure I've mastered one spiritual discipline before proceeding to one that is more advanced. Then I won't become discouraged in my climb to maturity. Spiritual growth occurs a step at a time.

One of the dangers often repeated in the Bible (I Corinthians 3:1–3; Hebrews 5:11–14) is the scourge of spiritual stagnation, when the believer doesn't grow but stays the same. We might start out with milk (I Peter 2:2), but we need to grow into strong meat (Hebrews 5:14). This happens when we are "built up" in Christ feeding daily on this word (II Peter 3:18).

Christ said, *"I will build my Church."* (Matthew 16:18) As Dave Egner watched his granddaughter expand her abilities and boundaries, so, too, does Christ watch us as we walk through this life. Mr. Egner saw a tiny glimpse of the advancement of his granddaughter during their walk together along that channel in Michigan. So, too, does Christ see us being built up in Him even though, like the little girl, we never notice it ourselves. Ours is an observation that is made over time as we realize that we are not the same, our interests are not the same over time. Christ has the ability to see our slightest advancements, or steps enlarging, or interests expanding. Growing up is built up. Peter makes an interesting analogy to this concept in his first epistle to the scattered saints (I Peter 1:1). After speaking of the newborn (I Peter 2:2), he speaks of the saints as *"lively stones"* being built up as a spiritual house (I Peter 2:5). Ethel Barrett, in her book <u>It Only Hurts When I Laugh</u> tells the story of the king of Sparta and his boast to a Greek ambassador of the invincible walls of Sparta. The visitor quickly asked if he might see these walls. The king's reply was that in the morning the Greek ambassador would be taken on a tour of the walls of Sparta. The next morning, to the ambassador's surprise, the king of Sparta took his guest through the gates of the city onto the plains outside the town. There, standing in perfect order and attention, was the well-disciplined and world-famous army of Sparta. The king of Sparta pointed to his troops and proclaimed: "There they are! There are the walls of Sparta!" I have come to believe that we, too, are to be such walls. In the New Testament the Church of Christ is likened to a bride (Ephesians 5), a brotherhood (I Peter 2:17), a body (I Corinthians 12), but also a building (Ephesians 2:21–22). As we speak, the Good Lord through His Spirit is building up His "temple," a temple not made with brick and granite, timber or tile, but "lively stones," you and me. So as we are built up, we are being built into the building of God.

Believer by believer, Christ, too, is building up His Church. Has he put you into His building yet? Have you been built up into God's walls yet? If you haven't, my encouragement to you would be to yield to the Master bricklayer and let him use you to finish His wall (work). Mebunnai is a good example to us through the meaning of his name, but his other name is just as important (Jehovah is intervening). Only when the Father chooses the stone, and only when the Spirit convicts (prepares) the stone, will Jesus be able to take that stone and make it a part of His grand building, the Church.

I Peter 2:5: *"Ye also, as lively stones, are built up a spiritual house, an holy priesthood, to offer up spiritual sacrifices, acceptable to god by Jesus Christ."*

15.

ZALMON: ASCENT

II Samuel 23:28: *"**ZALMON** the Ahohite, Maharai the Netopathite."*

WE HAVE COME TO another unknown "mighty man," but not an unnamed "mighty man." If we compare the two lists (II Samuel 23:28 and I Chronicles 11:29), Zalmon is #15 on the Samuel list and 14th on the Chronicles list where he is called Ilai, and this is all we know of this "mighty man:"

1. In both lists this warrior is called an Ahohite. This is a patronymic derived from Ahoah, a grandson of Benjamin (I Chronicles 8:4). David had at least two other "mighty men" in his list that were Ahohites: Eleazar (I Chronicles 11:12) and Dodai (I Chronicles 27:4) so this would have made Zalmon a Benjamite (I Chronicles 12:1-7).

2. Zalmon can also be spelled Salmon. The original Salmon was the father of Boaz (Ruth 4:20), and both names mean "terrace" or "ascent."

3. Ilai, Zalmon's other name means "supreme" or "elevated." For our spiritual challenge would you permit me to put the two names together under the topic of a **"supreme ascent."**

I asked myself the question, "What was the supreme ascent of all times? *"Wherefore He saith, when He ascended up on high, He led captivity captive, and gave gifts unto men."* (Ephesians 4:8) Jesus told Nicodemus: *"And no man hath ascended up to heaven, but he that came down from heaven, even the Son of man which is in heaven."* (John 3:13) This name is without doubt linked to Christ in the marvelous doctrine of the ascension of our Advocate (I John 2:1). As we have seen already in our study of David's mighty men, so many of the meanings of the names of these men can be connected to the terms and titles that define our Lord and Savior Jesus Christ in His sojourn here on earth.

The Greek word in Ephesians 4:8 is *anabaino* which simply means **"to go or come up."** In the context of Ephesians 4:8 the word is used to describe the return of Jesus Christ to His Father in heaven. That event is better described in Acts 1:9 with this recording of Luke: *"And when He had spoken these things, while they beheld, He was taken up; and a cloud received Him out of their sight."* The return of Jesus to the right hand of the Father is a well-documented happening in Scripture, but what isn't mentioned much is the fact that when Christ returned to heaven, He didn't go alone. Do you realize that if Zalmon was a believer in Jehovah, and I believe that all of David's mighty men came to believe as David did, that Zalmon ascended with Jesus that day the Christ returned to the Father by way of the Mount of Olives? Amazing to consider!

The phrase **"lead captivity captive"** refers to the souls of the Old Testament saints released from Sheol, the place of departed souls (Ephesians 4:9–10), when Jesus visited that place between His death on Friday at Calvary and His resurrection on Sunday at the empty tomb. The idea of the phraseology is the imagery of a conquering king returning after a victorious campaign triumphantly leading those he had captured in battle. We must remember that no soul could gain access to heaven before Jesus had finished His redemptive work on the cross. That is why God created a place called Sheol, a place those souls could wait. Now granted, not all souls believed like Abraham, Isaac, and Jacob, and so many others, so Sheol had to have two compartments in it, one for the souls of the saved and one for the souls of the lost. The lost side was called "hades" or "hell," while the saved side was called "Paradise" or "Abraham's bosom," and between them *"a great gulf fixed."* The only good story that gives us a clear picture of this place called Sheol is Jesus' parable of the rich man and Lazarus (Luke 16:19–31). This is the same place Jesus told the repentant thief he would meet him after his death (Luke 23:43). Peter tells us clearly that Jesus visited this place (I Peter 3:19), and it was from this place the saved were delivered while the unsaved still wait for their day in court when finally "hell" and all in it will be thrown into "the lake of fire." (Revelation 20:11–15)

Where did Christ lead Abraham, Isaac, Jacob and all the other Old Testament Believers? On High! The Bible is very clear that there are three "heavens." The first heaven is the atmosphere apron that surrounds our little blue dot in the universe (Genesis 1:8). The second heaven is the great expanse of space with its population of planets, solar systems, and starry suns separated by light-years of time because this, too, is called heaven in the Word of God (Psalm 19:1). The third heaven is the abode of God, which is only reached beyond the first and second heavens through a different dimension, a spiritual one, a place Paul visited and told us about (II Corinthians 12:2-4). This is the home of God, and this is the place that Christ ascended to. I don't know for sure who exactly was on the "departure" list that day, 40 days after Christ's death (Acts 1:3), but with a name like **"ascent,"** you can't tell me that Zalmon wasn't on that list.

In an Our Daily Bread devotional, I found this bite of history that for me is a fitting illustration and application for our thoughts on David's "mighty man" named Zalmon. The writer was Henry Bosch, and he recorded these thoughts:

> Some time ago the New York Times reported that the former head of the Russian state, Mr. Khrushchev, smugly explained, "We sent up our explorer, Yuril Gagarin. He circled the globe and found nothing in outer space. It's pitch-black there, no Garden of Eden, nothing like heaven." Gagarin's successor, Russian cosmonaut Gherman Titov, said, blasphemously, "There is no god out there. I didn't see him." Oh, the folly of unbelief! Imagine intelligent men making such ridiculous statements. If they were familiar at all with the Bible, they would know that the all-pervading Spirit of God is not physical and material and so cannot be seen by our limited, human vision. Titov didn't see the cosmic rays either, but they were there nonetheless! As to the Second Person of the Trinity, the Lord Jesus Christ, He is now seated at the Father's right hand in glory (Colossians 3:1). Since heaven is located "up far above all heavens," he could never be seen by anyone who is only a few hundred miles away from this earth. Titov didn't go high enough to see Him, and, regrettably, unless he gets saved, he never will!

And neither will you!

In the same article Bosch also asked this question: "Are you among God's spiritual astronauts who by grace will one day take a celestial journey 'far above all heavens' [note the plural here speaking of the heavens we have described above] to be with Christ in glory?" Zalmon is not a household name, even among Christians, but I believe he was one of the first spiritual astronauts to make that journey. Will you be one as well? Will **"ascent"** be a word that will be used to describe your departure one day? Will you go up (heaven) or down (hades) to hell because hell is down for it tells us that Christ ***"descended"*** before He ***"ascended"*** (Ephesians 4:9). Let me encourage you to get your name on the "departure" list because if you are without Christ, your name is already on the "descended" list (John 3:18, 36). Granted, that departure could happen at any time as Paul describes in II Timothy 4:6, but there will be a special flight if you are one of the special astronauts that will not see death, but will be taken in the "rapture." (I Thessalonians 4:16–17) Amen!

Ephesians 4:10: *"He that descended is the same also that ascended up far above all heavens, that he might fill all things.*

16.

MAHARAI: SWIFT

*I Chronicles 27:13: "The tenth captain for the tenth month was **MAHARAI** the Netophathite, of the Zarhites: and in his course were twenty and four thousand."*

WE HAVE COME TO another of David's top commanders, a man by the name of Maharai. His name is only found three times in the Bible, but each time he is listed among David's "mighty men" (II Samuel 23:28 and I Chronicles 11:30). Here is what I was able to discover about this warrior:

1. In all three accounts, Maharai is called "the Netophathite." From this we can trace his place of origin, probably his hometown. Maharai was from the village of Netophah. Netophah was a small town in Judah, just south of Jerusalem, but very near David's hometown of Bethlehem. That same town is called Beit-Netiph today. The next "mighty man" we will highlight, Heleb, was also from Netophah (II Samuel 23:29). Warriors from this town were still being named late in the history of the country of Judah. When Nebuchadnezzar attacked the Kingdom of Judah, a soldier from this town by the name of Seraiah came to its aid (II Kings 25:23 and Jeremiah 40:8). Individuals from this town were also numbered among those that were exiled to Babylon (I Chronicles 9:6). Fifty-six men from Netophah were listed among those who returned from the Babylonian Captivity by the scribe Ezra (Ezra 2:22). Nehemiah also adds the men of Netophah with the men of Bethlehem together for a total of 188 in

his listings (Nehemiah 7:26). When Nehemiah records the singers that helped rededicate the walls of Jerusalem, the town of Netophah is mentioned again (Nehemiah 12:27–28).

2. In our key verse printed above, Maharai is also numbered among "the Zarhites." This simply refers to the fact that Maharai could trace his lineage back to Zarah, or Zerah, the son of Judah (Joshua 7:17). Genealogy and heritage was very important to the Jewish people. That is why so many genealogical lists in the Bible.

3. Later in Maharai's military career, he was put in charge of the national defense of the United Israel for the tenth month of the year. Maharai commanded a division of David's grand army numbering 24,000 soldiers, making Maharai one of David's top dozen generals.

4. Finally, as with the others named, but little known "mighty men," we have Maharai's name. Its meaning is simple: hasty or swift. I would like to make application to the importance of a soldier being swift. It has been my goal through this Scriptural exercise to underline various principles and precepts that will help us be *"a good soldier for Jesus Christ."* (II Timothy 2:3). So what can we learn from Maharai, one of David's exemplary soldiers?

"Wherefore, my beloved brethren, let every man be swift to hear, slow to speak..." (James 1:19). An important characteristic of a good warrior is the ability to hear swiftly. What was the young lad Samuel to learn the night the Lord God came calling? How to hear the voice of the Lord is the simple answer. I believe the youthful prodigy had already been taught to listen, yes, even swiftly, because he reacted quickly, in haste to the call, but: *"Samuel was laid down to sleep; that the Lord called Samuel: and he answered. Here I am. And he ran unto Eli, and said, here I am; for thou calledst me. And he said, I called not; lie down again. And he went and lay down. And the Lord called yet again, Samuel. And Samuel arose and went to Eli..."* (I Samuel 3:3–6). The one slow to listen was the old priest Eli, not the young gatekeeper Samuel. Despite Eli's shortcomings, he did teach Samuel the important concept: *"Speak: for thy servant heareth."* (I Samuel 3:9) Samuel's problem was not in listening, or in listening swiftly, but in who he was tuned into, who he was listening to. This is a problem that many of us have.

In Glyn Evan's great devotional book, <u>Daily With The King</u>, he makes this comment on Eli's advice to young Samuel:

> I pray that God will enable men to become a good listener. I must understand that God does not speak to me in the storm, the earthquake, or the fire, but in the 'still small voice' (I Kings 19:9–12). That is another way of saying that God does not speak to me through circumstances or through others unless there is an inner confirmation and explanation of what comes from the outside. Eli, the old priest, was wise enough to know that God's will for Samuel, his aside, had to come directly from God to Samuel. How do I learn to be a good listener? I must begin by giving Him time and attention; that is the critical part of the battle. Next I must develop a sense of awe and reverence for God, which is a natural preparation for silence, which in turn is essential to proper listening."

What made Samuel such a mighty and affective servant of Jehovah was his ability to be swift to hear God. Even as a young man, he had a wonderful attribute as a swift soldier. David had that same ability as a young man, and I often wonder with their towns being so close together if Maharai and David had met before, as boys, and had grown up together listening to God in the fields around their towns. It is the warrior that hears God's instructions quickest that will in haste apply them that will come forth victorious and *"more than conquerors"* (Romans 8:37).

Another spiritual warrior that was swift to hear was the great Jewish prophet Isaiah. *"Whom shall I send, and who will go for us? Then said I, Here am I; send me."* (Isaiah 6:8) Only those who are listening will hear. How often does my wife yell at me from the kitchen, and only after much shouting does she get my attention. Why? I am not listening to her; I am listening to the television. Oswald Chambers in his famous devotional book, <u>My Utmost For His Highest</u>, makes this wonderful observation on Isaiah's ability to hear swiftly:

> God did not address the call to Isaiah; Isaiah overheard God saying, "Who will go for us?" The call of God is not for the special few, it is for everyone. Whether or not I hear God's call depends upon the state of my ears; and what I hear depends upon my disposition. "Many are called but few are chosen," that is, few prove themselves the chosen ones. The chosen ones are those who have come into a relationship with God through Jesus Christ whereby their disposition has been altered and their ears unstopped, and they hear the still small voice questioning all the time, "Who will go for us?" The majority of us have no ear for anything but ourselves, we cannot hear a thing God says. To

be brought into the zone of the call of God is to be profoundly altered. As we listen, our ears get acute and, like Jesus, we shall hear God all the time!

Amen and Amen!

Might I add this thought to Chambers challenge in the light of the meaning of Maharai's name? Being swift to listen to that "still small voice" in the night or at any time is the key ingredient to hearing that "still small voice" in the first place. I have come to the conclusion that like the other great listeners of the Bible, Maharai attained to

the position in David's Army because he was "swift to hear" and "slow to speak;" an attribute any commander would love to have in his soldiers, as does Jesus. (II Timothy 2:4)

Isaiah 55:2: *"...hearken diligently unto me..."*

17.

HELDAI: ENDURING

I Chronicles 27:15: "The twelfth captain for the twelfth month was **HELDAI** *the Netophathite, of Othniel: and in his course were twenty and four thousand."*

WE ARE TAUGHT CLEARLY in the Bible (II Peter 1:20) that every verse in the Holy Writ can only be of *"private interpretation,"* so on this the last of David's divisional generals I have come to this personal conclusion. Take what I write for what it is worth, with a measure of salt. I have come to believe that the Heldai of I Chronicles 27:15 is the same as Heled of I Chronicles 11:30 and Heleb of II Samuel 23:29. The common denominator among these three names is that they were all from Netophah, a town in Judah just south of Jerusalem (more of David's kinsmen). Their placement in the list of David's "mighty men" would also suggest that they are one and the same man. Both Heleb and Heled came from the same father, Baanah. In the case of Hedai, it says "of Othniel." I feel this is referring not to his father, but to his famous ancestor "Othniel," the first judge of Israel (Judges 3:9), one of the most famous men of Israel's first tribe, so this would connect all three to the tribe of Judah. Biblically speaking, however, Heldai's only call to fame is his being numbered among David's greatest warriors, top commanders, and elite soldiers, but as with so many of David's men, it is in the meaning of his name that I would like to inspire you. Heldai simply means "enduring." One of the greatest attributes needed in a soldier fighting the spiritual battles for the cause of Christ is endurance.

William Barclay once wrote: **"Endurance is not just the ability to bear a hard thing, but to turn it into glory."** Paul put it best when writing to the young warrior (I Timothy 1:18): *"Thou therefore endure hardness, as a good soldier of Jesus Christ."* (II Timothy 2:3) Mrs. Charles Cowman quoting Martin Luther in her famous devotional <u>Springs in the Valley</u> quotes:

> The post of honor in war is so called because attended by difficulties and dangers to which but few are equal; yet generals usually allot these hard services to their favorites and friends, who on their part eagerly take them as tokens of favour and marks of confidence. Should we not, therefore, account it an honor and a privilege when the Captain of our salvation assigns us a difficult post, since he can and does inspire His soldiers which no earthly commander can with wisdom, courage, and strength suitable to their situation? Listen to Ignatius shouting as the lion's teeth tear his flesh, **"Now I begin to be a Christian!"** The Christian's badge of honor here has ever been the Cross. The Bishop of Winchester says, "No church or movement can survive unless it is ready to be crucified."

We must endure the agony of the spiritual warfare, hardened to the difficulties and the dangers, if we like Heldai are to attain the place of honor numbered among Jesus' "mighty men." Irene Brock McElberen once wrote in a poem called <u>A Song of the Road</u> these lines: **"Let me but walk with my face to the wind; keen though it be, and strong; let my way lead up the hill all the while, rough through the path, and long!"** For me this is the abiding meaning of the word enduring. It was men like Heldai who endured with David through the long years of exile and exodus from their tribal lands as King Saul and his army chased them about from cave to cave. The sleepless nights they endured to gain the kingdom; the countless hungry days they endured to gain the throne; and the constant fear of death they endured to see David as king. Endurance will survive when nearly all other soldierly qualities fail.

Mrs. Charles Cowman seemingly liked to write about endurance (was it because she became a widow at a very early age and her life was an example of enduring faith?) because I found another challenge about endurance in her devotional <u>Mountain Trailways</u> where she wrote:

> Die hard, my men, die hard!" shouted Colonel Ingils of the 57th Division to his men on the heights behind the River Albuhera. The regiment was nicknamed "the Die-Hards" after that. The

tale may have been forgotten, but the name lives on; and in spite of foolish uses, it is a great name. It challenges us. We are called to be the Lord's "die-hards," to whom can be counted upon to stand firm no matter what happens. It is written of Oliver Cromwell: "He strove to give his command so strict a unity that in no crisis should it crack." With this aim in view, he made his "Ironsides!" The result of that discipline was seen not only in victory but in defeat; for his troops "though they were beaten and routed, presently rallied again and stood in good order until they received new orders." This is the spirit that animates all valiant life; to be strong in will, to strive, to seek, to find, and not to yield is all that matters. Failure or success, as the world understands these words, is of no eternal account. To be able to stand steady in defeat is in itself a victory. There is not tinsel about that kind of triumph. "It's a fight and a hard fight, and a fight to the end, for life is no sleep in the clover; it's a fight for a boy and a fight for a man, and a fight until days are all over.

To fight that kind of fight (I Timothy 6:12) you must have godly endurance. It was that kind of enduring fight that David and his men had in order for them to overcome all foes and come through victorious. How often David wanted to quit (I Samuel 27:1 and read his psalms), we don't know, and I wonder how many times it was his "mighty men" that rallied him, strengthened his spirit, and with a name like "Enduring" I wonder how many times Heldai was leading the chorus and counseling his captain to press on, go on, endure to the end.

It was said of Abraham, *"And so, after he had patiently endured, he obtained the promise."* (Hebrews 11:27) Abraham and Sarah had to endure nearly a third of their lives after they heard the promise of a child. Granted, they failed along the way, but in the end they got their promised boy because of patient endurance. This quality was also seen in Christ and encouraged in us: *"Looking unto Jesus the author and finisher of our faith; who for the joy that was set before him endured the cross…"* (Hebrews 12:2). As with all the godly characteristics, Jesus is our example (I Peter 2:21), and who of us can't endure with Christ? Bishop Quayle writes:

> Luxuriousness is rarely the cradle of giants. It is not unsuggestive that the soft and beautiful trophies are not in the home of the strong, indomitable, and progressive peoples. The pioneering and progressive races have dwelt in sterner and harder climes. The lap of Luxury does not afford the elementary iron for the upbringing of strong and enduring life. Hardness hardens;

antagonism solidifies; trials insure and confirm. Thou, Great God, who girdest the soul as Thou does gird the world by zones of stars and glories of star-sown night, gird us with godly endurance so that we shall feel, as we go into battle with tightened girdles at our loins, that God is our strength and makes war through us. Amen.

Was Heldai such a man? When you read of those that have done for God in the difficult and dangerous assignment, the characteristic of endurance is foremost in the example of such believers. Abraham had it, Moses had it, Jesus had it, and I believe men like Heldai had it. Do we have it?

II Thessalonians 1:4: *"So that we ourselves glory in you in the churches of for your patience and faith in all your persecution and tribulation that ye endure."*

18.

JONATHAN: THE LORD HAS GIVEN

II Samuel 21:21: "And when he defied Israel JONATHAN the son of Shimeah, the brother of David slew him."

THERE ARE PLACES WHERE the Christian should fear to go, but never dares to go. Places where the wicked one has controlled, dominated, and demons have infested such places for years. These are the places where the men and women of God have taken the Gospel at the peril of their own lives. Though fewer and isolated now, it has only been because of the courage of Christ's soldiers that these strongholds of Satan have been conquered, wicked places like Gath of Philistia. Gath was the hometown of the last group of diabolical giants, a superhuman race of people, the offspring, I believe, of fallen angels and wicked women (Genesis 6:4 and Jude 6). It was Satan's first attempt to pollute the stock of Adam and from keeping the Seed of the woman (Genesis 3:15 and Galatians 4:4) from coming into the world, our Lord Jesus Christ Himself. One by one their places of influence and control were conquered by God's giant-killers. Time would fail me to speak of Joshua and Og (Deuteronomy 3), Caleb and Arba (Joshua 14), David and Goliath (I Samuel 17), Abishai and Ishbibenob (II Samuel 21), Sibbechai and Saph (I Chronicles 20), and Elhanan and Lahmi (II Samuel 21). Each of these men took on a demonic giant and won, but there was still one giant left in Gath after all these encounters, a giant for Jonathan to kill at the Battle of Gath.

Paul taught us through his epistle to Timothy that we, too, are to be soldiers of a kind: *"Thou therefore endure hardness, as a good soldier of Jesus Christ."* (II Timothy 2:3) When you fight giants on their own turf, it is a hard struggle, a hard fight. No man is sure of the outcome of a battle fought against a giant in his hometown unless you have God on your side: **"If God be for us, who can be against us?"** (Romans 8:31) I believe this promise is true even if the one against you is a home-grown giant. We are also promised that we can be *"...more than conquerors through Him* [Jesus] *that loved us."* (Romans 8:37) It is important that we take care to prepare not only for an attack, but the possibility and opportunity to attack. It was time to conquer Gath, giants and all, and David's nephew would do his uncle proud and honor his country by killing the last giant.

In all my study (I have actually written a book on the topic of Biblical giants I call Satan's Super Soldiers) I have not found one giant to ever be an ally of God or God's people; they were all foes, enemies of God and God's chosen race. I also never found a giant in any of God's armies throughout history. Even Samson, the world's strongest man, was not a giant, a man of superior height and size, because we learn through a study of Samson's life (Judges 13–16) that Samson got his supernatural strength through the Spirit of God, not his makeup or muscles. The giant of Gath was "a man of great stature." This is the difference between Satan's Super Soldiers and God's warriors. Satan produces fear by size (Numbers 13:33), but God produces faith by His Spirit: *"Not by might, nor by power, but by my Spirit saith the Lord."* (Zechariah 4:6) We should conclude right now that our foes will always seem bigger, better, and more boastful (prideful): *"...and he defied Israel"* (II Samuel 21:21), just like Goliath defied Israel (I Samuel 17:45).

I believe Jonathan, like David, was provoked by this boasting giant. Remember David's words at the Battle of Elah: *"For who is this uncircumcised Philistine that he should defy the armies of the Living God?"* (I Samuel 17:26) Like David, Jonathan was just a young man at the Battle of Gath (the son of David's brother Shimeah-I Samuel 16:6–10). So despite his unusual height and shape (more fingers and toes than the normal person-II Samuel 21:20), Jonathan, like David, was willing to attack and kill this monstrosity from Gath. Unparalleled insolence has always been a characteristic of God's foes, our foes. Being the last giant, this freak of Satan had either seen or heard of the death of all the other giants (a careful read of II Samuel 21:15–22 will convince you that the other giants named in that passage, and Goliath himself, were all brothers), yet instead of being humbled, this giant was more defiant (II Samuel 21:22). If Satan was their creator, then it is not surprising that they, like their father, would be so prideful because this was the trait of Lucifer (Isaiah 14:12–15) in heaven. So it is with all our foes, but we can boldly proclaim that we have yet to find a giant that ever won, not even once, over a man of God in the Bible. They can taunt, they can tease, and they can tempt us into fearing them or doubting God, but in reality all they are doing is bragging and boasting to their own destruction. We are not told how Jonathan slew this giant, but like the other giant-killers before him, this giant was no match for God's giant-killer because **the Lord had given** Israel Jonathan for this!

What should the giant of Gath tell us about facing fearful foes on their own doorstep? What should the death of the last giant tell us about the end of the greatest giant of them all, death? And what should the Battle of Gath tell us of the conflicts yet to come with giants? First, we must conclude that it is folly to fear that which only glories in flesh and blood. If we are foolish enough to wrestle in flesh and blood, we will be defeated by Satan's giants every time (Ephesians 6:12). But our fight is not in flesh and blood, but in the Spirit, and we are promised: *"Greater is He that is in me than he that is in the world."* (I John 4:4) Read carefully these instructions by Paul in II Corinthians 10:3–4. Second, we must conclude that like the last giant, our last enemy, one of the greatest giants we face, death, will also be destroyed (I Corinthians 15:26). There is an appointed time for all giants to die, including Satan (Revelation 20:10). I like the way Ezekiel describes their destruction: *"And they shall not lie with the mighty that are fallen of the uncircumcised, which are gone down to hell with their weapons of war; and they have laid their swords under their heads, but their iniquities shall be upon their bones, though they were the terror of the mighty in the land of the living."* (Ezekiel 32:27) What a great description of the end of a gigantic warrior. There was and still is only a season for giants, and, when Christ finally destroys them, we will see them no more because their destination is different than ours. (Matthew 25:41) Lastly, we must conclude that the most powerful enemies will probably be faced in life's final battles. I write this while my father of 91 is facing his toughest foes in a VA home in northern Maine. A man of great health and strength well into his mid-80s, Dad is now being subjected to weakness that requires help, and a mental disability that is taking away his memory and his recognition of family. He is confused and paranoid, enemies he never thought he would face, foes his family never thought he would face. A simple study of the lives of the saints in the Scriptures will reveal that life's battles get tougher and life's foes get more numerous. Satan will always keep a giant in reserve to face us in life's final skirmish.

Let us remember today that God is our strength and our stronghold and our skill set even when we are fighting in our enemy's last bastion. (This world is not our home, it is Satan's home.) Fear not, nor faint in the battle of life; we are already promised victory!

Acts 2:35: *"Until I make thy foes they footstool."*

19.

ELHANAN: GOD IS GRACIOUS

II Samuel 21:19: *"And there was again a battle in Gob with the Philistines, where **ELHANAN** the son of Jaareoregim, a Bethlehemite, slew the brother of Goliath the Gittite, the staff of whose spear was like a weaver's beam."*

I PROMISED YOU A few articles ago that we would be coming back to this name. David had two mighty men named Elhanan. One the son of Dodo from Bethlehem (II Samuel 23:24 and I Chronicles 11:26), and Elhanan the son of Jaareoregim or Jair (I Chronicles 20:5). Before, we spoke on the graciousness of God as seen in the meaning of their names, but in the case of this Elhanan, we have a battle to fight. In this battle we learn that sin has many brothers and each of them is a giant.

"*Then he* [DAVID] *took his staff in his hand, chose five smooth stones from the stream, put them in the pouch of his shepherd's bag, and with his sling in his hand, approached the Philistine.*" (I Samuel 17:40 NIV) Have you ever considered why David took five stones out of the Brook of Elah? An interesting answer to that thought provoking question, if not a scriptural one, is because Goliath had four brothers. Whether any of them were at the Battle of Elah, we don't really know because it isn't until we get to the Third Battle of Gob, much, much later in David's reign, that we even discover that Goliath had brothers. There is speculation that David took the extra stones just in case he missed, but knowing what we know of David, he rarely missed, especially when God was directing the shot. Personally, I have come to the conclusion that this concept is one of the reasons we need to study "the giants of the Bible." When Satan makes something, he never makes just one. Goliath had brothers and these brothers, like Goliath, needed to die.

So, did Goliath have four huge brothers just like himself? This might be one of those questions where the admonition of Paul can be applied: *"Let every man be fully persuaded in his own mind."* (Romans 14:5) I have become fully persuaded that Goliath (I Samuel 17:4), Ishbibenob (II Samuel 21:16), Saph (II Samuel 21:18), Lahmi (I Chronicles 20:5), and a six-fingered monstrosity from Gath (II Samuel 21:20) were all the sons of a giant named Rapha. It is easy to connect the last four because we read: *"These four were born to the giant of Gath, and fell by the hand of David, and by the hand of his servants."* (II Samuel 21:22) We add to that verse these verses: *"…And Ishibibenob, one of the descendants of Rapha…"* (II Samuel 21:16) and *"…Lahmi, the brother of Goliath the Gittite…"* (I Chronicles 20:5), and I come to the conclusion that all five giants were related. You also need to consider that David never killed any of the last four giants, and yet it speaks of the giant David killed. That could only be Goliath, and for me the connection is made. Also, the last giant was actually killed in Gath, Goliath's hometown, and it seems quite clear that we have been dealing with a family of giants.

Just because David killed the giant Goliath, doesn't mean that giants were finished. They kept coming because there was a giant for Abishai (II Samuel 21:17), a giant for Sibbechai (II Samuel 21:18), and a giant for Elhanan; and there will be a giant for us as well because sin has many brothers, and they are all giants. I believe sin is a giant and can be defined by this precept from the pen of Paul in Hebrews 12:1: *"Wherefore seeing we are compassed about with so great a cloud of witnesses, let us lay aside every weight, AND THE SIN WHICH DOTH SO EASILY BESET US, and let us run with patience the race that is set before us."* How many saints have been deceived into thinking just because Goliath is dead, there are no more giants to fear or face? How many Christians after conquering one bad habit have been trapped by a second brother, equal to or more powerful than the first?

Jesus shares this insight into the concept I am trying to illustrate in the life of Elhanan: *"When the unclean spirit is gone out of a man, he walketh through dry places, seeking rest, and findeth none. Then he saith, I will return into my house from whence I came out; and when he is come, he findeth it empty, swept, and garnished. Then goeth he, and taketh with himself seven other spirits more wicked than himself, and they enter in and dwell there: and the last state of that man is worse than the first. Even so shall it be also unto this wicked generation."* (Matthew 12:43–45) Iniquity has many brothers and each is as formidable as the first. At the Battle of Elah, David cut off the head of Goliath, yet many years later David almost got his head cut off by Goliath's brother (II Samuel 21:15–17). It seems each time David and his army attacked Philistia, or was attacked by Philistia, there was a giant to face. So it is with us in our battles with sin. I wondered if David thought with each encounter if he was seeing a clone of Goliath because if they were brothers then they might have looked alike. Dressed in similar armor and carrying familiar weaponry, David and his men might have thought, "Didn't we kill that giant in the last battle?" Yet, battle after battle, a recognizable mountain of a man seemed to be at the forefront of battle. On the eve of each of the Battles for Gob stood another giant, another goliath with a gigantic weapon in hand; another foe, another formidable fen just as furious as the one before. There seems to be always one more giant to kill. I found this poem that might help us understand this parallel between giants and sins:

> It's a fight and a hard fight, and a fight to the end.
> For life is no sleep in the clover;
> It's a fight for the boy and a fight for the man,
> And a fight until days are all over.

Remember, our last enemy, death: *"The last enemy that shall be destroyed is death."* (I Corinthians 15:26)

Today, as we put on our "dress for success" (Ephesians 6:10–18) against the giants that stalk us, let us be conscious of the fact that despite our past victories over sin yesterday, we will no doubt have to reface its brother today. And because "God is gracious," we will leave the battlefield a victor with another giant lying at our feet defeated. And even after our latest victory, we cannot rest in the afterglow of success because tomorrow another giant will block our path to a righteous life. If we read carefully the stories of II Samuel 21, we count three giants in three battles (II Samuel 21:15–19), and, yet, when David's army attacked the stronghold of the giants (Gath) there is still another brother of his archenemy waiting to take him on (II Samuel 21:20–21). If this is true of David, let us not be surprised if this is no less true of us. Sin like giants has many brothers even though they might have different names: Covetousness,

Wickedness, Murderous, Fornication, Blasphemy, Disobedience, Maliciousness, Unrighteousness, and so many more. Each must be faced and destroyed before they are no longer a threat to us. For me the story of Elhanan is the story of a victor, not a victim. So, too, with us as we rely on the graciousness of God, we, too, can be a winner in the confrontations with sin and its evil brothers, but it is *"the sin that so easily besets us"* that is our giant. It knows our weaknesses and it waits its chance, but let us never forget that Elhanan (God is Gracious) is on our side. It is when we take up His graciousness that we can be confident that our "giant" sin will be defeated.

> Psalm 56:2: *"Mine enemies would daily swallow me up, for they be many that fight against me, O thou most High."*

20.

ITTAI: EXISTING

II Samuel 18:2: *"And David sent forth a third part of the people under the hand of Joab, and a third part under the hand of Abishai the son of Zeruiah, Joab's bother, and a third part under the hand of **ITTAI** the Gittite. And the king said unto the people, I will surely go forth with you myself also."*

HUMBOLDT, THE GREAT NATURALIST and world-wide traveler, once said that the most wonderful sight he ever saw in his trips was a primrose flourishing on the bosom of a glacier. Ittai was a primrose in David's garden because when things got rough and out-of-hand, Ittai rose to the occasion, and though most of Israel had abandoned David in the Absalom revolt, this stranger from the land of his archenemy (Philistia) proved to be a friend in deed as well as a friend in need. A poet once penned this line: "The brightest souls which glory ever knew were rocked in storms and nursed when tempests blew!" This was the mighty man Ittai in all his splendor and support for King David. His existence in the camp of David was a bright hope in a troubled time.

Someone else once said: "It takes hard times to know who your true friends are." And King David was facing hard times, perhaps, the hardest of his reign. His kingdom had just been ripped from his hands by his oldest son, the handsome and ambitious Absalom (II Samuel 15:6). Absalom was also David's favorite because he had a blind spot for Absalom and was totally ignorant just how far Absalom's revolution had gone. Fearing the safety of the residents of Jerusalem, David decided it was best to retreat than to resist the huge army Absalom had mustered to dethrone his father. Jerusalem was a mighty fortress, and it would have taken months, if not years, to overcome, but David, the wile fox that he was, knew his best strategy was to retreat across the Jordan because that would give him time to muster his forces. As David prepared to leave the city of God undefended, who stepped forward as his most faithful and loyal supporter? A Philistine by the name of Ittai. Since childhood, David had been fighting Israel's enemy to the southwest, Philistia. His first encounter with the Philistines was perhaps his most famous, the Battle of Elah where he took on Philistia's champion Goliath and won (I Samuel 17). Who knows, but Ittai could have been at that battle and his admiration for David might have started.

Yet as the years passed and the fame of David grew, David's charisma drew to him men from almost every race known in Palestine at the time. A careful check of David's mighty men of war (I Chronicles 11-12 and II Samuel 23) will unveil this often overlooked truth that David had Ammonites, Hittites, Moabites, Gibeonites, and, yes, Gittites, men from Gath, the hometown of Goliath. Dig a bit deeper and you will uncover the amazing fact that within the battalions of David mighty army was a regiment of 600 Gittites, natives of the Philistine city of Gath in his army (I Samuel 15:18), and Ittai was their commander. Not only were they from Philistia, but they had become David's personal bodyguard. This simple poem from the pen of J. P. McEvery tells us what might have happened between Ittai and David: "I could sail the waters of the world, bitter and wild and blue, and never I'd find a friend to love, like the friend I've found in you. I could walk down all the roads of the world, and knock on doors forever, and never I'd find a friend like you. Never, never, never." We are not sure when or where David met Ittai; it was probably while he was fleeing King Saul. The Bible is very clear that David did spend at least one year and five months in Philistia (I Samuel 27:7). Perhaps, it was then he met the loyal Ittai. It was not unusual in those days that men of different nations fought for other nations as mercenaries. Often people would fight for a cause or the right man and most found in the young man David a person of integrity (Psalm 78:72) and a true follower of the One True Living God. Ittai saw beyond his nation, his race, his nationality to a higher good, and a greater God, a true cause to which to give one's life and sword. I am convinced that these mighty men not only came to believe in David, but they also came to believe in David's God.

Remember during those turbulent years that David was a man without a country, and despite David's plea for Ittai to take his men and

ITTAI: EXISTING

return home, Ittai refused. Despite the fact the cause seemed to be lost (II Samuel 15:19–20), Ittai had hitched his cart to the fortunes of David and David alone so he refused to abandon David then or ever no matter the odds against them. They had seen tough and rough days before so Ittai re-pledged his allegiance to David. The situation looked hopeless, but Ittai and his men knew that as long as David was alive there was hope. This is the attitude of a man who had been brought up to believe in a half-man, a half-fish, a god called Dagon (I Samuel 5:1–9). This is a great example of a man that existed in a different mindset, a warrior that believed not in an idol made by human hands, but in the God of Israel. I have come to the belief that Ittai and Ruth were two heathens cut from the same spiritual cloth. Oh, one was a Philistine and one was a Moabite, but they both became proselytes to the Hebrew faith. Ruth's statement to Naomi might just as well be Ittai's statement to David (Ruth 1:16–17). In my opinion they join Rahab the Amorite, Nebuchadnezzar the Babylonian, and Darius the Mede who also through the testimony of another came to a belief in Jehovah. It is not strange that a relationship that developed into a friendship would also develop into a fellowship with the Almighty. Friendship evangelism has been around for a long time and continues to this day. It is my firm belief when Ittai switched loyalties, he switched lords. The leaders of the five city-states (including Gath) of Philistia were called "lords" (Judges 3:3), but now Ittai had a new lord (David) and a new Lord (Jehovah). Have you established such friendships yet? It is still a wonderful way to witness and share your faith in the Lord Jesus Christ.

David not only had the personality to command such soldiers, he also had a God they could believe in. Ittai must have witnessed numerous time the hand of God on his captain. So, whether good days or bad days Ittai was determined to follow David because David was following God (I Corinthians 11:1). Isn't it sad that we don't see this same loyalty in the church today? Granted, there are some leaders not worth following, but there are some. There are so many fair-weather friends today and, like what happened to Jesus, they will depart when times get tough (John 6:66). Eventually, David would give Ittai command of a third of his army and at the battle of the Ephraim Woods, he with the brothers Joab and Abishai would valiantly win back the kingdom for David (II Samuel 18:6). As soldiers of Christ (II Timothy 2:3), we, too, must exhibit such loyalty and devotion to our "Friend" (John 15:14). We need to press the attack and win back what has been lost over the years of rebellion and revolt in the Church of God. I ask you, what kind of friend are you to your commander-in-chief? Today, I challenge you to become "a friend of the Friend." There are people out there that need a friend before they can fully understand "What a Friend we have in Jesus."

Proverbs 18:24: *"...and there is a friend that sticketh closer than a brother."*

21.

ITHAI: LIVING

I Chronicles 11:31: "***ITHAI** the son of Ribai of Gibeah, that pertained to the children of Benjamin, Benaiah the Pirathonite.*"

ITHAI, THE MIGHTY MAN, is only mentioned twice in the Bible. His name appears on both lists in Scripture of David's famous warriors, but with a variation in the spelling of his name. In I Chronicles 11:31 his name is spelt with an "h" while in the II Samuel 23:29 account it is spelt with a "t" (Ittai). The meaning is basically the same with Ithai meaning "being or existing" while Ittai means "being or living" or existing and living. In both of the passages Ithai's father, tribe, and hometown is given so despite the spelling we are talking about the same soldier. I have come to believe the spelling of Ithai is to help us not get confused over the more famous soldier Ittai, the Philistine, and one of David's top generals (II Samuel 15, 18). So what do we know about this "mighty man?"

Along with the meaning of his name, we also know these three Biblical facts:

1. Ithai was the son of a man named Ribai, which means "Jehovah contends." Ribai is only mentioned in Scripture in relationship to his son. In the Biblical accounts often the father's name is mentioned as if the reader would recognize the father's name over the son. Also, it was traditional to name the father out of respect.

2. Ithai was from the town of Gibeah, one of the most famous villages in all of Israel. This town was given to the tribe of Benjamin

in the allotting of the land by Joshua (Joshua 18:28). This town was nearly wiped out because of a gross sin committed by the residents of Gibeah (Judges 19:12-30 and 20:1-48) during the age of the Judges. Gibeah was also the birthplace of Israel's first king, Saul, and it would become the first capital of Israel, the dwelling place of King Saul (I Samuel 10:26, 11:4, 23:19, 26:1). The inhabitants of this hamlet were called Gibeathites (I Chronicles 12:3). Gibeah was still being mentioned well into the prophet's age (Hosea 5:8, 9:9, 10:9). So Ithai came from an important place.

3. Ithai was also a Benjaminite. So Ithai was just one of many who rejected the kingship of Saul, their kinsman, and followed the standard of David (I Chronicles 12:2-3). Ithai might be considered a traitor, but his loyalty was to God first.

So as with so many of David's mighty men, I choose to focus in on the meaning of his name in relationship to his faith, not just in David, but in David's God. Ithai means "living." *"I am the living bread which came down from heaven: if any man eat of this bread, he shall live forever..."* (John 6:51). As with so many of David's mighty men, Ithai reminds me of another characteristic of God and His Son Jesus Christ.

I was raised in the philosophy of the 1960s which promoted along with many other things that "God was dead." When I was 15 (1966), a Time Magazine article was published with the title <u>Is God Dead?</u> As in the Garden of Eden when Satan first caused man to question his God (Genesis 3:1), during my teenage years the Wicked One was bold enough to publish his new battle plan against Christianity, and I quote: **"The notion that henceforward Christianity could flourish only by transforming itself into a more secular enterprise, dedicated to building the kingdom of God in this life rather than preparing believers for the afterlife. In this secularized faith, Christ would be invoked 'as a spiritual HERO [think Jesus Christ Superstar] whom even non-believers can admire,' while God and transcendence would be associated with the modern hope for a better future-a hope that would be achieved through progressive politics and enjoyed by a human race that has 'taken responsibility for the world.'"** Throughout my life many of many generations and others have tried to destroy the reality of God simply by declaring Him dead, pronouncing Him deceased. Some wrote and published God's obituary, while others even had mocking funerals for the eternal God. I still can't imagine that such things did happen and will probably happen again, yet, the Bible is clear, crystal clear, on this subject, He is living, God is alive and well!

Now that I look back 50 years, I see that this manifesto has been fulfilled. Mankind has determined that he is smart enough to take care of himself, and that the planet is his only world, and he needs to care for it. (This whole global climate change controversy is part of mankind "taking responsibility for the world!") Jesus is now just another one of the world's heroes, (Jesus is Islam's second greatest prophet) a good man who did his best and is worthy of emulation as a man, but certainly not as God. Besides, if God is not dead, He is just a being that is "watching us from a distance." For along with the death of God has come the burial of the clearly taught doctrine of the Bible on the depravity of man. Yet I maintain my belief and witness in the reality that

> I serve a risen [alive] Saviour, He's in the world today.
> I know that He is living whatever man my say.
> I see His hand of mercy; I hear His voice of cheer.
> And just the time I need Him He's always near.
>
> He lives. He lives. Christ Jesus lives today!
> He walks with me and talks with me along life's narrow way.
> He lives. He lives. Salvation to impart!
> You ask me how I know He lives. He lives within my heart!

God might be dead to many in the world, but He is very much alive!

When mankind turned from the supernatural to the natural, from theology to anthropology, and from the Kingdom of God to the City of Man, he had to disregard the sinful nature and depravity of the nature of man. Putting it another way, I have come to believe that the root problem with Christianity today, and, it matters not whether we are talking about moderate, liberal, or conservative Christianity, Christianity is no longer God-centered, but man-centered (think of the exaltation of the Pope in the eyes of most today). We have developed a theology of man and in that theology man is inherently good, not bad; evolving upward versus spiraling downward; capable of improvement and certainly not as Paul taught: *"O wretched man that I am…so than they that are in the flesh cannot please God."* (Romans 7:24, 8:8) Man is only looking to please himself, certainly not God, and this is not the first time in history man has set his own rules and established his own standards. I have been preaching for years that it appears to me that we are returning to the Age of the Judges of Israel: *"In those days there was no king in Israel* [note, not only have we dethroned

God we have also dethroned Jesus as King of our lives]: ***EVERY MAN DID THAT WHICH WAS RIGHT IN HIS OWN EYES.*** " (Judges 21:25) Is not this the philosophy of this age? Surely, you see it, don't you?

Let us never forget. Because He lives, so will we. Remember, Jesus taught us that *"God is not the God of the dead, but of the living."* (Matthew 22:32) Whether living bread or living water (John 4:10–11 and John 7:38), they are one and the same for us to believe in the Living God. I hope this mighty man of David has reminded us of an important truth when it comes to our relationship with the Almighty God, and that being that He is the ever "existing one," the always "living one," and no matter what man says He is still alive and watching over us whether we think He is or not. He is our only hope to live forever!

John 6:57: *"As the living Father hath sent me, and I live by the Father…"*

22.

BENAIAH: WHOM JEHOVAH HAS BUILT UP

> I Chronicles 27:14: *"The eleventh captain for the eleventh month was **BENAIAH** the Pirathonite, of the children of Ephraim: and in his course was twenty and four thousand."*

THIS BENAIAH IS NOT to be mixed up with the more famous Benaiah, the captain of David's personal bodyguard (II Samuel 23:20–22). Despite the fact there was a better known Benaiah in the ranks of David's "mighty men," this Benaiah was still one of David's top dozen generals. This is what I have been able to discover from God's Word about this "mighty man":

1. In all three accounts where Benaiah's name is mentioned, he is always called "the Pirathonite" (II Samuel 23:30, I Chronicles 11:31, and I Chronicles 27:14). A Pirathonite was a resident of the town of Pirathon. Abdon, after judging Israel for eight years, was buried on this Amalekite site (Judges 12:15). The land on which this Canaan town was located was given to the tribe of Ephraim (Judges 12:13).

2. This is also the first soldier from the tribe of Ephraim that we have highlighted in this series (I Chronicles 12:30). Eventually, the tribe of Ephraim would be the dominate tribe of the ten northern tribes that would break away from Judah during the kingship of Rehoboam. Another famous warrior from this tribe was Joshua (Numbers 13:8), the leader of Israel after the death of Moses.

3. Lastly, Benaiah means *"who Jehovah has built up."* Because we never dealt with the meaning of Benaiah in our last devotional on the first mighty man Benaiah, it will be the focus of our thoughts on this mighty man named Benaiah. As I was pondering this meaning, I remembered this verse from the pen of Paul about our Lord and Savior Jesus Christ: *"Rooted and 'built up' in Him, and stablished in the faith, as ye have been taught, abounding with thanksgiving."* (Colossians 2:7)

Christ said, *"...I will build my church..."* (Matthew 16:18). Today, there seems to be much conflict between those who are building the local churches and the Builder of the Church. The tragedy is that we in America have focused so much of our attention on the brick and mortar, the plank and timber, and the glass and marble of the physical church building, we have failed to realize that it is the spiritual church God is concerned about. We have beautiful spired cathedrals, and fancy wooden churches, and lovely architectural chapels doting our native land, but empty of the key building material of the true Church, people. The Apostle Peter writes in his first epistle: *"Ye also, as lively stones, are built up a spiritual house..."* (I Peter 2:5). When will the average church member return to the Master Builder the responsibility of building His Building (I Corinthians 3:11, Acts 2:47, and Ephesians 2:20–22). Our responsibility is to share; His responsibility is to add.

In our land the use of the word **"church"** more often than not refers to some building or a set of buildings on some corner or in some lane in a city or town. Never in the New Testament is the word **"church"** used to describe a building. That fact alone is a powerful theological truth in the doctrine of the Church. The best thing to happen to our American churches might be the demolishing of all so called church buildings. It was way into the second century in Church history before the Church of Christ had an established church meeting place, and there was and probably never will be an era like it for church growth and expansion. And to think our forefathers did it without a permanent church structure, something we couldn't even imagine today. What is the first thing we do today when we have a church plant? We find a place to gather. In 1973, my wife and I started a new assembly of believers in Pembroke, New Hampshire. As was the custom of the day, the first thing I did was to spend my time trying to find a place to meet. There were already four families ready to worship together, but we never thought once about meeting as the early church did *"...from house to house..."* (Acts 2:46). We had to find a neutral site to start our local church. Why? Even though we were all about establishing a New Testament style fellowship, we never once used the New Testament method. After meeting in a small community center for a couple of years, we moved into an old bed and breakfast hoping it would become our permanent meeting place, but within two years we couldn't afford the building and finally we moved into one of the member's homes. Only then did we realize just how the New Testament church started. It was then we learned that the time and gifts and tithes of the early church were all focused on one thing, adding *"...to the church daily such as should be saved."* (Acts 2:47) Today, when most ask about a local assembly, the first questioned asked is "What kind of building do you have or what are your facilities like?" Truly, the modern 21st century church has become like the Church of Laodicea: *"I am rich, and increased with goods, and have need of nothing..."* (Revelation 3:17) How sad it is when it should be "Christ has built up."

I don't know about you, but even as a pastor of 43 years, I get discouraged into thinking that the church isn't being "built up" as it should because I see very little adding going on around me. Oh, we are building a new kitchen and nursery in the basement, but where are the new members? Even when we get new members it is one local assembly passing on their members to our membership. Nothing seems to be happening here in America, but does that mean nothing is happening elsewhere? I have come to believe in the promise of God when he told His infant church that he would *"add daily..."* (Acts 2:47). I read this article by Dave Egner in which he wrote:

> Recently I came across some startling statistics in my reading, and they should produce a surge of optimism. Consider these facts: in Korea, the number of Christians has doubled every 10 years since 1940s to more than 11 million today. That's 25% of the population of Korea. The number of Christians has doubled in Indonesia since 1965. In Africa there were 10 million Christians in 1900; today there are 203 million. From less than a million in 1900 in Latin America, the number of Christians has grown to 18 million. But the most growth has taken place in China. At the time of the Communist takeover in 1949, there were about a million Chinese Protestants. But now there are an estimated 35 to 50 million believers!

When one puts these figures in context, we find that the areas mentioned were under opposition and persecution all the time, yet Christ was still building His Church, not church buildings. Church building growth is weak in China and India and in Muslim lands, but the Church continues to grow. When will us in America wake up to the reality that it is not mortar and money, but the moving of the Spirit that builds up. It is time we allow the Master Builder to use "lively stones" instead of limestone to build His Church. Believer by believer, Christ is building up his church, and though we might not see it here, over there it is happening. As I finish this devotional I am getting ready to leave for a land like I am describing: India. India is a place that still believes in allowing Christ to build up, the Master Bricklayer to use souls, not stone, to the building of his house. Like Benaiah!

I Peter 2:5: *"Ye also, as lively stones, are built up a spiritual house, an holy priesthood, to offer up spiritual sacrifices, acceptable to God by Jesus Christ."*

23.

HIDDAI: MIGHTY, CHIEF

> II Samuel 23:30: *"Benaiah the Pirathonite,*
> **HIDDAI** *of the brooks of Gaash."*

CALLED HURAI, MEANING "FREE or noble," in I Chronicles 11:32, this mighty man of David is also called Hiddai meaning "mighty or chief," in II Samuel 23:30. The common link which persuades me that we are talking about the same soldier is that both accounts place Hiddai in the same general order of David's listings and both accounts tell us that he was from "the brooks of Gaash." So, what can we glean from these few details?

Joshua, the great warrior of the days of the conquest of Canaan, was buried "on the north side of the hill of Gaash." (Joshua 24:30) Hills usually produce brooks or streams so this is simply a geographical location. Most of David's mighty men are recorded as having come from a town or a village or they are connected with some clan or tribe, but for Hiddai, David chose to give us just a place. In my research, Gaash was in a territory allotted to the tribe of Ephraim (Judges 2:9); Joshua was from the tribe of Ephraim. David must have thought that the mentioning of "the brooks of Gaash" would bring an understanding where Hiddai was from. Were the Brooks of Gaash famous? With this single detail to go on, we must, as we have so often before, focus our attention on the meaning of Hiddai's name. We have four to choose from: free, noble, chief, or mighty. I decided to see where the words "mighty" and "chief" will lead us. If you haven't noticed yet, I believe I have found a pattern in the names of David's "mighty men" that link up with our Lord and Savior Jesus Christ and the characteristics of his character. The meaning of David's mighty men's names is helping us define the Person of Christ.

David writes in his great Messianic (the song of Jesus in the Old Testament) Psalm: *"Gird Thy sword upon Thy thigh, O most mighty, with Thy glory and Thy majesty."* (Psalm 45:3) The term "mighty" is a constant name for God throughout the Old Testament. Ponder and consider for a moment these examples:

1. He is the Mighty God (Isaiah 9:6).
2. He is the Mighty One of Jacob (Isaiah 63:1).
3. He is the Mighty One of Israel (Isaiah 1:24).

When this word is added to the most Mighty and the Almighty (Revelation 1:8), the conclusion is an easy one and the verdict is clear. This is another name for Jesus!

Horsley translates Isaiah 9:6 this way: "God the mighty man!" Horsley feels it is the equivalent to the name "Immanuel" (Isaiah 7:14 and Matthew 1:23), "God with us" or "the mighty man of God with us." For us, this is the only category of God as mighty we could possibly come close to understanding. How can we relate to the mighty God with Him being infinite and we being finite? In His purest state it is certainly beyond our comprehension. Even the Apostle Paul came to this deduction: *"O the depth of the riches both of the wisdom and knowledge of God! How unsearchable are His judgments, and His ways past finding out!"* (Romans 11:33) Is not that one of the reasons that God became man? He sought not only our redemption, but our recognition. He already knew us (John 2:24), but He also wanted us to understand Him. So He became like us (Philippians 2:6), yet even in that he had to be more than an ordinary man, he had to come as a mighty man, but not a mighty man in the definition of the world.

In the world a man becomes mighty by deeds or device, by the positions he holds or the people he controls. Alexander the Great was a mighty man in the ancient world, *"and Cush begat Nimrod: he began to be a mighty one in the earth."* (Genesis 10:8) David numbered his "mighty men" (II Samuel 23:8–39) by their amazing exploits on the battlefield. But the Christ became mighty not by climbing a ladder of achievement, but by humbling Himself (Philippians 2:7–8). Yes, the mighty God became a lowly lamb, the envied evangelist, and the play thing of Pilate.

He yielded to the disgrace of the cross, but in His fall He rose to heights and might no man who ever lived on this planet ever did. Is there today a name that has lasted more in the changing social or political climate of this world? Nations have come and gone, generals have lived and died, and kings have been crowned and removed, yet, in all the years since the angels first called Him Jesus no name has outlived or outperformed His. Philosophers and philosophies have come and gone, teachers and teachings have had their day, yet, the doctrines of Christ remain to this day after two thousand years of critics and criticism. Generations have lived and died, yet the mighty man of Galilee lives on in His disciples, His followers, to this hour!

The Psalmist wrote: *"The stone which the builder's refused is become the headstone of the corner."* (Psalm 118:22) Cornerstones are foundation stones: *"For other foundation can no man lay than that is laid, which is Jesus Christ."* (I Corinthians 3:11) Despite being rejected by the leadership of Israel, Jesus still became the cornerstone of a new faith. He was not flawed because the problem was with the inspectors of the stone, not the stone, (Matthew 21:42 and Mark 12:10) so the cornerstone was the first stone in the building of a stone foundation, but the chief cornerstone can also refer to the last stone of the building. So there is a connection between the mighty and the chief. The chief cornerstone can also refer to the top-stone or the capstone. This is the stone that ties together the last pieces of the structure. Like the cornerstone which ties together the first stones of the building, the chief cornerstone is important to the structural integrity of the structure. To me these concepts are talking about the great, all completeness of Jesus Christ so in the meaning of the name of Hiddai we have this concept clearly revealed: Jesus is *"the Alpha and Omega, the beginning and the end"* (Revelation 1:8), and, may I add, the middle as well. He is the whole, not just a part or a piece. If any other gospel or any other gospelaire comes into the structure of the faith, then it will weaken the whole. That is why only Jesus can be the whole. Without this precept, the Christian Faith would have crumbled ages ago, as so many of the world's religions have. Why else would Paul say: *"In whom* [Jesus] *all the building fitly framed together regrowth unto a holy temple in the Lord."* (Ephesians 2:21) Jesus is the mighty chief of the world and the Church!

Our challenge today from the mighty man Hiddai must be of the reality of the unity we have in Christianity. Satan and sin and self will try to divide us, but with the mighty chief cornerstone as our base, we cannot be split. Jesus is not only chief, but He is a mighty chief. More than just a name or the meaning of a name, Jesus is the real power that holds our world together (II Peter 3:7) and holds the church together (Ephesians 1:20–23). So let us focus on the fundamentals of our faith and sing out loudly the words of John Fawcett's famous Church hymn: "Blest be the tie that binds our hearts in Christian love, the fellowship of kindred minds is like to that above." Once again we have to thank a mighty man like Hiddai for allowing us to walk down an inspiring path that has taught us a bit more of just who our Lord and Savior Jesus Christ really is, mighty chief!

I Peter 2:6: *"Wherefore also it is contained in the scripture, behold, I lay in Zion a chief cornerstone, elect, precious: and he that believeth on Him shall not be confounded.*

24.

ABIEL: MY FATHER IS GOD

I Chronicles 11:32: *"Hurai of the brooks of Gaash, **ABIEL** the Arbathite."*

The next "mighty man" on David's impressive list of his top warriors is a man named Abiel, or Abialbon (II Samuel 23:31). I believe they are the same soldiers because of these three reasons:

1. They appear in the same order on both lists (compare I Chronicles 11:32 and II Samuel 23:31). Note the men listed before and after them are also the same.

2. They are both called "the Arbathite." This simply means "belonging to Arabah." Arabah means "plain or wilderness." This name was given to the sunken valley on both sides of the Jordan River from the Sea of Galilee to the southern extremity of the Dead Sea. Though translated "plain" in many places like Joshua 18:18, it seems to denote a particular place. It is also used in Jeremiah 51:43 to describe a place of beauty. I believe that is a reference to the town where Abiel was from. If so, then Abiel was from the tribe of Judah or Benjamin. Located on the border between the two tribes, Betharabah, or "the house of the desert," is included in the towns of Benjamin (Joshua 15:6, 61). Again this is one of those unknowns that must be left to the precept of Romans 14:5.

3. Both names given in the two accounts basically mean the same thing. Abiel means "my father is God, or father of might" while Abialbon means "father of strength." The pattern must then continue as we search for why this list of names was so important to David.

They were his famous soldiers, but in their names, or in the meaning of their names, we get a broader understanding into *"the man after God's own heart"* (Acts 13:22). But as we have been highlighting and underlining in other devotionals, not so much David's heart but the heart of Jesus.

Isaiah prophesied: *"And His name shall be called...the everlasting Father."* (Isaiah 9:6) After wonderful, counselor, the Prince of Peace, and the mighty God, Isaiah tells us that the Christ will also be called Father. There can only be one aspect to which this title can be placed on the head of Jesus; there is only one doctrine that this title can be applied and that is in the relationship of the unity of the Godhead.

The first interesting aspect about this name for Jesus is that in the same verse Christ is called "a child" and "the Father" at the same time. In the Godhead we can confidently say that Christ, the second Person of the Trinity, had a part in His own birth. It is in the unity of the three Persons of the Godhead that we realize some amazing doctrines, especially in the relationship to Christ and "the Father." This is why Jesus could stun His disciples and the Pharisees when He proclaimed: *"I and my Father are one."* (John 10:30) Not only are these titles interchangeable, but so are the terms. Jesus would say to Philip on the evening of the Passover meal: *"Have I been so long time with you, and yet hast thou not known me Philip? He that hath seen me hath seen the Father; and how sayest thou then, show us the Father? Believe thou not that I am in the Father, and the Father in me?"* (John 14:9–10) Yes, the disciples had a hard time with this concept of Christ and there are a lot of people today both within and without the Church that can't get their heads around this issue. Oh, they can understand the Christ-child, but when it comes to the Father in the Christ-child (Colossians 2:9) they fall far short of this amazing truth.

The second interesting aspect of this connection between the Christ and the Father is the adjective that precedes it, everlasting. Jesus in the end will not simply be known by the title of Father, but "the everlasting Father," literally, **"Father of eternity."** For me, there are two wonderful teachings here. First, our relationship with Jesus as the Father will last forever, and second, He is the producer of eternal life to those who have been redeemed. In the scope of eternity, the Scriptures are very, very clear. In Micah's great prophecy concerning the birth place of the Christ, he states: *"Whose going forth have been from of old, from everlasting!"*

(Micah 5:2) There can be no doubt that He is the eternal Father as well as the eternal Son, but is He your Father yet?

But it is in the aspect of the author of life I feel most compelled to make comment in this devotional about Abiel (my Father is God). Mary was a barren virgin until she was overshadowed by the Holy Spirit of God (Luke 1:35). Then life began in her womb that would eventually bring forth Jesus Christ, the Son of God, and so, too, in the Church of God. It, too, was a barren virgin until it was overshadowed by the Holy Spirit (Acts 2:4); as with Mary, the Holy Spirit indwelled (her womb, our lives). Then that Bride of Christ began to produce life, and Christ became the Father to a vast multitude of children "born again" over the last 20 centuries. I believe Isaiah spoke of this aspect in his classic chapter on Christ: *"Yet it pleased the Lord to bruise Him; He hath put Him to grief: when thou shalt make His soul an offering for sin, HE SHALL SEE HIS SEED..."* (Isaiah 53:10). I am convinced that these ideas are drawn together in the Apostle Paul's letter to the church of Galatia: *"But when the fulness of time was come, God sent forth His Son, made of a woman, made under the law, to redeem them that were under the law, that we might receive the adoption of sons. And because ye are sons, God hath sent forth the Spirit of His Son into your heart, crying, Abba, Father!"* (Galatians 4:4–6)

As Jesus submitted unto the relationship of the Son to the Father (II John 3), so, too, we must submit under the relationship as sons to God (John 1:12 and Romans 8:14–17). Because I have had the privilege and honor to have been raised in a two-father family, my father Wendell and my grandfather Carroll, I understand this concept because I saw it played out in my boyhood on the family homestead in northern Maine. I called both Wendell and Carroll father. Though Carroll was my grandfather and Wendell was my father, both in a way gave me life, both were fathers to me biologically as well as socially, and, for me, also spiritually. Both hold a very special place in my heart because of what they did and were to me in my youth and the impact they had on my life. So, too, with the everlasting Father, who revealed Himself to me through two forms, the Son and the Spirit. Have you come to understand this relationship yet? Maybe, you never had a relationship like I had with my father and grandfather, but that doesn't mean that you cannot come to such a relationship. The Bible will take you step by step through this amazing relationship if you are willing to take the journey.

Can you truly say with Abiel, "My Father is God?" I thank God for my earthly father every day, and at the writing of this devotional he is still alive (I have had an earthly father for 65 years), but I must also proclaim that I have had a heavenly Father in the Person of Christ since 1958. I have had two Fathers for a long time, but do you? If you only have one father, you are lost, but when you are "born again" you get a second Father!

Romans 8:15: *"...But ye have received the Spirit of adoption, whereby we cry, Abba, Father!"*

25.

AZMAVETH: COUNSEL

II Samuel 23:31: *"Abialbon the Arbathite, **AZMAVETH** the Barhumite."*

AZMAVETH WAS "THE BARHUMITE," or "the Baharumite," depending on which "mighty men" list you are reading from (compare II Samuel 23:31 and I Chronicles 11:33) denoting a person from the town of Bahurim. This unknown town (meaning we don't know it's exact geographical location in Israel) has some very interesting Biblical events connected to it:

1. Phaltiel, the husband of Michal (the daughter of King Saul and David's first wife) followed Michal to Bahurim when David demanded her return to him after King Saul had married her off to Phaltiel after Saul's and David's split over Saul's fear that David was looking to overthrow him (II Samuel 3:16).

2. David passed through Bahurim and stopped for a drink there as he fled from his son Absalom during Absalom's infamous revolt (II Samuel 17:18).

3. It was also in Bahurim that Shimei made his curse on David as David fled Absalom (II Samuel 16:6), a curse he would later regret (II Samuel 19:16).

4. It is also the hometown of one of David's mighty men, Azmaveth. It is always interesting to me just how a town can produce a Shimei and an Azmaveth. This village probably was located on a road from the Jordan River Valley up to Jerusalem probably making Azmaveth a Benjaminite (I Kings 2:8).

Checking my reference books on the meaning of the name Azmaveth, I have discovered two basic definitions. First, Azmaveth can mean "strength of death" or it can mean "counsel." Following Abiel in both "mighty men" lists, I will use the direction that I have set for myself in this series of devotional. Anything that sounds or hints like a term or title connected with Christ, I will use.

Isaiah prophesied, *"...and his name shall be called...Counsellor..."* (Isaiah 9:6). Another reason I have chosen to write about Jesus the "counselor" today is the simple fact that counseling is on my mind. Last night I got a call from a young man in the church that was troubled over the breakup of a marriage of two of his good friends. The time was late, and I had just settled in to relax and calm down after two hours with six 9-year old boys, my Pal's Awana group. But like the friend that came to his friend at midnight (Luke 11:5–8), I couldn't pass him over or say wait until tomorrow. I couldn't tell him I was tired and exhausted and couldn't we talk later. Why? Not because I consider myself a counselor, but I do know the Counselor very well, and now I had another opportunity to point Him out and give this young man some sound Biblical advice.

The Psalmist states: *"Thou shalt guide me with thy counsel..."* (Psalm 73:24). After Christ fulfilled the position of *"...the captain of our salvation..."* (Hebrews 2:10), He assumed the position as counselor. *"Counsel is mine, and sound wisdom: I am understanding..."* (Proverbs 8:14). What a nice crossover verse to link the two mighty men, Abiel and Azmaveth, who inhabited the same verse we have printed at the top of this devotional. Their names are found in the same verse as are the two titles for Christ found in Isaiah 9:6. The tragedy is that most people, including Christians, spend time and money (sometimes a lot of money) on the counsel of men, when the best counsel is found in the Word of God from the lips of God because nobody can claim what Solomon wrote of the Almighty in relationship to wisdom, understanding, or counsel.

The world has discovered a lucrative business in the area and arena of counseling. Even a few Christians are tapping into the huge resources of the people who will pay for a bit of advice or some counsel in certain areas of their lives. Business men seek financial counsel, husbands and wives seek martial advice. Every once in a while young people even seek it, but where most seek a so-called professional all they need is Christ because his name shall be called Counselor. Most will not come to Christ's free client of counsel, the Word of God, but He is always available and ready with some good advice, much better than the ones that seek me out for a little counsel. So what makes Jesus such a good counselor? What makes Jesus the one you ought to seek out for advice?

Jesus Christ has the ability no human counselor has ever had. Jesus' disciple John described this unique ability in these words about Christ: *"But Jesus did not commit himself unto them, because He knew all men, and needed not that any should testify of man: for he knew what was in man."* (John 2:25) David recognized this about God when he wrote: *"O Lord, though hast searched me, and known me. Thou knowest my downsitting and my uprising, thou understandest my thoughts afar off....For there is not a word in my tongue, but, lo, O Lord, thou knowest it altogether."* (Psalm 139:1–2, 4) While human counselors waste valuable time evaluating, running tests, and asking questions, Jesus is able to cut straight to the heart of the matter, and what He can do. So can His Word: *"...piercing even to the dividing asunder of soul and spirit, and of the joints and marrow, and is the discerner of the thoughts and the intents of the heart."* (Hebrews 4:12) Both Christ and the Word are able to put their finger on the problem from the very beginning. Remember Jesus' encounter with the woman at the well outside that Samarian village? Remember how often the woman tried to side-track Christ? He was able to bring the conversation back to the real problem, and He certainly had the best advice for her. Jesus has never been wrong with His diagnose, and He is spot-on with the best counsel and best advice for any situation or circumstance. He knows when to be tough, when to push, and when to back away, and certainly when to be tender. Consider again the numerous encounters with people described in the Gospel, and you will see the Master Counselor at work. Despite the best advice many walked away with (like the rich young ruler), the sad truth is that many still walk away from Godly, Biblical counsel.

For me, counsel is simply the giving out of good Scriptural advice. I like the story out of the life of Elizabeth Kenny, the famous Irish-Australian nurse. Once asked by a friend how she managed to stay so constantly cheerful, no matter what the provocation. The friend said, "I suppose you were just born calm and smiling!" "Oh, no," laughed Kenny. "As a girl my temper often got out of control, but one day when I became angry at a friend over a very trivial matter, my mother gave me advice that I stored in my mind and have called upon it for guidance ever since. Mother told me, "Elizabeth, anyone who angers you, conquers you!" It is such advice that you can get if you go to the great Counselor because I suspect that is where Elizabeth's mother got her advice for her daughter. I had parents like that, and I know from where their wisdom, understanding, and counsel came.

Now, for those of us who are human counselors, that doesn't mean we are not needed. The Bible speaks of many. David had them (II Samuel 15:12), and Joseph of Arimathaea was "an honorable counselor" (Mark 15:43). I wonder how many of David's mighty men became his counselors? Our best source for advice or counsel is God (Romans 11:34)!

Psalm 119:24: *"Thy testimonies also are my delight, and my counselors!"*

26.

ELIAHBA: HIDDEN OF GOD

I Chronicles 11:33: *"Azmaveth the Baharumite,* **ELIAHBA** *the Shaalbonite."*

NEXT IN OUR TWO lists (II Samuel 23:32) of David's "mighty men" is a man from Shaalabbin, a city of Dan near Aijalon, on the slopes of Mount Ephraim (Joshua 19:42). Besides his hometown, Eliahba is only known in Scripture by the meaning of his name, "hidden of God." But as we have seen, a name can lead us to some wonderful thoughts and teaching about God and His Son Jesus Christ.

I have been fascinated for years to discover why some of my favorite Church hymns, choruses, and spiritual songs (Colossians 3:16) were created. I have been singing the traditional Church songs all of my life, but when one knows the circumstance behind the hymn, or the history surrounding a familiar church song, it makes the singing of that song that much more meaningful. Kenneth W. Osbeck, in his church hymn devotional, Amazing Grace, tells us how Fanny Crosby's inspiring hymn, He Hideth My Soul, was written:

> The beloved blind American poet Fanny Crosby did not begin writing Gospel texts until her mid-forties. But from then on inspiring words seemed to flow constantly from her heart, and she became "the happiest creature in all the land." Friends stopped in frequently to see her with requests for new texts for special occasions. One day Fanny was visited by William Kirkpatrick, a talented Gospel musician who had just composed a new melody that he felt needed suitable words to become a sing able hymn.

As William sat at the piano and played the tune for Fanny, her face lit up. She knelt in prayer, as was always her custom, and soon the lines to this lovely hymn began to flow freely from her heart: a wonderful Saviour is Jesus my Lord, a wonderful Saviour to me; He hideth my soul in the cleft of the Rock, where rivers of pleasure I see. He hideth my soul in the cleft of the Rock that shadows a dry thirsty land; He hideth my life in the depths of His love, and covers me there with His hand, and covers me there with his hand.

So how can such inspiration and truth flow from a blind lady?

Fanny Crosby was no doubt thinking (she was a great student of the Word and her poetic lines reflect that study) of Moses experience with Jehovah on Mount Sinai when the great Lawgiver asked to see God, to which *"the Lord said, Behold, there is a place by me, and thou shalt stand upon the rock: and it shall come to pass, while my glory passeth by, that I will put thee in the cleft of the rock, and will cover thee with my hand while I pass by: and I will take away mine hand, and thou shalt see my back parts: but my face shall not be seen."* (Exodus 33:21–23) David also spoke of this concept of "hidden of God" when he wrote in one of his psalms: *"Thou shalt hide them in the secret of thy presence..."* (Psalm 31:20). The meaning of Eliahba's name is certainly a clearly define teaching in the Bible, but how can we make an application to our Christian walk?

If there is a key verse in the Scriptures on this subject for me as a New Testament believer, it has to be these words from the pen of Paul: *"For ye are dead, and your life is hid with Christ in God."* (Colossians 3:3) Like Eliahba, we, too, are soldiers of a great Captain (Hebrews 2:10), and though our name might not be Eliahba, in the practical truth of the doctrine of "hidden in Christ," we are through our relationship with Christ. We live in a world with many enemies, and those enemies would do us harm if they could, but like the man who puts on the armor of God (Ephesians 6:10–18), we are hidden behind the armor, and we are hidden in Christ. To get to us our enemies must get through the armor, and they must be able to get through Christ. There is no greater protection in the world than that. In Oswald Chambers' classic work, <u>My Utmost for His Highest</u>, he writes this on the topic of "hid with Christ:"

> The Spirit of God witnesses to the simple Almighty security of the life hid with Christ in God and this is continually brought out in the Epistles. We talk as if it were the most precarious thing to live the sanctified life. It is the most secure thing because it

has the Almighty God in and behind it. The most precarious thing is to try and live without God. If we are born-again, it is the easiest thing to live in right relationship to God and the most difficult thing to go wrong, if only we will heed God's warnings and keep in the light. When we think of being delivered from sin, of being filled with the Spirit, and of walking in the very high and wonderful, and we say "Oh, but I could never live up there!" But when we do get there by God's grace, we find it is not a mountain peak, but a plateau where there is ample room to live and to grow. "Thou hast enlarged my steps under me." When you really see Jesus, I defy you to doubt Him. When He says, "Let not your heart be troubled," if you see Him I defy you to trouble your mind, it is a moral impossibility to doubt when He is there. Every time you get into personal contact with Jesus, His words are real. "My peace I give unto you," it is a peace all over from the crown of the head to the sole of the feet, an irrepressible confidence. "Your life is hid with Christ in God" and the imperturbable peace of Jesus Christ is imparted to you.

What a wonderful place to be found, "hid with Christ," "hidden of God!" It reminds me of the wonderful promise that Jesus gave His disciples just before they left the upper room: *"My sheep hear my voice, and I know them, and they follow me: and I give unto them eternal life; and they shall never perish, neither shall any man pluck them out of my hand. My Father, which gave them me, is greater than all; and no man is able to pluck them out of my Father's hand. I and my Father are one."* (John 10:27–30) Do you see the double hiding in these verses, what I like to call "double security?" My favorite devotional writer, Vance Havner, also makes comment on this doctrine in his devotional book <u>Day by Day</u>:

> Some escape the tyranny of self to a great degree by a new vocation, a new love. But some day the vocation may have to be abandoned, the loved one may die. Christ offers us the highest deliverance, not in a cause or in a philosophy or even in "Christian work," but in Himself. Some dear souls become interested in a new truth like the victorious life and make a fad of it, but still do not get through to Him who is our life. We are dead, our old self has been nailed to the cross and we are to reckon it a fact, yield ourselves to God and obey Him. It is the message of this third chapter of Colossians as of the sixth chapter of Romans. Self does not crucify self, but submits to crucifixion as the Spirit works it out in experience. But we do not major on dying; we rise from the grace to walk in newness of life, freed from the

shackles of the old life. If we lose ourselves in anything less than Christ Himself there is no full deliverance. Only "with Christ in God" are we in a safe hiding place!

Isn't it wonderful what a simple meaning of a mighty man's name can be to us? We must realize that even the names of the Bible contain a depth of purpose to bring us back to the reality of what we have in the Person of the Son and the Person of the Father. Go forth my friend in the sure assurance that we are "hidden with Christ in God!"

Psalm 32:7: *"Thou art my hiding place; thou shalt preserve me from trouble; thou shalt compass me about with songs of deliverance."*

27.

JONATHAN: JEHOVAH IS GIVEN

II Samuel 23:32: *"Eliahba the Shaalbonite, of the sons of Jashen, **JONATHAN**."*

WE HAVE COME TO our second Jonathan in David's massive army that was numbered among David's elite force called "the mighty men." We know that they were different warriors because of their family reference. One was the son of Shimeah, the brother of David (II Samuel 21:21), but this Jonathan was from the household of a man by the name of Jashen. If we add the information given about this soldier in I Chronicles 11:34, we only know this: *"...Jonathan the son of Shage the Hararite...."* Despite the different names given in relationship to the father, I have come to believe they are one and the same "mighty man." The order of the lists suggests that we are referring to the same fighter. It is not unusual in the Bible for one individual to have two names. Jashen and Shage could be a nickname for the other. Hararite means "mountaineer." It is a Hebrew word thought to denote a native of the hill-country of Judah or Ephraim. It is not a place, but a title. We have seen this title before in II Samuel 23:11, and we will see it again in I Chronicles 11:35, seemingly, an area where David recruited a number of his super soldiers. Mountaineers have been considered elite warriors in many countries around the world for millennium. But unlike the other Jonathan and his fight against one of Goliath's giant brothers, we know of no feats of valor or brave exploits of this Jonathan that caused his name to be added to David's lists. So, like so many before him and most after him, we must find our inspiration in the meaning of his name, "Jehovah is given."

Once again I have found it easy to link the definition of his name to the life of Christ. I think we all know when Jehovah was given, when the Almighty became a gift to mankind. Jesus told the woman at Jacob's well: *"If thou knewest **the gift of God**, and who it is that saith to thee, Give me to drink; thou wouldest have asked of Him, and he would have gen thee living water."* (John 4:10) Commenting on this, the great English devotional writer F. B. Meyer had this to say:

> God's best things are gifts. Light, air, natural beauty, elasticity of the spirits, the sense of vigorous health, human love, and, above all, His only begotten and beloved Son. Among all other gifts is there one to be compared to this? The living spring of eternal life, which Jesus opened up in our hearts, and which so greatly differs from the pit of outward ordinance, is an altogether unspeakable bestowment. Nothing can purchase it. If a man would give all the substance of his house for it, it would be utterly condemned. It must be received as a gift, or not at all. God's gifts must be asked for. "Thou wouldest have asked and He would have given." This is the law of heaven. Prayer is a necessary link between the divine hand that gives and the human heart that receives. We have not, because we ask not. There is nothing in our Lord's words of the dreamy and languid pietism which refuses to ask because it will not dictate to the perfect wisdom of God.

It is important that we understand the precept that Meyer is highlighting in his comment of God's gift of Christ, what I believe Paul called "an unspeakable gift" (II Corinthians 9:15). Meyer was referring to James' concept of James 4:2–3. The problem that has developed in man is the "I can do it without God" attitude. Most men don't want the helpful hand of God. Oh, man is ready at times to pay God for his services, but to accept a gift is beneath him. That is why so many have troubles with *"[T]he wages of sin is death, but the gift of God is eternal life through Jesus Christ our Lord"* (Romans 6:23), why work's salvation is more popular in the world today than grace (Ephesians 2:8–9) salvation. Mankind just wants to think he has done it on his own, worked with his own hands, and accomplished his own missions. He just wants God out of the picture so in the end, whatever end that might be, he can claim his own success, triumph, victory.

The tragedy today is that there are still a lot of people who don't even know about the gift that Jehovah has given. How can they ask for it, or how can they thank God for it, if they don't know about it? I am convinced that is why the Apostle Paul made this challenge in Romans: *"How then shall they call on Him in whom they have not believed? And how shall they believe in Him of whom they have not heard? And how shall they hear without a preacher? And how shall they preach, except they be sent? As it is written, How beautiful are the feet of them that preach the gospel of peace* [part of the Gospel is the truth that Jesus was a gift, and that His salvation is a gift]*, and bring glad tidings of good things! But they have not all obeyed the gospel. For Isaiah saith, Lord, who hath believed out reports?"* (Romans 10:14–16) The irony of this reality is illustrated by this story out of the life of the famous English pastor and preacher, Charles Haddon Spurgeon, in his classic book <u>All of Grace</u>. He writes of "…a minister who went to the home of a poor woman to give her some money that she desperately needed. When he knocked at her door, she did not answer. He felt sure that she was home, so he knocked again. Still no response. After more knocking, he left. On Sunday, he saw her in church and said, 'I called at your home last Friday. I supposed you were not at home, for I knocked several times and you did not answer. I had some money for you!' 'What time were you there?' she asked. 'About noon,' the minister replied. 'Oh, dear,' said the woman, 'I heard you, but I did not answer. I thought it was my landlord calling for the rent.'" How often have we made the same mistake not knowing the gift was just on the other side of the door, in the unanswered phone call, or in the unopened envelope?

The answer to all your problems is a gift that Jehovah has given to us: *"…and they shall call his name Emmanuel, which being interpreted is God with us."* (Matthew 1:23) All anybody has to do is open their heart's door and receive the free gift. W.Y. Fullerton was finally saved when he stopped trying to save himself, and heard the words of a preacher say: "All you have to do to be saved is to take God's gift and say, Thank You!" What we need to realize is that "the gift" (Jehovah is given) comes with "a gift" (the gift of eternal life), and all we have to do is believe and receive the first gift to get the second gift. We often forget that one of the first names Jesus ever received (Emmanuel) was wrapped up in the meaning of Jonathan's name, but will we take this gift is the $64,000 question. This gift has been laying under a tree (Calvary) for two millennia now and some have taken it, but there are still many that have not! Can you imagine a gift lying under a Christmas tree that long or a gift given to a spouse waiting very long before it is unwrapped and opened? Then what about those who have believed and received, but have never given thanks? I still sing that old children's chorus: "Thank you Lord for saving my soul.

Thank you Lord for making me whole. Thank you Lord for giving to me, thy great salvation so rich and free!" I am coming to the belief that it is just as disgraceful to not take God's gift as to take it and not give thanks for it. The greatest gift of all time should not go unopened or un-thanked for!

> James 1:17: *"Every good gift and every perfect gift is from above, and cometh down from the Father of lights, with whom is not variableness, neither shadow of turning."*

28.

THE SONS OF HASHEM: SHINING

I Chronicles 11:34: *"**THE SONS OF HASHEM** the Gizonite, Jonathan the son of Shage the Hararite."*

WE HAVE COME TO a very unique section in the listing of David's "mighty men." Up until this point in our research, and, may I add after this point as well because I have checked, we have been dealing with named individuals. We might not know the exact acts of bravery or a specific exploit of valor that caused these warriors to be numbered on David's "mighty men" list, but at least we had been given their names, and in most cases their father's name and where they were from. Now we have before us a group. We don't know how many, but at least two or more. All we are told is they were the sons of a man by the name of Hashem, which means "shining," and that he was a Gizonite. There are no other Gizonites mentioned in the Bible, and about all I could find out is that it is a patronymic, "a name showing descent from a given person as by the addition of a prefix or suffix." I find no Gizon in my concordance or any other reference book I have looked at. David writes of them as if they would be recognized, not as individuals, but as brothers or the sons of Hashem. The sons and brothers idea has provoke me with this challenge for you in relationship to the overall theme of this book and that being the connection of the meaning of the names of David's "mighty men" with the mightiest Man of them all, the Lord Jesus Christ.

I like the story told of a man who saw a small lad carrying a bigger boy on his shoulders. Puzzled, the man asked, "Son, isn't that boy you're carrying too heavy for you?" The reply was a classic, "He's not heavy.

He's my brother!" Jesus tried to build a BROTHER/brother relationship with His disciples: *"For whosoever shall do the will of my Father which is in heaven, the same is my brother, and sister, and mother."* (Matthew 12:50) I believe David probably did the same with his "mighty men." Jesus' top disciple Peter speaks of *"loving the brotherhood"* (I Peter 2:17). I believe David tried to build a brotherhood as well among his warriors, but the Hashem boys came into David's army already a brotherhood. Peter learned about the true meaning of a brotherhood from Christ even though he had a brother in Andrew, and, perhaps David learned of the true brotherhood among soldiers from the Hashem brothers. Even though David had older brothers, there didn't seem to be a brotherhood among them (I Samuel 17:28). Wordsworth once described the relationship Jesus had with His disciples as: **"Partners in faith and brothers in distress!"** This could also be said of David and his "mighty men." We have in our country today an organization call "Big Brothers." Its goal is to match up men with boys who have no fathers. We all know you can't replace a father because only one man can really be your dad, but we all can have a big brother to be a mentor to us when other important male influences are absent. This is why we as a church have a tremendous responsibility to others who are lacking some important person in their lives. We have great opportunities today in this area because of the breakdown of the home and the lack of true role models, especially to young men and boys. I believe one of the things we learn from Jesus' thirty years of silence in Nazareth was a ministry of being a big brother. Have we forgotten that Jesus had four brothers: James, Joses, Juda, and Simon (Mark 6:3)? We need to remember that Jesus was a brother long before he became a healer, a preacher, a teacher, and yes, even our Savior.

There is an old saying that goes, **"The glory of the father is in the son!"** In the case of Christ this proverb is especially true in every aspect, and I am not talking about Jesus' adopted father Joseph, but His Heavenly Father. This same aspect is seen in the unnamed sons of Hashem, as if the reader of David's list would recognize the father's name over the sons. One of the most often used terms for the Christ is "Son of the Most High God," but Jesus was also called:

1. The Son of the Living God (Matthew 16:16)
2. The Son of the Highest (Luke 1:32)
3. The Son of the Father (II John 3)

4. The Son of the Blessed (Mark 14:61)
5. The Son of Mary (Mark 6:3)
6. The Son of man (John 3:13)
7. The Son of Joseph (Luke 3:28)
8. The Son of God (Revelation 2:18)
9. The Son of David (Matthew 21:9)
10. The Son, Jesus Christ (I John 3:23)

The term "son" refers to that blessed relationship between a boy and his parents. For those of us who are sons, we can relate to this marvelous union we have with our father and our mother. There has always been a debate which relationship is strongest (the relationship of a mother with her son or the relationship of a son with his father), but in the case of Jesus there is no doubt. I am not saying that Jesus didn't have a great relationship with Mary, but from age twelve Jesus was clear: *"I must be about my Father's business!"* (Luke 2:49) Six of the eleven phrases in which the "Son" is mentioned are spoken of in the relationship with the Eternal Father and Jesus Christ.

I like what Herbert C. Gabhart has to say on this relationship, and I quote:

> The father tends to see in his only son (John 3:16) a continuity of the family name, the posterity of the family. The only son gives strength and security to the family, especially to sisters (Mark 6:3), and more especially if the sisters are unmarried. The only son is looked upon to carry on the work of the father (Luke 2:49), to preside over the affairs of the family in lieu of the father. As God's only Son, Jesus fulfilled all of these roles admirably. He has borne His Father's name with dignity and honor (Revelation 5:12). He has given strength (Philippians 4:13) to all the children of God and has provided security-eternal life, to all who believe (John 10:28–29). He continues to preside over the activities of the kingdom of God with infinite wisdom and everlasting love (I Corinthians 1:24).

Let us never forget that when we believe in Jesus as our Savior, we, too, become known as *"the sons of God."* (John 1:12) *"Behold what manner of love the Father hath bestowed unto us, that we should be called the sons of God…"* (I John 3:1). Brothers with Christ and sons of God are a clear doctrine in the Bible: *"For as many as are led by the Spirit of God, they are the sons of God. For ye have not received the spirit of bondage again to fear; but ye have received the Spirit of adoption, whereby we cry, Abba, Father. The Spirit itself beareth witness with our spirit, that we are the children of God: and if children, then heirs; heirs of god, and joint-heirs with Christ."* (Romans 8:14–17) Whether brother or son, may we try each day to develop stronger ties, not only with our Father as sons, but with Christ and our fellow brothers as brothers.

Matthew 12:50: *"Whosoever shall do the will of my Father… the same is my brother…."*

29.

SHAMMAH: RENOWN

II Samuel 23:33: *"**SHAMMAH** the Hararite,
Ahiam the son of Sharar the Hararite."*

WE ARE BEGINNING TO get some repetition in the names on David's "mighty men" lists, not in men because I do believe these are all different warriors. Today our devotional thoughts are on a man whose name has now appeared three times on our list:

1. Shammah the son of Agee, one of David top fighters (II Samuel 23:11).
2. Shammah the Harodite, a little known soldier (II Samuel 23:25).
3. Shammah the Hararite, the warrior of this article (II Samuel 23:33).

As with the first Shammah, this Shammah is only listed in the II Samuel 23 account, and, like the first Shammah, he, too, was a Hararite, a mountaineer and a native of the hill-country of Judah or Ephraim. These simple facts and the meaning of his name are the only things we really know about this third Shammah.

With the first Shammah we were able to look at a specific battle that brought him fame and recognition in the eyes of David. With the second Shammah, we looked into the meaning of his name, renown or fame, or the greatness of his fame. For our last Shammah we will look into the meaning given to his name in the context of "renown" or a question that has been asked throughout the ages, "Who is the greatest?" Ali, the boxer claimed he was! Many throughout history have been given the title of "the Great:" Alexander the Great, Herod the Great, Alfred the Great, Fredrick the Great, and many, many more. However, keeping with our pattern of thought, we turn again to the life of Jesus Christ for our answer to who really is the greatest.

Often, we, like the disciples of Jesus, get into a debate of *"...who should be the greatest..."* (Mark 9:34). We put people into categories like baseball players (Ruth or Bond), basketball players (Jordan or James), football players (Brady or Manning), politicians (Lincoln or Washington), war heroes (Alexander or Hannibal), and musicians (Bach or Mozart), to name a few. When in reality it is but another distraction on the real question that should be asked, **"What do you do with Jesus?"** Until Jesus becomes the greatest of them all, we have not really looked at life or history in the right way. Even in the Bible, the Man of God was compared to the great Hebrew king Solomon: *"The queen of the south shall rise up in the judgment with this generation, and shall condemn it: for she came from the uttermost parts of the earth to hear the Wisdom of Solomon; and, behold, **a greater than Solomon is here**."* (Matthew 12:42) Yet, even the wise man Solomon said this as he dedicated the Temple of God: *"For great is our God above all gods. Who is able to build Him a house, seeing the heaven and heaven of heavens cannot contain Him?"* (II Chronicles 2:5–6) Solomon had wisdom enough not to compare or even ponder the greatest of others (gods or men) in the presence of the greatest of them all, but do we? Solomon realized as we must that God cannot be confined to four walls and a roof, no matter how beautiful, elaborate, or ornate those four walls and roof. Solomon's spiritual observation was much like Isaiah's statement of *"...the whole earth is full of His glory."* (Isaiah 6:3) So how does one rightly explain the great God, the God of renown?

First, we have to note that in the original Greek, there is but one Greek article for "God" and "Savior." Titus 2:13 says: *"Looking for that blessed hope, and the glorious appearing of the GREAT God and Saviour Jesus Christ!"* This verse underlines and highlights the first concept of greatness we must consider when speaking of God. This is but more evidence to prove that the Man of Galilee was not an ordinary man, but a great man, the Son of Man and the Son of God both! The so-called great men of history can't even stand in the shadow cast by the Christ; as a matter of fact they get lost in the darkness of that shadow. Jesus was great, Jesus is great, not greater, or the greatest compared to others because he is the only great one, because there are no others like Him!

Second, we have the Greek word itself to consider, **megas**. In Acts 8, we have the story of Simon Magus. He was called "great" because he *"...giving out that himself was some great one..."* (Acts 8:9). It is far easier to call yourself great than to actually be great. Was Ali the greatest boxer ever? He thought so, but I dare think he wasn't. Interestingly, unlike Simon Magus, Jesus Himself never called Himself great. When you are really great, there is no need to actually call yourself great. You need no proclamation, no prophecy, and no proclaimer. Others like Simon have over the years called themselves great, but a simple reading of the life of Christ and one should conclude that he alone is worthy of the name Magus. Through demonstration, not dictation, Jesus proved His greatness in the villages and town of Galilee and beyond. Jesus the Great stands alone against all those that might claim the title.

If this is true, and I believe it is, then our conclusion must be: *"Great is the Lord, and greatly to be praised!"* (Psalm 48:1) I ask you again, *"Who is so great a God as our God?"* (Psalm 77:13) The Scriptures speak fully of the great God: His salvation is called great (Psalm 21:5); His mercy is called great (Psalm 57:10); His name is called great (Psalm 76:1); His works are called great (Psalm 111:2); His power is called great (Psalm 147:5); and His wonders are called great (Psalm 136:4). I would challenge you as I have done to get out your concordance and trace this adjective in relationship to the attributes of God. If you do, you will come to the same conclusion and summary as I have that God is great and His Son Jesus Christ is great.

Homer J. R. Elford tells this story:

> At the funeral of Louis XIV the great cathedral was packed with mourners paying their final tribute to the king whom they all considered great. The room was dark, save for one lone candle which illumined the great gold casket that held the mortal remains of the monarch. At the appointed time, Massillon, the court preacher, stood to address the assembled clergy of France. As he rose, he reached from the pulpit and snuffed out the one candle which had been put there to symbolize the greatness of the king. Then from the darkness came just four words:

"God only is great!"

Oh, that there would be a few more court preachers that would acknowledge that in the courts and cathedrals of today's Christendom.

Today, all I hear is, "Isn't that pastor great," or "That preacher, isn't he great?" And don't get me on my soapbox in relationship to how many think the current pope is great!

When Christ is compared to any other, He will always be greater. He is greater than Abraham, Isaac, and Jacob in the Hebrew faith, yes, even greater than Moses. For sure, Moses was a great man, but Jesus was greater, better, as Paul says in Hebrews. Then what of the great preacher Jonah who God used to bring about the greatest revival of the ancient world (Jonah 3), yet Matthew clearly states that a greater than Jonah had come in the person of Jesus Christ (Matthew 12:41). Any name connected with greatness, all the Shammah's of the world, fall far short when compared to Jesus Christ.

Matthew 12:42: *"And, behold, a greater than Solomon is here."*

30.

AHIAM: A MOTHER'S BROTHER.

I Chronicles 11:35: *"**AHIAM** the son of Sacar the Hararite, Eliphal the son of Ur."*

AHIAM IS LISTED IN both listings of David's "mighty men." The only difference between the two lists is in the spelling of Ahiam's father's name, Sacar in I Chronicles 11:35 and Sharar in II Samuel 23:33. Being a Hararite (note the connection of the last few "mighty men;" this grouping highlights for me that they were not only from the same region of Canaan, but they might have been a part of a special regiment of "mountaineers"- II Samuel 23:11, 33 and I Chronicles 11:34), Ahiam was a man from the hill-country of Judah or Ephraim, which leaves us with only one form of practical application to his being numbered among "the mighty men," and that being the meaning of his name: "a mother's brother."

A story was told in the Christian magazine called the <u>Baptist Observer</u> about a little boy who after reading John Bunyan's Pilgrims Progress asked his mother which of the characters she liked best. "Christian, of course," she replied. "He is the hero of the story." To which the lad responded, "Mother, I like Christiana best because when Christian set out on his pilgrimage he went alone, but when Christiana started, she took her children with her!" (I would just note here that there are still a lot of Christians who don't know that Pilgrims Progress was written in two parts. Most only read of Christian's journey, but there was a sequel to Christian's trip from the City of Destruction to the Celestial City which was Christian's wife Christiana and her four boys that also made the trip after him. At the writing of this devotional I have just finished putting the first half of the story into a PowerPoint course.) Such is the meaning to me of the name of Ahiam.

Ahiam is only known in the Bible through the lives of two men, his father Sacar and his unnamed, and might I add, unknown mother's brother. We know absolutely nothing about this father or the uncle. Nevertheless, this mother reminds me of this Biblical, historical account: *"Josiah was eight years old when he began to reign, and he reigned thirty and one years in Jerusalem. And his mother's name was Jedidah, the daughter of Adaiah of Boscath."* (II Kings 22:1) When Jedidah's son Josiah was only eight, she was left a widow when her husband was assassinated, (II Kings 21:23-26) and, despite her husband's wicked example, her son turned out to be one of the finest kings Judah ever produced. I have come to the belief that Jedidah had a lot to do with the sterling reign of Josiah. A godly mother can make a big difference in a godless house. A good mother can change the course of a home off course. A great mother can turn a household back to the faith. In my opinion Jedidah has to be added to the list of great mothers numbered in the Bible because as the little child observed in the story of Pilgrims Progress, Christiana "took her children with her!" Did Ahiam's mother have that same effect on him?

Every day ought to be mother's day, not just one Sunday in May. Have you pondered today just how much you owe to your mother? Jedidah was one such mother. I read once of a minister who gave this tribute to his mother by saying: **"My mother practiced what she preached!"** It was said of Jedidah's son Josiah: *"And he did that which was right in the sight of the Lord, and walked in all the ways of David his father, and turned not aside to the right hand or the left."* (II Kings 22:2) Actually, David was Josiah's 15th great grandfather, but he mirrored his great ancestor's qualities and godly character. I believe Josiah learned this at the feet of his mother, and so did Ahiam. Maybe this testimony of the great inventor Thomas Edison concerning his mother will better explain what I am trying to say about Ahiam. Edison wrote: "I did not have a mother long, but she cast over me an influence which has lasted all my life. The good effects of her early training I can never lose. If it had not been for her appreciation and her faith in me at a critical time in my experience, I should never likely have become an inventor." Me either!

I do not know if Ahiam did as Solomon did to bestow upon his mother this honor, but I do believe that she deserved it. The Scripture says; *"The king* [Solomon] *rose up to meet her* [Bathsheba]*, and bowed himself unto her, and sat her down on his throne, and caused a seat to be set*

AHIAM: A MOTHER'S BROTHER.

for the king's mother, and she sat on his right hand." (I Kings 2:9) Perhaps you are no king, but you, too, can realize the role your mother played in your upbringing. Honor her as the Lord commands (Exodus 20:12), and rise up as Solomon did and call her blessed (Proverbs 21:28). A mother like Ahiam had was worthy of both. There is no doubt some very poor mothers are out there, but I choose to focus our attention on the special one the Lord has given the world. Behind any good man, any good warrior, stands a wonderful woman we call mother. My mother was named Phyllis Barton.

Ahiam's mother, though unknown and unnamed, was a Hannah in relationship to her son Ahiam. Have you ever noticed the connection between great men and their mothers? Let me remind you of a few:

1. Could Abel have become the man of Faith (Hebrews 11:4) he was without the influence of his mother Eve?
2. Moses wouldn't have even lived beyond infancy (Exodus 2:1–10) if it wasn't for the protection of his mother Jochebed.
3. What was it about the lady Rahab (Matthew 1:5) that produced the mighty man of integrity, Boaz (Ruth 2–3)?
4. Samuel became the great judge, an amazing prophet, and a spectacular priest because he was taught about God at the feet of Hannah (I Samuel 1–2).
5. What part of the life of Elizabeth was mirrored in the life of John the Baptist, the greatest man born of a woman according to Jesus (Luke 1)?
6. God saw something in the devotion of Mary that committed Jesus to her care and upbringing (Galatians 4:4).
7. Finally, but certainly not the last, it was the two generations of mothers (Lois and Eunice-II Timothy 1:5) that created the young missionary Timothy.

I do not know why this unnamed mother named her child "a mother's brother," but it might just have to do with this concept that comes from the prayer of the mother of Pierre Loti, the famous French novelist, when she wrote on the flyleaf of a Bible she gave him: "May these words of our Saviour strike you most specially, my son, and make a deep impression. Let this book never be closed. Each day mediate on some passage for your strength. If I could have the certainty that you would be a true disciple of Christ, how my pain in being separated from you would lose its bitterness."

I close this devotional on the "mighty man" Ahiam with these words from the pen of T. DeWitt Talmage, the great preacher, on a mother's love: "Mother-love: abuse cannot offend it; neglect cannot chill it; time cannot effect it; death cannot destroy it. For harsh words it has gentle chiding; for a blow it has beneficent ministry; for neglect it has increasing watchfulness." Good and godly mothers produce "mighty men."

Proverbs 21:29: "Many daughters have done virtuously, but thou excellest then all."

31.

ELIPHAL: GOD IS JUDGE

I Chronicles 11:35: *"Ahiam the son of Sacar the Hararite,* ***ELIPHAL*** *the son of Ur."*

I HAVE COME TO a disagreement with others who have written on David's "mighty men" in connection to the next man on David's lists. There are some that believe that Eliphal in I Chronicles 11:35 is the same warrior listed in II Samuel 23:34 as Eliphelet. The only evidence most give is the fact that they are numbered in the same slot in David's order and that their names have a similar spelling. I have three reasons why I believe they are different warriors:

1. David's two lists do not list perfectly his "mighty men." We have arrived in a section of the listings where the two lists are differing more and more. I believe this is such a case in the naming of Eliphal and Eliphelet.
2. There is no similarity in the other facts connected or associated with these two soldiers. Eliphal's father was a man by the name of Ur, which means "light or brightness," while Eliphelet's father was Ahasbal, and he was a Maachathite. There is no connection in the two families.
3. Finally, their names mean different things. Eliphal means "God is Judge," while Eliphelet means "God is Deliverance."

It is for these three reasons that I will deal with these two "mighty men" separately. First, Eliphal and the mighty meaning of his name, God is Judge, and truly He is!

Jesus once told his generation: *"For the Father judgeth no man, but hath committed all judgment unto the Son: that all men should honor the Son, even as they honor the Father."* (John 5:22-23) Jesus is the Judge by order of the Father, and this is the truth behind the Biblical doctrine of the Judgeship of Jesus. Whether in name or title, we must recognize that Jesus is the appointed Judge of the world (II Timothy 4:1). I know the world doesn't believe this or they would be dealing with Jesus differently than they are, but whether the United Nations disapproves or the Supreme Court of this land approves, it matters not because Jesus has already taken the Moses' Seat (Matthew 23:2).

Paul continues this teaching of Christ with his own recognition of this position given to Jesus by His Heavenly Father in a sermon recorded in Acts 17:31: *"Because He hath appointed a day, in the which He will judge the world in righteousness by that Man whom he hath ordained...."* Yes, one day the Lord Jesus Christ will hold court and the destiny of every living soul will be in the hands of the Judge, the Lord Jesus Christ. He will pronounce sentence in each case based on what that individual did or did not do with Him. And for those who think that death will make a difference should note carefully the word recorded in the book of Second Timothy: *"I charge thee therefore before God, and the Lord Jesus Christ, who will judge the quick and **the dead** at His appearing and His kingdom."* (II Timothy 4:1) The key word for those that think death will somehow make them ineligible, note **"dead."** Peter also has a sermon recorded in the book of Acts that highlights and underlines this truth: *"And He [Jesus] commanded us to preach unto the people, and to testify that it is He which was ordained of God to be the judge of the quick and **dead**."* (Acts 10:42) Peter would verify this truth again in his first epistle with he wrote: *"Who shall give account to Him that is ready to judge the quick and the **dead**."* (I Peter 4:5) Even death itself cannot separate you from the judge. One day all men will face Jesus' judgment and justice, even believers.

Paul speaks of this doctrine in Romans as well: *"But why doest thou judge thy brother? Or why doest thou set at nought thy brother? For we shall all stand before the judgment seat of Christ."* (Romans 14:10) So all shall be included, the good, the bad, and the ugly; the righteous, the good, and the perfect; and whether you are a sinner or a saint, a just man or an unjust man, a righteous woman or an unrighteous woman, Christ will be your judge, but unlike the judges of this present world, Christ is a "righteous judge" (II Timothy 4:8). Paul made this statement when Nero was the judge of the world. Like those before Nero and those after Nero, he perverted judgment and justice. His judgments were based on greed, self-interest, and bribery. In contrast, Jesus Christ will judge each case on its merits, righteousness, and true justice. Could anybody ask for a fairer trial than one played out before a righteous judge? Christ will bring into the court case of each of us an insight into the truth behind every defense. No matter how you dealt with Christ will change the outcome, and I have come to believe that even the plaintiff will say in the end, "It was fair, I got what I deserved, my sentence was right." Don't get me wrong, the world will hate, does hate, the Judge. Micah prophesies: *"They shall smite the Judge of Israel with a rod upon the creek."* (Micah 5:1) For me, this prediction was fulfilled at the trial of Jesus. Amazingly, the world put the Judge of the world on trial, and Matthew tells us that they *"... smote him on the head..."* (Matthew 27:30). The Judge being judged is an irony the world never saw, but we see it clearly through the microscope of the Bible.

Despite what the world did to Him the first time around, Jesus isn't coming back to judge the world in malice or hatred or even revenge. The Christ will judge in fairness, favor, and fidelity. This is why it is so important to know the judge before you stand before his judgment seat. It is not just important that you know Him, but that He knows you (Matthew 7:21–23). Whether we like it or not, we all await a court date; it has been set, but we don't know it as yet. The verdict is clear that every one of us will someday stand before Christ, but we all will not stand before Him at the same time. I see clearly two dates. If you are a Christian, a believer in Jesus Christ, you will stand before Him in what the Bible calls "the judgment seat of Christ" (II Corinthians 5:10), and if you are a non-Christian, an unbeliever in Christ, you will stand before the Great White Throne judgment seat of Christ (Revelation 20:11–15). We are charged, both groups, the wheat and the weeds, the sheep and the goats, to get ready because judgment day is coming, and there is no force or power on earth or in the universe that can stop it from happening.

Eliphal was a good soldier that understood by the very meaning of his name that he would one day give an account to one greater than his king. I am writing this article at the time of the death of the longest serving Justice on the United States Supreme Court (Anthony Scalia). For nearly thirty years he made judgments on the toughest cases of the land, but now he waits his date with the Chief Justice of the Universe. They eulogized him as a good man, a godly man, a religious man, but I am wondering which judgment seat he will be standing before. Americans are now fighting over who will replace him to the neglect of preparing to face the highest court, not in the land, but in time; the greatest court system, not at The Hague, but in Heaven, and to ultimately face the Chief Justice, not Roberts, but Jesus Christ. It will be before His court we will stand one day even if our name is Eliphal. I have one final question: Are you ready for your court date?

James 5:9: *"Grudge not one against another, brethren, lest ye be condemned: behold, the Judge standeth before the door."*

32.
ELIPHELET: GOD IS DELIVERANCE

*II Samuel 23:34: "**ELIPHELET** the son of Ahasbai, the son of the Maachathite, Eliam the son of Ahithophel the Gilonite"*

As I said in the previous chapter, I believe that Eliphelet and Eliphal are two different soldiers in David's listings of his "mighty men." I gave my reason for this interpretation in our last devotional so let us zero in on the challenge we can get from the warrior Eliphelet.

All we know about Eliphelet can be summarized in three names. They are:

1. Maachathite: a patronymic of the residents of Maachah, a town near Mount Hermon (Deuteronomy 3:14). Young's concordance lists a number of Maachathites in the Bible, but the most famous is our soldier Eliphelet.
2. Ahasbal: the father of Eliphelet. The name means "blooming or shining." Whenever a father's name is given in connection with his son, I often wonder if the reason for that is simply that the father was better known than the son when the list was first published. Now Eliphelet is the more famous of the two. Also, it seems in Biblical times it was proper to recognize the father in relationship to the

son. You see this both in the Old Testament as well as in the New Testament.

3. Eliphelet: the "mighty man." Why he was listed will never be known this side of eternity, but his name gives us all we need to know for a challenge from God's Word: God is Deliverance.

Is there any doubt that mankind is in need of a Deliverer? Since the exploits of Eve and the actions of Adam in the Garden of Eden, the human race has needed someone to save them from themselves. We are still in need of a Deliverer that can deliver us from self-destruction. Because the Creator was an all-knowing God, a plan has been in place since the beginning of time (Genesis 1:1) which included "the Deliverer:" *"And I will put enmity between thee and the woman, and between thy seed and her seed; it shall bruise thy head, and thou shalt bruise his heel."* (Genesis 3:15) Those words to the serpent Satan were the first hints given to mankind that a Deliverer would come, and names like Eliphelet kept that precept and concept alive until that Deliverer in the person of Jesus Christ came to execute our deliverance.

As time passed since that early mention in God's judgment upon Satan, Adam, and Eve, the Hebrew prophets started to take up the theme: *"And the Redeemer [Deliverer] shall come to Zion, and unto them that turn from transgression in Jacob, saith the Lord."* (Isaiah 59:20) Even the Psalmist David began to openly write of a Deliverer: *"And he said, The Lord is my rock, and my fortress, and my Deliverer."* (II Samuel 22:2) The Hebrew word used most often in the Old Testament for "Deliverer" is **palat,** which means **"to let escape."** I even found a few references for Eliphelet with his name meaning **"God is escape."** Because the Bible likens the human race chained in sin, imprisoned by transgression, and in restraints by iniquity, it is in need of someone to release them, provide liberty for them, to provide a way of escape for them. Isaiah would write of one that was to come that would do just that: *"...proclaim liberty to the captives, and the opening of the prison to them that are bound..."* (Isaiah 61:1). Centuries after these words were written, a man speaking in a Jewish synagogue in Nazareth of the Galilee reread these words of Isaiah and proclaimed: *"This day this scripture is fulfilled in your ears."* (Luke 4:21) The long awaited Deliverer had come, and his name was Jesus!

Yes, Jesus the carpenter was claiming He was the long expected one; the one that would set the captives free, would open the doors of sin's prison house, and deliver those who had been in Satan's jail (Luke

4:16–21). Throughout the Old Testament, the principle of deliverance had been taught, a Deliverer had been foretold, and a name had been given, but nobody knew until Jesus' arrival that he really was the Son of God Himself. Standing in the wings of history before the foundation of the world stood "the Man of Sorrows" ready, willing, and able to deliver mankind. Throughout ancient history we had seen glimpses of what he would do for us. I think of the dramatic deliverance of Daniel from the lion's den (Daniel 6:20). Perhaps there is someone reading this devotional and they are wondering if God is powerful enough to deliver someone from a den of drugs, from the depravity of lust, or from the lord of lying himself (John 8:44). As Daniel was delivered from the mouth of the king of beasts and as the children of Israel were delivered from Pharaoh's elite chariot squadron at the Red Sea, and as the three Hebrew children were delivered from Nebuchadnezzar's fiery furnace, so, too, can He deliver you from any prison you might find yourself. Remember, Jesus taught us to pray: **"...*Deliver us from evil...*"** (Matthew 6:13). Paul gave us this concept through Timothy and a wonderful promise as well: *"The Lord shall deliver me from every evil work, and will preserve me unto his heavenly kingdom."* (II Timothy 4:18) What is it that you need to be delivered from? Do you even know you need a Deliverer?

William Williams wrote in his great church hymn, <u>Guide Me, O Thou Great Jehovah</u>: "Open now the crystal fountain, whence the healing stream doth flow; let the fire and cloudy pillar lead me all my journey through; **strong Deliverer**, be thou still my strength and shield!" If you believe the same as Williams, then you must cry with the Psalmist: *"But I am poor and needy: make haste unto me, O God: thou art my help and my Deliverer; O Lord, make no tarrying."* (Psalm 70:5) Interestingly, the only time the word is used in the New Testament in the context of Christ, is the Greek word *ho rhuomenos* which means **"the rescuer:"** *"And so all Israel shall be saved: as it is written, There shall come out of Sion the Deliverer, and shall turn away ungodliness from Jacob."* (Romans 11:26) Christ came to rescue us from sin, from ourselves, and from Satan: *"And that they may recover themselves out of the snare of the devil, who are taken captive by him at his will."* (II Timothy 2:26) Rescued is now the question. If you need to be rescued from something, do as any who need rescue from drowning, cry out, call out for help because we are taught that whosoever shall call on the Lord will be rescued (Romans 10:13). The Word of God promises us that anyone that cries out will be heard by the Deliverer, and He will immediately come to your rescue. He will find you, and he will deliver you from whatever, whenever you call.

I have come to believe that names like Eliphelet were given throughout the Old Testament to keep alive the hope of a coming Deliverer. Whenever Eliphelet's name was pronounced, it proclaimed the marvelous truth that God is deliverance, that God would deliver, and that God was a Deliverer. At the time they never fully understood the fulfillment in the person of Jesus, but the belief was alive and well and still is today!

Psalm 40:17: *"But I am poor and needy; yet the Lord thinketh upon me: thou art my helper and my Deliverer; make no tarrying, O my God."*

33.

ELIAM: PEOPLE'S GOD

II Samuel 23:34: *"Eliphelet the son of Ahasbai, the son of Maachathite,* **ELIAM** *the son of Ahithophel the Gilonite."*

ONLY MENTIONED ONCE IN Scripture, this "mighty man" is only known through his relationship with his father and the meaning of his name.

This is a case in point when the father was more famous, Biblically speaking, than the son. Ahithophel the Gilonite (II Samuel 15:12) was one of David's most trusted and influential counselors. Ahithophel comes upon the Biblical scene during the troublesome time of the Absalom rebellion. When Absalom conspired to overthrow his father David, it was to Ahithophel he first went to for advice, and from all accounts Ahithophel became a part of the revolt (II Samuel 15:31). However, at the critical time of the revolution, Absalom rejected Ahithophel's advice and decided to his own death to take the advice of the spies David left behind in Jerusalem to delay Absalom's assault on David's forces (II Samuel 15:32-37; II Samuel 16:15-23; II Samuel 17:1-21). When Absalom decided not to take the advice of Ahithophel, he decided to *"...put [his] household in order, and hanged himself, and died and was buried in the sepulcher of his father."* (II Samuel 17:23) Why such an end to a successful politician?

Ahithophel knew that when Absalom refused to pursue David immediately, as he had advised Absalom (II Samuel 17:1-4), the revolt was doomed (as it was). Ahithophel's answer to this crossroad in his life, however, was suicide. As with Judas, when caught in his betrayal of Jesus, hanging seemed to be the best answer for his dilemma (Matthew

27:1–5). So, too, with Ahithophel; suicide would claim another victim. What is sad to me is the known fact that suicide is still one of the greatest killers of our day, and suicide is still doing its ghastly work in the young as well as the successful politicians. Like Ahithophel, most suicides go to their death without fanfare, without grief, and without spectators. It is always amazing to me how easy it seems to be to go from a simple setback to suicide. The Bible says this of Ahithophel's reason for suicide: *"And when Ahithophel saw that his counsel was not followed, he saddled his ass, and arose, and got him home to his house, and to his city..."* (II Samuel 17:23). And as the saying goes, "the rest you know." You would think he was going home for lunch. One simple rejection resulted in Ahithophel murdering himself. He calmly returned home and did it. In my only direct suicide in my ministry, a seventeen year old that also simply went home from school one day and took his father's revolver and shot himself. There was no suicide note, and the only thing we could figure out why he did it was the fact that he had just been rejected by a girlfriend and had been cut from his high school football team. Not enough for you or me, but for this young man enough.

We are never told (as with most suicides) in the Bible why Ahithophel changed his allegiance or why he committed suicide and it seems strange to me with his son being one of David's "mighty men." The indication is that up to the revolt he had been a good counselor of David's and that most were surprised when he sided with Absalom over David. Even when he was summoned by Absalom, he is recorded to have been making sacrifices (an indication that he was at least a religious man) (II Samuel 15:12). Do spiritual people commit suicide? They do including my 17-year old church kid. There was a great preacher in Ireland named Willie Mullen that killed himself in his church study. Did Eliam attend his father's funeral or was he with David preparing for the battle of the Ephraim Woods? (II Samuel 18:6) Despite Ahithophel's sad ending, his son Eliam attained a wonderful end numbered among David's greatest warriors. Ahithophel also gave his son a wonderful name, the people's God.

If you would put the Bible in chronological order, the first verse in the Bible would be John 1:1, *"In the beginning was the Word, and the Word was with God, and the Word was God,"* not Genesis 1:1. When you ponder before creation, there is only one and that is God, and we know now that Jesus was God. In Isaiah's famous list of the names of God, he calls Jesus Christ "the mighty God," (Isaiah 9:6) and he certainly is the people's God. In one of the most famous of the Messianic Psalms, the Psalmist writes: *"Thy throne, O God, is forever and ever: the scepter of Thy kingdom is a right scepter."* (Psalm 45:6) As Jesus responded to his accusers he said: *"Hereafter shall ye see the Son of man sitting on the right hand of power, and coming in the clouds of heaven."* (Matthew 26:64) This is more fully described in the Revelation with these words: *"And I saw heaven opened, and behold a white horse; and He that sat upon him was called Faithful and True....And out of His mouth goeth a sharp sword, that with it He should smite the nations: and He shall rule them with a rod of iron: and He treadeth the wine press of the fierceness and wrath of Almighty God."* (Revelation 19:11, 15) Paul also verifies this title of God on Jesus Christ when he said, *"And without controversy great is the mystery of godliness: God was manifest in the flesh..."* (I Timothy 3:16). Paul continued in Timothy to say: *"For this is good and acceptable in the sight of God our Saviour..."* (I Timothy 2:3). We know of the name Emmanuel or "God with us." (Matthew 1:23) Only Jesus is worthy to be called God, not these myriad of impostors parading themselves through the world's religions including the 330,000,000 in India. (I have just returned from my fifth trip to that nation and every time I come back I have learned of a new "god!") Do you know Jesus as God, the people's God?

What this tells us about our Christ is that eternal self-existence belongs to Him and Him alone. It was upon this point Jesus stunned his own people the Jews when He said: *"Verily, verily, I say unto you, before Abraham was I am."* (John 8:58) The reason they took up stones to kill him (John 8:59) because to them this was blasphemy, and Jesus was making himself God, their God! He was using the holiest name for God known to them: *"I Am!"* (Exodus 3:14) But Jesus could use that name because it was his name. Paul writes: *"...Christ Jesus, who, being in the form of God thought it not robbery to be equal with God."* (Philippians 2:5–6) That will bring us to one conclusion and that being either Jesus was a liar, a lunatic, or He is Lord of all, the people's God! Most of the leadership of Israel in the days of Jesus thought him a liar. Some of his own family thought him a lunatic, but those who believed saw him as the people's God!

John Wesley was probably the greatest evangelist of his generation next to George Whitefield. Despite our disagreement on Arminianism, there is one thing we heartily agree on and that is the last words this great man of God said before his departure to glory, and I quote: "Best of all, God is with us!" I believe it, too. Do you? I believe Jesus came to show us the meaning of Eliam because in all his teachings, miracles, and redemptive work on Calvary He proved himself to be "the people's God!"

Titus 2:13: *"Looking for the blessed hope, and the glorious appearing of the great God, and our Saviour Jesus Christ."*

34.

HEPHER: A WELL

I Chronicles 11:36: *"**HEPHER** the Mecherathite, Ahijah the Pelonite."*

Hepher the Mecherathite is the least known of the "mighty men" of David to this point in our journey through David's listing of his most famous warriors. Mecherathite is a patronymic of Hepher, but this place is also unknown to Biblical scholars, the geography uncertain. Hepher is also only recorded in the Chronicles account so we don't even have another reference to help us know this valiant man of battle any better. So once again we are left with the meaning of his name, "a well."

When I have been limited in information connected to one of David's "mighty men," I have fallen back on my theme for this series of devotionals that David and his men mirror some aspect of my Lord and Savior Jesus Christ. So with that mind-set, I see in the meaning of Hepher another spiritual precept connected to the life of Jesus. Remember, Jesus said to the Samaritan woman at Jacob's well: *"But whosoever drinketh of the water that I shall give him shall be in him a well of water springing up into everlasting life."* (John 4:14) When we believe in Jesus as we should and allow Him into our lives, He is like "a well," a Hepher.

Whenever I get stumped on what to share in the devotional themes, I often turn to a favorite author and a favorite devotional to help me understand what it is I am trying to get across. A case in point is the "mighty man" Hepher and the meaning of his name. I found these thoughts from the pen of the great English preacher, author, and pastor, Charles Haddon Spurgeon, and I quote:

He who is a believer in Jesus finds in his Lord to satisfy him now, and to content him evermore. The believer is not the man whose days are weary for want of comfort, and whose nights are long from absence of heart-cheering thought, for he finds in religion such a spring of joy, such a fountain of consolation, that he is content and happy. Put him in a dungeon and he will find good company; place him in a barren wilderness, he will eat the bread of heaven; drive him away from friendship, he will meet the "friend that sticketh closer than a brother." Blast all his gourds, and he will find shadow beneath the Rock of Ages; sap the foundation of his earthly hopes, but his heart will still be fixed, trusting in the Lord. The heart is as insatiable as the grave till Jesus enters it, and then it is a cup full to overflowing. There is such fulness in Christ that he alone is the believer's all. The true saint is so completely satisfied with the all-sufficiency of Jesus that he thirsts no more-except it be the deeper draughts of the living fountain. The sweet manner, believer, shalt thou thirst; it shall not be a thirst of pain, but a loving desire; thou wilt find it a sweet thing to be panting after the fuller enjoyment of Jesus love. One in days of yore said, "I have been sinking my bucket down into the well full often, but now my thirst after Jesus has become so insatiable, that I long to put the well itself to my lips, and drink right on!" Is this the feeling of thine heart now, believer? Doest thou feel that all thy desires are satisfied in Jesus, and that thou hast no want now, but to know more of Him, and to have closer fellowship with Him? Then come continually to the fountain and take of the water of life freely. Jesus will never think you take too much, but will ever welcome you saying, "Drink, ye, drink abundantly, O beloved.

I can only add a hearty Amen to Spurgeon's challenge.

I can testify to this satisfying aspect of a relationship with the Lord. One of the early verses I learned as a kid was *"The Lord is my Shepherd, I shall not want."* (Psalm 23:1) It was nearly 60 years ago that I first drank from Jesus' well, and I have never sought another drink from any other religion or any other god. He has been my complete satisfaction, and I can verify that what Jesus said to the woman at the well has been true in my life. I found these thoughts in another favorite devotional, <u>My Utmost for His Highest</u>, by another favorite author, Oswald Chambers, and I quote:

HEPHER: A WELL

The picture our Lord gives is not that of a channel but a fountain. "Be being filled" and the sweetness of the vital relationship to Jesus will flow out of a saint as lavishly as it is imparted to him. If you find your life is not flowing out as it should, you are to blame; something has obstructed the flow. Keep right at the Source, and you will be blessed personally? No, out of you will flow rivers of living water (John 7:38), irrepressible life. We are to be centers through which Jesus can flow as rivers of living water in blessing to everyone. Some of us are like the Dead Sea, always taking in but never giving out [I had a chance to witness the selfish sea in 2010 on a trip to Israel. It is just as the books say, and over time it has made the sea so salty that you can't sink in it or drink it!] because we are not rightly related to the Lord Jesus. As surely as we receive from Him, He will pour out through us, and in the measure He is not pouring out, there is a defect in our relationship to Him. Is there anything between you and Jesus Christ? Is there anything that hinders your belief in Him? If not, Jesus says, out of you will flow rivers of living water. It is not a blessing passed on, not an experienced stated, but a river continually flowing. Keep at the Source, guard well your belief in Jesus Christ and your relationship to Him, and there will be a steady flow for other lives, no dryness and no deadness. Is it not too extravagant to say that out of an individual believer rivers are going to flow? "I do not see rivers," you say. Never look at yourself from the standpoint of –Who am I? In the history of God's work you will nearly always find that it has started from the obscure, the unknown, the ignored, but the steadfastly true to Jesus Christ.

The key is the Source, not the faucet!

Water is essential for the life of all living things. It is not by chance that in the Word of God water is used often to highlight and underline the truth that the Bible (also likened to water-Ephesians 5:26) is essential to our Christian purity. That Christ would liken Himself to the Water of Life, and all that we need will be found in the well of the Word (John 1:1–4) because in it we will find and have life. A sinner must be like a man dying of thirst, seeking and searching for a well in an arid land. As long as he sees the land dry and brown, he knows that water is still afar off, but when he sees green, he knows that water must be near. Often we must dig for it, but it is not a hopeless task when the signs are clear that water is near. A tragedy today is the fact that many are digging and finding dry wells, those who think that money will satisfy or passion and pleasure will satisfy or some other worldly desire that never quenches the thirst of the natural man. Some find momentarily satisfaction, but it is never lasting. Over my nearly 50 years preaching the Gospel of Jesus Christ, I have been trying to direct people to this Hepher, the well of Christ. Yet, most have sought to quench their thirst at other wells, but they have been empty cistern and containers with holes at best. Most seek only a daily quenching, an earthly satisfaction, little realizing that there is within their reach water that once received will allow them to walk away to never thirst again, an eternal water source that will change forever how they drink. Jesus taught clearly in John 6:53–56 that He was that drink, His blood was that water. There are wells, and then there is the Well!

II Peter 2:17: *"These are wells without water…."*

35.

AHIJAH: THE LORD IS BROTHER

I Chronicles 11:36: *"Hepher the Mecherathite, **AHIJAH** the Pelonite."*

A SIMPLE NAME NUMBERED among the "mighty men" of David's list in Chronicles. Ahijah is not mentioned in the II Samuel listing of David's famous warriors, and the only other link we can make to the list is that the mighty man Helez (I Chronicles 11:27), like with Ahijah, was called "the Pelonite." This is no doubt making reference to Ahijah's hometown of Pelon, but we know of no such town in the Bible which doesn't mean that there wasn't such a town. I have come to believe it was a small village in the territory allotted to the tribe of Ephraim (I Chronicles 27:10). When it is all we have in the Biblical narrative, we must turn to the meaning of Ahijah: "the Lord is Brother" or "a brotherly Lord." Sounds like a great title of Jesus to me!

By now you know that I like the devotional writing style of the British minister, F.B. Meyers. He once wrote this on the "brotherhood" and its relationship with the Lord Jesus Christ:

> Is not this the reason why God has set us in families? Had He so chosen, each of us might have been created alone as Adam was, and sent out with no special connection with others of our race. But instead, we are closely connected. It is very rarely that a man is so utterly bereaved as to be destitute of some relative. Between a man and his brother there is a special tie. It may be truly said, in the case of brothers, that a doorway has been made through the walls which ordinarily part men, which may be bricked up

or filled with debris; but the wall there will always be thinner than anywhere else, and someday the doorway may be opened from the passage of the messenger of peace. Men are always more inclined to follow the man of whom they can say, "He is our brother." Brotherhood, sisterhood, relationship of any kind, is therefore a very precious talent; and it becomes us solemnly to ask ourselves whether it has been put to use. Have you ever spoken or written to your brother or sister about Christ? This is the reason that Jesus has so strong a hold on human hearts. He is our brother, bone of our bone; not ashamed to call us brethren; and this constitutes a moving argument why we should be inclined to follow Him.

Jesus is not only our "Brother," He is also our "Lord!"

In answer to Meyer's question of "Have you ever spoken or written to your brother or sister about Christ," I remember early on in my witnessing that I came home one year from college with my youngest brother on my mind. Most of my family was saved by that time, but I didn't know of my youngest brother (there are 13 years between us). I recall to this day that it was while feeding our father's cows that I first brought up the subject of his soul's salvation, and though I didn't lead him to Christ that day, eventually, Michael would become a fine Christian. I can honestly say that I am proud and thankful to call him my brother, and that we are also brothers in Christ.

Abraham asked long ago, *"Lord God, what wilt thou give me?"* (Genesis 15:2) The Hebrew word is *Adonai-Jehovah*. According to Revelation 4:8, *Adonai-Jehovah* is the one worthy to receive glory, honor, and power. John went on to record these words from heaven: *"Thou art worthy, O Lord, to receive glory and honor, and power; for thou hast created all things, and for Thy pleasure they are and were created."* (Revelation 4:4) Add to these words of John in his Gospel, and we can draw a clear conclusion: *"All things were created by Him; and without Him was not anything made that was made."* (John 1:3) And now we have verification that Christ is not only our Brother, but he is our Lord. No other term for Christ appears more in Scripture in combination with the other names and terms associated with Christ than Lord. Here is a sample of the titles I have found:

AHIJAH: THE LORD IS BROTHER

1. He is Lord over all (Romans 10:12).
2. He is Lord of the dead and the living (Romans 14:9).
3. He is Lord God Almighty (Revelation 15:3).
4. He is Lord of the harvest (Matthew 9:38).
5. He is the Lord from Heaven (I Corinthians 15:47).
6. He is the Lord of Hosts (Isaiah 47:4).
7. He is the Lord Jesus (Acts 7:59).
8. He is the Lord Jesus Christ (Galatians 1:3).
9. He is the Lord our righteousness (Jeremiah 23:6).
10. He is the Lord of the Sabbath (Matthew 12:8).
11. He is the Lord God (Genesis 15:2).
12. He is the Lord of lords (I Timothy 6:15).
13. He is the Lord and Savior Jesus Christ (II Peter 1:11).
14. He is the Lord of glory (James 2:1).
15. He is the Lord mighty in battle (Psalm 24:8).
16. He is the Lord of all (Acts 10:36).
17. He is the Lord your Holy One (Isaiah 43:15).
18. He is the Lord your Redeemer (Isaiah 43:14).
19. He is the Lord strong and mighty (Psalm 24:8).
20. He is the Lord (Matthew 22:41–46).

What more proof than this overwhelming weight of Scripture to prove that Jesus Christ is Lord, a brotherly Lord. Truly, the angels announced it best on the night that Jesus was born when they proclaimed to the shepherds outside of Bethlehem: *"For unto you is born this day in the city of David, a Saviour, which is Christ the Lord."* (Luke 2:11)

Over the years I have enjoyed singing these words by Dottie Rambo:

> Master, Redeemer, Savior of the world.
> Wonderful, Counselor, Bright Morning Star.
> Lily of the valley, Provider, and Friend,
> He was yesterday, He'll be tomorrow,
> Beginning and the End.

Jehovah, Messiah, Mighty God and King.
Bread of Life, lasting words of love that I sing.
Light in darkness, Door to heaven, my home in the sky;
The Fountain of Living Water that never shall run dry.

But the angel called Him Jesus, born of a virgin.
Mary called Him Jesus, but I call Him Lord!

A simple study of the Life of Christ will reveal the duel aspect of the Christ as both "Brother" and "Lord" in relationship to the people of His day as well as with us today. As with the Lord's earthly brothers (James, Joses, Juda, Simon-Mark 6:3), we, too, have a connection in the spiritual sense to Jesus. When we became "sons of God" (John 1:12), we became brothers with Christ and heirs (Romans 8:17). Jesus came to be our "Brother-Lord," not some standoffish religious leader that always separates Himself from His followers. We are not servants, but friends (John 15:13–15). We are not even distant relatives, but brothers, part of the brotherhood of Christ (I Peter 2:17). Ahijah is a name that puts both the Lordship of Christ and the Brotherhood of Christ together, a relationship that is opened to anyone that will put his faith and trust in the "brotherly Lord." I have one final question, however: Do you live in this duel relationship with Christ?

I Kings 8:15: *"...Blessed be the Lord God of Israel...."*

36.

HEZRAI: BEAUTIFUL

II Samuel 23:35: *"**HEZRAI** the Carmelite, Paarai the Arbite."*

WE ARE BACK TO a double reference in our expedition into the Bible to uncover as many of David's mighty men as we can. Next on the chronological order of the two lists in II Samuel 23 and I Chronicles 11 is the man Hezrai, or Hezro, in I Chronicles 11:37. I believe that they are the same warrior because of their position in the listings, and they are both called "Carmelites." Because this is all we know of Hezrai or Hezro, let us first take a look at where this soldier was from before we look into the meaning of his name.

We have two possible meanings for the description of "the Carmelite." First, it could be talking about the region along the Mediterranean Sea famous for Elijah's remarkable demonstration of God's power against King Ahab, Queen Jezebel, 450 priests of Baal, and the 400 prophets of the groves (I Kings 18:19). I found this description of this region in <u>Robert Young's Analytical Concordance to the Bible</u>: "It is nearly always with the article –'the park', the well-wooded place. A mountain which forms a striking and characteristic feature of Canaan. It projects into the Mediterranean Sea, and stands as a wall between the maritime Plain of Sharon on the south, and the more inland expanse of the Esdraelon on the north. It is about 12 miles long from the sea till it terminates abruptly in the hills of Jain and Samaria, which forms at that part the central mass of the country. Its highest point is about 4 miles from the east end, at the village Esfieh, and measures in English feet 1728 above sea level." This is a great description and very accurate because I had a chance to visit this region of Israel in May of 2010 with a Biblical study group from Dallas Theological Seminary. It was a trip of a lifetime with the added bonus of being able to tour the area with my daughter, Marnie. We found only Dan to be more wooded than Carmel, and to climb to the top and see what Elijah saw when he saw the sea and the coming storm was a thrill. Whether Hezrai came from this region or not, I will never forget my visit and being a "Carmelite" for a day!

The second possible meaning of "the Carmelite" is that it could be referring to the town in the mountainous region of Judah where Nabal lived with his wife Abigail (Joshua 15:55). Only Nabal, Abigail, and Hezrai are called Carmelites in the Bible. Maybe Hezrai joined David's band while David was hiding out in that area, the story told in I Samuel 25. I find it interesting to wonder when familiar stories come to light in the study of David's mighty men. Was Hezrai somehow a part of the story that resulted in David taking Abigail for his second wife? I have always thought that if David would have stayed faithful to Abigail, the troubles he and his family got into would never have happened. You decide which of these two places Hezrai was actually from.

The last thing we know about Hezrai is the meaning of his name: both Hezrai and Hezro mean "blooming," but Hezrai can also mean "beautiful." It will be around these words I will develop this devotional, our next adjective describing our wonderful Lord and Savior Jesus Christ. For beside all of His other characteristics Jesus can also be seen as "beautiful." Isaiah wrote: *"In that day shall the Branch of the Lord be beautiful and glorious…"* (Isaiah 4:2). Add to this image this picture by Isaiah: *"And there shall come forth a rod out of the stem of Jesse, and a Branch shall grow out of his roots."* (Isaiah 11:1) There is no doubt the Branch is Jesus, and He is the most beautiful person that has ever come to this planet both in his personality and in His works. If the Rod speaks of Christ's womb life, and the Stem speaks of Christ's world life, then the Branch speaks of Christ's work life.

From His baptism to His burial, Jesus Christ's work was to proclaim the message of the Father, demonstrate who and what He was by His mighty miracles, and finish the redemption of mankind by His death on Calvary's tree. All this and more can be seen in the name of the "beautiful" Branch. Another Hebrew prophet proclaimed this: *"And speak unto him saying, thus speaketh the Lord of Hosts saying, behold, the man whose name is the Branch; and He shall grow up out of His place, and He shall build the temple of the Lord."* (Zechariah 6:12) Once this link is connected, we can return to Isaiah 4:2 and know we are correct to speak of the "beautiful" Branch. Now the context of our key verse referring to Hezrai is linked, we can go on to speak of the beautiful fruit that comes from the Branch. It was during Christ's ministry that He revealed to his hearer that in Him was *"...the spirit of wisdom, and understanding, the spirit of counsel and might, the spirit of knowledge and of the fear of the Lord."* (Isaiah 11:2) These fruits of God came to full "bloom" in the presence of the people of Palestine in the Person of God in Christ. If you place this verse alongside Isaiah 61:1, you will get a complete picture of the fruit of Christ's beauty and the fruitfulness of His ministry on earth. Jesus bore fruit throughout His earthly ministry as a proof that He was the beautiful Branch prophesied by both Isaiah and Jeremiah (Jeremiah 33:15).

Certainly Jesus did grow up out of His place, Heaven versus Nazareth. Though He spent the bulk of His life in Nazareth, His earthly hometown, He was rejected by His family and His friends (Luke 4:14–30). The fame of Jesus and the mighty miracles of the Christ were mostly outside his territory so whether Heaven or Nazareth this might be the saddest commentary on the people of God when they rejected God's most beautiful Branch: *"And they were offended in Him...and He did not many mighty works there because of their unbelief."* (Matthew 13:57–58) Those who had Him the longest got the least benefit out of His mighty power because they couldn't believe He was who He claimed to be. You would have thought his "beauty" would have been enough, but we are also told in Isaiah 53: *"For He shall grow up before Him a tender plant, and as a root out of a dry ground: He hath neither form nor comeliness; and when we shall see Him, there is no beauty that we should desire Him."* (Isaiah 53:2) Jesus' beauty was not external; fleshly, but internal; spiritual. Some picture the Christ as a charismatic, handsome human, but He wasn't. He was beautiful, but only in His fruits and those beautiful fruits could have been plucked from the Branch if they would have only believed.

Also, Jesus, the beautiful Branch, did build the temple of God. We are not talking about a temple of granite or cedar or stone, but of the souls of men. As with Christ, the beauty of God's work today is not the churches and chapels and cathedrals because as Paul writes: *"Know ye not that ye are the temple of God, and that the Spirit of God dwelleth in you?"* (I Corinthians 3:16) Peter echoed the doctrine of Paul when he wrote: *"Ye also, as lively stones are built up as a spiritual house..."* (I Peter 2:5). This is why the world is rejecting us because they are only looking on the outward man and not seeing the beauty of the inward man. Jesus also clearly proclaimed this teaching when he told His disciples just before Gethsemane: *"I am the true Vine* [the main Branch]..." (John 15:1), and like Him we are to produce fruit (John 15:2, 5, 8, 16). How beautiful is the fruit you are making?

Zechariah 3:8: *"...for behold I will bring forth my servant the Branch* [a beautiful Branch.]*"*

37.

NAARAI: PLESANTNESS OF JEHOVAH

I Chronicles 11:37: *"Hezro the Carmelite, **NAARAI** the son of Ezbai."*

ANOTHER ONE OF DAVID'S "mighty men" with two names is Naarai or Paaral (II Samuel 23:35). When you put the information of these two descriptive verses together, this is what we know about Naarai:

1. He was the son of a man by the name of Ezbai meaning "shining or beautiful." Jesus also came from a beautiful Father.

2. He was from the town of Arab (Joshua 15:52) in the territory of Judah making him an Arbite (II Samuel 23:35). Jesus also came from a town in Judah.

3. Naarai means "pleasantness of Jehovah" and Paarai means "revelation of Jehovah." Hebrew words translated "pleasant" in our Old King James Version of the Bible often mean "desire" (check your Young's Concordance). In keeping with our general application into the meaning of David's "mighty men" and their names and their connection to Jesus Christ, I would like to put together the word "revelation" and "desire" and the prophecy of *"And I will shake the nations, and the **desire** of all nations shall come: and I will fill this house with glory, saith the Lord of Hosts."* (Haggai 2:7)

The Hebrew word *chemdah* means "desirableness." This is also the Hebrew word translated "pleasant." (See Young's Concordance for Psalm 106:24 and other Scriptures.) The context of this powerful word suggests that it is the same as "deliverer" in Isaiah 59:20-21. The One who will cure all ills, right all wrongs, and exalt the nation of Israel in the last days. Even nature itself (Romans 8:19-23) has longed to see such a deliverance, and that is why Jesus is the desire of the Church, the created world, and the nations, or at least those who live in the nations that know Him. Naarai, Paaral, reminds us that in Christ is the pleasantness of Jehovah, the desirableness of God, and the revelation of Jesus Christ (Revelation 1:1).

For me both comings of Christ are mixed together in these great terms associated with Jesus. Truly, the Messiah was desirable to men like Simeon and the woman Anna (Luke 2) as Jesus took on human form and died for their sins and our sins (Philippians 2:7-8). Likewise, the Christ is desirable to us today as we see the world going into a self-destructive spiral; as the moral ozone hole on this planet gets bigger and bigger, and as man walks in the darkness with unsolved problem after unsolved problem that can only be corrected by the return of Christ. The United States has failed to solve the world's dilemmas. The United Nations has failed to solve the world's needs. The United Counsel of Churches has failed to solve the social issues of the world. Interestingly, the same Hebrew word is translated in the Song of Solomon as: *"He is altogether lovely."* (Song of Solomon 5:16) Place them side by side and you get this portrait of Christ: "the altogether desirable One," or "the object of all desires," the pleasantness of God revealed in the person of the Man from Galilee, the Lord Jesus Christ. How important it is for us to show the world that the Eternal God has no other candidates for this position. The world is hoping for an election, a multiple choice, a democratic wish list, and the world has brought forth other choices (Muhammad, Buddha, Braham, Confucius, etc.). There is only one desire of God the Father: *"This is my beloved Son, in whom I am well pleased!"* (Matthew 3:17 and Matthew 17:5) You have no other choice; you will either desire Him or be destroyed by Him. You will either confess Him or be judged by Him.

Finis Jennings Dake picks up this thought about "the Desire of the nations" with these words:

> The word "desire" is put here for the object of the desire, which does not consist of the things; it must refer than to Him alone [Jesus Christ], who can and will satisfy the desire of all nations. In the day of fulfillment there will be a universal longing for deliverance, peace, and safety which only God can bring. First, the world will be deceived into thinking that the Anti-Christ

can meet the universal desire, since he will claim to be God and Christ combined; but sudden destruction will come upon them. The "desire" which they thought would be realized in the Anti-Christ will be fulfilled in Jesus Christ, at His second advent. The longing really centers around that which the person will bring to the nations-not silver and gold, but light and truth to disperse darkness and ignorance, liberty to do away with slavery, moral restoration to dispel depravity, salvation to dispel ruin, and peace and prosperity to do away with wars and insecurity.

We know now that this seems impossible with all the various religions of the world promoting their champion, but Paul is clear in his theology that things will change one day. Why? *"Wherefore God also hath highly exalted Him, and given Him a name which is above every name: that at the name of Jesus every knee shall bow, of things in heaven, and things in earth, and things under the earth; and that every tongue should confess that Jesus Christ is Lord, to the glory of God the Father."* (Philippians 2:9–11)

Mrs. Rhea F. Miller wrote these memorable and inspiring words a number of years ago, words that would become a hymn:

> I'd rather have Jesus than silver or gold;
> I'd rather be His than have riches untold;
> I'd rather have Jesus than houses or lands;
> I'd rather be led by His nail pierced hands.
>
> Than to be a king of a vast domain,
> Or be held in sin's dread sway.
> I'd rather have Jesus than anything
> This world affords today!

Who of us hasn't heard George Beverly Shea sing that song in front of the massive crowds at a Billy Graham Crusade? From Shea's own words: "Over the years, I've not sung any more than I'd Rather Have Jesus, but I never tire of Mrs. Miller's heartfelt words." That is why George composed the music to those lovely words and was the first to ever sing them. A Christian's desire for Christ cannot be seen any clearer than that, yet there are still (I once used the word millions) billions in this world that have not as yet heard of Naarai, "the pleasantness of Jehovah."

The world, at least from my observation, has no such desire today. At the writing of this devotional I have just returned from a trip to the

Punjab in India. I watched thousands at the Golden Temple (the Mecca of the Sheiks) in Amritsar seeking forgiveness of sin by washing in the holy water that surrounds the temple or by giving their wealth to the temple in exchange of favor with their God. Jesus is not mentioned except under the breath of a pastor from Maine. My visit there and to other States (Uttar Pardesh, Orissa, Tamil Nadu, and Kerala) tells me the world is a long way from bowing to Jesus, or desiring Him, yet, following the rapture of the Church (I Thessalonians 4:13–17) there will come such a "tribulation" on the World that in the end they will "desire" Jesus. The sad truth is those billions I wrote of will have died long before they could praise His name. What is the desire of your heart (Psalm 37:4)? Only when you desire Him will you find the pleasantness that comes from knowing Him personally.

I Samuel 9:20: *"...And on Whom is all the 'desire' of Israel?*

38.

JOEL: JEHOVAH IS GOD

I Chronicles 11:38: *"**JOEL** the brother of Nathan, Mibhar the son of Haggeri."*

I HAVE COME TO another *"doubtful disputation"* (Romans 14:1) in our ongoing expedition into the listing of David's "mighty men." As I have done in the past, when I have come to an impasse, I have taken the advice of the Apostle Paul in answer to his own questioning of "doubtful disputations," and that being that each man should be fully persuaded in his own mind about the dispute (Romans 14:5). My judgment call is this: I believe that the Joel of I Chronicles 11:38 is the same warrior of II Samuel 23:36 named Igal. First, let me give my rational in this matter in this devotional.

My reasons for believing that Joel and Igal are the same soldier are these:

1. They fall within the same context; both names follow Paarai (II Samuel 23:35) or Naarai (I Chronicles 11:37).

2. They both are connected to a man by the name of Nathan. Granted, one says "brother" (I Chronicles 11:38) and the other says "son" (II Samuel 23:36), but this could simply be a contextual error.

3. Joel means "Jehovah is God" and Igal means "Deliverer," but as we have already seen in this study of the meanings of the names of David's "mighty men," Jehovah God is also "a Deliverer."

4. Lastly, Nathan is a name connected with King David. Could this solder be related

to the great Hebrew prophet of David's court, Nathan? This man of God came into Biblical light when King David asked if he should build a temple to Jehovah (II Samuel 7:1–17). This is also the same Nathan that pronounced the infamous rebuke on David after his affair with Bathsheba and the murder of Bathsheba's husband, Uriah (interestingly, one of David's "mighty men") (II Samuel 12:1–25). Nathan would also be the prophet that would anoint Solomon as David's successor (I Kings 1:45).

So whether or not Joel was connected to Nathan as a son or a brother or not at all, we know not, but what we are sure of is the fact that the meaning of Joel is another indicator that leads us back to the theme of this series of devotional and that being "Jehovah is God," and we can link this truth to Jesus.

When our 16th President, Abraham Lincoln, gave his famous Gettysburg Address, he

did it in brevity and relevancy, what I like to call short and sweet and to the point. Likewise, when Jesus decided to announce Himself to the world, He also did it in the tone of brevity and relevancy; two simple words, made up of three little letters, but consisting of one eternal name, Jehovah. *"Jesus said unto them, Verily, verily, I say unto you, before Abraham was, I Am* [Jehovah]." (John 8:58) The people listening to this declaration did not miss what Jesus was saying because they immediately picked up stones to kill Him (John 8:59). Jesus was saying in this title that He was Jehovah, and that He was God. The depth of this name is seen more clearly in the Old Testament.

When Moses asked the voice from the fiery bush His name, the reply was as simple as Jesus' reply to the crowd: *"I Am That I Am."* (Exodus 3:14) Though the Eternal God is known by many names recorded throughout the Bible (just like with His Son Jesus- Matthew 1:21), His first name is JEHOVAH (Psalm 83:18). Here are some of the variations I have been able to find in my tracing of God's given name:

1. Jehovah-JIREH-The Lord will provide (Genesis 22:14).
2. Jehovah-TSIDKENU-The Lord our Righteousness (Jeremiah 23:6).
3. Jehovah-ROPHEKA-The Lord our healer (Exodus 15:26).

4. Jehovah-SHALOM-The Lord our peace (Judges 6:24).
5. Jehovah-ROPHI-The Lord our Shepherd (Psalm 23:1).
6. Jehovah-NISSI-The Lord our banner (Exodus 17:15).
7. Jehovah-SHAMMAH-The Lord is there (Ezekiel 48:35).
8. Jehovah-SABAOTH-The Lord of hosts (Genesis 32:2).

These titles are given that we might understand all the fullness of Jehovah's name manifest in the Person of His Son Jesus Christ.

The name Jehovah comes from the Hebrew verb "to be" and means "I Am, I Was, and I Will." So what the voice was saying to Moses and what Jesus words were saying to the people is that He is the God of the Past, the God of the Present, and the God of the Future. Paul put this wonderful truth together in his classic verse: *"Jesus Christ, the same yesterday, today, and forever."* (Hebrews 13:8) When Jesus used the name "I Am," He was revealing to us the Biblical doctrine that in Him dwelt *"... all the fulness of the Godhead bodily."* (Colossians 2:9) Those who compile such lists tell me that the name Jehovah, in all of its forms, is used nearly 6,800 times in the Bible. "Jah," an abbreviated form of Jehovah, is used 50 times and is usually translated "Lord." In a recent restudy of the Book of Psalm I noted for the first time the phrase "Praise ye the Lord" psalms. These are the psalms that either end with this phrase or begin with this phrase (Psalm 104, 105, 106, 111, 112, 113, 116, 117, 146, 147, 148, 149, 150). This of course is where we get our word "halleluJAH." Some of the great men of the Bible have God's name in their name: EliJAH meaning "God of Jehovah."

What makes the connection to Christ even more amazing is His constant use of that eternal first name in so many of His descriptions of Himself. John's Gospel, which was basically written to verify the deity of Christ, is full of the variations of this name. You know them already, but to refresh your memory, here they are again:

1. I AM the bread of life (John 6:35).
2. I AM the light of the world (John 8:12).
3. I AM the door (John 10:7).
4. I AM the good shepherd (John 10:11).

5. I AM the resurrection (John 11:25).
6. I AM the way (John 14:6).
7. I AM the truth (John 14:6).
8. I AM the life (John 14:6).
9. I AM the vine (John 15:1).

These concepts of Christ were delivered in this form so that there would be no doubt who He was. And, if there is still any doubt in your mind, then hear this from Christ: *"I and my Father are One."* (John 10:30) Whether in its purest form JAH or Jehovah or in the name of Joel, "The Lord is God" is found in every jot and tittle of the Old Testament, and then when you get to the New Testament that same name is associated with "the carpenter from Nazareth." Joel, Jehovah, or Jesus, it makes no difference.

Psalm 83:18: *"That man may know that Thou, whose name alone is Jehovah, are the Most High over all the earth."*

39.

MIBHAR: YOUTH, CHOICE

I Chronicles 11:38: *"Joel the brother of Nathan,* ***MIBHAR*** *the son of Haggeri."*

THIS "MIGHTY MAN" OF David's army is not listed in the II Samuel 23 account of David's most impressive soldiers. Therefore, all we know about him is his father's name, Haggeri, which means "wanderer" and his name Mibhar, which means "choice" or "youth." With this being my only avenue for a devotional and my only hope for a challenge, I have chosen to combine the meanings of Mibhar's name with these two verses out of the life of Christ for our article: *"And the people stood beholding. And the rulers also with them derided Him, saying, He saved others: let Him save Himself, if He be Christ, the CHOSEN of God."* (Luke 23:35) and *"And when they were come into the house, they saw the CHILD with Mary His mother, and fell down, and worshipped Him: and when they opened their treasures, they presented unto Him gifts; gold, and frankincense, and myrrh."* (Matthew 2:11) "Choice" and "youth" are certainly two words that can be connected to the Christ, and, in keeping with our focus in these series of devotionals, we can see this out of the lives of the unique warriors of David's army as a portrait of Jesus.

Oswald Chambers once wrote: "The good is always the enemy of the best!" This is why we must let God choose for us. Such was the case in this term given to Jesus by the rulers deriding Him on the cross: "the chosen of God." For their lives and their nation's existence, they thought they had made the good choice in having Jesus crucified by the Romans. Their leaders had agreed together to this: *"Ye know nothing at all, nor consider that it is expedient for us, that one man should die for the people, and that the whole nation perish not."* (John 11:49-50) They chose the good, but God chose the best. It is interesting to me that in the Jew's decision they were fearful that Jesus would bring the wrath of Rome on them, but in reality they were bringing the wrath of God on themselves. Within a few years (33-70 AD) that nation they so feared would be used by God to bring punishment to Jerusalem and its inhabitants for making the wrong choice! Oh, that we would realize that Jesus is the best choice we can make.

Again, Oswald Chambers writing on this word in relationship with Christ says:

> Jerusalem stands in the life of our Lord as the place (Luke 18:31) where he reached the climax of His Father's will. "I seek not Mine own will, but the will of the Father which hath sent me." That was one of the dominating interests all though our Lord's life, and the things He met with on the way; joy or sorrow, success or failure, never deterred Him from His purpose. "He steadfastly set His face to go to Jerusalem."

In so many ways the Lord gave us countless examples of how our lives ought to be lived, and this is another of those ways. We, too, are to do the Father's will, and once we find it we are to focus on that will and not be distracted or detoured from it. I have come to the conclusion that this practice comes down to a simple choice, choices we make every day to stay on course. Oswald goes on:

> The great thing I remember is that we go up to Jerusalem to fulfill God's purpose, not our own. [Interestingly, this is both true in the literal sense as the spiritual sense. I had a chance in 2010 to visit Jerusalem, and no matter which direction you approach the City of Jerusalem you are going up because Jerusalem sits on a high hill and all roads lead upward. So it is in our spiritual lives.] Naturally, our ambitions are our own; in the Christian life we have no aim of our own. There is so much said today about our decision for Christ, our determination to be a Christian, our decisions for this or for that, but in the New Testament it is the aspect of God's compelling that is brought out: "Ye have not chosen me, but I have chosen you." But He must have been

unwise to have chosen me because in me dwells no good thing, I am of no value at all. But that is exactly why He did choose me and you. As long as we think that there is something in us of value He will never choose us (I Corinthians 1:27–29). If we come to the end of ourselves, then He can take us and do something in us and through us and by us and we can go up to Jerusalem (the heavenly one) with Him. Amen and Amen. We are apt to think because a man might have a natural ability, therefore he must be a good candidate for being a Christian. It is not a question of our equipment, our talents, our money in the eyes of God, but our poverty; not by what we can bring into the relationship, but by what God can put in us; not a question of natural virtues of strength or character, knowledge and experience-all that is of no avail in this matter. The only thing that avails is that we are taken up into the big compelling of God and made His comrades.

When the wise men finally found the Christ-Child, they found a youngster. There has been much debate through the centuries of Christianity just how old Jesus was when the men from the east showed up. Some say the child was a few months old and others go as high as two years. There is no way of saying for sure, but this one thing the Scriptures are very sure of, that Jesus was certainly a "youth;" that Jesus lived through babyhood, boyhood, and young adulthood. One of the tragedies of our age is the disrespect given to the young. This is not a characteristic just of our age, but of all ages. Herod cared little for the youth of his kingdom; that is why he was willing to sacrifice the young of Bethlehem to get rid of Jesus (Matthew 2:16). David was considered just "a youth" (I Samuel 17:33) when he stood against Goliath. Paul championed the cause of the young when he wrote: *"Let no man despise thy youth!"* (I Timothy 4:12) Let us never forget that our Lord and Savior was young once, too. Jesus is the Savior of all ages, including the young. That is why every age can relate to Christ. Jesus resisted instant maturity, what Adam had, for the opportunity to grow up and understand and feel as all feel, even those in their youth. For those who think that children are useless and helpless, I encourage you to read the Bible again and note how often God uses youth in his doings. We need to hear again this sharp rebuke from the Lord against Jeremiah's excuse: *"Then said I, Ah, Lord God! Behold, I cannot speak: for I am just a child. But the Lord said unto me, say not, I am a child: for thou shalt go to all that I shall sent thee, and whatsoever I command thee thou shalt speak."* (Jeremiah 1:6–7)

Being young is not a handicap as some adult think and some children have been taught. One reading through the Bible will reveal God's use of children as children. Jesus at twelve was already about His Father's business. We ought to make it our business to tell young people in their youth that God can use them, too. It says this about John the Baptist's younger years: *"And the child grew, and waxed strong in spirit..."* (Luke 1:80). And it is said of Jesus: *"And the child grew, and waxed strong in spirit, filled with wisdom: and the grace of God was upon Him."* (Luke 2:40) And: *"And Jesus increased in wisdom and stature, and in favor with God and man."* (Luke 2:52) Next time you despise the young, remember Jesus was young once also. Was Mibhar just a young soldier in David's army when he chose him to be a part of his elite group? I know not, but I do know Jesus chose me at seven years of age to join His army in my youth.

John 15:16: *"Ye have not chosen me, but I have chosen you."*

40.
BANI: POSTERITY

II Samuel 23:36: *"Igal the son of Nathan of Zobah, **BANI** the Gadite."*

IF SOMEBODY WOULD HAVE asked you how many men in the Bible are called "Bani," how many would you have said? I believe there are some who would have said none, but believe it or not, there are 10 men named Bani in the Bible:

1. An ancestor of a chief music minister under David (I Chronicles 6:46).
2. A Judahite, the ancestor of Uthai, who settled in Jerusalem (I Chronicles 9:4).
3. An ancestor of a family that returned to Jerusalem after the Babylonian exile; he is also called Binnui (Ezra 2:10). He is also numbered among those that married and divorced a foreign wife after the Babylonian exile (Ezra 10:34).
4. The father of a man by the name of Rehum (Nehemiah 3:17).
5. The father of Uzzi, a chief Levite in Jerusalem (Nehemiah 11:22).
6. A Levite that taught the Law under Ezra (Nehemiah 8:7).
7. A Levite that led the worship services in the days of Nehemiah (Nehemiah 9:4).
8. A Levite that signed the covenant with God in the days of Ezra (Nehemiah 10:13).
9. Another Levite that signed the same covenant (Nehemiah 10:14).

And then there was Bani, a man from the tribe of Gad that is numbered among David's "mighty men." Bani means "posterity." One's posterity is all of a person's descendants or all of one's succeeding generations, those future children versus your past ancestry. Your children and their children are your posterity. How can we make this application to Jesus Christ as has been our exploration in these "mighty men" seeing Jesus had no wife and thereby no children, or did he? Who are the children of Christ?

First let us highlight the concept of "child" in relationship with Jesus: *"The parents brought in the child Jesus, to do for Him after the custom of the Law."* (Luke 2:27) What a fitting name for Christ after His birth. It is in the name of a child that we can relate to the Person of Christ. As Christ lived a life as we did from childhood, there is no wonder that he is touched with the feelings of our infirmities, no matter the person, no matter the age, no matter the situation or circumstance: *"For we have not an high priest which cannot be touched with the feelings of our infirmities; but was in all points tempted like we are, yet without sin."* (Hebrews 4:15) But what of Christ's posterity?

Jacob answered his brother Esau's question of who are these people: *"The children which God hath graciously given thy servant."* (Genesis 33:5) We often forget that God gave us His Son through the form of a child. Maybe not at Christmastime, but most of us are guilty of this omission throughout the rest of the year. The Psalmist underlines Jacob's conclusion about children with this famous Biblical precept: *"Lo, children are the heritage of the Lord: and the fruit of the womb is His reward."* (Psalm 127:3) For most this is a personal gift; just think of the babies born into your family. At the writing of this devotional my wife and I are rejoicing in the joy of grandparenthood. Our daughter Marnie and her husband Josue presented us with a grandson a few months ago. Judah has become the joy of our lives despite the fact he lives in California, three thousand miles away. But through the miracle of FaceTime, we get to see him regularly to the point that he recognizes us and has even given us names, GiGi for my wife and BaBa for me. Judah Alan is our only posterity to date, but in the cause of Christ, it is a universal blessing!

Having been a pastor for 43 years now, I have had the privilege of watching new parents bringing newborns to church for the first time. The statements of "what a lovely baby" or "what a darling child" brings great joy to the father and the mother. But there has never been, nor will there ever be, a greater congratulation at any assembly as when Mary and Joseph brought the Christ child to the Temple to be circumcised and named. Little did Jesus' parents realize the scope of their child's effect on the crowd. The encounter with Simeon and Anna confirmed the prediction of Gabriel that this was no ordinary child; that He was the One long hoped for and the One few were still looking for. I think Charles Wesley expressed it best in his classic Christmas hymn, <u>Hail Thou Long Expected Jesus,</u> when he wrote these stirring words:

> Hail, thou long expected Jesus,
> Born to set Thy people free:
> From our sins and fears release us;
> Let us find our rest in Thee.
> Israel's strength and consolation,
> Hope of all the saints Thou art;
> Long desired of every nation,
> Joy of every waiting heart.

But what of Christ's posterity?

Simeon said in his prayer: *"...my eyes have seen your salvation."* (Luke 2:30) What an amazing statement from an old man to say about an eight-day old child. His story is rare in that he was only one in a handful that was still watching and waiting for the coming Messiah. He had been told by the Spirit that he would not see death until he saw the Lord's anointed. As he grew older and older he must have doubted, rethought the promise, yet, on the day of Jesus' arrival at Herod's Temple he was looking and only through the Spirit spotted Jesus in the crowd. The Temple area was huge and you can't tell me there were no other parents that day presenting their child to the Lord, yet, in all the mass of people and the many children Simon saw the child, and a man who had been taught no doubt from birth to keep the Law of Moses, to do good works among his neighbors, and to perform the religious rituals taught by Levi, was now putting his faith and hope in a child (Luke 2:34). But what of Christ's posterity?

Like Simeon, we, too, need to get our eyes off the crowds of the season called Christmas and onto the child of the season. It is time we refocus our celebration from the Claus to the Christ. A saying goes: **"Salvation is not giving up something, it is receiving someone!"** Have you received the child of Christmas yet? Christmas may be officially over, but finding the Christ-Child can still happen at any time of the year. Simeon and Anna are testimonies to this very truth. But I ask again, how in this can we see and understand that this child had any posterity?

Despite the fact that Jesus never had a wife (for those who think Mary Magdalene, no way!) or kids, He still had a posterity. Isaiah foretold this: *"Yet it pleased the Lord to bruise Him; He hath put Him to grief: when thou shalt make His soul an offering for sin, HE SHALL SEE HIS SEED..."* (Isaiah 53:10). Every believer that believes is Christ's posterity. Every sinner that gets saved is Christ's posterity. Every boy or girl, man or woman that puts their trust in Christ is part of Jesus' posterity. We are the future generations of the Christ Child. Since His death, burial, and resurrection there have been people of every generation that have become a part of the posterity of Jesus. As no doubt Bani had a posterity, so, too, did Christ, not in the physical sense, but through the spiritual process Jesus called "being born again" (John 3:1-16). Through our faith in the Christ Child we have become *"the children of God"* (John 1:12). As we grow in grace (II Peter 3:18), we like Bani are to become "mighty men and women," Christ's posterity!

Isaiah 9:6: *"For unto us a child is born..."*

41.

ZELEK: SPLIT OR RENT

I Chronicles 11:39: *"**ZELEK** the Ammonite, Naharai the Berothite, the armourbearer of Joab the son of Zeruiah."*

WHILE DAVID WAS AT the Cave Adullam, he began to gather around him a group of exceptional warriors (I Samuel 22:1-2). Then when Ziklag became his home away from home (Bethlehem), another group of courageous soldiers became a part of his small personal army (I Chronicles 12:1-7). Out of these men-of-war came David's intriguing list of "mighty men" (II Samuel 23:8). These were the men Jehovah built up to eventually make David king at Hebron and then a few years later at Jerusalem (I Chronicles 11:4-10). In the battles that they fought together that brought this story to God's appointed end, an elite group known as "the thirty mighty men" (II Samuel 23:23) emerged as David's bravest of the brave, David's heroes of heroes. As we have discovered, recorded in the Bible are actually two lists of these amazing warriors together with their genealogy or place of origin. In II Samuel 23:8-38 we have 37 soldiers listed (II Samuel 23:39) while in I Chronicles 11:11-47 there are an additional 16 who came from territories conquered by David's armies. David seemed to be no respecter of persons or race when it came to the makeup of his soldiers. David also seemed to have that rare gift (like with the famous Carthaginian general Hannibal) of being able to muster loyalty from a variety of nationalities once hostile to the country of Israel and the people of the Jews. Hannibal, the greatest general of his time and always found on history's top warriors' list of all time, merged together an army that constantly beat the Roman Army of African, Spanish, and

Celtic mercenaries. Unlike the Romans, Hannibal's forces were not heterogeneous in organization or armament, and their quality depended entirely on their own leaders and the general in overall command, of which Hannibal was one of the world's best if not the best, but I believe the world has overlooked the genius of David in this ability. When you consider what David did, though his armies were never as large as Hannibal's, the men he was able to meld together became exceptional in their warfare with David.

In our compiling of a combined list of David's "mighty men," we have come to a soldier whose only distinction in this famous brotherhood is his race. He was Zelek the Ammonite whose name means "split" or "rent." Perhaps the only way we can understand fully how amazing it was to have such a man like Zelek in David's Army, we must first share a brief history of the Ammonites written by Robert Young:

> Ammon-a fellow-countryman. The name of the descendants of Ben-Ammi, the younger son of Lot by his youngest daughter born in a cave of a mountain near Zoar, B. C. 1897.....Genesis 19:30-38. Their country lay at the northeast of Moab, and east of the tribes of Reuben, between the Arnon and the Jabbok Rivers. Their border was strong (Numbers 21:24); they were not distressed or meddled with by Israel; the original inhabitants of their country were the giants, and called Zamzummim (great and tall, and many as the Anakim), who were destroyed by the Ammonites (Deuteronomy 2:19, 20, 37); their chief city was Rabbath-Ammon, and it contained the gigantic bedstead of Og, King of Bashan (Deuteronomy 3:11)....none of their nation was to be allowed to enter the congregation of Jehovah to the tenth generation (Deuteronomy 23:3).....They along with Amalek, joined Eglon, King of Moab, B. C. 1354, and smote Israel, and took Jericho, the city of the palm-trees (Judges 3:13); their gods were served by the children of Israel, B. C. 1161, so that Jehovah sold the latter into their hands, and they served them 18 years, on both sides of the Jordan. Israel crying to Jehovah, the Ammonites encamped in Gilead, but were defeated by Jephthah, who drove them from Aroer to Minnith (Judges 10:6-8, 11:1-33); their chief national god was Chemosh (Judges 11:24); they besieged Jabesh-Gilead, when Nahash their king threatened its inhabitants with a severe penalty, but he was discomfited by King Saul (I Samuel 11:1-11; 12:12); they were accordingly vexed by Saul thereafter (I Samuel 14:47); their silver and gold taken in

battle were dedicated to Jehovah by David (II Samuel 8:12; I Chronicles 18:11); Hanun their king, the son of Nahash, having insulted the messengers of David, hired the Syrians to help him, but they were defeated by Joab and Ahishai (II Samuel 10:1–19); I Chronicles 19:1–9); who also besieged Rabbah his capital, and took it, whereon David went to complete the capture, and took all the spoil, and humbled the inhabitants (II Samuel 11:1, 2; I Chronicles 20:1–3).

And then there was Zelek! How does a man change sides after such a history of hostility? How does a citizen of one race switch his allegiance to another race? How does an archenemy flip to the side of an archenemy and become one of its king's greatest soldiers? Remember, we have already studied the Philistines that switched sides, those that became David's personal guard, but there was a group of them, well over six hundred, but Zelek was alone. The only other Ammonite I could find in the Bible that was friendly towards David was a man named Shobi, the son of Nahash, the brother of Hanun, of the city of Rabbah, who took supplies to support David at Mahanaim when David was fleeing from the Absalom rebellion (II Samuel 17:27). All other relationships between the Ammonites and the Israelites are negative in the Scriptures. Solomon would marry an Ammonite, no doubt a political marriage as were so many of Solomon's marriages. Naamah would give birth to Rehoboam, the next king of Israel and the king that would split Israel into two nations (I Kings 14:21,31; II Chronicles 12:13). Naamah was also one of Solomon's wives that turned his heart away from God in his older years (I Kings 11:1, 5, 7, 33). So there is quite a history between the Ammonites and the Israelites, and, yet, I come back to our hero Zelek. How does a single Ammonite, knowing the history between these two races, end up on a list of David's "mighty men?"

So, I ask you again, how does a man that worships the wrong god (Judges 11:24), from an incestuous beginning (Genesis 19:35), from a cursed nation (Genesis 12:3), from a hater of Israel, end up a celebrated soldier in David's divisions? I could come up with only one answer. A number of years ago after reading Elizabeth Elliot's 1956 book <u>Through Gates of Splendor</u> about her husband's death with his four friends at the hands of the Auca people and the reason that these five young Americans even went into the Amazon rain forest: *"...and hath redeemed us to God by Thy blood out over EVERY kindred...and nation."* (Revelation

5:9) They went so that a representative from the Auca people would be at the throne. I am convinced now that the Ammonites also needed a representative, and I am persuaded his name is Zelek. So God reached down His hand and "rent" an individual from the nation of Ammon to be present at His throne on that day.

Revelation 7:9, 10: *"After this I beheld, and lo, a great multitude, which no man could number, of all nations (including Ammon), and kindreds, and people, and tongues, stood before the throne, and before the Lamb, clothed with white robes, and palms in their hands; and cried with a loud voice, saying, Salvation to our God which sitteth upon the throne, and unto the Lamb."*

42.

NAHARAI: SNORTING ONE

II Samuel 23:37: *"Zelek the Ammonite,* **NAHARAI** *the Beerothite, armourbearer to Joab the son of Zeruiah."*

THIS "MIGHTY MAN" OF David presents, at least for me, some very interesting possibilities that I would like to explore.

First, I could seemingly do nothing with the meaning of his name which means "snorting one" as I have with so many others of his comrades.

Second, dealing with the matter of the spelling of his heritage, a "Beerothite" in II Samuel 23:37 and a "Berothite" in I Chronicles 11:39, David was no doubt writing of the village of Beeroth, a town in Benjamin (II Samuel 4:2, 3, 5, 9). Seemingly, just another one of the many Benjamites who switched sides seeing Israel's first king, King Saul, was a Benjamite, David mortal enemy.

Third, and for me the most intriguing description of Naharai is the fact that he was "the armor-bearer of Joab." Joab was our first "mighty man" in this series of devotionals on David's unique soldiers and David's top warrior (I Chronicles 11:4-9). It will be upon this military relationship that I would like to make my challenge for this soldier.

It was the Hebrew prophet Amos who first asked the classic question, *"Can two walk together, except they be agreed?"* (Amos 3:3) For most of my life that has been the Biblical concept that has been proclaimed to debate and discuss the principle of separation. Yet, over the years I have discovered that this question can also be applied to a number of other matters, and in particular this precept that is often ignored when this question is asked. For me it is the scriptural doctrine of "two." Solomon taught us this about this teaching: *"Two are better than one, because they have a good reward for their labour. For if one fall, the one will lift up his fellow; but woe to him that is alone when he falleth; for he hath not another to help him up."* (Ecclesiastes 4:9–10) The Bible often ponders and illustrates the power of "one" (James 5:16 and Joshua 23:10) and talks of the exploits of judges like Shamgar (Judges 3:31) and soldiers like Benaiah (II Samuel 23:20) and boys like David (I Samuel 17) and prophets like Micaiah (I Kings 22) and deacons like Philip (Acts 8) and writers like John (Revelation) and lads like the kid who offered Jesus his lunch for the feeding of the five thousand (John 6:9). But when was the last time we talked and discussed the teamwork of two? It was Moses who first brought up the topic when he wrote: *"How should one chase a thousand, and two put ten thousand to flight, except their Rock had sold them, and the Lord had shut them up?"* (Deuteronomy 32:20) (Note, a ten-fold effectiveness over one.) For me these questions and more about the possibilities and potential of "two" are answered by the relationship between the great Captain Joab and his little known armor-bearer Naharai.

In the <u>Illustrated Family Encyclopedia of the Living Bible</u> authored by Charles Kraft, this interesting and inspiring explanation of the importance of the armor-bearer is given:

> The function of the armourbearer depended on the nature of the ancient warfare. The limitations of the weapons of antiquity, each with its different range, obliged the individual warrior to equip himself with all the weapons that he was likely to need in the varying phases of the combat: the bow, for long range fighting; the javelin, for medium range; and the spear and sword for hand-to-hand combat. Hence, warriors of the upper class took with them men who carried these weapons and handed them to their masters, according to the requirements of the battle. The armourbearer accompanied the warrior in assaults on the enemy, serving him loyally and obeyed his orders in battle. The armourbearer did not desert his master in time of peril; and sometimes even death did not separate them, as was the case with Saul's armourbearer who fell on his own sword after his master's death. (I Samuel 31:5)"

For me there is in the Bible a better example and explanation of the value and importance of the armor-bearer found in the story of Jonathan and his armor-bearer recorded in I Samuel 14.

In this Biblical battle Jonathan takes on a force of Philistines in a field after climbing up a steep rock face with his armor-bearer as his companion (I Samuel 14:6–14). As one they fought back to back and won a great victory proving the worth of an armor-bearer even to an elite soldier like Jonathan. David was King Saul's armor-bearer when he was just a kid (I Samuel 16:21). It is my belief that when David was making his list, he recognized the importance of Naharai in his position as armor-bearer to Joab. And this precept that can be seen clearly in the Old Testament in a military sense is also seen in the New Testament in a spiritual sense as taught by Jesus.

The power of one is multiplied, not just one-fold by the presence of another, but depending on the individual many-fold. This was the reason that Jesus sent out his disciples into the spiritual battle (Ephesians 6:10–12) "two by two" (Luke 10:1). So as with Joab and Naharai, Peter and John (Luke 22:8) were just one of a variety of "twos" Jesus used. I can't find a time when Jesus sent the disciples out as individuals; there was always at least two. In order to function properly the two had to be in step, in unison, together in thought, and in purpose as Jesus taught the power of two: *"Again I say unto you, that if two of you shall agree on earth as touching anything that they shall ask, it shall be done for them of my Father which is in heaven."* (Matthew 18:19) Do you have a partner on earth? Do you have someone to fight life's battles side by side with? Do you have a companion you can pray together with? I feel the Scripture teaches that God rarely sends anybody alone into a difficult battle. Consider Moses and Aaron (Exodus 5), Paul and Barnabas (Acts 13), Peter and John (Acts 3), and what of Church history in Moody and Sankey? So was the case with Joab and Naharai.

Together, Joab and Naharai no doubt fought countless battles during David's fight to gain the kingdom and many more, no doubt, to secure the kingdom. All that time David was watching this exceptional armor-bearer helping and protecting David's key asset, underlining and highlighting the power of two. Paul wrote of a faith that *"…waxed valiant in flight, turning to flight the armies of the aliens…"* (Hebrews 11:34). Whether in prayer (Matthew 18:19) or battle (Deuteronomy 32:30), the potential of two in the mighty hands of God is limitless. So, as you read of the times Joab fought in the Biblical account, and he is named often in the battle reports, add in your mind the name Naharai because he, too, was there, even though he is unnamed in the accounting.

I feel the Good Lord is still looking for the couple to serve Him in battle; the duo that will fight for Him; a match set that can agree on a course, on the cost, and with God's commission; and twins in the tests, trials, and temptations of life. How much did Joab accomplish simply because he had a Naharai watching his back? How often was Joab saved from an unseen blow because Naharai was there to deflect it? Though this warrior went unrecognized in the shadow of the mighty Joab, David wanted us to know him.

> Mark 6:7: *"And He called unto Him, the twelve and began to send them forth two by two..."*

43.

IRA: WATCHER

I Chronicles 11:40: *"**IRA** the Ithrite, Gareb the Ithrite."*

THIS IS THE SECOND "mighty man" with the name of Ira. The other was Ira the Tekoite (I Chronicles 11:28 and II Samuel 23:26) while this Ira was an Ithrite. As with the other Ira, it is the meaning of Ira that inspires this devotional on David's super soldier.

The Bible gives us plenty of instruction and a number of lessons for this man's name, "watcher." Was Ira a guard, sentry, or sentinel? Most soldiers will during their service have to act as a "watchman" for the rest of the army, and, perhaps, Ira fulfilled the meaning of his name. I am still at loss at times just how to profile an unknown soldier who fought in unnamed battles. After much thought I have decided I would parallel this "watcher" with other Biblical watchmen from the pages of Holy Writ.

Better known as a prophet, Ezekiel was a unique "watcher." The final battle for Judah, during the age of the kings, was about ready to happen. The clock had been ticking since the days of King Hezekiah (II Kings 20:14–19), but the final days of the kingdom were at hand. Babylon was beginning to eye Judah and Jerusalem as its next conquest. The rebellious Jews were irritating Babylon's king, Nebuchadnezzar. As Babylon prepared, Jehovah had placed his sentinel in Babylon to warn the people of God of the impending attack. God's sentry, Ezekiel, had taken his post, but could he prepare the people for a battle that God didn't want them to fight? Like with Jeremiah, God's sentry in Jerusalem, the message was the same; surrender, yield to the control of Babylon and they would be saved as a nation; revolt and destruction would be the end. It was a hard message, seemingly a traitorous warning, yet God's watchmen knew the mind of God, the will of Jehovah, and they sounded forth the warning, but would the people hear and heed?

I once read of a reporter that was asked by his editor to go into the streets of the city and take a poll. The question he wanted asked was this: "What are the two greatest problems in the world today?" As the reporter stood on the local street corner, a man that was in a great hurry passed the reporter totally ignoring the reporter's attempt to stop him and ask the question. Walking beside the rushing fellow, the reporter asked: "What are the two greatest problems in the world today?" Irritated and mad that he had been distracted from his destination, the man disgustingly said as he moved on, "I don't know and I don't care!" After a bit of thought the reporter decided that he didn't need to ask anybody else the question because the indignant man had given him the answer to his editor's question. Times haven't changed that much from the days of Ezekiel or Ira, or us, because what was true then is true now. The two greatest problems in the world today are people who don't know and who certainly don't care. Most people just want to live in their own little bubble as did the children of Israel. Most people just want to continue on doing what they want to do versus what God wants them to do, so God's watchmen have a tough job trying to explain God's providence and God's purpose in the current world.

Ezekiel wasn't God's first watchmen over Israel. Back in the days of Hezekiah, Isaiah was the prophet and watchman warning the people of Israel about the coming Babylonians. Isaiah was God's sentinel for that generation of Jews, but Manasseh, Hezekiah's son, eventually killed that watchman (II Kings 21:16). Jeremiah would voice the mind of God when he wrote in his classic prophecy: *"Also I set watchmen over, you, saying, hearken to the sound of the trumpet. But they said, we will not hearken."* (Jeremiah 6:17) The sentry's job is not a popular one, especially if you're in God's Army. Often he must tell people what they don't want to hear. Jeremiah learned very early that he, too, was to be a watchman, and that his messages of warning would not be heard or heeded, and that his calls of danger would put him in danger. So by the time God said to Ezekiel, *"Son of man, I have made you a watchman for the house of Israel; whenever you hear a word from my mouth, you shall give them warning from me,"* (Ezekiel 3:17 RSV) the life expectancy of a Jehovah watchman was not very good. But someone had to do it, just like someone must do it today. We still need spiritual sentinels, spirit-filled sentries that will watch and warn about the pending judgments of God on our world despite the reality that only a few in our day will heed or hear the warning calls.

Despite Ezekiel's inability to stop the defeat of Israel in the battle of Judah (II Chronicles 36), he did by his example and writings lay down the Biblical ground rules and regulations for being a good "watcher." Ezekiel 33 is without doubt in my opinion the defining chapter on the doctrine of the watchman even though it contains the details of Israel's final defeat (Ezekiel 33:21). Ezekiel's journey to Babylon had taken place years before, but through the eyes of the Spirit (II Peter 1:21) he was able to see the coming battle, the battle, and the defeat in battle. Even in Babylon he remained a faithful sentinel where he would eventually die in the Babylonian Captivity never to see Jerusalem again. Sometimes death is the reward for a sentry that stays at his post overrun by the enemy. A good sentry will stay to warn to the last minute with retreat not being an option.

Nehemiah was another famous watchman, and he properly trained others to watch with him. They were so vigilant that their enemies never attacked (Nehemiah 4:9, 16, 17, 18, 23). Many times an enemy is heard before he is seen. Too many go ahead on their own to give an improper warning. To sound an uncertain sound can be dangerous (I Corinthians 14:8), but not men like Nehemiah, Jeremiah, Isaiah, Ezekiel, and I believe Ira as well. The priest and prophet Samuel was another one of these faithful sentries, a sentinel in the house of God (I Samuel 3:15). But before he could become a watchman for God (I Samuel 3:20), he had to learn how to listen for God (I Samuel 3:4–10). Sometimes our enemies sneak up on us and only betray themselves by the sounds they make. Sometimes they are disguised (II Corinthians 11:13–14), and they can only be recognized by their speech (Judges 12:1–16). A good watchman has good ears to listen, either for God or foe.

Despite people saying they don't know and they don't care, we must keep up the volume and voice the danger call anyway. The tragedy of our day is that too many voices have been silenced or are silent. Now few believe in sin and the danger of sin and the penalty of sin (Romans 6:23) or even a place called "the lake of fire" (Revelation 20:15). This world is like the great ocean liner the Titanic on a course to collide with an eternal iceberg while most of the passengers are unaware of the danger before them. The signs are there, the warnings broadcasted, but those on board have refused to understand the dangers or heed the warnings. The sentry on watch sees the iceberg too late to change the course, or the sentinel in charge is asleep having shut off the communication link to the other world. The watchman is snoring instead of shouting. Ira, where are you? Every age needs an Ira even if Ira isn't heard. Read carefully the warning given to the "watcher" recorded in Ezekiel 3:17–19 and see if you need not take up the post of "watcher."

Micah 7:4: *"The best of them is as a brier: the most upright is sharper than a thorn hedge: the day of Thy watchman and Thy visitation cometh; now shall be their perplexity."*

44.

GAREB: DESPISER

II Samuel 23:38: "Ira the Ithrite, **GAREB** an Ithrite."

INTERESTINGLY, BOTH ITHRITES IN David's "mighty men" are listed together in the two accounts of David's best soldiers (I Chronicles 11:40 and II Samuel 23:38). In our last devotional we profiled the warrior Ira; now our attention turns to Gareb. Let us first consider their family connection in Ithrite, or belonging to Jether, the patronymic of the family of Jether. Could they have been brothers or cousins? I could find only three possibilities of who Ira and Gareb's family was:

1. Gideon, the famous judge of Israel, had a son by the name of Jether (Judges 8:20). Could these "mighty men" have come from this Manassehite?

2. Ezra, a descendant of Caleb the spy, had a son by the name of Jether (I Chronicles 4:17). Could these "mighty men" have come from this Hebrew?

3. A descendant of the patriarch Asher was named Jether (I Chronicles 7:38). Could these "mighty men" have come from the tribe of Asher?

Robert Young in his analytical concordance states that he believed that both men belonged to the tribe of Judah linking them with the descendants of Caleb who was also from the tribe of Judah. Young also suggests that these warriors were from Jattir in the mountains of Judah where David had a very loyal following (Joshua 15:48). Take your pick; let each be persuaded in their own mind (Romans 14:5). As for me, I will once again focus on the meaning of Gareb (Despiser) and its connection to the Person of Christ: *"He is despised and rejected of men; a man of sorrows, and acquainted with grief..."* (Isaiah 53:3). Few consider the despisers of our Lord, but we will.

The word translated "despised" in our King James Bible is the Hebrew word *bazah* or "to distain or scorn." This word is used to help explain the prophet's prophecy of: *"He hath no form nor comeliness; and when we shall see Him, there is no beauty that we should desire him."* (Isaiah 53:2) It is amazing to me that after thousands of year's mankind still judges on the basis of the outward appearance. This lesson on the meaning of Gareb's name should once and for all illustrate the folly of this approach of judgment.

Jesus was despised because He was not attractive enough for the people of Israel. (Remember, they have always wanted a King Saul type.) What we forget is that there was nothing charismatic in Jesus' looks; I have come to believe that you could have never picked Him out in a crowd. Until Jesus began to perform miracles, few if any recognized Him. He spent 30 years in an out-of-the-way place, and, when Jesus became famous, his hometown neighbors questioned what had happened to the boy next door: *"From when hath this man these things? And what wisdom is this which is given unto Him, that even such mighty works are wrought by His hands?"* (Mark 6:2) The Bible would later record: *"And they were offended at Him."* (Mark 6:3) These were his own family and friends. One of the hardest emotional burdens carried by Jesus throughout His earthly life was the fact that even his closest relatives didn't believe in Him (John 7:5). To be despised by a stranger, and He was, is one thing, but to be despised by your sisters and brothers, that is another matter altogether. There is no evidence that Mary turned on Jesus, and we know not of Joseph, but as Jesus traveled throughout Galilee and often into Nazareth He faced more and more those that would come to despise Him, even some that at first followed Him, but would eventually abandon Him all because: *"Many therefore of His disciples, when they had heard this* [read John 6:52–58]*, said, This is an hard saying; who can hear it? When Jesus knew in Himself that his disciples murmured at it, He said unto them, doth this offend you?...From that time many of his disciples went back, and walked no more with Him."* (John 6:60–61, 66) There is an interesting verse in Mark's Gospel that goes like this: *"And when his friends heard it, they went out to lay hold of Him: for they said, He is beside Himself."* (Mark 3:21) They thought that Jesus had gone crazy; had lost it mentally; had gone off his rocker! They despised Him!

One of the reasons Christ is such a great Comforter to His Church is the fact He understands all the emotions we go through in this world, including being despised. Jesus taught: *"The servant is not greater than his Lord. If they have persecuted me, they will also persecute you."* (John 15:20) Could I make this interruption and application: as they have despised Him, they will also despise us. Paul would predict that in the last days there would be: *"...despisers of those that do good..."* (II Timothy 3:3). Jesus went about doing that which was good (Acts 10:38), and the world eventually hated Him for it: *"But though He had done so many miracles before them, yet they believed not on Him."* (John 12:37) Remember all those amazing exploits on the Sabbath day He performed and how they reviled on Him for them? Today, the Christian community is being despised because we want to save the life of a baby in its mother's womb, yet those same voices are screaming louder than we are to "save the whale," to "save the gorilla," and to "save the planet!" All our good works are being despised because what Jesus did is what we are doing, and, if they despised Him, they will eventually despise everything we do. Jesus revealed the wickedness in the hearts of men and thereby exposed the darkness they so loved. Jesus came to shed light, but because their deeds were evil they despised Him (John 3:19–21). Paul spoke of being despised in his generation (I Corinthians 4:10) so why do we think that we will go through our age without being despised?

Paul said of Christ: *"Who for the joy that was set before Him endured the cross, despising the shame..."* (Hebrews 12:2). This is how we will get through being despised, the joy that is set before us and that being the glorious appearing of our great God and Savior the Lord Jesus Christ (Titus 2:13). We have to, like the Christ, endure the mocking, the scorn, the distain of this present world and because He did we can. Are you despised by someone today? Never forget that you have a sympathizing shoulder, a concerned Christ who understands being despised. Is there a situation in your life that has resulted in you being despised by a family member or a friend? Never forget that you have an understanding Savior that knows all about your trouble. Is there a despiser in your life that continues to haunt you and harass you because of who you are or what you believe? Never forget that no matter what you face or who you face, you have a friend that sticks closer than a brother (Proverbs 18:24) that knows your every burden.

I know not why Gareb's parents named him Gareb or why that name has the meaning it does, but this I know; the name Gareb has allowed me to come to a better understanding of what my Savior went through and it has allowed me to grow in my knowledge of my Lord and Savior (II Peter 3:18). Perhaps, we need to pick out a few more names out of God's Word and discover their meaning and then trace them back to another aspect in the Life of Christ because to know Him better is to know ourselves better and to know the challenges we will face in our Christian life.

Psalm 22:6: *"But I am a worm, and no man; a reproach of men, and despised of the people."*

45.

URIAH: JEHOVAH IS LIGHT

II Samuel 23:39: *"**URIAH** the Hittite: thirty and seven in all."*

THE LAST "MIGHTY MAN" in the II Samuel 23 list is Uriah, perhaps, the most infamous man in this list; thirty-seventh in David's first list, but not the last. We will go on to find other names in I Chronicles, but for this list Uriah is the last. What I would highlight and underline first about this warrior is his race.

The Hittites were the descendants of Heth, the second son of Canaan. (Genesis 10:15) They were a peaceful and commercial people when they are first mentioned in the Scriptures as they sold to Father Abraham a burial place for his beloved wife Sarah (Genesis 23:7–10). It seems as with the Amorites in battle (Genesis 14:13), Abraham took the Hittites as commercial allies in business, and at the first there seemed to be no bad blood between the races. However, by the time Joshua and the armies of Israel arrived in Canaan to claim their Promised Land by conquest, the Hittites were well established in the mountain country that would become the possession of the Tribe of Judah. They were numbered with the *"…seven nations greater and mightier than…"* countries on God's hit list (Deuteronomy 7:1). Often times in the listing of these seven nations, the Hittites are named first (Deuteronomy 20:17). Why they rose to the top of God's list, we know not. So when the Israelites failed to utterly destroy the Hittites, a door was opened to reveal the most honorable Hittite of them all and certainly the most mentioned Hittite in Biblical history: the unsuspicious, self-denying, loyal, and honorable patriot in David's army, Uriah the Hittite, the husband of Bathsheba, and "Jehovah is Light."

Uriah, though a descendant of a cursed race, was himself a devout follower of David, and I believe David's God. He came up through the ranks until he attained a position numbered among David's elite troopers known as the "thirty" (I Chronicles 11:41 and II Samuel 23:39). It is interesting to note, as we have before in the listing of these warriors, that many of David's special soldiers were actually foreigners: Ittai, a Philistine, Ithmah the Moabite, and Zelek the Ammonite, but the most famous of the lot was Uriah the Hittite. The conclusion I have reached as I have surveyed these names is that David was looking for the best of the best no matter where they were from or what race they were from. Character and courage were the qualities David looked for, more than culture.

The Scripture is not clear when Uriah met and married the beautiful Bathsheba, or when Uriah joined David's Band and became one of his top officers, yet, both these situations play a part in the tragic tale that will unfold in Uriah's life. This story centers on this marriage and Uriah's loyalty and devotion despite the intrigue and suspicion that results in one of the most dramatic accounts of Holy Writ. For me, it is again in the meaning of Uriah that I have gotten insight for this devotional. Uriah means "Jehovah is Light." Uriah's devout and tender devotion for Bathsheba is seen in Nathan's description of Bathsheba in his parable: *"But the poor man [Uriah] had nothing except one little ewe lamb [Bathsheba] he had bought. He raised it, and it grew up with him and his children. It shared his food, drank from his cup, and even slept in his arms. It was like a daughter to him."* (II Samuel 12:3 NIV) Despite being the apple of his eye and the love of his life, Bathsheba was second on Uriah's love list because he loved his king even more. To me we have before us how we are to love our Lord and King, Jesus Christ. Do you love Him more than anyone or anything else? (John 21:15) Love and loyalty cannot be separated. Many forces try, but a genuine love and a faithful loyalty will win every time; will conquer every time even if in the end death comes to the champion of loyalty.

The story book romance takes a bitter and tragic twist when Uriah is off fighting the king's battle (II Samuel 11:1). As Uriah fights a dangerous and difficult siege of Rabbah, his king and his wife have an adulterous affair resulting in Bathsheba becoming pregnant with the King's child. To cover up the wickedness David hatches a plot to grant Uriah a special furlough from the battlefront in a vain attempt to make Uriah, not David, appear to be the father of Bathsheba's unborn baby. Though unaware of the scheme, Uriah demonstrates a quality trait rarely seen in the Bible, let alone in the world. At a moment's notice, Uriah's soldierly devotion and chivalrous character comes shining through: *"Uriah says to David, the ark, and Israel and Judah are staying in tents, and my master Joab* [his commanding officer] *and my lord's men are camped in the open fields. How could I go to my house to eat, and drink, and lie with my wife. As surely as you live I will not do such a thing."* (II Samuel 11:17 NIV) Truly, a man in whom David was not worthy, but a man that is worthy of the name "Jehovah is Light." So to cover and hide his shame and sin, David uses Uriah's loyalty and love to destroy him.

Unable to frame Uriah and unable to keep concealed his transgression, David plots a second time, a plan B if you will. David will turn the courage and bravery of Uriah into an instrument of murder: *"In the morning David wrote a letter to Joab and sent it with Uriah. In it he wrote, Put Uriah in the front line where the fighting is fiercest. Then withdraw from him so he will be struck down and die."* (II Samuel 11:15–15 NIV) In the daily war correspondence between Joab and David, Joab simply wrote at the end of the dispatch: *"And Uriah the Hittite died also."* (II Samuel 11:17 KJV) It is worth noting that what David ordered and what Joab did are not quite the same (Compare II Samuel 11:15 and 16). David ordered a retreat, an abandonment of Uriah, while Joab simply put Uriah in the hottest part of the battle, up against the best soldiers of Rabbah. Did Joab follow the order of David to the letter of the law or did he give Uriah a fighting chance against the best warriors of their enemy? I think this is another one of those situations where each must make up his own mind on this matter (Romans 14:5).

Loyal unto death and totally unaware, I believe, of the cloak and dagger plot whirling around him, Uriah is a good example of a "sealed orders" kind of faith (Hebrews 11:8). As Abraham left Haran "not knowing where he was going," Uriah left Jerusalem "not knowing he had been ordered to die." I hear a lot people saying that wasn't fair, and it wasn't, but Uriah was right; he did the right thing. It would have been dishonorable to have read the dispatch, and for the life of Uriah he never would have because in the mighty plan of God, Uriah was expendable. I hear a lot saying I would never let anyone misuse and abuse me like that, yet the Lord taught: *"And if someone wants to sue you and take your tunic, let him have your cloak as well. If someone forces you to go one mile, go with him two miles."* (Matthew 5:40–41) Our loyalty and honor reaches to God, not government; to our King, not our kinsmen. It is a far better thing to be faithful unto death than to be disloyal in life. When Nathan finally exposed David's sin and when he said: *"You are the man!"* (II Samuel 12:7 NIV), I believe David would have traded places with Uriah because the light of Jehovah shone brightly in the mighty man Uriah.

Revelation 2:10: *"Fear none of those things which thou shalt suffer: behold, the devil shall cast some of you into prison…be faithful unto death, and I will give thee a crown of life."*

46.

ZABAD: ENDOWER

I Chronicles 11:41: *"Uriah the Hittite, **ZABAD** the son of Ahlai."*

WE HAVE COME TO our first major crossroad in our study of David's "mighty men." Zabad is the first warrior's name we cannot trace beyond or back to David's first list of soldiers (II Samuel 23:8–39). The Second Samuel accounting of David's famous men ends with Uriah (II Samuel 23:39), but you will note in our key verse printed above there is a continuation with the warrior Zabad. The author of Second Samuel (and it couldn't have been Samuel because he dies in I Samuel 25:1) concludes his history by writing: *"...thirty and seven in all..."* (II Samuel 23:39), but as we have discovered in our cross matching the two lists that we are now at "mighty man" number forty-six. I have never found a good explanation for the two lists and why some names are on one list and not on the other. All I know for sure from a Biblical perspective is that the combined list continues in First Chronicles with Zabad, the son of Ahlai.

As with so many of David's fabulous fighters, all we know about Zabad is his father's name and the meaning of his name. His father is only known in the Bible in his relationship to his famous son, and Zabad means "endower." An endower is one who gives gifts. By now you know that my mindset in this study of David's "mighty men" has been to connect these men with our "Captain" (Hebrews 2:10), the Lord Jesus Christ. The minute I understood the meaning of Zabad's name I recalled these lines from Paul's pen in his epistle to the Ephesians: *"But unto every one of us is given grace according to the measure of the gift of Christ. Wherefore He saith, when He ascended up on high, He led captivity captive, and gave gifts unto men."* (Ephesians 4:7-8) Jesus is the great endower of all time, our Zabad, if you will.

Let us consider for a few moments the variety of gifts the Lord Jesus Christ has bestowed on His followers. Though there are similarities among us as believers, there are also huge differences. The problem today is that we as the Christian Church are allowing these differences to divide us which was never the intent of these gifts. Derived from the same Source, the gifts were designed for the good of the whole Body of Christ. Problems developed almost immediately as the Church began to pick their favorite gifted man to follow: *"Now this I say, that every one of you saith, I am of Paul; and I of Apollos; and I of Cephas; and I of Christ."* (I Corinthians 1:12) Men like Paul and Peter and Apollos became household names to the early Church as do men like Graham, Jeremiah, and Swindoll today. What Christians then and now miss in putting such men on a pedestal is that without the measure of grace gifted to these men they would have no fame or function in the Church of God. Whoever we are in the work of Christ, or whatever we have accomplished in the service of Christ, we owe to the Giver of gifts. I like what Vance Havner once wrote on this topic: "Some stop too soon in their quest for the satisfying experience of the Lord. They get this blessing or that and settle down there and make their blessing an end in itself and a yardstick by which they measure everybody else. The part is greater than the whole. **They major on the gift instead of the Giver.**" The Endower has become secondary in many churches today, and the gifts have become preeminent. I am thinking about the gifts of the Spirit that once defined the Christian community, but now they are a laughing stock because of their uses and misuses. Even the Spirit is to take a secondary role to the Person of Jesus Christ (John 16:13).

In my study of the "spiritual gifts" I have come to believe that they can be found in three chapters of the New Testament: Ephesians 4, I Corinthians 12, and Romans 12. It is not my purpose in this devotional on David's "mighty men" to debate the gifts or even to conclude how many there are or to name them, but from a study of them one can deduce that there were extraordinary abilities given to some and ordinary abilities given to others in the early Church and, I believe, down through the ages. Some gifts resulted in amazing feats while others were for daily, ordinary helps and uses to the Body of Christ. Like the soldiers of David, some we have traced their extraordinary acts while others we only know their name. Psalm 68:18, where Paul got the basis for his Ephesians verse, says,

"...received gifts for men." I feel the meaning of this phrase is that Jesus first received these gifts from the Father, and then He distributed them among His followers through the Holy Spirit (I Corinthians 12:1–8). The context of the verse in the Psalms suggests the picture of a conqueror giving out to his soldiers tokens of his victory from the spoils of his enemies. I wondered as I pondered this aspect of Zabad's name if David didn't do that with his warriors on numerous occasions after great victories. Paul often uses the analogy of the soldier in his writing (II Timothy 2:3–4 and I Timothy 6:12), and the phrase *"led captivity captive"* is also a reference to the concept we are trying to make.

Another problem that has come from these gifts is the idea that we no longer have to play a part in the administration of these gifts. Most of us in the Body of Christ have forgotten the admonition to Timothy by Paul: *"Wherefore I put thee in remembrance that thou stir up the gift of God, which is in thee by the putting on of my hands."* (II Timothy 1:6) We forget that in the early days of the Church the Spirit and its gifts was given by the leadership of the Church as described in Acts 8. Again, I like what the revivalist Vance Havner once wrote: "Sometimes your medicine bottle has on it, 'shake well before using.' That is what God has to do with some of His people. Paul wrote Timothy, 'stir up the gift of God, which is with thee.' We must stir up the gift of God. Like sugar in the lemonade, it may be there but it needs to be set in motion." Interestingly, Paul challenged Timothy in three vital areas of his life that stirring was necessary: Doctrine (I Timothy 4:16), Discipline (II Timothy 2:3), and Dynamics (II Timothy 1:6). All three are important and the lack of one will affect the others, and they all need to be stirred together in order to make the right "lemonade" for life.

So, too, must we allow the Lord to stir up our gifts as one stirs the coals in a fireplace. There is fire under the embers, just like there is power in our lives given by the Spirit. Matthew Henry wrote: **"We must exercise them, and so increase them!"** Gifts of the Spirit that have lain dormant since conversion can be stirred into activity at any time. Don't let the devil convince you that lack of service for years has destroyed the gift, put out the fire. Many are being told the gift is gone, dead because of lack of use; not true, not so! To destroy the gift you would have had to destroy the Spirit, and that can't be done by even the devil himself. To stir the gift is to simply use the gift, and we can take advantage of this at any opportunity that comes along. Just as a fire can be revived from the ashes of a campfire, so, too, can the gift of the Spirit be revived. Jesus Christ, our endower, left us for heaven, but by sending His Spirit He gave gifts to men, not every man or woman, but those that receive Him as their Savior.

I Peter 4:10: *"As every man hath received the gift, even so minister the same one to another, as good stewards of the manifold grace of God."*

47.

ADINA: THE ORNAMENT OF GOD

*I Chronicles 11:42: "**ADINA** the son of Shiza the Reubenite, a captain of the Reubenites, and thirty with him."*

David's next "mighty man" is Adina. It has been awhile since we have had as much information on one of David's great warriors as with Adina. We know at least five things about this soldier:

1. His father's name was Shiza, which means splendor.
2. He was a Reubenite. I believe this is the first Reubenite specifically mentioned in David's list. One of the interesting aspects of David's men is the presence of all the tribes of Israel. David would eventually be king of all the tribes, but that would take some years. Adina might have been the first, but he was not the last: *"And on the other side of the Jordan, of the Reubenites, and the Gadites, and of the half tribe of Manasseh, with all manner of instruments of war for battle, an hundred and twenty thousand."* (I Chronicles 12:37) We sometimes forget that two and a half tribes decided to stay on the east bank of the Jordan, and yet in this we see David's influence and fame even across the great water divide.
3. He was the Captain of the first Reubenites to follow David. The number was only thirty at first, but with that number rising as we just quoted did Adina rise in rank to command the entire Reubenite contingency?

4. He was named among a group of unnamed followers of David: "thirty." In our study so far only "the sons of Hashem" (I Chronicles 11:34) and these "thirty Reubenites" are unnamed. I have come to this opinion (Romans 14:5). I feel Adina joined David early in the struggle for the kingdom and brought along thirty of his tribesmen with him. Thereafter, they fought as a unit and are recognized together for their great feats of bravery. So, for me, this is not only an individual citation, but a group citation as well from the pen of David.

5. He name means **"an ornament of God."**

Webster's dictionary defines "an ornament" in the context of an individual as "a person whose character or talent adds luster to his surroundings." If this be true in the context of our study of David's "mighty men," then taken as a whole these men are like a string of pearls hung around David's neck with Adina being a single pearl. However, the context of this man's recognition is more than that to me. Combined with his men, Adina is not singled out alone, so we are talking about a section of pearls on David's string of "mighty men." That is the historical aspect of Adina, but again I looked deeper into the spiritual and Biblical significance, and the more I meditated and pondered and searched the Word of God, I asked myself the question, "Am I an ornament of God?" Have you ever considered this question about yourself? I decided to get out my concordance, find the meaning of this name, and make the application necessary to my own life. I hope this research will also help you. This is what I found:

1. *"As an earring of gold, and an ornament of fine gold, so is a wise reprover upon an obedient ear."* (Proverbs 25:12) Am I an ornament of God because I have an obedient ear? As I traced these verses on "an ornament," I realized that God through His Word was giving me an understanding of what He wants hanging around His neck. We know the Lord loves obedience over sacrifice (I Samuel 15:22). I still sing the children's chorus: "Obedience is the very best way to show that you believe. Doing exactly what the Lord commands, doing it happily. Action is the key to obedience, joy you will receive. Obedience is the very best way to show that you believe." No doubt one of the reasons Adina was acknowledged as a "mighty man" was

his obedience to his captain's orders. Are we as obedient to our Captain's orders (Hebrews 2:10)?

2. *"She shall give thine head an ornament of grace: a crown of glory shall she deliver to thee."* (Proverbs 4:7) The context of the "she" here is wisdom (Proverbs 4:7). Wise warriors are also an asset to any army, just like obedient soldiers. Whether wise in the use of weapons of war or wise in the fight, Adina was a leader that proved himself wise in the things of war. Note this ornament is called "an ornament of grace." If obedience is a favorite of God, so is grace. So I ask again, are we an obedient, gracious ornament around the neck of our Savior?

3. *"For they shall be an ornament of grace unto thy head, and chains about thy neck."* (Proverbs 1:9) The context of this verse on "an ornament" is different despite the use of "an ornament of grace." This verse has to do with following the instruction of a mother and a father (Proverbs 1:8). How much of Adina's success can we attribute to Shiza, his father? Good sons and daughters usually have good fathers and mothers. When a partnership of a man and a woman is focused on a child, good things can happen, and we know that our heavenly Father loves a good son because they are like a chain of gold around His neck.

4. *"As for the beauty of His ornament, He set it in majesty..."* (Ezekiel 7:20). Again, the context is the key to understanding this verse on "an ornament." I feel that God is talking about the things He gave to Israel to His glory. Instead, Israel used these ornaments to make idols and then worshipped them. It is the same as mankind worshipping the creature instead of the Creator (Romans 1:25). Do we worship the ornaments of God instead of God Himself?

5. *"I will greatly rejoice in the Lord, my soul shall be joyful in my God; for He hath clothed me with the garments of salvation, He hath covered me with the robe of righteousness, as a bridegroom decketh himself with ornaments, and as a bride adorneth herself with her jewels."* (Isaiah 61:10) Perhaps, this is where we make the application to our Lord and Savior, our Bridegroom, as we have throughout this series of devotionals. Ephesians 5 gives us this connection of Christ and His Church, and we, too, have been clothed and covered. Our "captain of salvation" (Hebrews 2:10) has covered us in His salvation

and righteousness (II Corinthians 5:21). Are these the garments you wear every day; are you one of the ornaments that He decks Himself with?

What a string of pearls we have been given to adorn ourselves with: a necklace containing obedience, wisdom, grace, instruction, beauty, majesty, salvation, and righteousness. Could these be what Jesus was talking about when he commanded: *"...neither cast ye your pearls before swine"* (Matthew 7:6)? Adina was an honorable ornament around the neck of David. Can we say the same about us? The Bible seems to be very clear; the Lord is looking for jewels for "an ornament" about His neck.

Ezekiel 16:7: *"I have caused thee to multiply as the bud of the field, and thou hast increased and waxed great, and thou art come to excellent ornaments..."*

48.

HANAN: MERCIFUL

*I Chronicles 11:43: "**HANAN** the son of Maachah, and Joshaphat the Mithnite."*

Our 48th "mighty man" (my order) is a warrior by the name of Hanan. His name means "merciful or gracious." A very easy application to fit into the topic of our "mighty men" series when you consider: *"The Lord is merciful and gracious, slow to anger, and plenteous in mercy."* (Psalm 103:8) And what can be said of the Almighty can be said of His Son the Lord Jesus Christ. Let us now consider these thoughts on the soldier Hanan.

Referring to our text, T. DeWitt Talmage, the famous minister of a former age, writes:

> I am told that the wonderful mercy of God is like an ocean upon which are placed four swift-sailing craft each with compass, sextant, choice rigging, and a skillful navigator. I tell them to launch away and discover for me the extent of this uncharted sea. The first ship puts out in one direction and sails to the north, the second to the south, the third to the east, and the fourth to the west. They crowd on all their canvas and sail 10,000 years and one day come up to the harbor of Heaven; I shout to them from the beach, "Have you found the shore?" and they answer, "There is no shore to God's mercy." Swift angels, dispatched from the throne, attempt to go across it. For a million years they fly and fly, but then come back, and bow their heads at the foot of the throne and cry, "No shore! No shore to God's mercy!"

There are those who like Talmage have been trying in some earthly illustration to describe the scope and depth of God's mercy, but all have failed because of the unfathomable dimensions of this attribute of the Almighty God.

Could there be a greater thought than that about God's mercy? No boundaries, no borders, no barriers! It is the fathomless virtue of our eternal Father and his exceptional Son, Jesus Christ. Richard DeHaan, commenting on Talmage's thoughts on the mercy of God, wrote this:

"Because our God is "rich" in this marvellous quality (Ephesians 2:4), He plumbed the depths of divine wisdom to devise a plan of redemption whereby salvation and forgiveness of sin might be made available for a lost and dying world. Yes, "God so loved us that he gave His Son." Such compassion is beyond human comprehension! It extends to everyone and provides for every situation in life. For those who gratefully respond to His love and grace, it will endure throughout the endless ages of eternity. How grateful we should be that there is **"no shore to God's mercy!"**

If we can't measure the height or depth or width or breadeth of God's love (Ephesians 3:17–19), then we can't measure the size of God's mercy either.

In recent weeks, I have been preaching at my little church through the book of Jonah at our weekly prayer meeting on Wednesday nights. I have come this week to Jonah's anger over the revival of Nineveh and his seeming displeasure with the Almighty. Citing his disagreement over God's merciful grace on the Ninevehites, Jonah opens his heart to God and tells his Lord why he fled to Tarshish in the first place (Jonah 1) and why he refused the first opportunity to preach in Nineveh: *"For I knew that thou art a gracious God, and merciful, slow to anger, and of great kindness, and repenteth thee of evil."* (Jonah 4:2) Jonah, instead of complaining of God's graciousness and mercifulness, he should have been singing with Chisholm:

> The mercies of God! What a theme for my song,
> O, I never could number them over!
> They're more than the stars in the heavenly dome,
> Or the sands of the wave-beaten shore!

As someone once stated it, "Let us never forget that mercy is infinite love expressing itself in infinite goodness." It is a virtue of God only surpassed by the love of God in my opinion.

We have before us today in our study of David's "mighty men," a grand Greek adjective associated directly with our Lord and Savior Jesus Christ. The Greek word is *eleemon* or merciful. W. E. Vine gives us this fine definition of this great word: "Not simply possessed of pity, but actively compassionate, is used of Christ our High priest (Hebrews 2:17), and of those who are like God." Jesus taught his early disciples and applied this teaching to his later disciples this concept: *"Blessed are the merciful: for they shall obtain mercy."* (Matthew 5:7) We are also challenged by Christ with this concept: *"Be ye therefore merciful, as your Father also is merciful."* (Luke 6:36) Once again an attribute of the Almighty is encouraged upon those who follow after the Lord. Christ demonstrated the merciful life, so, too, are we encouraged to duplicate that kind of life in our relationship with our brothers and sisters in Christ, but also with our unsaved neighbors. The question that remains, are we?

David wrote in a psalm: *"With the merciful thou wilt shew thyself merciful."* (Psalm 18:25) Being merciful frequently begets mercy. I found this article by Henry Bosch in an Our Daily Bread a few years ago, and I liked it so much that I saved it for an occasion like this:

> "The Christian should always show mercy. Since divine favor has been showered upon us by the Lord Jesus in saving us, we ought also to reflect a loving attitude towards others. As we do, they will be inclined to show us more consideration because of our graciousness towards them. Above all, God will reward us with additional blessings and increased happiness. Ralph Scott comments, **'Kindness is a hard thing to give away; it keeps coming back to the giver.'** In Les Miserables Victor Hugo tells the story of Jean Valjean. His only crime was the theft of a loaf of bread to feed his sister's starving children. After serving 19 years for his crime, he was released. Unable to find work because he was a convict, he came to the home of a Christian bishop who kindly gave him supper and a place to sleep. Yielding to temptation, however, Valjean stole the bishop's silver plates and slipped out into the night. But he was apprehended and brought back to the scene of the crime. The kind bishop did not want to prosecute the man. Deciding to try and win him to the Lord instead, he told the officers he wanted Valjean to have the silver plates.

Turning to the culprit, he said, 'And Jean, you forgot to take the candlesticks.' The criminal was astounded, and the kindness later resulted in his conversion. This brought a deep sense of joy to the compassionate bishop. Don't pass away any opportunity to be merciful. Each generous deed will brighten the life of another and enrich your own. The literal meaning of Jesus' words on the Sermon on the Mount are **Happy are the kind!**"

Today, most of us stand at a crossroad with an opportunity to show mercy while our High Priest is being merciful to us next to the throne of God (Hebrews 4:16). Why don't we channel that merciful spirit into the life of another knowing that mercy breeds mercy. If there is one attribute of God that is needed in this world, it is the virtue of merciful graciousness. How many ills of this world could be conquered if only this characteristic of God were being passed on through His Church? It is high time we as the followers of Christ share the ministries of Christ like gracious mercy. Hanan is another one of David's unknown "mighty men" with an amazing name (Proverbs 22:1).

Psalm 57:10: *"For Thy mercy is great unto the heavens…"*

49.

JOSHAPHAT: GOD HAS JUDGED

I Chronicles 11:43: *"Hanan the son of Maachah, and **JOSHAPHAT** the Mithnite."*

OUR NEXT "MIGHTY MAN" of David was a soldier by the name of Joshaphat, and his name means **"God has judged;"** another wonderful example of an application to our Lord and Savior Jesus Christ and our next 'mighty man" for our meditation.

Let us get something perfectly clear before we get too far into this devotional on one of David's "mighty men." God never destroys or judges the righteous with the unrighteous. Remember, as Abraham listened to the Almighty explain his plans for the divine judgment on the city-states on the southern tip of the Dead Sea, Abraham thought of his nephew Lot and his family living in Sodom. Abraham knew that Lot was a back-slidden-believer, but Abraham also knew that Lot was righteous in God's sight (II Peter 2:7–8) so Abraham asked God: **"Wilt Thou also destroy the righteous with the wicked?"** (Genesis 18:23) In the conversation that followed Jehovah God told Abraham that He wouldn't (Genesis 18:26–33) because God had already sent two of his messenger angels ahead to get the only righteous people out of the cities sentenced for destruction by fire and brimstone. As Lot and his two daughters fled Sodom, one of the angels proclaimed: *"Haste thee escape thither, for I cannot do anything till thou become thither."* (Genesis 19:22) This divine precept of the godly not being judged with the ungodly has always been the principle of God in determining judgment, and I believe that it is still in effect today. That doesn't mean that the godly and ungodly do not die together, say in a plane crash, but never in a divine judgment situation. God will always separate the two in divine judgment. To illustrate this concept consider if you will what took place in Egypt during the last judgment on the nation, the death of the firstborn. *"And they shall take the blood, and strike it on the two side posts and on the upper door post of the houses wherein they shall it."* (Exodus 12:7) It was God's way in that circumstance to separate the godly from the ungodly, the righteous from the unrighteous.

When God determines it is time for divine judgment, He always makes a way of escape even though that escape isn't always the same. For Lot and his daughters it was the intervention of guardian angels, for the Israelites in Egypt it was blood, but for Noah and his family it was a boat. Sometimes God provides protection through the judgment like with the blood on the posts of the doors of the homes of the Jews, or with Noah it was the ark that lifted the family and the animals above the judgment. As I always like to point out, the same water that judged the world of Noah protected the family of Noah (Genesis 6–8). Noah and his family were as safe as if God had come down in a spacecraft and taken them out of the world until the flood waters were no more. It is important for us to have these precepts in our minds before we talk about what God has judged.

There are many today who live in the terror of divine judgment that shouldn't because they are not the unrighteous, but the righteous. Not until Pharaoh woke up that morning in Egypt did he realize that judgment had come upon him and every member of his nation. The tragedy is still true today as most on this planet live under divine judgment, but don't believe that it will ever come. What is sad for me is that the preachers and prophets of today teach and preach that the righteous will suffer with the unrighteous in the coming judgment known as the Great Tribulation. Where they get this concept in the Bible I know not. Every story that I have been able to discover in Holy Writ that speaks of divine judgment contains a section telling how God separated the good from the bad, or protected the good from the judgment of the bad. To these false prophets and preachers I ask these simple questions. Did Noah get his feet wet? Did Lot have one hair of his head singed? Did one firstborn child of Israel die? What of Rahab's family in Jericho? As God protected His saints in the Old Testament, why wouldn't He protect his New Testament saints? I believe He did, and He will.

I am reminded of what Jesus did for His new Church when Jerusalem came under divine judgment at the hands of the Romans. Jesus had warned His disciples that He came to Jerusalem to die: *"For the days shall come upon thee that thine enemies shall cast a trench about thee and compass thee around and keep thee in on every side."* (Luke 19:43) Christ was foretelling the Roman siege on Jerusalem, and His advice to his followers was: *"And when ye see Jerusalem compassed with armies then know that the desolation thereof is nigh. Then let them which are in Judaea flee to the mountains, and let them which are in the midst of it depart out and let not them which are in the countries enter there into."* (Luke 21:20–21) History records that when the Jews rebelled, a Roman army under Cestius descended upon Jerusalem and laid siege to it. Then unexpectedly at a favorable moment of attack the Roman general withdrew his forces without any apparent reason. The reason I believe was to give the saints of Jerusalem a way of escape out of the doomed city. Taking heed of the warning of Christ, the Christians of Jerusalem fled so that when Titus returned to resume the siege, not one Christian perished in the destruction of Jerusalem in 70 AD.

God promised the church of Philadelphia: *"I also will keep thee from the hour of temptation which shall come upon all the world, to try them that dwell upon the earth."* (Revelation 3:10) To my knowledge only one more worldwide judgment is to come, *"for there shall be great tribulation such as was not since the beginning of the world to this time no more ever shall be."* (Matthew 24:21) I am of the persuasion that like Enoch I, too, will be translated from this world before that period of judgment comes (Genesis 5:24, Hebrews 11:5). Like Noah, I will be safe from the wrath of God (Genesis 6:16, Hebrews 11:7). Like Lot, I will escape from any justice unleashed upon my ungodly neighbors (Genesis 19:29, Luke 17:28–29). Like the firstborn of Israel in Egypt, I will be protected, not because of my worthiness, but because of the blood of my substitute Jesus Christ (Exodus 12:23, I Corinthians 5:7). Like the church in Jerusalem, I have been warned, and I only wait my "redemption" (I Thessalonians 4:13–17, Luke 21:28). God will not destroy the believer with the unbeliever, the wheat with the weeds, and the sheep with the goats.

Let us be at peace today concerning our gracious Lord's promise in dealing with the godly and the ungodly. We are His; they are not. Do you think He would change His ways and deal with us in any way differently than He did with our forefathers? He is the same God (Hebrews 13:8) so why should He or would He deal differently then or now? We need not fear or fret, worry or wonder, about this issue. I am trusting in the consistent judgment of God through the length of time. Judgment is firmly in the hand of my Savior (II Timothy 4:1), and why would He go to Calvary for us only to judge us with the ungodly (Psalm 1:3–6). We need to trust in the Word of God and the example it gives of **"God has judged,"** and believe that our loving and merciful God will not judge us with them. We will have our judgment (II Corinthians 5:10), but in heaven, not on earth!

Revelation 22:20: *"Even so, come, Lord Jesus."*

50.

UZZIA: JEHOVAH IS STORNG

I Chronicles 11:44: *"**UZZIA** the Ashterathite, Shama and Jehiel the sons of Hothan the Aroerite"*

WE HAVE ARRIVED AT "mighty man" #50, just about halfway through, and to a warrior by the name of Uzzia. As with so many of the first fifty, Uzzia is a relatively unknown Biblical character, but we do know three things about this fighter that rose in the ranks to become one of David's "mighty men":

1. He was numbered among David's elite soldiers.
2. His hometown is mentioned as Ashteroth (why he was an Ashterathite), of which we have two choices of where this town was located. There was a Jewish Levitical city (It was given to the children of Levi as an inheritance. Remember, the Levi's didn't get any particular territory, but they were scattered throughout the land to be priests to their brethren in the other tribes.) in the territory of Manasseh on the east bank of the Jordan River by this name (I Chronicles 6:71), and there was a city in the old kingdom of Bashan by the same name (Joshua 13:31). I am wondering if these are not the same places because Manasseh, remember, received land on both sides of the Jordan River (Numbers 32:20–28 and Joshua 17:1–11).
3. His name means "**Jehovah is Strong**." Once again, I find inspiration in this definition of Uzzia: *"The Lord is good, a stronghold in the days*

of trouble." (Nahum 1:7) We will share our thoughts on this powerful attribute of Jesus in this devotional.

There are many kinds of strongholds. I remember in the early 1960s attending classes at Perham Elementary in my home state of Maine on how to make a bomb shelter. It was to be a stronghold against the day of an atomic attack. The Cuban Missile Crisis was at its peak, and the fear of a Russian nuclear strike was a constant threat, but technology for making atomic bombs was rapidly outstripping the technology for making bomb shelters. I still remember coming home from school and asking my dad if we could build a bomb shelter. (There was a real danger even in Perham, Maine, because less than thirty miles away was a massive Air Force base in Limestone called Loring. This base was the eastern most air force base in the USA at the time, and the base was home to the mighty B-52, one of the triad weapons of our national defense. With silo missiles and submarine missiles, the B-52 could also carry nuclear warheads. The theory was that one of the first sites the Russians would target was Loring Air Force base.) My dad, a man of great trust in God, simply told me that we would be trusting in Jesus for our safety. And, as we know now, there was no nuclear attack in the 60s, or since, and we built no bomb shelter. As I write this devotional, the world is facing another day of trouble, or so they believe, the Y2K virus. As the earth nears the end of its second millennium, post BC, people are again in fear of the uncertainty of a major computer meltdown or shutdown. (As we know now, we had nothing to fear; just the fear promoted by all the computer companies who made billions off a false problem. The world is always looking for a stronghold in the wrong place.) In Nahum's day, a stronghold was a fortified city or town with a high, thick wall with powerful defensive gates and strong battlements. The reality is that no man-made stronghold has even fully protected its population. The mightiest of them all like Babylon and Constantinople have all eventually fallen. It is for this reason that we must look for another "stronghold" and for me the best is the Lord Jesus Christ Himself.

There are three basic standards by which all strongholds must be judged:

First, any stronghold must be adequate in power to protect in any kind of trouble that may come to those who live within its protection.

Only the Lord Jesus Christ is **"all-powerful!"** Jesus told His disciples: *"All power is given unto me in heaven and in earth."* (Matthew 28:18) How often did Jesus demonstrate to His followers that He had power, not only to protect Himself, but them as well? Whether in the midst of a storm on the Sea of Galilee, or in the midst of a group of lepers, or in the midst of demon possessed men, Jesus protected them from diseases, devils, and danger. This reminds me of something the Psalmist wrote about Jehovah: *"He shall cover thee with His feathers, and under His wings shalt thou trust: His truth shall be thy shield and buckler. Thou shalt not be afraid for the terror* [now there is a word for the 21st century] *by night; nor for the arrows that flieth by day; nor the pestilence that walketh in darkness; nor for the destruction that wasteth at noonday."* (Psalm 91:4-6) Does your stronghold provide you with such protection? How strong is your God?

Second, any stronghold must be accessible and available to all who would need its security. Only the Lord Jesus Christ is **"all-providing!"** Jesus said: *"He that cometh to me I will in no wise cast out."* (John 6:37) I love the old Church hymn <u>Whosoever Will</u>. It, perhaps, says it best with these words: "Whosoever hearth shout, shout the sound! Spread the blessed tidings all the world around. Tell the joyful news wherever man is found. Whosoever will may come." (Romans 10:13) No matter how big the world constructs its strongholds, somebody will be left out. Is your stronghold all-inclusive or is it exclusive?

Third, any stronghold must be abiding; it must stand the test of time. Only the Lord Jesus Christ is **"all-permanent!"** (Hebrews 13:8) The mighty walls and towers of ancient Babylon for decades kept Babylon's enemies at bay by its mighty stronghold, but in a night this fortress fell to the Medes and Persians (Daniel 5:30). The context of Nahum's burden was the seemingly impregnable stronghold of Nineveh (Nahum 1:1), the capital of the Assyrian Empire, but in the year 612 BC this stronghold ceased to exist. Hitler tried to fortify Europe against attack, but on June 6, 1944, that mighty stronghold was breached and eventually the whole structure crumbled. Only the Lord Jesus Christ has stood the test of time, the attack of all adversaries, and still to this day remains a stronghold in a day of trouble. Why? Because of the **"strong"** in the stronghold, the Lord God Himself. Even *"the gates of hell"* (Matthew 16:18) have tried their best to prevail against this stronghold, but to no avail! Has your stronghold such lasting endurance, such universal permanence, such everlasting strength, **God Strong**?

It was Isaiah who gave the best description of a stronghold in my opinion and would that we judge all "strongholds" by this standard: *"For thou hast been a strength to the poor, a strength to the needy in his distress, a refuge from the storm, a shadow from the heat, when the blast of the terrible ones is as a storm against the wall."* (Isaiah 25:4) I believe Uzzia and Uzzia's parents put their trust in the stronghold of Jehovah, the strength of God, just like my father put his trust in Jesus. I believe that Uzzia's name was a testimony to the belief of his parents in Jehovah. What does "strong" mean to you?

Zechariah 9:12: *"Turn you to the stronghold, ye prisoners of hope: even today do I declare that I will render double unto thee."*

51.

SHAMA: OBEDIENT

I Chronicles 11:44: *"Uzzia the Ashterathite, **SHAMA** and Jehiel the sons of Hothan the Aroerite."*

HERE IS WHAT WE know about this "mighty man" in David's list of his most important warriors:

1. Shama's brother was Jehiel, also a "mighty man" who we will deal with in our next devotional.

2. Shama's father was Hothan which means "determination." He is only mentioned in the Bible in connection to his two sons, but what a powerful name!

3. Shama's hometown was Aroer, of which we have three named in the Scriptures, and they are:

    A) A city near Rabbath Ammon, in the valley of Jabbok, now called Arieh (Numbers 32:34). If this was Shama's hometown, then this would make Shama from the tribe of Gad (I Chronicles 12:37).

    B) A city of the Amorites on the bank of the Arnon River and now called Arair (Judges 11:26). If this was Shama's hometown, then this would make Shama from the tribe of Reuben (I Chronicles 12:37).

    C) A city in the south of Judah, now called Ararah (I Samuel 30:28). If this was Shama's hometown, then this would make

Shama from the tribe of Judah. Take your pick (Romans 14:5). Each place would fit in perfectly with the pattern of David's "mighty men" because he had soldiers from all three tribes.

4. Shama's name means "**obedient**." I couldn't help but remember this New Testament verse when I discovered the meaning of Shama's name: *"And being found in fashion as a man, He humbled Himself, and became '**obedient**' unto death, even the death of the cross."* (Philippians 2:8) It will not be hard to connect Jesus to Shama.

Christ is the only person ever to live on this planet that was totally **"obedient."** This obedience began the moment He was born in Bethlehem. Even a man with the name of obedience can't be as obedient as Christ was because *"All have sinned* [always a direct result of disobedience] *and come short of the glory of God."* (Romans 3:23) Despite the fact that Jesus was superior (Luke 1:35) and smarter (Luke 1:47) than any adult He came in connect with, yet He humbled Himself and was in obedience to them as an example to us: *"And he went down with them* [His parents], *and came to Nazareth, and was subject* [obedient] *unto them..."* (Luke 2:51). It was Jesus Himself that gave His creation the first law of obedience (concerning the tree of the Knowledge of good and evil) in the Garden of Eden. For Jesus to shun the order He ordained would have been ungodly at best. So while Jesus lived on earth He was obedient to His elders, His parents, His law, and He taught us that obedience was the only "way to be happy in Jesus." As I watch the Church in action, I wonder if we have yet learned this lesson taught by the life of Christ.

What is the source of such obedience? In a favorite reference book (Herbert C. Gabhart's classic devotional on <u>The Name Above Every Name</u>) concerning the names of Jesus, I found this definition of obedience: "Obedience should stem from love not law. The heart should be satisfied with loving obedience. There is something lacking when fear is the source of obedience. Let love rule." Why did Christ practice obedience? Was He afraid of His parents; the doctors of the law in the temple; the soldiers of Rome; the Sanhedrin; His own disciples? None of the above! Jesus was obedient because Jesus loved the world (John 3:16). Jesus ultimately showed His love by becoming *"obedient unto death, even the death of the Cross."* John in his first epistle highlights this again as a demonstration of obedience when he writes of this love, this life, and eventually this lynching: *"He that loveth not knoweth not God; for God is love. In this was manifest the love of God toward us, because that God sent His only begotten Son into the world, that we might live through Him. Herein is love, not that we loved God, but that He loved us, and sent His Son to be a propitiation for our sins."* (I John 4:8–10)

Obedience stems from love, and love is demonstrated by obedience. We hear a lot about love today. We hear a lot of sermons on loving God, loving our neighbor, and loving ourselves, but unless we obey God we do not really love God, love our neighbor, or love ourselves. Jesus came to teach us how to love (John 13:34–35), but he also came to teach us to obey His Father's commandments: *"If you keep* [obey] *my commandments, ye shall abide in my love; even as I have kept* [was obedient] *my Father's commandments, and abide in His love."* (John 15:10) Jesus was very clear in His connecting the doctrine of obedience with the doctrine of charity. This truth was passed on to His followers, and men like Paul picked up the theme in their writings: *"For to this end also I write, that I might know the proof of you, whether ye be obedient in all things!"* (II Corinthians 2:9) When one looks at the commandments of the Father and the commandments of the Son, it seems a daunting task to keep them all, to find a desire to keep them all, even the will to keep them all, yet, if we really do love the Father and the Son, then we will have the motivation (obedience) to keep Their commandments!

Is there any true obedience until we give ourselves wholly to the love of Jesus Christ? Is there any true love until we wholly follow and obey the Lord Jesus Christ? In John H. Sammis' classic Church hymn, <u>Trust and Obey</u>, this is his theme in this meaningful and challenging song. The history of this hymn came from a testimony given at one of Dwight L. Moody's evangelistic meetings in Brockton, Massachusetts, in 1886. During that service a young man, during his conversion story, gave this observation: "I might not be quite sure of what happened tonight, but I am going to trust, and I am going to obey!" Daniel B. Towner was leading the music that night and jotted down the boys words, and later in a letter to a friend, John Sammis, rewrote the statement. As they say, the rest is history. Trust is sometimes easier than obedience, but neither is possible without the other and love! Use what Jesus used to gain your salvation; use what Jesus used to live in this world, and use what Jesus used to make Him obedient in every situation and circumstance in His pilgrimage, even to a death on a Cross. Perhaps, someone needs to write a song on "Love and Obey."

> When we walk with the Lord in the light of His Word,
> What a glory He sheds on our way!
> While we do His good will he abides with us still,
> And with all who will "love" and obey.
> "Love" and obey, for there's no other way
> To be happy in Jesus, but to "love" and obey!

I was taught this little chorus as a child:

> Obedience is the very best way to show that you believe.
> Doing exactly what the Lord commands doing it happily.
> Action is the key to obedience, joy you will receive.
> Obedience is the very best way to show that you believe.
> O-B-E-D-I-E-N-C-E,
> Obedience is the very best way to show that you believe.

Hebrews 5:8" "…*He was a Son, yet learned He obedience by the things which He suffered."*

52.

JEHIEL: GOD IS LIVING

I Chronicles 11:44: *"Uzzia the Ashterathite, Shama and **JEHIEL** the sons of Hothan the Aroerite."*

JEHIEL IS A VERY popular name in the Bible with a dozen individuals so named. This is a list of those Biblical characters and a wonderful example of the importance of names in the Word of God, especially when you consider the meaning of this name:

1. A Levite singer in the Tabernacle in the days of David (I Chronicles 15:8).
2. A Gershonite porter in the last days of David (I Chronicles 23:8).
3. A companion to the sons of David (I Chronicles 27:32).
4. A son of Jehoshaphat, a king of Judah (II Chronicles 21:2).
5. A son of Herman, the singer in the times of Hezekiah (II Chronicles 29:14).
6. A Levite set over sacred items in the days of Hezekiah (II Chronicles 31:13).
7. A chief priest in the days of Josiah a king of Judah (II Chronicles 35:80.
8. The father of Obadiah who returned with Ezra from exile (Ezra 8:9).
9. The father of Shechaniah who had a foreign wife (Ezra 10:2).

10. A priest who had also taken a foreign wife (Ezra 10:21).
11. A man of Elam's family that also took a foreign wife (Ezra 10:26).
12. The "mighty man" of David whose name means **"God is living."**

    In our last chapter, we studied Jehiel's brother and the family connections. Next to the sons of Hashem (I Chronicles 11:34) and the sons of Zeruiah (II Samuel 2:18), the sons of Hothan are only the third set of sons listed in David's "mighty men" list so far. There will be two more sets to come (I Chronicles 11:45–46). However, as before, my only course for a challenge comes from the meaning of Jehiel's name. What theology can we learn about this "mighty man" and the sample meaning of his name?

    The writing of this devotional comes on the heels of the Easter celebration of 1999. One of the songs we sing every year at the church I pastor in Ellsworth, Maine, is Alfred H. Ackley's famous Church hymn <u>He Lives!</u> This thrilling Easter song was written in answer to a question put to Mr. Ackley during an evangelistic service the author was conducting. A Jewish student challenged the composer with this question: "Why should I worship a dead Jew?" In George W. Sanville's book <u>Forty Gospel Hymn Stories</u> the answer to this sincere inquiry is given. Ackley is reported to have answered the young Jew with these words, "He lives! I tell you, He is not dead, but lives here and now. Jesus is more alive today than ever before. I can prove it by my own experience, as well as the testimony of countless thousands!" Sanville goes on to write: "Mr. Ackley's forthright, emphatic answer, together with his subsequent triumphant effort to win the man to Christ, flowered forth into song and crystallized into a convicting sermon on 'He Lives!' In his re-reading of the resurrections of the Gospels, the words **'He is risen'** struck him with new meaning. From the thrill within his own soul came the convicting song <u>He Lives!</u> The scriptural evidence, his own heart, and testimony of history matched the glorious experience of an innumerable cloud of witnesses that 'He Lives' so he sat down at the piano and voiced that conclusion in song. He says, 'The thought of His ever-living presence brought the music promptly and easily.'" God is Living is the theme of this challenge and at the heart of these stirring words by Ackley:

> I serve a risen Saviour, He's in the world today;
> I know that He is living, whatever man may say;

I see His hand of mercy, I hear His voice of cheer,
And just the time I need Him He's always near.

In all the world around me I see His loving care,
And though my heart grows weary, I never will despair;
I know that He is leading through all the stormy blast,
The day of His appearing will come at last.

Rejoice, rejoice, O Christian, lift up your voice and sing
Eternal hallelujahs to Jesus Christ the King!
The Hope of all who seek Him, the Help of all who find,
None other is so loving, so good and kind.

He lives! He lives! Christ Jesus lives today.
He walks with me and talks with me along life's narrow way.
He lives! He lives! Salvation to impart!
You ask me how I know He lives? He lives within my heart!

One of the verses of the Easter Story that struck me as ironic this year were these words by the High Priest, Caiaphas: "I adjure thee by THE LIVING GOD, that thou tell us whether thou be the Christ, the Son of God." (Matthew 26:63) The meaning of Jehiel's name is used to expose Christ when in reality He was "the Christ," "the Son of God," and "the Living God." (Matthew 16:16) Jesus had taught openly and clearly that He was the Son of the Living God (Luke 20:38). The tragedy of the Easter Story from the standpoint of the Jews was despite invoking the name of the Living God these men of the Sanhedrin acted as if God was dead. I like what F. B. Meyer writes on this subject:

> Since God spoke of Himself as the God of the patriarchs, centuries after they had been borne to their graves, it stood to reason that they were yet living; and on this ground our Lord met the allegation that there is no life beyond death. Death is not a state or condition, but an act. We speak of the dead; but in point of fact there are none such. We should speak of those who have died. They were living up to the moment of death; but they were living quite as much afterwards. Death is like birth, an act, a transition, a passage into a freer life. Never think of death as a state, but as resembling a bridge which, for a moment, casts its shadow on the express train, which flashes beneath, but does not stay.

If God breathed into man "the breath of life" (Genesis 2:7), it was His life, not human life, that was breathed. Therefore, there must be an eternal piece of God in all of us, the "living" part and, therefore, if that be true, death might have an effect on the flesh of man, but it can't have any effect on the "soul" of man. Paul confronted the crowds at Lystra with these words: *"Sirs, why do ye these things? We also are men of like passions with you, and preach unto you that ye should turn from these vanities unto THE LIVING GOD, which made heaven and earth, and the sea, and all things that are therein."* (Acts 14:15) Because He lives, we live, A LIVING God that brought life to all mankind. Remember, John wrote this of Jesus: *"In Him was life; and the life was the light of men."* (John 1:4) When God gave man his original life, he threw it away for a taste of the fruit of the tree of the knowledge of good and evil (Genesis 3). Mankind became spiritually dead in his trespasses and sins (Ephesians 2:1). There was only one that could bring life back into mankind, the original author of life, the Son of God. So the eternal Godhead came up with a plan to bring life back to man. It would require "a death" (Romans 6:23), but the reward for mankind would be a renewal of "eternal life" (Romans 6:23). On the first Easter Jesus gave His life that we might gain life and thereby fulfill the purpose and plan of the Almighty. "God is living" is the theology that begins Genesis, and it is the theology that ends the Revelation. The forever "Living One" is at the heart of all that is life both here and now. Jehiel's name is the name that highlights and underlines this theology.

Mark 12:27: *"He is not the God of the dead, but the God of the living: ye therefore do greatly err."*

53.

JEDIAEL: GOD KNOWS

I Chronicles 11:45: *"**JEDIAEL** the son of Shimri, and Joha his brother, the Tizite."*

THE NEXT "MIGHTY MAN" in David's Hall of Fame is the warrior Jediael, the son of Shimri. We have also come to another set of brothers that joined David's elite soldiers, and Jediael's brother Joha will be highlighted in our next chapter. All we know about Jediael is the meaning of his name: God knows. *"Now are we sure that thou KNOWEST all things, and needest not that any man should ask thee: by this we believe that thou camest for from God."* (John 16:30) Jesus was and still is the omniscient God. There is a trilogy of terms associated with the Godhead that are clearly seen in the attributes of the Christ: OMNIPOTENT (all-powerful): *"And Jesus came and spake unto them, saying, All power is given unto me in heaven and in earth."* (Matthew 28:18); OMNIPRESENT (all-present): *"... and, lo, I am with you always, even to the end of the age. Amen."* (Matthew 28:20); OMNISCIENT (all-knowing) which brings to light the truth of Colossians 2:9: **"For in Him dwelleth all the fulness of the Godhead bodily."** In this article we will highlight and underline the teaching of this third characteristic of Christ found in Jediael's name.

A man who had seen the famous painting the Mona Lisa come away from the experience and wrote down his thought: "Many who viewed the work did so with evident approval. All I saw, however, was a plain face of shallow complexion with scarcely a suggestion of a smile. Unmoved, I was about to turn away, when suddenly I noticed that the Mona Lisa seemed to be looking straight into my eyes! I took another position, and still another, but she stared at me no matter where I went. Turning to a gentleman next to me, I said: 'Is she looking into your eyes also?' 'Yes, my friend,' he replied, 'that is one of the marvels and mysteries of this painting; you always seem to be under her omnipresent gaze.'" I have come to the conclusion that the three divine attributes of the Almighty are connected. To know all you needed not only to be all powerful, but all knowing. The problem that arises in this theology is the fact that if people don't believe in the all present God, they will not believe that God is watching them and in watching them knows them, knows about them, and knows everything that is happening with them.

If a painting can affect people in this way, why is it so hard to get people to believe that God is not only watching their every action, but knows their every thought: *"O Lord, thou hast searched me, and known me! Thou knowest my downsitting and mine uprising, thou understandest my thoughts afar off. Thou compassest my path and my lying down, and art acquainted with all my ways. For there is not a word in my tongue, but, lo, O Lord, thou knowest it altogether."* (Psalm 139:1–4) Jesus demonstrated this attribute in a number of encounters described in the Gospels, like after healing the palsy man at Capernaum: *"Certain of the scribes said within themselves, This man blasphemeth. And Jesus KNOWING their thoughts said, Wherefore think evil in your hearts?"* (Matthew 9:3–4) This was the omniscient Christ in action. Not only did Jesus possess the knowledge of God and man, the facts and figures, if you will (Luke 2:47), but He also knew the hearts and intents then, and He knows the hearts and the intents of the hearts of all men now. There have been many a wise man that has lived among us, but no man, except Jesus, could read the thoughts of man.

The Bible is very clear in this aspect of the all-knowing God. Henry Clarence Thiessen defines "omniscient" this way: **"By the omniscience of God we mean that he knows Himself and all other things, whether they be actual, or merely possible, whether they be past, present, or future, and that He knows them perfectly and from all eternity. He knows things immediately, simultaneously, exhaustively, and truly. He also knows the best way to attain His desired ends."** Stephen Charnock writes in his The Existence and Attributes of God: **"God knows Himself, and He only knows Himself. This is the first and the original knowledge, wherein He excels all creatures. No man doth exactly know himself; much less doth he understand the full nature of the spirit; much less still the nature and perfection of God."** Christ verified this understanding when he said: *"No one knoweth the Son, save the Father; neither doth any know the Father, save the Son, and he to whosoever the Son willeth to reveal Him."* (Matthew 11:27) Paul brings in the Person of the Trinity to this omniscience when he writes to the Church at Corinth: *"Even so the things of God none knoweth, save the Spirit of God."* (I Corinthians 2:11)

God's knowledge reaches beyond the accepted knowledge of man to the foreknowledge of the future. For those who have misunderstood this aspect of God's omniscience, I like again what Thiessen writes: "But prescience is not itself causative; we must not confuse foreknowledge with the predetermining will of God. Free actions do not take place because they are foreseen, but they are foreseen because they will take place!" He of course is speaking of the great debate for years over the sovereignty of God versus the responsibility of man. It was when I came to an understanding of the omniscient God that I understood how God could predestinate. Not that He makes the choice because He certainly gave mankind free-will since the days of Eden, but that in His all-knowing He just knew how man would choose. That is why the Lamb of God was slain from the foundation of the world. God knew of Adam's choice before He created Adam, and He made provision to gain man back to Himself through the death of Christ on the tree.

Have you like the disciples of John 16 become aware of the perception of Jesus? Does Jesus answer your unasked questions before the question is even formulated in your mind? It was this attribute of Christ that finally caused His closest disciples to believe. Remember, by this time they had witnessed His omnipotence. Had He not come to them over the waters in the midst of a storm? But it wasn't until He revealed their thoughts and their thought-provoking questions that they knew they were dealing with the Almighty. For those who still doubt this amazing ability read the entire 139th Psalm. If after that you still doubt, then you will have to wait until the Day of Judgment when every word, every thought, you ever uttered or imagined will be revealed to you. You will stand amazed, but it will be too late then. Herbert Gabhart once wrote of this theology: **"Christ knows all He needs to know and all there is to know, and He knows me!"** Before Jesus had ever met the publican Zacchaeus He knew his name (Luke 19:5). Before Jesus had ever met the Samaritan woman He knew that she had had five husbands (John 4:18). Before Jesus had ever met Nathanael He knew of his character (John 1:47). Before Jeremiah was even born God knew that he would be a prophet to the nations (Jeremiah 1:5). Before Samuel had examined all the sons of Jesse God knew that David would be king (I Samuel 16:13). And if God knew all these things about them, He knows about us!

John 2:25: *"And needed not that any should testify of man; for He knew what was in man."*

54.

JOHA: JEHOVAH IS LIVING

I Chronicles 11:45: *"Jediael the son of Shimri, and **JOHA** his brother, the Tizite."*

I FIND IT INTERESTING that this is the fourth "mighty man" whose name has something to do with **"living:"** Ithai (I Chronicles 11:31) meaning **"living;"** Hepher (I Chronicles 11:36) meaning **"living well;"** Jehiel (I Chronicles 11:44) meaning **"God is living;"** and now Joha (I Chronicles 11:45) meaning **"Jehovah is living."** I will start this devotional singing with David: *"My soul thirsteth for God, for the LIVING GOD: when shall I come and appear before God?"* (Psalm 42:2)

I read a saying once that can be applied to God, and it also should be applied to us: **"Always live as if you expect to live always."** To me this is the real meaning of "the living God." God has always existed, and He will always exist. I have not always existed, but through Christ I will always exist. Anybody can have that hope if they will like David thirst after the LIVING GOD. For many today this thirst is only a goal or a temporary ambition, but for the real thirsty soul this is life itself. Dr. A. B. Simpson in one of his great devotionals tells this story:

> An eastern caravan was once overtaken in the desert with the failure to find a supply of water. The accustomed fountains were all dried, the oasis was a desert, and they halted an hour before sunset after a day of scorching heat to find that they were perishing for want of water. Vainly they explored the usual wells, but they were all dry. Dismay was upon their faces and despair in

their hearts, when one of the ancient men approached the sheik and counseled him to unloose two beautiful harts that he was conveying home as a present to his bride, and let them scour the desert in search of water. Their tongues were protruding with thirst, and their bosoms heaving with distress. But as they were led out to the borders of the camp and set free on the boundless plain, they lifted up their heads high, and sniffed the air with distended nostrils, and then with unerring instinct, with a course as straight as an arrow and with speed as swift as the wind, they darted off across the desert. Swift horsemen followed close behind; an hour or two later they hastened back with glad tidings that water had been found, and the camp moved with shouts of rejoicing to the happily discovered fountains.

I, too, believe that we have such an instinct buried deep in our soul which is the Holy Spirit of God. Like the harts of the story, we, too, will travel straight to the LIVING God if we simply allow the Spirit to lead us. The Spirit knows that Jehovah is the only one that can satisfy our spiritual thirst. Jesus knew that when He told the woman at the well to ask of Him and He would give her water in which her would never thirst again (John 4). Heaven contains eternal springs (Revelation 22:1). Are we traveling towards them or are we wandering in the wasteland of this world dying of spiritual thirst? Many years ago John W. Peterson wrote a wonderful hymn with these words:

> I thirsted in the barren land of sin and shame,
> And nothing satisfying there I found;
> But to the blessed cross of Christ one day I came,
> Where springs of LIVING water did abound.
>
> How sweet the LIVING water from the hills of God,
> It makes me glad and happy all the way;
> Now glory, grace, and blessing mark the path I've trod,
> I'm shouting hallelujah every day.
>
> O sinner, won't you came today to Calvary,
> A fountain there is flowing deep and wide;
> The Saviour now invites you to water free,
> Where thirsting spirits can be satisfied.

Drinking from the springs of LIVING water,
Happy now am I, my soul they satisfy;
Drinking from the springs of LIVING water,
O wonderful and bountiful supply!

The Psalmist also sung this: *"My soul longeth, yea, even fainteth for the courts of the Lord: my heart and my flesh crieth out for the LIVING GOD."* (Psalm 84:2) Are there two more powerful instincts in the human soul than thirst and longing? In the great conversion stories of Church history that I have read, these two aspects are the driving force behind most of them. Even after salvation these are the motivations behind those who have done great and wondrous things for the cause of Christ. At the writing of this chapter in my David's Mighty Men book, I have just finished reading two books on the life's story of the amazing woman missionary Gladys Alyward. This small, frail English woman survived in hostile China between the years of 1930 and 1950. Vance Havner once wrote of such Christians: **"A Christian ought to live with a sense of wonder, always expecting God to do some marvellous thing. We really do not expect much from God these days. We pray for rain and leave our umbrellas at home. We pray for revival but don't really expect one to start today. We have been told that whatsoever we ask in prayer, believing, we shall receive, but we ask, doubting, or, at the most, we ask, merely hoping, and our expectation is not unto Him."** It is refreshing to read of those whose only purpose in life was a longing after the LIVING GOD. Perhaps, that is why the living Savior demands a living sacrifice. (Romans 12:1)

Havner also wrote: **"God wants our bodies as a living sacrifice, not corpses!"** It is only reasonable that a LIVING GOD would want a living offering. What good would a dead sacrifice be to a LIVING GOD? When David finally came face to face with his terrible sin against Bathsheba and Uriah, he wrote: *"For thou desireth not sacrifice; else would I give it: thou delighteth not in burnt offerings."* (Psalm 51:16) David realized that Jehovah didn't deal in dead things, but *"...the sacrifices of God are a broken spirit: a broken and a contrite heart..."* (Psalm 51:17). God wants a living heart that is broken to His will, not a dead heart without function or purpose. James H. McConkey tells this story:

A missionary to the Indians from the north country related the following incident which took place during a consecration service. As he was speaking, an old Indian chief arose, walked forward, and laid his tomahawk at the feet of the missionary. "Indian chief give his tomahawk to Jesus Christ," he said, and sat down. Still the missionary spoke of the love of God in Christ Jesus. Rising from his seat the old chief walked forward once more to the front. Unwrapping his blanket from his shoulders, he laid it at the feet of the preacher's feet. "Indian chief give his blanket to Jesus Christ." As the preacher continued on to speak of how God had rifled heaven of its choicest gift, the old chief got up and left the meeting. By and by he came leading his pony to the tent door. He tied it to a stake and again walked down the aisle. Facing the missionary, he said, "Indian chief give his pony to Jesus Christ." As he sat down, the missionary told how Jesus had died for the sins of all men. It was then the old chieftain rose for the last time. He walked forward with tottering steps to the front and said. "Indian chief give himself to Jesus Christ!"

A LIVING JEHOVAH needs a living life. How did the old hymn writer put it? **"Love so amazing, so divine, demands my heart, my soul, my all!"** We are living in an age where the giving of self like the old Indian chief is a rare thing even in the Church of God. It seems we always want to hold something back or give God that which we have already discarded. It is time for us to see clearly that God demands only one thing, and the little drummer boy of Christmas fame got it right when he gave himself.

Jeremiah 10:10: *"But the Lord is the true God, He is the LIVING GOD..."*

55.

ELIEL: MY GOD IS GOD

I Chronicles 11:46: *"**ELIEL** the Mahavite, and Jeribai, and Joshaviah, the sons of Elanaam, and Ithmah the Moabite."*

THIS "MIGHTY MAN" IS one of ten so named in the Bible. His patronymic, Mahavite, is unknown so that leaves us once again with the meaning of his name as all we know about this super soldier of David. What a great name: My God is God. This brings out the personal relationship we are to have with the Almighty, but the question remains, Is God your God?

Atheism is rising in this world. The more and more we become self-sufficient, or we think we can be self-sufficient, the more we feel we don't need any god, let alone the true and living God. As I write this article, I have just been confronted with another atheist attempt to disrupt the work of God. Child Evangelism Fellowship is facing a direct assault on the heart of their ministry, Good News Clubs in the public school. A lady who claims to be an atheist is trying to start Satanic Clubs to counter the Good News Clubs. What she has revealed in this attempt is who the god of the atheist is: *"In whom the god of this world hath blinded the minds of them which believe not, lest the light of the glorious gospel of Christ, who is the image of God, should shine unto them."* (II Corinthians 4:4) Interestingly, these very non-god believers have as the center of their beliefs god. Hetwood Broun said it best when he wrote: **"Nobody talks so constantly about God as those who insist that there is no God!"** If He doesn't exist, then why are they so worried about praying to a non-existing God or believing in anon-existing God? Why do they worry about prayer in school or God clubs after school if there is no such being, deity as God?

HE DOESN'T EXIST, REMEMBER, MY ATHEIST FRIEND! Franklin P. Jones once said: "An atheist is one who hopes the Lord will do nothing to disturb his disbelief." A story out of the life of the great American Benjamin Franklin as told by W. J. Isbell in the <u>Southern Baptist Brotherhood Journal</u> highlights the choice we all must make in our relationship with the existence of God:

> Charles I of England had proclaimed that the people could return to sports in England on Sunday. All clergymen were to read the proclamation, and to the amazement of one congregation their clergyman read the royal edict in church, which many clergy had refused to do. But he followed it with the words, "Remember the Sabbath day to keep it holy," and added, "Brethren, I have laid before you the commandment of your king and the commandment of your God. I leave it to you to judge which of the two ought rather to be observed."

After reading this story I was reminded of the great instruction Peter gave to the Church early in its infancy: **"We ought to obey God rather than men!"** (Acts 5:29) I guess that Eliel's parents wanted no doubts when it came to neither their belief in Jehovah God, nor who their son's God would be when he grew up. So, whenever their son's name was shared, their faith was shared, and whoever heard Eliel's name, they heard a testimony of faith.

The Psalmist writes: *"I was cast upon Thee from the womb: thou art my God from my mother's belly."* (Psalm 22:10) So many only come to the realization of God in adulthood, or worse still, after adulthood: death! Many more only come to belief in God through terrible experiences. Vance Havner once wrote:

> Isaiah has come to the end of himself. Like Moses and Midian, like Job when he saw God, like Daniel with his comeliness turned to corruption and Habakkuk with rottenness entering his bones; like Peter at Tiberias and Paul with his thorns, he has come to the end of all feeling and trying and praying, the end of all he is and has, to where God begins.

But there are a few like David and Timothy that learned and believed in God from an early age: *"And that from a child thou hast known the holy scriptures, which are able to make thee wise unto salvation through faith which is in Christ Jesus...When I call to remembrance the unfeigned faith that is in thee, which dwelt first in thy grandmother Lois, and thy mother Eunice: and I am persuaded that in thee also."* (II Timothy 3:15 and 1:5) From their coming into the world, these men and women have seen the hand of the Lord upon their lives, and I can add to their statement of Faith that "Thou art my God" as well. I was seven when I placed my trust and faith in the carpenter from Galilee, and 68 years later I am writing of that same statement of my Faith.

This great personal relationship mirrored in the name of Eliel has as its benefit the concern and care of the Great God for us. We love Him, but He first loved us (I John 4:19). The reality of this marvelous bond is illustrated for us by Ralph W. Sockman when he wrote: "Julia Ward Howe one day was talking to Charles Sumner, the distinguished senator from Massachusetts. She asked him to interest himself in the case of a person who needed some help. The senator answered, 'Julia, I've become so busy I can no longer concern myself with individuals.' Julia replied, 'Charles that is quite remarkable. Even God hasn't reached that stage yet!'" David, the great king recognized that his God was interested in him when he wrote: *"I said unto the Lord, Thou art my God: hear the voice of my supplication, O Lord."* (Psalm 140:6) If the Lord is your God, then you have direct communication with Him. He will never be too busy; He will never be out-of-town; and He will never be asleep (Psalm 121). He will never put you on hold; He will never tell you to return tomorrow; and He will never hang up on you. He is your God and He takes personally your needs, your petitions, your wants as if they are His very own. Your case is special to Him and though He has billions to deal with, He will deal with your issue as if it were the only one He was dealing with.

A Sunday school teacher suddenly stopped reading a passage out of the Bible and asked her class, "Why do you believe in God?" She got a variety of answers, some full of simple faith, others obviously insincere. The one that stunned her most came from the son of the pastor. He answered apologetically, "I guess it runs in the family!" As one reads through the Holy Writ, this personal belief in the Almighty God does run through the family of those who believe in a personal God. I find it hard to believe that there are some that feel to have a proper relationship with God you must keep Him at arm's length or put some kind of barrier between you and Him. That is how it was before Calvary; a great gulf fixed (Luke 16:26); a veil in-between (Matthew 27:51, but Jesus died to bridge that gap and open the veil for all to enter the Holy of Holies into the very presence of God Himself. It is time that we take seriously our

God's desire to have a personal relationship with us, and that He loves for us to call Him our God. My God is God!

As I end this 55th "mighty man," could I once again encourage you to consider making Jesus your God? It must start with you making him your Savior, the one that took away your sins (Romans 3:23) by dying (Romans 6:23) for you on Calvary. While you were still a sinner Christ died for you (Romans 5:8), but has that become personal for you yet? It is time to consider this amazing truth, this stunning theology that My God is God!

Psalms 63:1: *"O God, thou art my God…"*

56.

JERIBAI: JEHOVAH CONTENDS

I Chronicles 11:46: *"Eliel the Mahavite, and **JERIBAL**, and Joshaviah, the sons of Elanaam, and Ithmah the Moabite."*

WE HAVE ARRIVED AT another brother team that made David's famous warrior list. We shall leave the family history to our consideration of Joshaviah in our next chapter and go straight to the doctrine of "**Jehovah contends.**"

Isaiah gets us started with this verse: *"But thus saith the Lord…I will contend with him that contendeth with thee…"* (Isaiah 49:25). The Hebrew word for our King James Version "**contend**" is "**strive**." It was Isaiah who underlines the significance of striving with God when he writes again: *"Woe unto him that striveth with his Master! Let the potsherd strive with the potsherds of the earth. Shall the clay say to him that fashioneth it, What maketh thou? Or thy work, He hath no hands?"* (Isaiah 45:9) The great English devotional writer of the nineteenth century F. B. Meyer says this about this teaching:

> God moulds us as a plotter does his clay. In doing this, He comes to a point where our nature seems entrenched in all its might. We can yield everything but this. But not to yield this is to neutralize our yielding in all beside. That is where the soul strives with God. It is the battlefield, the crisis, the crease-line of destiny. We may strive with God in two ways, saying, what makest Thou? or, He hath no hands; either by accusing Him of not having a definite purpose, or by alleging that He is not taking the best method of accomplishing it. Have you ever questioned

the love, or wisdom, or purpose of God, in the moulding and education of your soul? Or have you questioned the benevolence and wisdom of His methods? To do either of these is disastrous to peace of heart and growth in grace. We must will and dare to believe that God is doing His very best for us, and doing it in the very best way. The fate of those who strive against their Maker is very terrible. They are counted as potsherds. 'Let the potsherd strive with the potsherds of the earth.' What is a potsherd? A shred of pottery, which may have been part of the beautiful vase, but now as a broken fragment is good for nothing but the rubbish-heap. See it protruding from the cinders! This is the fate of the castaway, which the apostle feared. The image says nothing as to our eternal destiny, but assures us that we may miss all opportunity of serving the purposes of God. Agree, therefore, with thy divine Adversary quickly, lest He cast thee aside, or touch thee in the sinew of the thigh that shrinks, and thou limp through the remainder of thy days!

Interestingly, another definition I have found for Jeribai was "my adversary." We know from I Peter 5:8: *"Be sober, be vigilant; because your ADVERSARY the devil as a roaring lion walketh about, seeking whom he may devour."* I know this might be hard for anyone to hear, but I believe it is true. It would be better to have Satan as your adversary then to have Jehovah as your adversary. Contending with God can be a very dangerous conflict, and wise is the man that fears such an awesome confrontation. I have come to believe in the great story of God as Satan became the adversary of Job, God became the adversary of Job's friends. They had so missed the trial of Job seeing Job as a hypocrite in that he must have committed a great sin to be in so much trouble. The reason I believe this is what God said to them at the end of the story: *"And it was so, that after the Lord had spoken these words unto Job, the Lord said to Eliphaz the Temanite, My wrath is kindled against thee, and against thy two friends: for ye have not spoken of me the thing that is right, as my servant Job hath."* (Job 42:7) Eliphaz, Bildad, and Zophar had so misread Job's situation, they eventually ended up contending with God and striving with the Almighty. This is a circumstance we should try to avoid at all cost.

It was the Apostle Paul that feared being a castaway. Why? *"But I keep my body, and bring it into subjection: lest that by any means, when I have preached to others, I myself should be a castaway."* (I Corinthians 9:27) For me, the key phrase of this revealing verse is *"lest that by any means."* Paul wanted no confrontations with Jesus. He had experienced

JERIBAI: JEHOVAH CONTENDS

that on the road to Damascus when he found himself in conflict with the Christ (Acts 9:4–5). In a way Saul had been contending with God when he persecuted the Church. Blindness was the result, and even though he got his sight back, I am a believer he suffered the after effects of that confrontation with Jesus for the rest of his life (II Corinthians 12:7). Jacob had a similar experience when he contended with God in the event we call Jacob wrestling with the angel. Remember the end of that story as Jacob leaves the battlefield limping, a limp he would have for the rest of his life (Genesis 32:32). The Almighty warned through Isaiah: *"Thou shalt seek them, and shalt find them, even them that contended with thee; they that war against thee shall be as nothing, and a thing of nought."* (Isaiah 41:12) Despite this being a warning to those that would contend with the people of God, I am convinced that this is also a warning against those that would strive with God. Have you noticed a similarity between the Abrahamic curse in Genesis 12:3 and Isaiah 49:25 and the verse we just quoted? Wise is the man that heeds these warnings and runs to God and makes peace with God quickly, the quicker the better!

The good news on this doctrine is this promise also recorded in Isaiah: *"For I will not contend for ever, neither will I be always wroth: for the spirit should fail before me, and the souls which I have made."* (Isaiah 57:16) Another great devotional writer of the 19th century, C. H. Spurgeon, made these comments on this divine promise:

> **Our Heavenly father seeks our instruction, not our destruction.** His contention with us has a kind intention towards us. He will not be always in arms against us. We think the Lord is long in His chastisements, but that is because we are short in our patience. His compassion endureth forever, but not his contention. The night may drag its weary length along, but it must in the end give place to a cheerful day. As contention is only for a season, so the wrath which leads to it is only for a small moment. The Lord loved His chosen too well to be always angry with them. If He were to deal with us always as He does sometimes, we should faint outright and go down hopelessly to the gates of death. Courage, dear heart! The Lord will soon end His chiding. Bear up, for the Lord will bear you up and bear you through. He who made you knows how frail you are and how little you can bear. He will handle tenderly that which he has fashioned so delicately. Therefore, be not afraid because of the painful present, for it hastens to a happy future. **He that smote**

you will heal you; His little wrath shall be followed by great mercies!

It is wonderful to know as with all God's negative emotion against us because of our rebellion and wickedness that His positive attributes will always overcome in the end. Let us strive little against Him lest we be found contending with the Almighty. Let us contend not with Jehovah lest we be found striving with God. And even if we like Paul or Jacob find ourselves in such a place, let us remember that God's anger will only last for a season.

Job 40:2: *"Shall be that contendeth with the Almighty instruct Him? He that reproveth God let him answer it."*

57.

JOSHAVIAH: JEHOVAH IS EQUALITY

I Chronicles 11:46: *"Eliel the Mahavite, and Jeribai, and **JOSHAVIAH**, the sons of Elanaam, and Ithmah the Moabite."*

WE CAN ONLY HONESTLY write three things about this "mighty man" of David: 1) He was the brother of Jeribai, the "mighty man" we highlighted in our last article; 2) He was the son of a man named Elanaam, which means "God is pleasant;" and 3) His name means: Jehovah is Equality. As my mind set has been since the beginning of this book on the Person of Christ with the "mighty men" of David being the stimulus, my mind immediately drifted to this verse from the pen of Paul. Paul wrote to the Church at Philippi these classic words: *"Who, being in the form of God, thought it not robbery to be equal with God."* (Philippians 2:6)

In a passage that has as its primary interpretation "the humility of the Christ," we also get a glimpse of the unity and equality of the Godhead. We are confronted today with those that place Christ a little lower than God and a little higher than the angels. Some say that Christ was the first creation of the Almighty using verses like Colossians 1:15 (*"Who is the image of the invisible God, the firstborn of every creature"*) as the basis of their teaching. Others speak of Christ's incarnation as making Him smaller than God, but Paul makes it very clear in his theology that equality abides in the Godhead. He also wrote to the Church at Colosse: *"For in Him dwelleth all the fullness of the Godhead bodily."* (Colossians 2:9)

Despite the humility and humanity of Jesus Christ, He was no less God Himself. No matter which aspect of the Godhead you are talking about there was and there remains equality among the three Persons of the Godhead. Joshaviah simply puts this doctrine into one word, or should we say one name. I like the way Edward Hindson writes on this topic in his comments on our key verse of Philippians 2:6:

> To be equal with God; this confirms the meaning of the form. Christ was on an equality with God. He laid aside His divine glory, but He did not and could not lay aside His divine nature. He laid aside the expression of deity, but he did not and could not lay aside His possession of deity. He laid aside His rights as the Son and took His place as a servant. He put aside the insignia of deity and put on the robes of humanity.

Without a doubt, the Scriptures are very clear, equality is now and has always and will forever be a part of the makeup of God. The Godhead can be no more parted than God can lie (Titus 1:2). Babyhood, boyhood, adulthood could not change His equality with His Father and with the Spirit. Interestingly, it was this complex truth that got Jesus into trouble with the religious elite of His day. Remember the charge they laid against Him: *"Therefore the Jews sought the more to kill Him, because He not only broke the Sabbath, but said also that God was His Father, MAKING HIMSELF EQUAL WITH GOD."* (John 5:18) What this shows to me is another attribute of the Almighty we often overlook. There is not only a relationship between the three Persons of the Godhead, but there is equality in God's dealing with us as well. Remember this statement by the workers in one of Jesus' famous parables: *"Saying, these last have wrought but one hour, and thou hast made them equal with us, which borne the burden and heat of the day."* (Matthew 20:12) I must admit that upon my many readings of this parable of the workers in the vineyard I, too, have sided with those who had worked all day versus those that only worked one hour or a few hours, and yet the owner gave all the same daily wage. I have seen it as unfair as have many, and unless we understand this doctrine of the equality of Jehovah, we will not understand. How can the thief on the cross get into paradise after a few hours of belief and be on equal footing with those that believed for decades? Logic would tell us that it is unfair, wrong, but the doctrine of the equality of God tells us something different. If you factor in this attribute of God, then this explanation of the husbandman is understandable: *"Friend, I do thee no wrong: didst not thou agree with me for a penny? Take that thine is, and go thy way: I will give unto this last, even as unto thee. Is it not lawful for me to do what I will with mine own? Is thine eye evil, because I am good?"* (Matthew 20:13–15) Sometimes we make the mistake of stepping on God's toes. He is God, and He can do what He wants with what is His. Take forgiveness. He can forgive those He wants to forgive, and I really can't complain, yet we often do. There are still those who will never think the mass-murderer Bundy should be forgiven, and yet it appears before his execution he sought forgiveness from his crimes from God.

I have become convinced that what Jesus was trying to tell the human race in that controversial parable is that He recognizes no arbitrary designations and labels or classes or races or groups. We see through the eyes of the characteristics of human equality, but there is a grander equality that was established when God created the Church. I like the way Phillips' translation defines this form of equality in Colossians 3:10–11: *"In this new man of God's design there is no distinction between Greek and Hebrew, Jew and Gentile, foreigner and savage, slave and free man. Christ is the great equalizer in the human race, and if this be true in Christ than this ought to be true in Christians."* I know that God is the great equalizer, but I believe the human race has a long way to go before it will see equality as God sees equality. Jesus came to give us an example of this truth, remember, as to how He saw man. There was no partiality with Jesus whether Samaritan or sinner, Greek or Gentile, woman or man. It goes back to the meaning of Joshaviah's given name: Jehovah is equality. It is not only what He is, but how He treats everyone.

Why is it that Christ's Church is not practicing this standard, this attribute of the Almighty? There ought not to be such a thing as high and low birth, rich or poor people, honored or dishonored individuals. Such distinctions within the Body of Christ ought not to be. James wrote of this problem, and I like the way the New English Bible says it: *"My brothers...you must never show snobbery. For instance, two visitors may enter your place of worship, one a well-dressed man with gold rings, and the other a poor man in shabby clothes. Suppose you pay special attention to the well-dressed man and say to him, 'Please take this seat,' while to the poor man you say, 'You can stand; or you may sit here on the floor by my footstool,' do you not see that you are inconsistent and judge by false standards?"* (James 2:1–4) I found this interesting application in a book called <u>Smart Sayings of Great Personages</u>: "Alexander the Great, seeing Diogenes looking attentively at a large collection of human bones piled one upon another, asked the philosopher what he was looking for. 'I am searching,' said Diogenes, 'for the bones of your father, but I cannot distinguish them from those of his slaves.'" That is the equality that God would have us have in our relationship with others because that is the equality God has towards us. Is not this what Peter learned in his great vision? (Acts 10:34)

II Corinthians 8:14: *"But by an equality, that now at this time your abundance may be supply for their wants, that their abundance also may be a supply for your want: that there may be equality."*

58.

ITHMAN: PURITY

I Chronicles 11:46: *"Eliel the Mahavite, and Jeribai, and Joshaviah, the sons of Elanaam, and **ITHMAN** the Moabite."*

WHO OF US HAS not studied the exemplary life of Ruth the Moabite? Who of us has not admired the tremendous faith it took for Ruth to follow her mother-in-law back to Bethlehem? Who of us has not read the story of Ruth and held our breath, would she or wouldn't she be Boaz's bride? Ruth has gone down in Hebrew history as one of the great proselytes to Judaism and even entering the Messianic Line (Matthew 1:5). I have come to believe in my study of David's "mighty men," another Moabite is worthy of our attention and study, Ithmah.

The first thing we need to record is the ever growing list of foreign mercenaries that are numbered among David's elite troopers. Remember these famous warriors:

1. Ittai the Gittite (II Samuel 18:2), the soldier from Gath, a Philistine.
2. Zelek the Ammonite (I Chronicles 11:39), a race from Lot's incest.
3. Uriah the Hittite (II Samuel 23:39), a race that was condemned by God.
4. Ithmah the Moabite (I Chronicles 11:46), another race from Lot's incest.

The only other information we can glean from the Scriptures about Ithmah is the meaning of his name, purity. How does a man from a cursed race (*"An Ammonite or Moabite shall not enter into the congregation of the*

Lord; even to their tenth generation shall they not enter into the congregation of the Lord forever." Deuteronomy 23:3) get pure? I feel like Ruth before him, Ithmah came into contact through his relationship with David with the Purifier: *"And He shall sit as a Refiner and Purifier of silver: and He shall purity the sons of Levi, and purge them as gold and silver…"* (Malachi 3:3). I have come to believe that as Peter would finally understand through his vision in Acts 10 that *"of a truth I perceive that God is no respecter of persons* [Ithmah]: *but in every nation* [Moab] *he that feareth Him, and worketh righteousness, is accepted with Him."* (Acts 10:34–35)

    I found this poem by an unknown author a number of years ago, and for me it speaks volumes about the meaning of Ithmah's name and its connection to Jesus Christ and us:

> He sat by a fire of seven-fold heat,
> As He watched by the precious ore,
> And closer He bent with a searching gaze
> As He heated it more and more.
> He knew He had ore that could stand the test,
> And He wanted the finest gold
> To mount as a crown for the king to wear,
> Set with gems with a price untold.
> So He laid our gold in the burning fire,
> Though we fain would have said Him, "Nay,"
> And He watched the dross that we had not seen,
> And it melted and passed away.
> And the gold grew brighter and yet more bright,
> But our eyes were to dim with tears,
> We saw but the fire, not the Master's hand,
> And questioned with anxious fears.
> Yet our gold shone out with a richer glow,
> As it mirrored a Form above,
> That bent over the fire, though unseen by us,
> With a look of ineffable love.
> Can we think that it pleases His loving heart
> To cause us a moment's pain?
> Ah, No! but He saw through the present cross
> The bliss of eternal gain.
> So He waits thee with a watchful eye,
> With a love that is strong and sure,
> And His gold did not suffer a bit more heat,
> Than was needed to make it pure.

Ithmah was a jewel set in refined gold in the crown of David's "mighty men." Unlike the men of Judah or any other tribe of Israel, Ithmah was a traitor to his race and nation when he joined the army of their enemy. Like Ruth, only a spiritual conversion could have motivated such a revolt against home and homeland. Ithmah found faith I believe and was numbered among David's famous soldiers.

Isaiah wrote this in his classic book: *"And I will turn my hand upon thee, and purely purge away thy dross, and take away all thy sin."* (Isaiah 1:25) As New Testament saints, Christ's work in us has a similar theme according to Peter: *"That the trial of your faith being much more precious than of gold that perisheth, though it be tried with fire, might be found unto praise and honor and glory at the appearing of Jesus Christ."* (I Peter 1:7) As saints of God, we will often endure the fires of sickness, suffering, and severe pain that the impurities of our lives might be purged away. These trials will not be pleasant, but the Purifier knows that they are necessary, and He will only make the process as hot as it necessary to get the cleansing done, the dross out, and the purest product refined. Jesus would teach in his classic Sermon on the Mount: *"Blessed are the pure in heart; for they shall see God."* (Matthew 5:8) Oswald Chambers writes on this concept: *"We have to grow in purity. God makes us pure by His sovereign grace, but we have something to look after, this bodily life which we come in contact with other people."* Life itself is a purifier, but it is used by the Master Purifier to make us *"...conformed to the image of His Son."* (Romans 8:29) That kind of purity takes a lot of purging and refining.

Let us today allow the Purifier to turn up the heat on our lives so that in the end we will come forth as gold. A young man on my hall in college, Ron Hamilton, wrote this grand song after losing an eye:

> God never moves without purpose or plan,
> When trying his servant and molding a man.
> Give thanks to the Lord though your testing's seems long;
> In darkness He giveth a song.
> I could not see through the shadow ahead;
> So I looked at the cross of my Saviour instead.
> I bowed to the will of the Master that day;
> Then peace came and tears fled away.
> Now I can see testing comes from above;
> God strengthens His children and purges with love.
> My Father knows best, and I trust in His care;
> Through purging more fruit I will bear.
> O rejoice in the Lord, He makes no mistakes.

> He knoweth the end of each path that I take.
> For when I am tried and purified,
> I shall come forth as gold!

I believe Ithmah was a product of this process, but have you been?

I Timothy 4:12: *"But be thou an example of the believer...in purity..."*

59.

ELIEL: MY GOD IS GOD

I Chronicles 11:47: *"**ELIEL**, and Obed, and Jasiel the Mesobaite."*

THE ONLY FACT THAT separates this Eliel from the Eliel of I Chronicles 11:46 are "the Mahavite" of verse 46 and "the Mesobaite" of verse 47. They are not the same "mighty men" because they come from two different places. Why would David repeat such a name so close together in his famous listing of his elite soldiers? They were two exceptional warriors that happen to have the same name, and what a name it is, what a good name it is: "My God is God." Though we dealt with this meaning just a few chapters ago it is worth a second look, a revisiting.

"A good name is rather to be chosen than great riches…" (Proverbs 22:1). And the name Eliel is a great statement of faith, given from parents that must have loved Israel's Jehovah. They wanted everyone to know of their belief in the True and Living God. Eliel had to be born in a very low spiritual period in the history of the Hebrews (the reign of Saul), and the parents of Eliel proclaimed "My God is God" the best way they could. No doubt a first born son, Eliel was a living testimony to his parent's faith, and I suspect by the time he had attained "mighty man" status in David's Army, his statement of faith as well. How can we acknowledge today that Jesus is our God? We like Eliel's parents do it through a name, the name "Christian" (Acts 11:26). We like Eliel take on the name of our God, Jesus Christ. Despite the fact that the name "Christian" has been dragged through the media mud and the social slime of our day, it is still the good name that was given to us by the world nearly two thousand years ago.

It is my desire to live such a life that the name "Christian" will at least be respected by those that witness my life. I, like Eliel, need to uplift the meaning of my name "My God is God."

In our other article on a "mighty man" named Eliel we focused on "My God," but in this article I would like to draw your attention to "is God." Though the Bible doesn't try to defend the existence of God, it simple states: *"In the beginning God..."* (Genesis 1:1) and *"in the beginning was the Word and the Word was with God and the Word was God."* (John 1:1) The Bible then goes on in great length to describe who and what "God is." As we have tried to highlight and underline this truth through the Person of the Son in the Triune God, I will once again bring this to light in relationship to Jesus. Let us do this through this great explanation by the pen of Paul when he wrote to Timothy this amazing description of Christ: *"Which in His times He shall shew, who is the blessed and only Potentate, the King of kings, and the Lord of lords."* (I Timothy 6:15) It is around this title of "Potentate" that I would like to develop this wonderful concept on Christ.

Potentate is only used once in Scripture. The Greek word is *dunastes* which means "one that is powerful." Interestingly, from this Greek word we get our English word of "dynasty." In Acts 8:27 the same word is translated "of great authority." This is why Jesus Christ is considered the only true Potentate because He "is God!" *"And Jesus came and spake unto them saying: All power is given unto me in heaven and in earth."* (Matthew 28:18) It was a young 18th century pastor by the name of Edward Perronet that gave the Church of God these stirring lines to sing:

> All hail the power of Jesus name!
> Let angel's prostrate fall;
> Bring forth the royal diadem,
> And crown Him Lord of all.
> Ye chosen seed of Israel's race,
> Ye ransomed from the fall;
> Hail Him who saved you by His grace,
> And crown Him Lord of all.
> Let every kindred, every tribe,
> On this celestial ball;
> To Him all majesty ascribe,
> And crown Him Lord of all.
> O that with yonder sacred throng
> We at His feet may fall;
> We'll join the everlasting song,

ELIEL: MY GOD IS GOD

And crown Him Lord of all.

First published in 1779, this song, sometimes called the "National Anthem of Christendom," exalted Christ as the Almighty Potentate of all. Edward Perronet, a companion and fellow evangelist with John and Charles Wesley, was only echoing heaven with his great hymn of faith in the matchless truth of "Christ is God." It was John the Apostle who first heard these inspiring words: *"Thou are worthy, O Lord, to receive glory and honor and power…"* (Revelation 4:11). Like with Perronet's words, heaven's words were also put to song. It was Oliver Holden that gave Perronet's poem life, and in heaven John heard the angel choir sing: *"Worthy is the Lamb that was slain to receive power…"* (Revelation 5:9–12). You better learn this song because we will sing it in heaven!

It was Paul who called Jesus *"the Power of God"* (I Corinthians 1:24). Despite the many who have tried to claim that position, the Eternal Father gave it only to His Son. The reason is that only Jesus could be the only blessed Potentate. Most human potentates, powerful, authoritative rulers, have not been blessed. History tells us that one of the most powerful, longest reigning potentates was Louis XIV of France. This grand monarch, sometimes called "the sun King," ruled France in its heyday for 72 years. His call to fame rests in the palace he built for himself, the renowned Palace of Versailles. Not known for reform or helping his people out of poverty, he was a potentate, but not a blessed potentate. Then there was the first Czar of Russia known as Ivan IV. This absolute ruler of Russia did much to bring his country into the modern age. He had all power and authority in his land. His word was law, yet he, too, was no blessed potentate. History remembers him best as "Ivan the Terrible!" As his reign lengthened so did his violence and hatred. In a fierce fury he even killed his own son. No blessed potentate there! Our list of earthly potentates could go on and on, but we will not find one like Christ; even the best potentates would never match the blessed Potentate.

I have come to like the translation of a man by the name of Moffat. I would have you consider in the light of our topic Isaiah 40:15,17 and how Moffat translates these verses in relationship of "God is God" and other worldly rulers: "O thou Eternal, our own God, others have been ruling us; but thine authority alone today we own. These lords are dead and gone, ghosts that return no more." One day it says *"that at the name of Jesus every knee should bow, of things in heaven, and things in the earth, and things under the earth, and that every tongue should confess that Jesus*

Christ is Lord, to the glory of God the Father." (Philippians 2:10–11) Then and only then will the world be thankful for a loving, caring, gracious and blessed Potentate that will rule and reign so much differently than the other kings and lords and potentates have throughout world history. Granted, Christ will have to rule with a rod of iron (Psalm 2:9), but none will be able to say that He was not a blessed Potentate. Time has proven that no earthly ruler has been able to bring to his citizens what is necessary to the happy fulfillment of life. Oh, that mankind would recognize now the Christ and prepare for His rule as Potentate.

Philippians 2:9: *"Wherefore God also hath highly exalted Him, and given Him a name which is above every name."*

60.

OBED: SERVANT

I Chronicles 11:47: *"Eliel, and **OBED,** and Jasiel the Mesobaite."*

A SIMPLE NAME IS all we have to go on in our consideration of David's 60th "mighty man." His name is only found in David's second list and found nowhere else in the Scriptures. All we have to go on is the meaning of Obed which means "servant." I would like to develop this devotional around this simple question: Is a soldier a servant?

As I ponder this article on David's "mighty men" and in particular Obed, I recall Jesus' encounter with a Roman soldier early in his ministry. I have come to the belief that this centurion was one of the mighty men of the New Testament. The story is a simple one, but the recognition by Jesus makes this warrior unique: *"And when Jesus was entered into Capernaum, there came unto Him a centurion, beseeching him, and saying, Lord, my servant lieth at home sick of the palsy, grievously tormented. And Jesus saith unto him, I will come and heal him. The centurion answered and said, Lord, I am not worthy that thou shouldest come under my roof: but speak the word only, and my servant shall be healed. For I am a man under authority, having soldiers under me: and I say to this man, Go, and he goeth; and to another, Come, and he cometh; and to my servant, Do this, and he doeth it."* (Matthew 8:5–9) Take note of how this centurion makes no distinction between his servant and his soldiers. Not all servants are soldiers, but all soldiers are servants. Obed was a servant of David, and I believe like the centurion's servant, Obed was faithful and useful to David as such. I also believe that David loved his soldiers like Obed just as this centurion loved his servant to seek the best for him. I think you know how this story of the centurion ends with the greatest testimony of faith given to any man by Jesus Himself: *"Verily I say unto you, I have not found so great faith, no, not in Israel."* (Matthew 8:10) This was not the faith of a Jew, but a Gentile, and I believe David recognized this "mighty man" Obed for his servant-like characteristics.

I also find in this meaning a connection to Christ Himself. In the Matthew Gospel numerous Old Testament prophecies are said to have been fulfilled in the Life of Christ. One of them is a reference to Jesus as a servant: *"That it might be fulfilled which was spoken by Esaias* [Isaiah] *the prophet, saying, Behold, my servant, whom I have chosen; my beloved, in Whom my soul is well pleased: I will put My Spirit upon Him, and He shall shew judgment to the Gentiles. He shall not strive, not cry; neither shall any man hear His voice in the street. A bruised reed shall he not break, and smoking flax shall He not quench, till He sent forth judgment unto victory. And in His name shall the Gentiles trust."* (Matthew 12:17–21 and Isaiah 42:1–6) Is not this exactly what the Capernaum centurion did? What a wonderful example and role model for all that would be a servant to Jesus Christ? Is not this what He loves best, a trusting servant that will take Him at His word, "speak the word only?"

Servant here means "one under the authority of another." In the case of Jesus Christ it is referring to God the Son's subjection to God the Father in His coming to earth to fulfill the eternal purpose and plan of the Almighty. Paul the Apostle said it best when he wrote to the believers of Philippi: *"Let this mind be in you, which was also in Christ Jesus: who being in the form of God, thought it not robbery to be equal with God: but made Himself of no reputation, and took upon Him the form of a servant, and was made in the likeness of men, and being found in fashion as a man, He humbled Himself, and became obedient unto death even the death of the cross."* (Philippians 2:5–8) Who knows better the role of a servant than a servant? Jesus was a servant on earth before He became Master, and David, too, would be able to recognize a servant because he was first a servant to Saul before he was Master to his "mighty men."

When Christ came to earth, He was under no illusions of why He had come. His goal was to do the Father's will; His messages were to speak the Father's words; and His mission was to fulfill the Father's plans. Christ was in every sense and in every action a servant. Peter says that Christ *"...has left us an example, that we should follow His steps."* (I Peter 2:21) For most of us this is one of the hardest patterns He left for us to follow. Even Jesus' closest disciples had a hard time with the example of servant. On one occasion the disciples were confronted with the power-seeking John and James. Whether through their mother or on their own they sought positions above the others, and the other apostles were mad, but Jesus rebuked them all and taught us a valuable lesson on servant-hood when He said: *"And whosoever of you will be the chiefest, shall be servant of all."* (Mark 10:44) Jesus not only left the example of being a servant to His Father, but He was also a servant to His friends (John 15:5). When none of His disciples would wash the feet of their brethren at the last supper, Jesus took up a towel and water and washed the disciples' feet (John 13:4–5). What a rebuke that must have been to them, and to us today!

The great prophet Isaiah wrote centuries before the first coming of Christ this truth concerning the stewardship of our Savior: *"Behold, my servant, whom I uphold; mine elect, in whom my soul delighteth; I have put my Spirit in Him…"* (Isaiah 42:1). This one verse gives us perhaps the best description for a servant found in the Bible. First there is the word "elect" referring to Christ as being the selected one as a sacrifice for the sins of the people (Matthew 1:21). The word "delighteth" refers to Christ being the satisfier of the demands of the Father. The word "spirit" refers to the fact that Jesus became a servant, but the spirit of servant-hood came from the Father. There has been and there will not be a greater example of the servant spirit than given by Christ Himself!

So if our Savior was a servant and we are exhorted to follow His example, doesn't that mean we are also to be a servant to God and our fellowman? Not just playing the servant, but being a servant both in hand and heart. Jesus worked the deeds of a servant while on earth because He had the heart of a servant. The same Spirit that indwelt Him indwells us so we ought to be about the business of serving God and others, and as Paul puts it: *"…as we have therefore opportunity, let us do good unto all men, especially unto to them who are of the household of faith."* (Galatians 6:10) Remember, in the real world a servant is considered on the bottom rung of the social ladder, but in the eyes of God he is on the top rung of that same ladder. For me there only remains one more question in this devotional: In whose eyes do you want to be recognized? Most would say God, but live just the opposite. Are you like Obed in the Army of God? We know that we are called soldiers (II Timothy 2:3–4), and most of us would rather be a soldier than a servant (II Corinthians 4:2), but hopefully I have demonstrated enough in this chapter and shared enough in this devotional to convince you that a soldier is a servant. If the centurion of Capernaum and the "mighty man" Obed isn't enough examples, then you must look to the One who certainly was above all, who didn't have to be a servant, yet He was.

Isaiah 53:11: *"He shall see the travail of His soul, and shall be satisfied: by His knowledge shall my righteous servant justify many; for He shall bear their iniquities."*

61.

JASIEL: GOD IS MAKER

I Chronicles 11:47: *"Eliel, and Obed, and **JASIEL** the Mesobaite."*

OUR JOURNEY THROUGH II Samuel 23 and I Chronicles 11 has traced the "mighty men" of David. We have reached the final name in these two parallel chapters listing and in some warriors describing their amazing exploits as soldiers under David's command. We will discover some other names in I Chronicles 12 that we will add to our "mighty men" list, but if we would stop where David stopped, the last name would be Jasiel the Mesobaite. Mesobaite is the patronymic of Jasiel, but the location of Jasiel's hometown is still unknown to us to this day. That leaves us, as so often in this study, with only the meaning of Jasiel's name to provoke a devotional. Jasiel simple means "God is Maker." I believe a reference to the Creator God.

The world would debate me, but the Bible has always been very clear who the Creator is. Paul writes in his epistle to the Romans: *"Who changed the truth of God into a lie, and worshipped and served the creature more than the Creator, who is blessed forever. Amen."* (Romans 1:25) At the writing of this devotional I have just returned from three glorious days on the Miramichi River in New Brunswick, Canada. I was black salmon fishing with my father-in-law, Stacy Meister, and our good friend and guide Irving Vickers. During those three days, I witnessed again the magnificence of God's creation in the foothills and hallows of central New Brunswick. We saw animal life galore, like owl, eagle, beaver, muskrat, deer, and partridge, not to mention a salmon or two. We landed 53 of the greatest fish in the sea! On our way up to Upper Blackville, we traveled through a hundred miles of the Renuos Highway. From the beginning to the end, there was no sign of civilization, no homes, no telephone or electrical poles, no towns or villages, just a road that cuts through the dense forest in central New Brunswick from Plaster Rock to Renuos. A massive ice storm had hit the area over the weekend and left the trees in one section covered in a layer of ice. It was like driving through a crystal woodland; what a sight and site! All I could think to do was to thank and praise the Almighty for the opportunity to witness another aspect of His grand creation.

For *"all things were made by Him; and without Him was not anything made that was made,"* (John 1:3) and *"For by Him were all things created, that are in heaven, and that are in the earth, visible and invisible, whether they be thrones, or dominions, or principalities, or powers; all things were created by Him, and for Him."* (Colossians 1:16) These verses ought to be a constant reminder to us that this world is not our own, but just given to us to enjoy, not destroy. Mankind hasn't been the good steward he was supposed to be (Genesis 1:28). I recently found this warning in the Revelation: *"...and should destroy them which destroy the earth."* (Revelation 11:18) God takes seriously those that would harm His creation, but mankind has tried to claim it as his own. Mankind has tried to ignore, shut-out, and theorize away the Creator of this planet, the real owner by creation of this earth. Why? Because man wants to be his own creator! They tell me that if you would go to Kyoto, Japan, you would find a temple which contains over a thousand images of Buddha and each image is different than the others. The individual that goes to this shrine is encouraged to look at each of the Buddha's until he finds one that most resembles him and then he is to worship that image. How true this is today in the worship of man versus the worship of God. Someone has written fittingly of this phenomenon: **"Today's idols are more in the self than on the shelf."**

In Greek mythology, there was a fictional character called Narcissus. This god would spend its days gazing at his own reflection in a pool. Perhaps our era will be called "the age of narcissism." Instead of seeing God in creation, man has begun to see himself. This was not true of the Psalmist David as he wrote this: *"The heavens declare the glory of God; and the firmament sheweth His handiwork."* (Psalm 19:1) There was no doubt in David's mind who the Creator was and who created the creation. Is there a doubt in your mind? The scientific world and the political world and the educational world have been casting doubts for nearly a century now. I still remember when the creation was taught in public schools, but no more. The world is casting more doubt in the minds of the rising generations than ever before. It will not be surprising that there will arise a generation that knows not where it came from and who created them. My wife and I were just talking today how ignorant our AWANA (our youth ministry to three to twelve year olds) kids are to the things of the Bible, including creation. Paul writes: *"For the invisible things of Him from the creation of the world are clearly seen, being understood by the things that are made, even His eternal power and Godhead; so that they are without excuse."* (Romans 1:20) So where are you on creation and the Creator? What are your excuses not to believe?

Interestingly, the Creator is not through. F. B. Meyer, a favorite devotional writer, makes some amazing comments on Isaiah 65:17, a prophecy that will be fulfilled according to Revelation 21:1: *"Behold, I create new heavens and a new earth…"* This is what Meyer has to say about this:

> The heavens and earth that are now were not produced in their present shape in a day; but through a week of time which is chronicled in the strata of the earth. God was at work building them up. So beneath the scaffolding of history and human affairs it may be that the Creator is already at work laying the foundation of the new era which shall soon be unveiled. But the new creation is much more difficult than of the old, because there is so much undoing to be done. Amid the crash of empire, the rock of revolutions, the blood, and tears, and anguish of the present, God is making room for and preparing for the new heavens and earth in which dwelleth righteousness…We turn to the book of the Revelation for further particulars, and there learn that the blessed future can only be explained in negatives. What heaven will really be is as yet hidden, that the surprise may be the greater; but it is certain that each of the elements of the present distress will be eliminated. No more sorrow, pain, death, curse, tears, or separating sea. Christ will make, is making, all things new; and, best of all, he is making us new to enjoy them. Oh, blessed conditions, in which God will not remember our sins, and we shall not remember the former things, of pain, and sorrow, and death!

When I think that the creative work of the Almighty is not over, I can't wait to see what He does create out of the fiery end to the heavens and earth as we know them (II Peter 3:5–10). Someday the world will know the true Creator as He really is!

When I walk in nature, I see Jesus' hand; do you? Around every bend of the river, I see His handiwork; do you? As the birds sing I hear Him speak; do you? Watching a rising or setting sun I see His paint brush; do you? A full moon or a star-studded sky reveals to me the Maker's masterpiece, but does it to you? The world might deny the Creator, but one day, even in the mind of the world, there will be no doubt who the Creator is!

Isaiah 43:15: *"I am the Lord, your Holy One, the Creator of Israel, your King."*

62

AHIEZER: HELPING BROTHER

I Chronicles 12:3: *"The chief was **AHIEZER**, then Joash, the sons of Shemaah the Gibeathite; and Jeziel, and Pelet, the sons of Azmaaveth, and Berachah, and Jehu the Antothite."*

FOR MANY, THE LIST of "mighty men" stops with I Chronicles 11 or II Samuel 23. On a fishing trip with a pastor friend, Dave Natalie, from Pennsylvania to the woods of Northern Maine, I was introduced to I Chronicles 12 in a series of messages my friend shared around the campfires we had during that week-long trout fishing trip. The focus of his sermonettes was on the "mighty men" and their special gifts, military gifts they used to help David win the kingdom. Though they might not have received as much press as the 61 soldiers we have already highlighted, they were certainly important in David's strategy in claiming the rule over Israel. After that week of devotional, I was determined to add these men to my list of David's "mighty men."

This is how the chronicler introduced the first series of men we will underline in our continual research into David's top warriors: *"Now these are they that came to David at Ziklag, while he yet kept himself close because of Saul the son of Kish: and they were among the mighty men, helpers in war. They were armed with bows, and could use both the right hand and the left in hurling stones and shooting arrows out of a bow, even Saul's brethren of Benjamin. The chief was Ahiezer..."* (I Chronicles 12:1–3). In David's first lists the "mighty men" were listed individually by order of their mighty deeds. In I Chronicles 12, the men are listed by their tribes and their unique abilities for warfare, or what I would like to call David's special units (like our Navy Seals or Army Rangers, Special Forces). The first unit mentioned was a group of 23 men from the tribe of Benjamin, Saul's home tribe. The leader of this unit of "mighty men" was a man by the name of Ahiezer, and, unlike the last series of David's "mighty men," we are able to get a profile of this mighty warrior through the deals describing the men he led.

First, when did Ahiezer became a part of David's army? According to the text it took place at Ziklag (I Chronicles 12:1). The history of this town is given in the accounting of David's flights from Saul in I Samuel. David had been on the run from Saul for what I believe was a decade or more. In frustration, David moved into Philistia, the territory of his archenemy the Philistines and became a mercenary for Achish the King of Gath (yes, the hometown of Goliath!). While there, Achish gave David and his 600-man battalion (I Samuel 27:2) a place to call their own, Ziklag (I Samuel 27:6). *"And the time that David dwelt in the country of the Philistines was a full year and four months."* (I Samuel 27:7) So it seems to fit that it was during this period of time Ahiezer and his troop joined David. This would also parallel the final 16 months of Saul's reign, and for me what is eye-opening is the fact that some of Saul's own tribesmen were beginning to switch sides. Do you remember the time and place when you switched sides, from your father the devil (John 8:44) to making Jesus the Captain of your life (Hebrews 2:10)?

Second, what did Ahiezer excel in militarily? Ahiezer and his men were extraordinary archers (bow) and slingers (hurling stones) (I Chronicles 12:2). The Benjamites were known throughout Hebrew history as men exceptionally skilled in the use of the sling which was David's favorite weapon in his youth. (Remember what he did with a single stone against the famous giant warrior Goliath in I Samuel 17?). David would have had a special place in his heart and in his ranks for slingers. The Bible records in the days of the judges a unique unit of slingers that were Gibeathites (Ahiezer and his brother Joash were Gibeathites-I Chronicles 12:3) who were described with this amazing description: *"the inhabitants of Gibeah"* (Saul's hometown) (I Samuel 10:26) which were numbered seven hundred chosen men. *"Among all these people there were seven hundred men left handed; every one could sling stones at an hair breathed, and no miss."* (Judges 20:15-16) Over the years, their skill with a sling was also matched by their skill with the bow and arrow. You add to this their unique ability to be ambidextrous with both weapons systems, and you have some very useful warriors. Their ability did not diminish with their use of their right hand or left hand. This ability would be very helpful in a long battle in which one arm or the other would get tired. This Benjamite battalion led by Ahiezer must have been a great help to David in the battles he fought. I am wondering if you are not numbered with one of Christ's great battalions. We call them "local churches" today.

Third, where did Ahiezer come from? As we have seen, not only was Ahiezer from Saul's home tribe, but he was from Saul's hometown (I Chronicles 12:1–3). Gibeah was a small town. I was able to visit the archeological site of Gibeah on a trip to Israel in 2010 and found it like my hometown of Perham, Maine. There is no way that Saul didn't know Ahiezer, and I am wondering with such skills if Ahiezer was not a part of Saul's original army. Whether or not Ahiezer and his men saw "the handwriting on the wall" or they had simply become disillusioned with Saul's rule, the text doesn't say, but we do know they abandoned their leader and their homes to follow David and re-establish themselves in the Philistine town of Ziklag. Many years after Ahiezer chose David over Saul another Benjamite (Philippians 3:5) would switch sides choosing Christianity over Judaism (Acts 9). I am wondering, have you switched sides yet?

Lastly, who was Ahiezer really? Would you allow me to make these spiritual applications to the final facts of what we know of this "mighty man?" First, he was a son of a man named Shemaah the Gibeathite. When we join Christ's army we become "sons:" *"But as many as receive Him, to them gave he power to become the sons of God, even to them that believe on His name."* (John 1:12) Second, he was a "brother," a brother of Joash (we will deal with this "mighty man" in our next devotional). When we join Christ's army, we, too, become "brothers:" *"Love the brotherhood."* (I Peter 2:17) Third, he was "chief." Ahiezer attained to this position perhaps by his leadership ability or his skills, we don't know for sure, but we do know how we become "chiefs" in Christ's army: *"And whosoever of you will be the chiefest, shall be servant of all."* (Mark 10:44). Lastly, Ahiezer was "a helper of the war" (I Chronicles 12:1) as were his brethren, which bring us to the most interesting fact about Ahiezer: his name means "helping brother." He was not only a brother to Joash, he was a brother to his fellow soldiers, and I believe he was a brother to David. When we join Christ's army, we, too, are supposed to be helpers. One of the overlooked gifts of the Spirit is "helps:" *"And God hath set some in the Church…helps…"* (I Corinthians 12:28). God needs many followers like Ahiezer in His army, especially in this last characteristic of this "mighty man." We know nothing more of the help of Ahiezer, but this introductory verse to the "mighty men" says it all: *"These also are the CHIEF of the mighty men whom David had..."* (I Chronicles 11:10).

II Corinthians 1:11: *"Ye also helping together by prayer for us, that for the gift bestowed upon is by the means of many persons that thanks may be given by many on our behalf."*

63.

JOASH: JEHOVAH SUPPORTS

> I Chronicles 12:3: *"The chief was Ahiezer, then **JOASH**, the sons of Shemaah the Gibeathite; and Jeziel, and Pelet, the sons of Azmaaveth, and Berachah, and Jehu the Antothite."*

As we continue to look into the "mighty men" of the Benjamin Battalion, the second man on this list was Joash. Joash was the brother of the captain of the battalion, a man by the name of Ahiezer, the sons of a man named Shemaah. All we know about this warrior is "then Joash." I have come to the belief (Romans 14:5) that Joash was second in command of the unit of Benjamites that joined David's Band at Ziklag towards the end of King Saul's reign (II Chronicles 12:1). Like the others, Joash was an expert with the bow and the sling with either his right or left hand (I Chronicles 12:2) which made him a very dangerous enemy, a man you would want on your side in a fight. The other Biblical connection I would remind you of is the other important brothers found in the Bible text, especially in the New Testament, Peter and Andrew, James and John come to mind--like Abiezer and Joash. But once again, as we have so often in this series of devotionals, we focus our attention on the meaning of Joash: "Jehovah supports." As with the God he served and the king he was loyal to, it is an important, if not a primary, quality necessary for a support role, a second place position, to serve the God of the seconds.

In 1969, I attained my high school basketball goal by playing in the Eastern Maine Tournament at the Bangor Auditorium. Despite losing in the opening round, a disappointment to this day, I played well enough to be named to the second team of all-stars picked by the basketball committee for the tournament. I was an all-star, but I was not the best of the best. I didn't win, I was a loser, yet there still lingers nearly 60 years ago that second place: "then Barry." I did play. I did participate and for that I am still proud. Many despise second place, but over time I have come to honor and respect those who are able to stand in the shadows, to accept the position of "second." Maybe, that is the reason I love to write about men like Joash and all the other "second place" people found in the Bible. One of my favorites is the friend and companion of Joshua, Caleb.

Christ had come and gone leaving the apostles to wait at Jerusalem for the promised coming of the Holy Ghost (Acts 1:8). As they waited, they prayed (Acts 1:140 and planned the evangelization of the world. At the heart of this Christ-given commission were the twelve men Jesus had called from among His disciples (Luke 6:13). They would lay the foundation upon which the Church would be built (Ephesians 2:20). However, there was a big problem. There were only eleven of them now, not twelve. Judas needed to be replaced because of his treachery and eventual suicide (Matthew 27:3-5). It was then that Peter recalled the Old Testament Scripture of Psalm 109:8 (Acts 1:20). This is a great precept when we don't know what to do. The Bible is still the answer book! Once the passage was applied to the situation the other disciples agreed to give Judas' position to someone else, but who would or could qualify?

Before there were any nominations certain guidelines were selected and established to even choose the candidates for the vacant office. How we need to revisit this concept in the Church of God today. The reason most churches and church related organizations are in so much trouble today is because they have put "anybody" in a position of authority. The days for choosing Church offices by Biblical guidelines seems to be over. As long as she or he looks good, acts good, and possesses a good personality and resume, we put them in. No longer does the Church look for God's man or God's woman for the job. I wonder how many offices the Apostle Paul would have been nominated if he were alive today. I suspect not many being the jailbird he was, not a good speaker, and always making trouble. Despite modern trends, the Bible still teaches about certain qualifications for certain Church offices. Look up I Timothy 3 and Titus 1 as some examples, and you might be surprised just how disqualified your pastor is, your deacon is, or that missionary you support is to the spiritual offices they are holding in your church.

JOASH: JEHOVAH SUPPORTS

In the case of Judas' replacement, five very tough requirements were established by the apostles (Acts 1:21–22). This is how I explain these qualifications:

1. A godly man. Sorry, no women could apply even though there were some good women among the group (Acts 1:14), including Jesus' mother. I Timothy 3:2. We often forget that man's barriers are down in most places today, but God's barriers to certain positions are still up Biblically.

2. A called disciple (Luke 6:13 and Luke 10:1). We often forget that Christ called more than twelve disciples and the replacement for Judas had to have been specifically called by Jesus Christ Himself.

3. A mature believer (John 6:66). We also forget that not all of Christ's called disciples stayed true to their original calling. Disciples can fall away, too!

4. A grounded person (John 1:36–37). One of the things that many believers overlook is that a group of John the Baptist's disciples would become Jesus' disciples as well. We know of Andrew and John, but we forget about Matthias and Justus.

5. A special witness (Acts 1:3). These candidates had to personally witness the bodily resurrection and the bodily ascension of Christ, something that only a few actually did. So the field of qualified candidates was actually maybe as low as two?

No doubt there were many that qualified on a point or two, but seemingly only two qualified on all five characteristics, Barsabas (also known as Justus) and Matthias. We know they both met the qualifications, but in a two-man race with only one winner somebody has to come in second, whether to replace Judas or to be second in command of the Benjamin Battalion. Paul would write to the Church at Corinth: *"Knew ye not that they which run in a race run all, but one receiveth the prize."* (I Corinthians 9:24) So we are to run that we might attain, but every race has the possibility of loss. When we traveled from northern Maine to central Maine for the basketball tournament I wrote of at the beginning of this article, my teammates and I thought we would win. We were the higher seed with only two season losses, but we lost! I am reminded of Jonathan's aspiration of being second in David's kingdom (I Samuel 23:17), even though he was in line to be the next king after his father Saul. He understood that with Jehovah's support second is not a bad place.

Today, let us so live like Joash, Justus, and Jonathan that in the end, though we might not get the command, the position, the kingship, we will nevertheless at least qualify for the job. I believe in all three cases they did though they were never chosen. Ours is not to claim the job, ours is but to be prepared for the job, calling or no calling. Knowing this, it is far better to be in second place on the Lord's team than in first place on the devil's squad. So, let us live our lives and prepare our race even if we end up in second place.

Colossians 1:10: *"That we might walk worthy of the Lord unto all pleasing, being fruitful in every good work…"*

64.

JEZIEL: GOD GATHERS

I Chronicles 12:3: *"The chief was Ahiezer, then Joash, the sons of Shemaah the Gibeathite; and **JEZIEL**, and Pelet, the sons of Azmaaveth, and Berachah, and Jehu the Antothite."*

ALL WE KNOW ABOUT this third mighty man of the Benjamin Battalion is that he was the son of Azmaveth, that he joined David in Ziklag (I Chronicles 12:1) with his brother Pelet, the subject of our next "mighty man" devotional. Like his companions, Jeziel had exceptional fighting skills (I Chronicles 12:2), and the final Biblical fact we can glean from Scripture is the meaning of his name, God unites or God gathers. As with so many of David's "mighty men," I have drawn a connection to this warrior and the Person of Christ. I would have you consider this application in our relationship with Jesus.

Isaiah said of the coming Christ: *"He shall feed His flock like a shepherd; he shall gather the lambs with His arms…"* (Isaiah 40:11). I would like for us to consider the action of the word "gather" in the meaning of Jeziel's name as well as the ministry of Christ. I am very thankful for the gathering ministry of my Savior, both in this life and in the life to come. To start with I am going to turn your attention to these words written from the inspiring pen of the great English pastor and author Charles Haddon Spurgeon:

> Our good Shepherd has in His flock a variety of experiences, some are strong in the Lord, and others are weak in faith, but He is impartial in His care for all His sheep, and the weakest lamb is as dear to Him as the most advance in the flock. Lambs

are wont to lag behind, prone to wander, and apt to grow weary, but from all the danger of these infirmities the Shepherd protects them with His arm of power. He finds new-born souls, like young lambs, ready to perish: He nourishes them till life becomes vigorous; He finds weak minds ready to faint and die, He consoles them and renews their strength. All the little ones He gathers, for it is not the will of our Heavenly Father that one of them should perish (II Peter 3:9). What a quick eye He must have to see them all! What a tender heart to care for them all! In His life time on earth He was a great gatherer of the weakest sort, and now that He dwells in heaven, His loving heart yearns towards the fainting here below. How gently did He gather me to Himself, to His truth, to His blood, to His love, to His church! With what effectual grace did He compel me to come to Himself! Since my first conversion, how frequently has He restored me from my wanderings, and once again folded me within the circle of His everlasting arms! The best of all is, that He does it all Himself personally, not delegating the task of love, but condescending Himself to rescue and preserve His most unworthy servant. How shall I love Him enough or serve Him worthily? I would fain make His name great unto the ends of the earth, but what can my feebleness do for Him? Great Shepherd, add to Thy mercies this one other, a heart to love Thee more truly as I ought.

What more can I write, except to ask, have you been gathered into the fold of Christ yet? Have you allowed the mighty, all-powerful arms of Jesus to embrace you yet? Has the Shepherd's fold become your gathering place week after week, day after day, yet? If the answer is yes then you know of the joy and happiness of this sacred place, but if the answer is no then I would have you consider right now letting the Shepherd find you, gather you up in his arms, and bring you home (Luke 15:1-3-6). All you have to do is cry, make you silent heart-felt call, and He will be at your side. I have preached for nearly 60 years now that a seeking sinner will always make contact with a seeking Savior. We are told that Jesus came to *"seek and to save"* those who are lost (Luke 19:10). If you will but reach out to Him, He will come to you and gather you into His Almighty hands and lift you with His Almighty arms and place you on His Almighty shoulders and carry you into His eternal sheepfold. David wrote of this wonderful concept in his classic Psalm 23. There is never a place you have wandered to that He will not find you. He will never stop searching and seeking for you, and He will overcome every obstacle and

JEZIEL: GOD GATHERS

barrier to gather you unto Himself. If you but yield to Him in this life, there is another gathering that you will also participate in.

I believe if you have been a part of this first gathering that Spurgeon writes about, then you will also participate in another gathering that Mrs. Charles Cowman once wrote about in her wonderful devotional, Springs in the Valley. She writes of a coming gathering that each and every one of Christ's living followers is looking forward to, including this author.

> What a scene of unimaginable grandeur that will be, when at last all nations are gathered to His feet! That will include representatives from all the European States, from Ireland in the far north to Greece in the south, and from Portugal in the west to the hidden saints of God in the Soviet Russia in the east. There will be many from Algeria, Morocco, and the Atlas mountains; from Egypt and the Nile Valley; from the sandy deserts and the mountains of the Sahara; from the lakes in central Africa, from the banks of the Niger, the Calabar, the Congo, and the Zambezi rivers; and from the uplands of South Africa. There will be gathered to Christ many from Palestine, Transjordan and Arabia; India will contribute her millions; and even from closed lands like Nepal, Sikkim and Tibet, Christ will gather His own. From the islands in the Dutch East Indies they will come, Java, Sumatra, Bali, Celebes, Lombok, Sumbawa, Borneo, and the rest, and will be gathered to the feet of the Redeemer. From the teeming millions of central Asia, from China, Japan, Korea [and could I add North Korea for Cowman didn't know of the split], Manchukuo, and Mongolia, there will be an immense home-going to the Saviour. From the myriad islands of the Pacific the people of Polynesia and Melanesia will be gathered to the Lord who redeemed them. From Australia and New Zealand there will be multitudes who will join in the glad song of praise. From every republic of Central, South, and North America, and from the West Indies Islands: Cuba, Haiti, Jamaica, Porto Rico, and the Lesser Antilles, they will come. From the far-off forests and lakes of Canada there will be a similar home-going. Whether be those of the white race, or the red, or the black, the gathering to Christ will be overwhelmingly splendid. [Revelation 5:9, 7:9]

What a day that will be when we who believe in the Christ will be gathered from far and wide to meet our Lord and Savior, our eternal Shepherd, face to face. There are those that see this as an impossibility, but for those of us who believe, this is what a great Shepherd (Hebrews 13:20) can do. Jesus taught clearly that He was the good Shepherd (John

10), and what kind of a Shepherd would He be if He couldn't gather His sheep and His lambs? Gathering is one of the functions of any shepherd, and, if the natural shepherd knows where his sheep are at any time, so does the spiritual Shepherd. The day is coming when that Shepherd will return for His sheep (I Thessalonians 4:13–17), and I ask again: Are you one of his sheep? Will you be numbered among the gathering?

Isaiah 66:18: *"For I know their works and their thoughts: it shall come, and will gather all nations and tongues; and they shall come, and see my glory."*

65.

PELET: ESCAPE

I Chronicles 12:3: *"The chief was Ahiezer, then Joash, the sons of Shemaah the Gibeathite; and Jeziel, and **PELET**, the sons of Azmaaveth, and Berachah, and Jehu the Antothite."*

THE FOURTH NAME DAVID recorded on the Benjamin Battalion roster was Pelet. He was the brother of our last "mighty man" Jeziel, and the son of a man named Azmaveth. Pelet's biography reads like the three men listed before him. The only difference is the meaning of his name, escape. As with the others, it is around this meaning that I would like to challenge my reader today.

For me, one of the best *"…exceeding great and precious promises…"* (II Peter 1:4) of God's Holy Word is this wonderful truth recorded in Paul's letter to the Church at Corinth: *"There hath no temptation taken you but such as is common to man: but God is faithful, who will not suffer you to be tempted above that ye are able; but will with the temptation also* **make a way of ESCAPE***, that ye may be able to bear it."* (I Corinthians 10:13) Despite memorizing this classic verse at a very early age, I still stand amazed with each new Scriptural discovery I make in relationship to this great promise. The theme I am referring to is God's "escape routes" which we see again in the meaning of Pelet's wonderful name. Did Pelet have such an experience in the Davidic Wars? Did he find a way out of a tight situation as he fought alongside his lord and king? No matter the situation or the circumstance, it is important that the man of God looks for "the way of escape," the way out if you will, in the spiritual struggles he has to face. Like the children of Israel on the banks of the Red Sea when it appeared there would be no escape from Pharaoh's massive army and his elite chariot corps. I am actually provoked to write on this precept because just last night I preached on this concept at one of my monthly nursing home services in Ellsworth, Maine. Is there escape for people surrounded by aging bodies, weakening minds, and a society that locks them away in old-age prisons?

I have come to believe that every area of Egyptian life had been defeated in the famous "ten" plagues of Egypt, but one. The world's most powerful nation at the time had the world's most powerful army, some would say invincible army. One by one God through Moses' rod had taken on Egypt's "gods" and won, including Pharaoh himself, a king seen as a god with the death of the future Pharaoh. Only one power in the land seemingly had been left intact, the military. Because of the devastating destruction of the plagues Pharaoh eventually let the people go, but within a short time Pharaoh's heart was hardened again, and he called for his generals. He remembered his elite chariot corps and the 600 special units that led his army (Exodus 14:5-7). I believe because of the death of his son revenge was in his heart. He gave his chariot captains orders to pursue the Israelites while he followed with his army. Those orders would hammer the final nail in the coffin of Egypt, and would show clearly that God can make a way of escape for any one of his children at any time no matter the difficult traps in life.

When Pharaoh's chariots finally reached the encamped Israelites, his angry heart must have laughed for joy. With the Red Sea before them, the Egyptian army behind them, and Egyptian military forts beside them (Exodus 14:2), the children of Israel were boxed in with no way of escape or so Pharaoh thought. What we want to always remember, this is where the Good Lord had actually led them. This was not Pharaoh's trap, but God's trap (Exodus 14:4). It reminds me of Job and the trap Satan set for this man of God. A careful reading of Job 1-2 reveals this was all permitted by God, like with Israel on the banks of the Red Sea. The next time God seemingly leads you into a box canyon, a blind alley with no way out, remember, it might not be you he is trying to impress, but your enemy. Remember what David wrote in his classic Psalm: *"He prepareth a table before me in the presence of my enemies."* (Psalm 23:5) Could I also add, He prepares a way of escape also in the presence of your enemies.

So what do you do when you are surrounded with no way to go, no way out? Some would say turn and fight. Israel could have, but we learn from studying the beginning of the journey to Canaan that God

PELET: ESCAPE

had taken Israel on a circular course to Canaan: *"lest peradventure the people repent when they see war, and they return to Egypt."* (Exodus 13:17) We are told from the book of Numbers that the number of fighting males was over 600,000, yet at this time they were slaves, not soldiers. This experience, surrounded and boxed in, wasn't a lesson about fighting, but not fighting. This was a lesson on "a way of escape." Pharaoh's chariots were manned by veterans, well-trained, well-equipped, and accustomed to war. If they would have fought, they probably would have been massacred. If you can't fight or flee, there is only one course left for you. You must look for God's way of escape (Exodus 14:15). But do we?

Alexander MacLaren once said: "Those who know the way of God can find it in the dark!" Matthew Henry once wrote: "The God of Israel, the Saviour, is sometimes a God that hideth Himself, but never a God that absenteth Himself; sometimes in the dark, but never at a distance!" (I would just like to remind you that the story of Israel at the Red Sea took place at night.) And then it was the poet Annie Johnson Flint who composed:

> Have you come to the Red Sea in your life, where, in spite of all you can do, there is no way out, there is no way back, there is no other way through? Then wait on the Lord with a trust sincere till the night of your fear is gone; He will send the wind, He will heap the floods, when He says to your soul, "Go on." And His hand will lead you through-clear through-ere the watery walls roll down, no foe can reach you, no wave can touch, no mightiest sea can drown; the tossing billows may rear their crests, their foam at your feet may break, but over their bed you shall walk dry shod, in the path that your Lord will make.

Read again this classic tale that many have tried to explain away, but have never been able to remove from the Holy Text. It remains to this day one of the best examples of our exceedingly great promise in I Corinthians 10:13.

There have been secular scholars and even Biblical experts who have tried to put some logical explanation on this "way of escape" saying it was but through a marsh, the result of an earthquake, but if one clearly examines the script and puts Israel in the right geographical place, no explanation will do other than the miracle it was. This event was a God-thing, a way of escape. For Paul it was a basket through a window in Damascus (Acts 9:25). For Peter it was the help of an angel out of his prison cell (Acts 12), and for the spies of Jericho it was a scarlet rope

(Joshua 2:18). For David fleeing an angry Saul it was an open window (I Samuel 19:12). I don't know what way God will prepare for you, and I know not if it will be clearly revealed to you or if you will have to look for it, but I do know it is there, every time and in every situation. Robert Frost once wrote: "The best way out is always through." God's way of escape is through His way of escape, and it always is! Today, if you stand on the shore of a sea with no way across, wait on God's way of escape!

Isaiah 43:2: *"When thou passeth through the waters, I will be with thee…"*

66.

BERACHAH: BLESSING

I Chronicles 12:3: *"The chief was Ahiezer, then Joash, the sons of Shemaah the Gibeathite; and Jeziel, and Pelet, the sons of Azmaaveth, and* **BERACHAH**, *and Jehu the Antothite."*

NAME NUMBER FIVE ON the Benjamin Battalion honor roll is Berachah. No brothers named; no hometown named; no father named; no acts of bravery named, like so many of the others on David's "mighty men" roll. We can, as with those numbered before him, highlight and underline the characteristics of his fighting skills, but we have already highlighted and underlined those special qualities in the previous articles on his companions in this special group of Benjamites that switched sides even before King Saul was killed. So, it is once again the name Berachah and the meaning of his name that will direct our focus in this devotional on the 66th man named in David's famous "mighty men."

    I discovered in looking up the name Berachah in Young's Concordance that Berachah means "blessing," and that he is the only Biblical character with that name in the Bible. His name only appears once in Holy Writ, here in the names given under David's Benjamin Battalion. However, upon further research I did discover that this name does come up in one other story in Scripture, but the name is not given to a person, but a place. Jehovah would win a great victory for King Jehoshaphat in a valley they would call the valley of Berachah or blessing (II Chronicles 20:26). Besides this, I can think of only one more application I can make to Berachah and that is in connection to my Lord and Savior Jesus Christ. How do I make that connection? One day a new song is going to be sung in heaven, a song about Jesus that John heard when he was ushered into the heavenlies and saw and heard things yet to come. Here are some of the words of this new song as recorded in the Revelation: *"Saying with a loud voice, Worthy is the Lamb that was slain, to receive power, and riches, and wisdom, and strength, and honor, and glory, and* **"blessing!"** (Revelation 5:12) One day the Lord Jesus will receive "berachah."

Again in the Revelation we can read the words, but not hear the melody to a new song about Jesus: *"And every creature which is in heaven, and on the earth, and under the sea, and such as are in the sea, and all that are in them, heard I saying,* **blessing,** *and honour, and glory, and power, be unto Him that sitteth upon the throne, and unto the Lamb forever and ever."* (Revelation 5:13) I found this anonymous writing about the Lord that for me fits here:

> He who is the Bread of Life began His ministry hungering. He who is the Water of Life ended His ministry thirsting. Christ hungered as man, yet fed the hungry for God. He was weary, yet He is our rest. He paid tribute, yet He is the King. He was called a devil, but He cast out demons. He prayed, yet He hears prayer. He wept yet He dries our tears. He was sold for 30 pieces of silver, yet He redeemed sinners. He was led as a lamb to the slaughter, yet He is the Good Shepherd. He gave His life, and by dying He destroyed death!

Could I add to these thoughts, "What a Blessing!" Jesus was spit on, cursed, rebuked, and railed during the first time He came, but the second time He comes He will be seen as a blessing. Amen and Amen.

Paul first spoke of this blessing in his letter to the Church at Ephesus when he wrote and added a wonderful application to the meaning of this word in relationship to Christ: *"Blessed be the God and Father of our Lord Jesus Christ, who hath blessed us with all spiritual* **'blessings'** *in heavenly places in Christ."* (Ephesians 1:3) Charles Haddon Spurgeon (by now you must know that when I am stumped I look up what Charles might have written on the topic I can't seemingly get my head around) makes for me this thrilling observation on this **"blessing,"** our Berachah:

> All the goodness of the past, the present, and the future, Christ bestows upon His people. In the mysterious ages of the past the Lord Jesus was His Father's first elect, and in His election He gave us an interest, for we were chosen in Him from before the foundation of the world. He had from all eternity the prerogatives of Sonship, as His Father's only-begotten and well-beloved

Son, and He has, in the riches of His grace, by adoption and regeneration, elevated us to Sonship also, so that to us He has given "power to become the sons of God." The eternal covenant, based upon suretiship and confirmed by oath, is ours, for our strong consolation and security. In the everlasting settlements of predestinating wisdom and omnipotent decrees, the eye of the Lord Jesus was ever fixed on us; and we may rest assured that in the whole roll of destiny there is not a line which militates against the interests of His redeemed. The great betrothal of the Prince of Glory is ours, for it is to us that He is affianced, as the sacred nuptials shall ere long declare to an assembled universe. The marvellous incarnation of the God of heaven, which all the amazing condescension and humiliation which attended it, is ours. The bloody sweat, the scourge, the cross, are ours forever. Whatever blissful consequences flow from perfect obedience, finished atonement, resurrection ascension, or intercession, all are ours by His own gift. Upon His breastplate He is now bearing our names; and in His authoritative pleadings at the throne He remembers our persons and pleads our cause. His dominion our principalities and powers, and His absolute majesty in heaven, He employs for the benefit of them who trusts in Him. His high estate is as much at our service as was His condition of abasement. He, who gave Himself for us in the depths of woe and death, doth not withdraw the grant now that He is enthroned in the highest heavens.

And what could we add more to the multitude of divine blessings that are ours through the blessed "blessings" that are ours now through our Lord and Savior. Take some time today and think about what blessings have come to you personally because I also believe that in most cases our blessings from God are custom-made.

In my personal study of the names given to Christ in the Bible (Over a few years I wrote a devotional on 366 names, terms, and titles given to Christ in the Word of God.) I added to the great phrase of Isaiah: *"And His name shall be called…"* (Isaiah 9:6) **"Blessing."** Interestingly, there are two people in India where their parents gave them the name of "blessing" or in India it is "Blessen." Little did I know when I compiled that list of names for Jesus that I had missed one, Berachah. Once again I have discovered in another Biblical search that truly the Person of Christ is underlined in the lives of David's "mighty men." When God told Abraham that he would bless *"all families of the earth"* (Genesis 12:3) through him, little did Abraham realize that blessing would be highlighted through the

Bible even in the naming of people's children. Yes, even in the accounting of a brave man in David's Army, we are reminded of God's "blessings" on us and in us through Christ. He is deserving of all blessings, and we are undeserving, yet as Spurgeon so elegantly put it, these blessings are now ours because Jesus was willing to share them with us. So now we are a part of all heavenly blessings through our Berachah! What blessings are you missing out on because you are not a Child of the King?

Revelation 7:12: *"Saying, 'Amen!'* **Blessing***, and glory, and wisdom, and thanksgiving, and honour, and power, and mighty, be unto our God forever and ever! Amen."*

67.

JEHU: THE LORD IS HE

*I Chronicles 12:3: "The chief was Ahiezer, then Joash, the sons of Shemaah the Gibeathite; and Jeziel, and Pelet, the sons of Azmaaveth, and Berachah, and **JEHU** the Antothite."*

THE SIXTH BENJAMITE TO join David at Ziklag (I Chronicles 12:1–2) was an Antothite named Jehu. This makes Jehu a resident of Anathoth, a Levitical city (I Chronicles 6:60) in the territory of Benjamin (Joshua 21:18) which was located about three miles north of Jerusalem in David's day. There is still a town there today, but it is called Anata. In 2010, I was able to travel throughout Israel and in particular around Jerusalem. Though I never stopped in Anathoth, I drove by it making this "mighty man" a bit more personal than some of the others (so you will note a personal devotion). David's high priest Abiathar was also from Anathoth (I Kings 2:26), and the great prophet Jeremiah (Jeremiah 1:1) was also born there. The other significant Biblical event is the return of 128 men from Anathoth after the Babylonian captivity (Ezra 2:23 and Nehemiah 7:27). Then there was a man named Jehu, a mighty man, whose name means "the Lord is He" or "He is Lord."

One of the better modern hymns written in 1986 is the beautiful song with the same name <u>He is Lord</u>. Three writers put their musical skills together to compose this popular song and chorus, as well as the memorable melody and tune. Linda Lee Johnson, Claire Cloninger, and Tom Fettke based their song on two Scriptural passages: Isaiah 53 and Philippians 2:6–11. There is no doubt who they thought the Lord was, as there is no doubt in my mind that the Lord is Jesus Christ of Nazareth. This for me is the challenge from Jehu in the meaning of his name.

> Emptied of His glory; God become a man,
> To walk on earth in ridicule and shame.
> A Ruler, yet a Servant; a Shepherd, yet a Lamb;
> A Man of Sorrows, agony and pain.
> Humbled and rejected, beaten, and despised.
> Upon the cross the Son of God was slain.
> Just like a lamb to slaughter, a sinless sacrifice;
> But, by His death His loss became our gain.
> Satan's forces crumbled like a mighty wall.
> The stone that held Him in was rolled aside.
> The Prince of life in glory was lifted over all,
> Now earth and heaven echoes with the cry.
> He is Lord, He is Lord!
> He is risen from the dead and He is Lord!
> Every knee shall bow, every tongue confess
> That Jesus Christ is Lord!

The "He" of Jehu is the "Him" of Hebrews 11:27: *"...for he endured, as seeing Him who is invisible."* Amen and Amen!

As I write this devotional, my Grandmother Barton is dying. When I think of her 91 years, the verse above came to my mind. To her the "Him" was Jesus Christ, as with Moses, as with Jehu: *"Esteeming the reproach of Christ greater riches than the treasures in Egypt: for he had respect unto the recompense of the reward."* (Hebrews 11:26) To her He made all the difference; He was the difference in her life. A widow of 34 years, she maintained her faith so wonderfully seen in her marriage that had been cut short in 1958. Like the rest of her family: who *"...have not seen, and yet believed..."* (John 20:29). Grammy kept her focus on Him all her life and gave to those of us who know Him and her an example of faith to follow (I Corinthians 11:1). I have said for years that if I should choose to depart from the faith, I would be without excuse before the Lord simply because of the example of my one grandmother. I had plenty of examples in my life, but one example like Maude would be enough. She could have used a number of excuses to denounce the Faith, but she didn't and for that I am grateful because, when it has gotten tough, I have thought back on Grammy's life, and I have said if she could stay focused on Him so can I, and I have because it is all about Him, not about us, and if we stay true to Him, then we will stay true to the Faith!

Jesus used a very special word to describe those who, though not seeing Him, still believed in Him, and that word was **"blessed"** (John 20:29). So many have faltered and fallen since they believed. If you would reread I Timothy, you will find the word **"some"** repeated over and over again (1:3, 1:6, 4:1, 5:15, 6:10, and 6:21). There has been and always will be **"some"** of every generation who depart, turn back, fall, but there will also be **"some"** that will not, like Grammy, who kept her eye on Jesus, her heart in the Faith, and her mind set on things above (Colossians 3:2). Grammy never saw Jesus like Thomas, but she still believed. Her faith was never reinforced with a visit like Paul, but she still trusted Him to the end. Grammy had a long pilgrimage turning her sin over to Him in her teens and accepting His Spirit into her life as a young person. Some lives are sprints while others like Grammy's are marathons. The words of James McGranatan say well what my Grandmother Barton believed, and how she lived her marathon, and I quote: **"I believed His reconciled face; believed in His message of pardon and peace; I believed, and I kept on believing!"**

I have decided that at her funeral I have been given the privilege of leading by my family, I will share with her loved ones a poem I found in the flyleaf of her husband Roy's Bible that she gave to me many, many years ago. In that old, well-worn Bible, I learned of an uncle I had never heard of before because he had died nearly thirty years before I was even born. His name was Benjamin Barton, and he was a World War One veteran that had after "the war to end all wars" decided to be a pioneer missionary to Peru. However, less than a year after he arrived in Peru he came down with a lung condition that took his life before he was able to return to Maine. It seems at his funeral this poem was read, and my grandfather had kept it in his Bible till his death when his first grandson was given the Bible. I will resurrect the poem at Grammy's funeral. The poem is all about those who would desire and delight in being "...*faithful unto death*" (Revelation 2:10) and for those who lived "...*as seeing Him!*" I believe that even to a soldier like Jehu these words would have a familiar ring to them.

> We weep not for him [her] that his [her] warfare is done,
> That the battle is finished, and the victory is won;
> For to those that his [her] heart loved the most,
> He [she] never gave up, he [she] died at his [her] post.
> Almost gone is his [her] family, and the friends of his [her] youth,

Yet there remains a legacy of love, loyalty, and truth.
His [her] faith put to flight the alien host,
But he [she] died like a soldier, he [she] fell at his [her] post.
He [she] asks not for statute, or sculpture, or verse,
He [she] asks not his [her] life or merits rehearse.
He [she] asks but when he [she] would have given up the ghost,
That his [her] family might know he [she] died at his [her] post.
Victorious he [she] died, for he [she] rose as he [she] fell,
With Him thou unseen, in heaven to dwell.
He [she] has crossed the great sea, he [she] has stepped on golden coast,
To take up station there, to claim his [her] new post.
And shall we the words of our loved one forget,
Oh, no, they be fresh in our memory yet.
An example like his [hers] shall be our constant boast.
We shall return to our work, we shall return to our post!

Are you at your post? Are you still serving the One that died for you? Is Jesus your "Him?" You might not have seen Him, but that doesn't mean you still can't believe in Him.

John 3:16: *"For God so loved the world, that He gave His only begotten Son, that whosoever believeth in Him should not perish, but have everlasting life."*

68.

ISMAIAH: THE LORD HEARS

I Chronicles 12:4: *"And **ISMAIAH** the Gibeonite, a mighty man among the thirty, and over the thirty; Jeremiah, and Jahazial, and Johanan, and Josabad the Gederathite."*

AFTER DAVID FLED FROM King Saul in his early twenties, he began to assemble a mercenary army around him of "mighty men of valor" who would eventually assist him in attaining the throne of Israel (I Chronicles 11:10). The first group joined David at the Cave of Adullam and was a force of *"…about four hundred men."* (I Samuel 22:2) I have come to believe that these four hundred were actually an answer to David's prayer recorded in Psalm 142: *"I looked on my right hand, and beheld, but there was no man that would know me; refuge failed me, no man cared for my soul."* (Psalm 142:4) Like Elijah after him, David felt he was alone, just like Elijah felt he was alone, but neither was alone. Remember, Elijah had seven thousand friends (I Kings 19:18), and David's friends would soon number in the thousands as well. God had heard their supplications.

A number of years later David had moved out of Israel because the threat on his life had intensified with King Saul's passionate pursuit of his former armor bearer (I Samuel 16:21). David fled with his men to the king of Gath and became a mercenary captain for King Achish (I Samuel 27). Hiring his men out to Achish resulted in the Philistine king giving David his own town, a place called Ziklag. It was to that place the second great group of men joined David's band (I Chronicles 12:1–2), and these are the men we have been highlighting and underlining in the past few devotionals. By now David's force had grown to over 600 (I Samuel 27:2).

If we compare the two numbers, 400 at Adullam and now 600 at Ziklag, we come to the conclusion that I Chronicles 12 is giving us some of the names of the two hundred plus that come to David at Ziklag. We have already introduced to you the Benjamin Band, now it is time to introduce you to the Gibeonite Group, and we will start with their commander Ismaiah. Again, I believe this leader and his men were in direct answer to David's appeal to God for helpers (I Chronicles 12:18).

As we have shared many times throughout this lengthy expedition into the history of David's "mighty men," David drew warriors to his side not only from the tribes of Israel, but from indigenous people groups from Canaan itself. Ismaiah was not a Benjamite or even from David's tribe of Judah. The first thing mentioned about this "mighty man" is his race, Gibeonite, or a resident of the Amorite city of Gibeon. It was Ismaiah's ancestors that had tricked Joshua into making an alliance with them in the early days of the war for the control of Canaan. These crafty people had survived annihilation by convincing Joshua that they actually lived in a far off and distant land (Joshua 9), when in reality they were just a few miles from Joshua's latest conquest, Ai. If the march of the Hebrews would have continued as God had originally planned, the next city on Joshua's hit list was Gibeon. If that peace treaty hadn't been signed, then Ismaiah would never have been born. In an amazing twist of God's providence, Ismaiah's forefathers lived to produce a soldier that would eventually help David attain what Joshua and his armies never did--the mastery of Canaan.

Though we have no knowledge of any of Ismaiah's military exploits, we are told that he was given command over a group called "the thirty." We have seen this number used before in a description of the first group of "mighty men" (II Samuel 23:24). I have come to believe that "the thirty" was a unit description or a grouping of David's warriors that fought together. Maybe, a special force unit (I Chronicles 11:25) that was called on for dangerous missions when a small group was needed versus the entire army. Ismaiah was "a mighty man among the thirty" and "over the thirty." David seemingly chose his "mighty men" based on ability, not race; skills, not residence, and character, not background. Men like Ismaiah should be an inspiration to us all. Despite his background (from a cursed race) and his birth certificate (born among slaves-Joshua 9:21), Ismaiah attained to a position of honor for himself and his race by turning to and accepting God's man for the kingship of Israel. So, too, must we. We are born into a cursed race (John 8:44) and born into the depraved family of sinners (Ephesians 2:1). God sent His only begotten Son to be the captain of our salvation (Hebrews 2:10). Have you joined Jesus' band yet? Have you taken up arms against your old master? If like Ismaiah, you switch sides, you, too, will one day be a part of the winning side!

I find it interesting that every time we begin another group of "mighty men," the meaning of their names fit in nicely to the narrative of our spiritual thoughts. David's "mighty men" were in direct results to intercession and supplication, and Ismaiah means "The Lord Hears." David would write in another psalm: *"The Lord will hear when I call unto Him."* (Psalm 4:3) I do not know when the Lord heard the heart cry of David for the first time, and I know not when the Almighty heard the heart cry of Ismaiah for the first time, but I believe there was a time like with me. Jew or Gentile, it makes no difference because God is always listening for a genuine call, a soul's cry. We have highlighted before God's tasks as He gathers and gains a representative from every nation and race (Revelation 5:9 and 7:9). I don't know if Ismaiah was the first Gibeonite saved, just like I don't know if Ruth was the first Moabite saved, but I do know this, it all started when a cry was made to a listening God. Because God never slumbers or sleeps, the cry will be heard. I love the story of Elijah on Mount Carmel when he gave the priests of Baal the first chance to stir their god into action. They cried and call for most of a day, but no response from the fire god of Canaan. Surely, it would be easy for a fire god to give fire, but there was no reply to their prayers and supplications (I Kings 18). It appeared that Baal couldn't hear.

Then it was Elijah's turn and after constructing the altar, he made a short supplication and before he ended his prayer the fire fell (I Kings 18:36–38). Why? Because Elijah believed in the Lord that hears. Do you believe in such a God? Is that the reason Ismaiah's parents gave him the name they did? Had they converted first? If they did, they were not the first to switch gods because of what Jehovah had done. Remember Rahab converted, not because of the spies, but because of what she had heard about what Jehovah had done for the children of Israel (Joshua 2:8–11). I find it interesting that in many of the conversion stories of the Bible the one that converts, converts because of some attribute of God. The seeing God was the reason that Hagar converted (Genesis 16:13). How many convert because the Almighty has a great ear? He is a great listener! It is so nice to know that when I open my heart, I know someone is listening to my plea, my concerns, my needs, and my feelings. As I rewrite (I first compiled this series in 1998, but updated the series in 2016 and now finally getting it to press in 2025) this article, I am watching my 39-year-old son die of lung and liver cancer. (2017) It has been a comfort to know that I can share my heart concerns and my questions about this trial to "a listening God."

Psalm 65:2: *"O thou that hearest prayer, unto Thee shall all flesh come."*

69.

JEREMIAH: JEHOVAH IS HIGH

I Chronicles 12:4: *"And Ismaiah the Gibeonite, a mighty man among the thirty, and over the thirty;* **JEREMIAH**, *and Jahazial, and Johanan, and Josabad the Gederathite."*

THE SECOND MAN IN the Gibeonite Group, as I am calling them, is the first of the "four Js: Jeremiah. Note, unlike so many of these "mighty men," there is nothing added, just *"...and Jeremiah..."* Interestingly, before we are through our search we will discover that David had three "mighty men" by the name of Jeremiah (I Chronicles 12:10, 13). Jeremiah is a popular Biblical name with at least nine men recorded, including the most famous Jeremiah of them all, the "weeping" prophet of Israel (Jeremiah 1:1). The others are:

1. The grandfather of King Jehoahaz of Israel (II Kings 23:31).
2. A man who was the head of the Manassite family (I Chronicles 5:24).
3. The father of Jaazaniah (Jeremiah 35:3).
4. A priest who settled in Judah (Nehemiah 12:1).
5. A leader who helped to rebuild the walls of Jerusalem (Nehemiah 12:34).

For this Jeremiah, we will simply focus our attention on the basic meaning (Jehovah is High) of the name Jeremiah as we have on other "mighty men" in whom we only have a name. Paul wrote this in Hebrews

7:26: *"For such an High Priest became us, who is holy; harmless, undefiled, separate from sinners and made 'higher' than the heavens."*

I know that I am sounding like a broken recorded after this lengthy expedition and exploration into a list of David's "mighty men" by showing you again another meaning of one of David's famous soldiers with a connection to Jesus Christ, or at least a connection to the meaning of their name. Paul also wrote to the Church at Ephesus these words: *"And what is the exceeding greatness of His power to us-ward who believe, according to the working of His mighty power, which He wrought in Christ, when He raised Him from the dead, and set Him at His own right hand in the heavenly places, far above all principalities, and power, and might, and dominion, and every name that is named, not only in this world, but also in that which is to come: hath put all things under His feet..."* (Ephesians 1:19–22). Perhaps, there is no better definition or description given in the Bible for the doctrine of "higher" than these stirring words by the pen of Paul. In the original, Greek, the word is *hupselos* which means "high or lofty." Certainly this is a fitting adjective for the exaltation due our Lord Jesus Christ, our Jeremiah.

Paul would go on to write to the saints in Ephesus these thoughts: *"He that descended is the same also that ascended up far above all heavens, that He might fill all things."* (Ephesians 4:10) We could look at this attainment of Christ as a form of edification of the position and place Christ now holds in the heavenlies, but I have decided in this chapter on the "mighty man" Jeremiah to look at this truth as a form of encouragement. I take my inspiration from the writing of the great English preacher and author Charles Haddon Spurgeon. Whenever I come up short on a particular Scriptural subject, I get out my Spurgeon books and see what this mighty man of letters writes on the topic I am seeking a truth about. Spurgeon makes these marvelous observations on "Jehovah is High," and I quote:

> Most of us know what it is to be overwhelmed in heart; emptied as when a man wipeth a dish and turneth it upside down; submerged and thrown on our beam ends like a vessel mastered by the storm. Discoveries of inward corruption will do this, if the Lord permits the great deep of our depravity to become troubled and cast up mire and dirt. Disappointments and heartbreak will do this when billows after billow rolls over us, and we are like the broken shell hurled to and fro by the surf. Blessed be God, at such seasons we are not without an all-sufficient solace, our

> God is the harbor of weather-beaten sails; the hospice of forlorn pilgrims, higher than we are is He: His mercy higher than our sins, His love higher than out thoughts. It is pitiful to see men putting their trust in something lower than themselves, but our confidence is fixed upon an exceeding high and glorious Lord. A Rock He is since He changes not and a high Rock, because the tempests which overwhelm us roll far beneath at His feet; He is not disturbed by them, but rules them at His will, if we get under the shelter of this lofty Rock we may defy the hurricane; all is calm under the lee of that towering cliff. Alas! Such is the confusion in which the troubled mind is often cast, that we need piloting to this divine shelter!

Did I not say these were meaningful and inspiring words to a troubled soul?

The key is the understanding of the concept of "higher" and its relationship to our High Priest and the lofty position He now holds at the right hand of the Father. How is it possible for any enemy, including Satan himself, to soar higher than where Christ sits? Any military man would tell you that the "high ground" is always the best ground in a fight. If Christ commands the "high" ground in every battle, and He is always looking down and not up at our problems or trials, surely, we can see how this would be the greatest news to any child of God. It is time we teach this doctrine, expound this theology to our brothers and sisters in Christ. I believe this was the purpose of William G. Fischer's classic Church hymn entitled <u>The Rock That is Higher Than I</u>. I have loved theology put to music for most of my life, but music without a message is just a tune. Note carefully the doctrine of this hymn with the meaning of Jeremiah.

> O sometimes the shadows are deep,
> And rough seems the path to the goal;
> And sorrows, sometimes how they sweep,
> Like tempests down over the soul!
> O sometimes how long seems the day,
> And sometimes how weary my feet;
> But toiling in life's dusty way,
> The Rock's blessed shadow, how sweet!
> O near to the Rock let me keep,
> If blessings or sorrows prevails;
> Or climbing the mountain-way steep,
> Or walking the shadowy vale.
> O then to the Rock let me fly,
> To the Rock that is higher than I;

O then to the Rock let me fly,
To the Rock that is higher than I!

Fischer had but one source for the theme of his song and that was the word of God itself. I believe that it was David, the David of the "mighty men," that first recognized this truth about his Jehovah. It was not Spurgeon either, but the master of the mighty men that found in his God a level that was far above anything he would face. Have you the Rock?

Psalm 61:2: *"From the end of the earth will I cry unto Thee, when my heart is overwhelmed: lead me to the Rock that is higher than I."*

70.

JAHAZIEL: GOD REVEALS

I Chronicles 12:4: *"And Ismaiah the Gibeonite, a mighty man among the thirty, and over the thirty; Jeremiah, and **JAHAZIEL**, and Johanan, and Josabad the Gederathite."*

THE SECOND OF THE four 'Js' is Jahaziel and like the man before him his name is all we have with its meaning, "God reveals." I will once again make an application to the Person of Jesus Christ in this meaning. As we know, the Lord Jesus Christ came to "reveal" the Father and His message to mankind: *"For He taught them as one having authority, and not as the scribes."* (Matthew 7:29)

The story is told about the famous eighteenth century philosopher and skeptic David Hume that underscores this term associated with the Christ and the meaning of Jahaziel's name, as well as the strange relationship the man Jesus had with the people of His day. It seems that David Hume use to go to church on Sundays to hear the equally famous Scottish minister John Brown. David Hume's friends often rebuked him for this because it seemed to them a contradiction to Hume's philosophy. One day, David explained his unusual actions with these words: **"Well, I don't believe all that he says [speaking of the ultra-orthodox Brown], but he does! And once a week I like to hear a man who believes what he says."** Such was the case of the many that came to hear Jesus speak, to listen to His teaching and sermons. Few by the numbers ever believed what Jesus said, believed enough to follow him, but they knew He believed, and He was so much unlike the scribes of their day it was refreshing to hear a man that believed what He said.

I have always loved the response of the soldiers that were sent to arrest Jesus in the Temple: *"Then came the officers to the chief priests and Pharisees; and they said unto them, why ye have not brought him? The officers answered, NEVER MAN SPAKE LIKE THIS MAN."* (John 7:45-46) Christ's authoritative manner so captivated his audience that even His enemies were impressed. The soldiers were so caught up in what Jesus was saying they forgot why they had been sent to get him. Christ spoke in clear and confident tones, gracious and gentle sentences, and direct and dynamic speech. The people were so use to the uninspiring instruction of their scribes, when men like John the Baptist and Jesus of Galilee came along, they were captivated and drawn to them. Granted, they all didn't believe and become followers and many came for the miracles versus the messages (John 12:37), but they could tell between the sincerity of the Savior versus the insensitivity of the scribes. Someone has put this concept in this simple proverb: **"If you believe what you say, what you say will be more believable."**

What is exciting about this name for me is that we, too, have the authority to reveal God to others. Paul spoke of this when he wrote to the Church at Corinth these words: *"And my speech and my preaching was not with enticing words of man's wisdom, but in demonstration of the Spirit and of power."* (I Corinthians 2:4) One of the examples of the powerless Church in the 21st century is the lack of conviction in the pews and the pulpit. There were times when men of God spoke with authority, and the world listened, the saved and the unsaved alike. Dennis DeHaan wrote this little poem with this theme:

Christ spoke with great power to all who drew near,

> His message was one that they needed to hear.
> And we who share the good news of His love,
> Must speak with conviction and power from above!

We must like Christ speak in simplicity of speech and message. We must open our hearts to our audience, as well as our heads. We must demonstrate to them that we really believe in what we are sharing with them; that the Christ we are telling them about is our best friend and that what He can do for them He has already done for us. Only then will they realize that what we are saying to them about our Savior is true and right and the best thing they, too, can believe in. Only then will they see and understand the authority by which we speak, and the authority that can be theirs in a heart-felt belief in the Lord Jesus Christ as their Lord and

Savior. Only then can we sincerely reveal the revealing God to a people lost in sin and blinded by Satan (II Corinthians 4:4).

"And when He was come into His own country, he taught them in their synagogue, insomuch they were astonished, and said, whence hath this man this wisdom, and these mighty works?" (Matthew 13:54) Wherever and whenever Jesus taught the people, the Gospel writers seem to agree on the crowd's reaction with astonishment. Why? Because he was revealing God to them in Himself. *"And they were astonished at His doctrine: for He taught them as one that had authority, and not as the scribes."* (Mark 1:22) *"And they were astonished at His doctrine: for His word was with power."* (Luke 4:32) The Greek word here is *ekplessomai* meaning "to strike significantly, to be exceedingly struck in mind." Today, we might simply use the word "amazed." *"And were beyond measure astonished, saying, He hath done all things well: He maketh both the deaf to hear, and the dumb to speak."* (Mark 7:37) His message not only brought amazement, but His miracles had the exact same effect on the people. Though He impressed the people in general, the Bible also tells us that not all the people were impressed. *"And the scribes and chief priests heard it, and sought how they might destroy Him: for they feared Him, because all the people were astonished at His doctrine."* (Mark 11:18) Still today, there are those who stand back and mock the miracles and the message of the Christ. I wonder if there are those who can never be astonished at anything or that anything or anyone could really reveal God to them?

One day you, too, will stand before Him, but will you like Charles Gabriel say in song:

> I stand amazed in the presence
> Of Jesus the Nazarene,
> And wonder how he could love me,
> A sinner condemned unclean.
> How marvelous! How wonderful!
> And my song shall ever be:
> How marvelous! How wonderful!
> Is my Savior's love for me!

Will you be astonished or will you, like the scribes and the Pharisees, be unaffected and unimpressed before the Almighty God? Jesus came as a trial run to see the reaction of the human race to "God with Us" (Matthew 1:23). One day we will be with God. What an honor, what a privilege, that God revealed Himself through His Son to us, and just as honoring is the commission He gave us to reveal the Almighty God through Jesus Christ.

We have some even among the Church that teach that God keeps secrets, but at the core of "God Reveals" is the truth that we have a God that loves to reveal: *"...He giveth wisdom unto the wise, and knowledge to them that know understanding. He revealeth the deep and secret things..."* (Daniel 2:21–22). There you have it, "the revealing God," and He did it best when He sent His only begotten Son to earth at Christmas time to reveal God to us. As I write this article it is Christmas time again, and once again the world is more astonished about Santa Claus than the babe of Bethlehem. Despite a revealing, some things never change!

Matthew 7:28: *"And it came to pass, when Jesus had ended these sayings, the people were astonished at His doctrine."*

71.

JOHANAN: THE LORD IS GRACIOUS

I Chronicles 12:4: *"And Ismaiah the Gibeonite, a mighty man among the thirty, and over the thirty; Jeremiah, and Jahaziel, and* **JOHANAN***, and Josabad the Gederathite."*

OUR THIRD "J" WARRIOR is Johanan. Someone has defined "grace" as "that action of God by which He withholds a deserved penalty and alleviates suffering and distress." The Psalmist wrote of God with these glowing words: *"The Lord is merciful and gracious, slow to anger, and plenteous in mercy."* (Psalm 103:8) In the life of this single "mighty man" the depth of this kind of grace can be clearly seen in the meaning of his name, the Lord is gracious. Would you return with me once again to the Life of Christ and witness the wondrous attribute of grace demonstrated in the meaning of this warrior's name.

After having been rejected by the leaders of his hometown of Nazareth (Matthew 15:1–20), Jesus left Galilee for a short trip into the region of Tyre and Sidon, the ancient territory of the Phoenicians. We would call this area Southern Lebanon today. Laidlaw in his fine commentary says that "Jesus' ministry was going through a 'change' in relationship between the balances between the message of Christ and the miracles of Jesus; that the year of success and the year of opposition had changed. That His labors consist henceforth of a succession of tours and journeys." I, too, believe that Jesus had left his home country for a period of rest and concealment (Mark 6:31). His grueling schedule often forced Him into periods of relaxation (we often forget that despite being the Son of God, Jesus had humbled Himself into the body of mortal man with all of its limitations and restrictions), and His new-found fame into a needed quiet place where nobody knew Him; however, "...*His fame went throughout all Syria.*" (Matthew 14:24) With Syria being to the east of Galilee, Jesus decided to go west into a region with perhaps less recognition, but it seems, though He wasn't as well known, He wasn't unknown. Lockyer writes: "He could not hide. Concealment for Him was impossible the more He became known. Who can hide the glory of the sun? As Light, Jesus could not be buried in a world of darkness. So great a Physician could not be unnoticed in a world of suffering! As the fragrance of flowers cannot be hid, how could He?" As Johanan has seemingly been hidden in the middle of a long list of the names of David's "mighty men," he can't be hidden despite being 71 on that list, just like God's great grace cannot be hidden. As with Johanan, so with God's grace; everybody eventually come to it and finds in it the warmth and glow of a warming attribute of God that is beyond deserving and favor.

How often people fail to get God's amazing grace simply because they have not come in genuine faith. Grace is a valuable virtue that Christ gives out to those who sincerely want it and reach for it by faith. Jesus meets a woman on His journey to the seaside of the Mediterranean. What makes this a wonderful story is how Jesus was able to look beyond the physical need of her daughter because to heal the daughter was the easy part, but to heal the soul of this lady, therein lies the greatest miracle of this story. So what are the qualities that bring the grace of God out into the light of any given day?

First, **there has to be worship** (Matthew 15:25). Three times this Gentile addresses Jesus as "Lord" (Matthew 15:22, 25, 27). Until we see Jesus for who He really is, grace cannot really be revealed or received! "Lord" is a title that reveals the woman's respect and reverence for the Christ. Also in recognizing the Christ as "the Son of David," she acknowledged in this Prophet of Nazareth as one who was willing to go beyond the limits of Galilee and, perhaps, help her in her need. Oh, that we would realize that our Blessed Lord was willing to cross the frontier of space, leave the glory of Heaven, and die on a cruel cross to heal us from the disease of sin. Surely such a one is worthy of worship! The Lord of grace!

Second, **there has to be humility** (Matthew 15:27). Instead of being insulted by Jesus' statement, she humbled herself to the designation and seeing the insult of being called "a dog." Someone has written this about Jesus' demeanor in His encounter with the Canaanite woman: "Behind a frowning countenance, He hides a smiling face!" Did this mother see through the exterior of harshness to the interior of grace? Humility is a basic virtue that few possess, but this hurting mother had plenty of it. So many like Naaman (II Kings 5) reject God's cure at first because they can't humble themselves to take a dip in a dirty Jordan. One must be humble to receive grace (James 4:6).

Third, **there has to be faith** (Matthew 15:28). *"But without faith it is impossible to please Him, for he* [or she] *that cometh to God must believe that he is, and that he is the rewarder of them that diligently seek Him."* (Hebrews 11:6) Was it a desperate faith like the woman with the issue of blood or a dynamic faith like the Roman centurion with the sick servant? This mother was certainly desperate over the fact that her daughter had a demon that couldn't be controlled, but like the Gentiles before her this lady did possess a marvelous faith, an exemplary faith like the mother of Zarephath (I Kings 17) and the mother of Shunem (II Kings 4). This mother from Tyre and Sidon was willing to overcome all obstacles and endure all insults to see that her daughter was healed, even if that meant trusting in a total stranger from Galilee. Note carefully that like the centurion her faith was acknowledged by Jesus as something special.

This Canaanite mother met and adhered to all the major precepts needed to fulfill the requirements for grace to flow freely from Jesus to her daughter. I like the way Mark addressed this principle when writing of the woman with the issue of blood: *"And Jesus, immediately knowing in Himself that virtue had gone out of Him…"* (Mark 5:30). What virtue? The virtue of grace had left Him triggered by the faith of the lady. Is the reason you have not received grace because you have no faith, no humility, and no worship in you? The Psalmist has written: *"But I have trusted in thy mercy; my heart shall rejoice in Thy salvation* [deliverance which might include healing]. *I will sing unto the Lord, because he hath dealt bountifully with me."* (Psalm 16:5–6) In the conclusion of his commentary on this miracle Herbert Lockyer gives this insightful observation on the lessons we must learn from this woman from Lebanon, and I believe from the meaning of "The Lord is gracious."

> The secret of blessing is lying low at the feet of Him from whom we deserve nothing. Born of a sinful stock and individually guilty of sin, we have no claim on God except for judgment. But if we humbly acknowledge our guilt and need in virtue of

all He accomplished on our behalf, He will abundantly pardon. Another lesson is that of the reward for persistent faith-the faith that changes despair into the full assurance of hope-the faith that overcame all obstacles like silence, exclusion, and apparent reproach- the faith in Christ's willingness and ability to understand us!

What more can I say about this wonderful attribute of our gracious God other than to ask if you have yet applied for it. A day is coming when you will not be able to help yourself or another, so where will you turn for help. The mother of the demonic daughter turned to Jesus through worship, humility, and faith. You would do well to do the same.

Exodus 22:27: *"When he crieth unto me, that I will hear; for I am gracious!"*

72.

JOSABAD: THE LORD HAS BESTOWED

I Chronicles 12:4: *"And Ismaiah the Gibeonite, a mighty man among the thirty, and over the thirty; Jeremiah, and Jahaziel, and Johanan, and **JOSABAD** the Gederathite."*

Our last "J" of the quartet of "Js" that were led by David's "mighty man" Ismaiah is a "mighty man" from the village of Gederah (Joshua 15:36) by the name of Josabad. A simple name with this simple meaning, "the Lord has bestowed." I draw this connection with Jesus and Josabad with this verse in John's first epistle: *"Behold, what manner of love the Father hath **bestowed** upon us, that we should be called the sons of God; therefore the world knoweth us not, because it knew Him not."* (I John 3:1) Come along with me again as I try to make a link between the meaning of Josabad's name and our Lord and Savior Jesus Christ.

There is no doubt, I believe, in the Bible that the Eternal Lord is a great **"bestower."** The very first thought that came to me as I began to ponder the significance of this name and the meaning of this name were the words of Annie Johnson Flint put together with the music of Hubert Mitchell in the song <u>He Giveth More Grace</u>:

> He giveth more grace when the burdens grow greater;
> He sendeth more strength when the labors increase.
> To added affliction He addeth His mercy;
> To multiplied trials His multiplied peace.
> When we have exhausted our store of endurance,
> When our strength has failed ere the day is half done.

> When we reach the end of our hoarded resources,
> Our Father's full giving is only begun.
> His love has no limit; His grace has no measure;
> His power has no boundary known unto men.
> For out of His infinite riches in Jesus,
> He giveth, and giveth, and giveth again!

That song, to me, speaks of the many virtues God **bestows** on mankind through Jesus Christ: grace (Titus 2:11), strength (Philippians 4:13), mercy (Romans 9:15), and peace (John 14:27), but the one that I would like to zero in on in this devotion is love (John 3:16) (*"Behold, what manner of love the Father has **bestowed** upon us...".*). In my opinion, there is no greater honor a human being can have than to be *"called the son[s] of God"* (John 1:12). This distinction granted to the believer in Christ is **bestowed** in love because there is no worthiness in ourselves (Romans 3:23). Phillip's paraphrase of I John 3:1 says this: "Consider the incredible love that the Father has shown us in allowing us to be called 'children of God'-and that is not just what we are called, but what we are!" I love that thought, "but what we are." An old song of my youth says: **"Now I belong to Jesus, Jesus belongs to me; not for years of time alone, but for eternity!"**

As I continued to ponder the meaning of this name, another song came to my mind. Perhaps, there has been no better defining of God's love in a hymn than Frederick M. Lehman's classic <u>The Love of God</u>. Kenneth W. Osbeck gives these insightful thoughts on the history behind this wonderful song:

> Never has God's eternal love been described more vividly than in the words of this greatly loved hymn: "measureless," "strong," "evermore endure." The unusual third stanza of the hymn was a small part of an ancient lengthy poem composed in 1096 by a Jewish songwriter, Rabbi Mayer, in Worms, Germany. The poem entitled <u>Hadamut</u> was written in the Arabic language. The lines were found one day in revised form on the walls of a patient room in an insane asylum after the patient's death. The opinion has since been that the unknown patient, during time of sanity, adapted from the Jewish poem what is now the third verse of "the Love of God." The words of this third stanza were quoted one day at a Nazarene camp meeting. In the meeting was Frederick M. Lehman, a Nazarene pastor, who described his reaction: "The profound depths of the lines moved us to preserve the words for future generations. Not until we had come

to California did this urge find fulfillment and that at a time when circumstances forced us to hard manual labor. One day, during short intervals of inattention to our work, we picked up a scrap of paper and added the first two stanzas and chorus to the existing third stanza.

Pastor Lehman completed the hymn in 1971. His daughter Claudia (Mrs. W. W. Mays) assisted with the music:

> The love of God is greater far than tongue or pen can ever tell.
> It goes beyond the highest star and reaches to the lowest hell.
> The guilty pair, bowed down with care, God gave His Son to win.
> His erring child He reconciled and pardoned from his sin.
> When years of time shall pass away and earthly thrones and kingdoms fall.
> When men, who here refuse to pray, on rocks and hills and mountains call.
> God's love so sure shall still endure, all measureless and strong.
> Redeeming grace to Adam's race-the saints and angels song.
> **Could we with ink the oceans fill and were the skies of parchment made.**
> **Were every stalk on earth a quill and every man a scribe by trade.**
> **To write the love of God above would drain the oceans dry.**
> **Nor could the scroll contain the whole though stretched from sky to sky.**
> Oh, love of God, how rich and pure!
> How measureless and strong!
> It shall forevermore endure
> The saints and angel's song.

I will give the last word of this devotional into the skilled hands of the great English pastor and author, Charles Haddon Spurgeon, and his comments on John's classic verse in I John 3:1: "'Behold, what manner of love the Father hath bestowed upon us.' Consider who we were, and what we feel ourselves to be even now when corruption is powerful in us, and you will wonder at our adoption. Yet we are called 'the sons of God.' What a high relationship is that of a son, and what privileges it brings! What care and tenderness the son expects from his father, and what love the father feels towards the son! But all that and more than that, we have through Christ."

II Corinthians 8:1: *"Moreover, brethren, we do you to wit of the grace of God bestowed on the churches of Macedonia."*

73.

ELUZAI: GOD IS MY STRENGTH

I Chronicles 12:5: *"**ELUZAI**, and Jerimoth, and Bealiah, and Shemariah, and Shepatiah the Haruphite."*

WE CONTINUE ON WITH just a list of names that are associated with David's "mighty men" (I Chronicles 12:1) in connection to David's adopted home of Ziklag. The next in this accounting is the "mighty man" Eluzai and all we have to go on is the meaning of his name. We know not of his hometown, but he might be a part of the Benjamin Battalion (I Chronicles 12:2). We know not of any military exploits, but the one thing we do know is his name gives us another connection to the Christ: *"Saying, Amen: Blessing, and glory, and wisdom, and thanksgiving, and honour, and power, and might, be unto our God forever and ever. Amen."* (Revelation 7:12) The Greek word here for "might" is the word *ischus* which denotes according to Vine: "might, strength, power inherent and in action as used of God." *"And what is the exceeding greatness of his power to us-ward who believe, according to the working of His mighty power?"* (Ephesians 1:19) We have before us again a wonderful attribute and marvelous characteristic of our Lord and Savior Jesus Christ in the "mighty man" Eluzai.

Moses also asks a self-answering question: *"For what God is there in heaven and earth, that can do according to Thy works, and according to Thy might?"* (Deuteronomy 3:24) I like David's definition of "might" when he wrote: *"Thine, O Lord, is the greatness, and the power, and the glory, and the victory, and the majesty: for all that is in the heaven and in the earth is Thine; Thine is the kingdom, O Lord, and thou art exalted as head above all. Both riches and honor comes to thee, and thou reigneth over all; and in Thine hand is power and might; and in Thine hand it is to make great, and to give strength unto all."* (I Chronicles 29:11–12) King Jehoshaphat continued this theme when he said: *"O Lord God of our fathers, art not thou God in heaven? And in Thine hand is there not power and might, so that none is able to withstand Thee?"* (II Chronicles 20:6) It is for me the great prophet Isaiah that brings together the connection of God and Christ and this godly quality when he prophesied: *"And there shall come forth a rod out of the stem of Jesse, and a branch shall grow out of his roots: and the Spirit of the Lord shall rest upon Him, the Spirit of wisdom and understanding, the Spirit of counsel and might…"* (Isaiah 11:1–2). There is no question in the Old Testament that the Almighty God has all the power and strength, and now it was foretold in the coming of His Son that He would also have the Spirit of power, and might, and strength!

Christ is without a doubt "the strength of God." From His works of creation to His work of salvation, Christ demonstrated His might without question: *"Forasmuch as there is none like unto Thee, O Lord; Thou art great, and Thy name is great in might."* (Jeremiah 10:6) This would go along with Peter's conclusion when he made this statement to the Sanhedrin: *"…neither is there salvation in any other: for there is none other name under heaven given among men, whereby we must be saved."* (Acts 4:12) It is the might in the name of Jesus whereby our prayers are answered: *"If ye shall ask anything in my name, I will do it."* (John 14:14) That is our strength in prayer! Daniel, the great Babylonian politician, once said: *"Blessed be the name of God forever and ever; for wisdom and might are His!"* (Daniel 2:20) Besides the might of salvation and supplication, we also can be strengthened with His might" *"That He would grant you, according to the riches of His glory, to be strengthened with might by His Spirit in the inner man."* (Ephesians 3:16) Only by turning to Christ and relying upon His might can we have the strength to resist the pressures of temptation, the problems of tests, and the persistence of trials. The Lord God is our strength, and He is willing to strengthen us against all onslaughts, attacks, and assaults by the wicked one and the wicked ones. We desperately need in this age a strength that can overcome all pitfalls and plots against us. The theme of Christ's strength runs from one end of the New Testament to the last end. In the *"great" "new song"* (Revelation 5:9) that one day we will sing with the *"thousands and thousands"* of heaven (Revelation 5:11) this is a reoccurring stanza: *"…and strength…"* (Revelation 5:12–13). What a day that will be!

So in what areas did Jesus demonstrate His power, might, and strength? First, the Christ has strength over the dynamics of nature. His control over the terrible storms He and His disciples encountered at the Sea of Galilee demonstrates this power and strength (Mark 4:35–41). When He shouted: *"Peace, be still!"* (Mark 4:39) and the raging waves went dead calm and the howling wind dried up, this is power, this is might, this is strength! Certainly, only the Creator of wind and waves could accomplish such a feat. Add to that Jesus' amazing walk across that same body of water (Matthew 14:25); His feeding of the five thousand and the four thousand; and the changing of the water to wine (John 2:1–11), and you have enough illustrations to verify that the Christ was given *"...all power..."* (Matthew 28:18) over nature.

Second, the Christ has strength over the demonic spirits and Satan himself. There are countless examples in the Gospels of this power and strength, but the most dramatic in my opinion is the time Jesus released a man who was controlled by "a Legion" of demons (Mark 5:9). Not only did Jesus deliver that man from the grip of these creatures of hell, but in Jesus' conversation with this "legion" we discover in the verbal exchange that the devils must obey Christ, and they believed he was *"...the Son of the Most High God..."* (Mark 5:7). James tells us they "tremble" (James 2:19), and they certainly did that day because they knew that Jesus had the power and strength to cast them that moment into hell's fire. He cast them into the pigs instead, but never once was Jesus ever overpowered by a satanic spirit, not once, because of the strength of God in Him.

Third, Christ has strength over the diseases of the flesh. *"And His fame went throughout all Syria: and they brought unto Him all sick people that were taken with diverse diseases and torments...And those that had the palsy; and He healed them."* (Matthew 4:24) There was not a weakness of the flesh that Jesus could not heal. There was not an aliment of body or mind that Jesus could not cure. Jesus never missed a diagnosis, and He never failed to destroy all abnormalities of any man or women. Jesus was certainly "the Great Physician" because of his great power and Godly strength.

Fourth, Christ has strength even over death. First there was Jarius' daughter (Mark 5:21–43); then there was the widow of Nain's son (Luke 7:11–17); and of course Jesus' good friend Lazarus (John 11:1–46). Then there was Jesus' own death (John 10:17–18)! Each was a different case in detail and demonstration, but bottom line, they prove that Christ had and still has *"the keys of Death"* (Revelation 1:18). He still has the power and the might and the strength because Jesus Christ is the "God of my strength!"

Matthew 28:18: *"And Jesus came and spake unto them, saying, all power is given unto me in heaven and in earth."*

74.

JERIMOTH: ELEVATION

I Chronicles 12:5: *"Eluzai, and **JERIMOTH**, and Bealiah, and Shemariah, and Shepatiah the Haruphite."*

THE THIRTEENTH MEMBER OF what we are calling the Benjamin Battalion that followed David to the Philistine town of Ziklag was a "mighty man" named Jerimoth. Once again, all we know about this super soldier is the meaning of his name, elevation. One of my favorite new choruses was written by Jack Hayford, and it proclaims this message:

> Majesty, worship His majesty.
> Unto Jesus be all glory, honor, and praise.
> Majesty, kingdom authority,
> Flows from His throne unto His own;
> His anthems raise!
> So exalt, lift up on high the name of Jesus.
> Magnify, come glorify Christ Jesus, the king.
> Majesty, worship His majesty.
> Jesus who died, now glorified,
> King of all kings!

David might have been one of the first to use this grand word to describe the Almighty, but he would not be the last: *"Thine, O Lord, is the greatness, and the power, and the glory, and the victory, and the majesty..."* (I Chronicles 29:11). I believe this is at the heart of the meaning of Jerimoth's name, majesty, being lifted up, the One worthy to be elevated far above all others. Did not Paul say this about Jesus: *"Wherefore God also hath highly exalted him, and given Him a name which is above every name?"* (Philippians 2:9) The elevated One!

Rev. Jack Hayford gives this accounting of his writing the chorus of <u>Majesty</u>:

> In 1977, my wife Anna and I spent our vacation in Great Britain, travelling throughout the land from the south country and Wales to the northern parts of Scotland. It was the same year as Queen Elizabeth's 25th anniversary of her coronation, and symbols of royalty were abundantly present beyond the usual. As Anna and drove along together, at once the opening lyrics and melody of <u>Majesty</u> simply came to my heart, I seemed to feel something new of what it meant to be His: to be raised to a partnership with Him on His throne. Upon returning to our home in California, I was finally able to complete the song. <u>Majesty</u> describes the kingly, lordly, gloriously regal nature of our Saviour, but not simply as an objective statement in worship of which He is fully worthy, when begotten in spirit and in truth, can align us with His throne in such a way that His kingdom authority flows to us, to overflow us, to free us and channel through us. We are rescued from death, restored to the inheritance of sons and daughters, qualified for victory in battle against the adversary, and destined for the Throne forever in His presence.

I think why this song has become so special to me after the reading of its history is the fact that my wife and I spent our vacation in England, Scotland, and Wales in 2003 celebrating our 30th wedding anniversary. We, too, saw the royalty as we visited Buckingham Palace, the queen's ship the *Britannia*, and Hampton Court. But I came to the same conclusion that Hayford came to: **the royalist have nothing on the royalty of Christ**. They might be lifted high, elevated in the eyes of man, but Jesus Christ was exalted, elevated far above all other by the Father. It does us good to know where true elevation comes from!

In David's version of <u>Majesty</u>, he wrote such stanzas as: *"His glory is great in Thy salvation: honor and majesty hast thou laid upon Him."* (Psalm 21:5) *"The voice of the Lord is powerful; the voice of the Lord is full of majesty, with Thy glory and Thy majesty...And in Thy majesty ride prosperously because of truth and meekness and righteousness..."* (Psalm 45:3-4). *"Honor and majesty are before Him: strength and beauty are in His sanctuary."* (Psalm 96:6) *"Bless the Lord, O my soul. O Lord, my God, thou art very great; Thou art clothed with honor and majesty."* (Psalm

104:1) David recognized the exalted and elevated position of His God, and in word and song he proclaimed this truth. I often wonder if it wasn't the presence of Jerimoth and the meaning of his name that provoked David to speak so often of the uplifted Lord, the majesty of God in the truth of His great majesty. I feel that this truth also has a very practical application for our everyday lives.

When you see a friend or a family member discouraged, despondent, depressed, or dejected, his or her head is often bowed. I don't know what it is about our physical makeup that causes this, but when we are downcast, or cast down, often we demonstrate our emotional state by this physical reaction. Remember the classic 60's folk song that went: "Hang down your head, Tom Dooley, hang down your head and cry, hang down your head, Tom Dooley, poor boy you're going to die." Who of us has not felt that way a time or two? Yet David's psalm proclaims another truth: *"But Thou, O Lord, art a shield for me; my glory, and the lifter up of mine head."* (Psalm 3:3) I still remember this line from another boyhood song that said: "Hold your head up high. You'll never walk alone!" David was fleeing his own rebellious son, Absalom, when he wrote what has become known as the Third Psalm. He had every right to hang his head down low, feel defeated, yet he had someone on his side to keep his head lifted high. We, too, have "a lifter of the head" in the Person of Jesus Christ and his other name is Jerimoth, the elevator of the soul! Have you yet to experience the up life, the elevation you can get from the Christ?

F. B. Meyer, a favorite devotional writer of mine, once wrote this about "the lifter up of mine head:" "Thy head is drooping like a flower cup-it sadly needs the dexterous hand of the Gardner. God lifting up the tired and sorrowful face." James Rowe perhaps put it best in his classic Church hymn:

> I was sinking deep in sin, far from the peaceful shore.
> Very deeply stained within, sinking to rise no more.
> But the Master of the sea heard my despairing cry,
> From the waters lifted me, now safe am I.
> Love lifted me, love lifted me,
> When nothing else could help, love lifted me.
> Love lifted me, love lifted me,
> When nothing else could help, love lifted me.

Jamieson, Fausset, and Brown in their helpful commentary simply added these few words to the concept of the elevation of the Eternal One: **"One who raises me from despondency!"** How often I remember that at different periods of my life when things were not going as good as I had hoped, they would, too, get me "down;" down in the mouth, down in the heart, and downcast in my soul. My head would drop and droop, my step would slow and stutter, and my heart would ache and skip a beat. Without fail, God would send someone along to meet me on that difficult road that would quicken my step, soothe my soul, and lift my head! Unlike most animals on this planet, the Good Lord, the Great Creator, made us with an upward, forward, and onward look. Granted, you can look down, but, unlike most creatures, we can also look up. Our head and eyes were created to look up, not down. However, at times our head becomes so heavy with worry and fear that it becomes too burdensome to look up. Our shoulders droop, and our heads drop, and our eyes darken. Instead of seeing the "Son," we only see the gloom that has invaded our lives. That is when we need "the Lifter."

What do you see today? Only the ground before you; only the trouble about you; only the fear before you? What you need is to be elevated, lifted up, by the great "Lifter." Read carefully Matthew 11:28–30, and, if you will come to Jesus, He will lift you up!

Psalm 102:10: *"For Thou hast lifted me…"*

75.

BEALIAH: THE LORD IS LORD

I Chronicles 12:5: *"Eluzai, and Jerimoth, and **BEALIAH**, and Shemariah, and Shepatiah the Haruphite."*

Another name, another "mighty man," another interestingly meaning: "The Lord is Lord," and another opportunity to refocus our attention away from an unknown soldier to a known Savior. From the pen of Paul I was reminded of this: *"Which in His times He shall shew, who is the Blessed and only Potentate, the King of kings, and the Lord of lords!"* (II Timothy 6:15) I am only about three quarters of my way through this study, and I still am so amazed just how many of the men of David, through their names, have an application to my Lord and Savior Jesus Christ.

We will first start this insight into the meaning of **"the Lord is Lord"** with a few comments by a favorite devotional writer, a man you have heard from before, F. B. Meyer, a man of the nineteenth century that speaks a lot to us in the 21st century. I think his thoughts on *"No man can say that Jesus is Lord, but the Holy Ghost!"* (I Corinthians 12:3) apply here:

> Jesus is Saviour, but is He Lord? Have thou yielded to Him in Lordship? Nothing short of this will give thee true peace and power. Thou must be brought to say with the psalmist "other lords beside Thee have had dominion over me, but by Thee only will I make mention of Thy name." Jesus must be Lord of thy heart; every affection must be brought under His most wise and loving control. He must be Lord of thy home, so that no conversation may be indulged, no recreation set afoot, no society entertained, which is inconsistent with his character and claim.

He must be Lord in thy business and its return, so that thou shalt live in perpetual communication with Him, along the lines of the Heavenly Telephone; and in the use of all its proceeds He must have the supreme voice. He must be Lord of thy plans. It is for Him to say "go," "come," or "do this." That was a true message which Ahaseuerus sent though the good Ezra to the Jewish people, "Whatsoever is commanded by the God of Heaven, let it be done exactly for the house of the God of Heaven." I like the word **"exact!"** But this perpetual recognition of the Lordship of Jesus is only possible to those who have yielded their entire nature to the gracious influence of the Holy Spirit, who loves to glorify Christ. Doest thou seek the attitude of consecration which thou honours thy Lord? Then let the Holy Spirit work it for thee! Wouldst thou have it maintained? Let Him maintain it! And if thou askest thyself, whether thou hast received the Pentecostal endowment, be sure that thou hast, if with all thine heart thou sayest that Jesus Christ is Lord, to the glory of God the Father. This is the certain test!

Have you made Him "Lord" in the areas that Meyer suggests? If you haven't, then I feel you need to consider each category.

An unknown song writer many years ago gave the Church this simple, yet powerful chorus: "He is Lord, He is Lord! He is risen from the dead and He is Lord! Every knee shall bow, every tongue confess that Jesus Christ is Lord." No doubt inspired by these verses in Philippians: *"Wherefore God also hath highly exalted Him, and given Him a name which is above every name: that at the name of Jesus every knee should bow, of things in heaven, and things in earth, and things under the earth; and that every tongue should confess that Jesus Christ IS LORD, to the glory of God the Father."* (Philippians 2:9–11) If not now, there is a day coming when Jesus will be known as "The Lord is Lord!"

I will turn the next part of this article over to another favorite devotional author, and another author I have quoted often in this series of chapters on David's mighty men, Vance Havner. I feel he gives another insightful observation on the Lordship of Christ with these words:

> If I had only one sermon to preach it would be on the Lordship of Christ. When we get right on that point we are right all down the line. God honors the exaltation of His Son. Jesus Christ demands more complete allegiance than any dictator who ever lived. The difference is, He has a right to it. The heart of revival, of the deeper Christian life, of Christianity, is making

> Jesus Lord. Has He taken over in your heart? Perhaps He resides there, but does he preside? I came to Christ as a country boy. I did not understand all about the plan of salvation. One does not have to understand it; he has only to stand on it. I do not understand all about electricity but I do not intend sitting around in the dark until I do. But one thing I did understand even as a lad. I belonged to Christ and He was Lord. Here is the key to the sad state of many Christians and churches. There is a cheap, easy believism that does not believe and a receivism that does not receive. There is no real confession of Christ as Lord. It is significant that the word Saviour occurs only 24 times in the New Testament, while the word Lord is found 433 times...On the Damascus Road Paul started right when he asked: "Who art thou, Lord? Lord, what wilt thou have me to do?" He began by confessing Jesus as Lord. Thomas cried: "My Lord and my God!" John Wesley tells us that several mornings after Aldersgate he awoke with "Jesus, Master" in his heart and mouth. The Holy Spirit had done His work. Dr. E. Y. Mullins says: "In applying for membership in a Baptist Church, faith in Christ and acceptance of His Lordship is a prime condition.

I can only add a hearty Amen to everything Vance has written because I, too, believe the missing link today in Christianity is the importance of the doctrine and the theology in the Lordship of Christ.

I will give the final word in this chapter to another favorite devotional writer who wrote in a favorite devotional book, <u>Daily With My Lord</u>, W. Glyn Evans:

> So I must not cheat Jesus Christ, or myself. I must never bring myself down to the place where I say dismally: He bought my heart and I didn't love Him; He bought my body and I didn't serve Him; He bought my mind and I don't think of Him; He bought my will and I didn't yield to Him.

Oswald Chambers (another favorite spiritual writer of mine) said:

> The passion of Christianity is that I deliberately sign away my own rights and become a bond-slave of Jesus Christ. Until I do that, I do not begin to be a saint...The Cross of Christ-and its power-is fulfilled in me the moment I say yes to the sovereignty of Jesus Christ over me.

The sovereignty of Jesus Christ is the Lordship of Jesus Christ to me.

Until we see Jesus as Lord, until we accept Jesus as Lord, until we acknowledge Jesus as Lord, we will never be able to fulfill the purpose by which the Son of God died on Calvary for us. The Lordship of Jesus over my life is the key to a successful and victorious Christian life. Many see it as a burden, a restriction on their life, but in reality it is just the opposite because the Lordship of Christ brings with it amazing benefits that can only be enjoyed when Christ is "Lord of your life," "the Lord is Lord!" Have you ever noticed just how many of the epistles start with Jesus as Lord (Romans 1:3-I Corinthians 1:2, II Corinthians 1:2, Galatians 1:3, Ephesians 1:2, Philippians 1:2, Colossians 1:2, I Thessalonians 1:1, II Thessalonians 1:1, I Timothy 1:1, II Timothy 1:2, Philemon 3, James 1:1, I Peter, II Peter 1:2) and all within the first three verses!

Jude 4: *"...the only Lord God, and our Lord Jesus Christ."*

76.

SHEMARIAH: JEHOVAH GUARDS

I Chronicles 12:5: *"Eluzai, and Jerimoth, and Bealiah, and **SHEMA-RIAH**, and Shepatiah the Haruphite"*

SHEMARIAH'S NAME REMINDS ME of this verse from the Psalmist: *"He only is my Rock, and my Salvation; He is my Defense; I shall not be greatly moved."* (Psalm 62:2) The Hebrew word here is *misgab* which means "a place of defense, or a high tower." In the days of the writings of the Psalmists, a high place was usually an impregnable fortress. Without siege weapons, airplanes, or other mechanical devices like artillery to scale or break down a walled fort, a high place was a great refuge, whether manmade like David's fortress at Jerusalem or a natural sanctuary like Masada, these were defensive positions from which offensive attacks could also be launched. Our next "mighty man" in David's I Chronicles list is Shemariah and what a meaning we have in his name: Jehovah Guards. I feel we can turn this meaning into another wonderful challenge into the attributes of the Almighty. If you have God guarding you, who can get at you? I for years have claimed the amazing truth of: *"...except the Lord keep the city, the watchman waketh but in vain."* (Psalm 127:1) **Unless the Lord is your guard you guard in vain!**

David wasn't the first, or the last, to believe in this concept that "Jehovah is our Guard," but I believe he spoke of it more than any other Biblical writer. Because the old King James Version of the Bible only uses the word "defense," we sometimes miss out in the vast scope of this precept about Jehovah God. When David wrote: *"My defense is of God..."* (Psalm 7:10), he uses the Hebrew word *magen* which means shield. A shield in David's time was a defensive weapon used to protect the warrior from objects thrown at him by his enemy. So, not only will God be a high tower to you, He will also be a shield for you, a kind of double security, if you will. Picture a soldier inside a fort with a shield in his hand. The Detroit News once carried an article on the heliosphere, the magnetic force shield which protects our entire solar system from harmful cosmic rays. Generated by our own Sun, it is so huge that the US spacecraft Pioneer 10, which at that time had traveled more than 23 trillion miles, had not as yet passed beyond its protective shield. Without its protection, life on the earth, as we know it, would not exist. I stand amazed every time I learn something new about God's creative power and how He shielded our tiny planet from all harm, our position in our galaxy, the tilt of our earth, the distance from our Sun, and now this protective shield; certainly Jehovah Guards!

What is true of the heliosphere shield is also true of the divine shield. The Psalmist writes constantly in the Psalms: **"The Lord is my shield!"** Without Him, spiritual life as we know it could not exist on this wicked planet. Dangers more harmful than cosmic rays would soon destroy us. If it were not for the greatest protective defense of all, the Lord Jesus Christ, we would be open for attack and an assault by demonic forces beyond imagination. Jesus is our defensive shield, our defensive armor on this cruel and corrupt earth. In a recent study of the Christian armor described by the Apostle Paul in Ephesians 6:10–18, I came to the conclusion that when we put on that massive spiritual armor, we are simply putting on Christ. I feel Paul confirms this truth in this statement: *"And let us put on the armor of light…but put you on the Lord Jesus Christ, and make no provision for the flesh, to fulfill the lust thereof."* (Romans 13:14) And again: *"For as many of you as have been baptized unto Christ have put on Christ."* (Galatians 3:27) With these truths in mind, we can say with David: *"But Thou O Lord, art a shield for me…"* (Psalm 3:3).

This shield is no guarantee that we won't be attacked or assaulted, but behind it is a perfect safety place from which all assaults and attacks can be repelled, all advances of the Wicked One stopped. Like the *"shield of faith"* (Ephesians 6:16), it will be able to *"…quench all the fiery darts of the wicked."* As the earth is being bombarded with cosmic rays constantly, so, too, Satan and his demons are bombarding the Christians with temptations, evil thoughts, and wicked trials of every sort daily. But as most of us take no notice of the cosmic rays or the heliosphere, so, too, most of the temptations, evil thoughts, and wicked trials go unnoticed.

Remember Job's "hedge" (Job 1:10)? Long before these "fiery darts" reach us they are deflected, or quenched, by the protective shield, defense of the Holy Spirit of Christ, and only those that God allows will be let through for the trying of our faith (I Peter 2:6). I like this concept through the pen of Paul: *"For the mystery of lawlessness* [that hidden principle of rebellion against constituted authority] *is already at work in the world, but it is restrained only until He* [the Holy Spirit] *who restrains is taken out of the way."* (II Thessalonians 2:7) As the heliosphere restrains the solar system's cosmic rays from getting to us, so, too, does the Holy Spirit restrain Satan's system of corruption from getting to us.

David also writes this about "Jehovah Guards:" *"Be Thou my strong Rock, for an house of defense to save me."* (Psalm 31:2) Here David uses an entirely different Hebrew word, *metsudah*, which means "a fortress or a stronghold." It appears to me that David saw his God as a multi-defense; not just one line of defense, but several lines; not just one obstacle to the enemy, but a series of obstacles. Picture, if you will, David standing in a high tower, inside a fortress with a shield held high. When David eventually captured Jerusalem from the Jebusites, he built a place they called Millo (II Samuel 5:9). It says he built on a high place (Mount Zion-II Samuel 5:7) a fortress they would call "the city of David" (II Samuel 5:7, 9), and from the description David built a defense they called "in depth," a multi-layer of defense so that even if the enemy broke through one structure, he would face a second and a third. Most fortresses like this end in a "keep," the final defense line, normally a castle or a fort. David was a military man so he knew how to construct such a fortress, but what I find amazing is that David spends more of the written word speaking about Jehovah as his defense than his citadel of Jerusalem. I feel he did this because he knew that there was a much surer defense than moats, walls, and towers. He knew that walls could be overrun, but not God. Moats could overcome, but not Jehovah, and even the impregnable fortress could fall, but the Almighty, never!

This defense reminds me of the protection we have in Christ, the Father, and the Holy Spirit. David speaks of a triple defense and so does the New Testament. First there is the double defense found in the hands of Jesus and His Father: *"And I give unto them eternal life; and they shall never perish, neither shall any man pluck then out of MY HAND. My Father which gave them me is greater than all; and no man is able to pluck them out of MY FATHER'S HAND."* (John 10:28–29) And then John tells us of the third line of defense when he wrote: *"Because greater is He* [Holy

Spirit] *that is in you, than He that is in the world.*" (I John 4:4) Like with David, our enemies have to go through the Son, the Spirit, and the Sovereign before they can get to us. What a guard we have in our lives!

Job 22:25: *"Yea, the Almighty shall be thy defense…"*

77.

SHEPHATIAH: THE LORD IS JUDGE

I Chronicles 12:5: *"Eluzai, and Jerimoth, and Bealiah, and Shemariah, and **SHEPHATIAH** the Haruphite."*

OUR JOURNEY CONTINUES THROUGH David's list of "mighty men" with the Haruphite (?), Shephatiah. I feel we also have before us today another great title for Christ in the meaning of the name of this "mighty man." Even though Job didn't know about Shephatiah, or Christ, he is the one that draws a connection between the two in my opinion. Bear with me for a moment, and I think you will see what I am getting at by linking Shephatiah and our Savior and this comment by Job about a "daysman:" *"Neither is there any daysman betwixt us that might lay his hand upon us both."* (Job 9:33) Shephatiah means "the Lord is judge," and a daysman is a kind of a judge.

The word first derives from the word "day" as in a day of trial. In the verse from the very first chronological book of the Bible, this Hebrew word is only used here: *yakach*. At the core of its meaning is "to reason, reprove, or to decide." My old King James Version of the Scriptures uses the word "umpire." Now there is a word that all Americans can relate to when you consider our national pastime. What I found most interesting was the custom Job was writing about when he invoked the term "daysman." It seems that in Job's day a daysman was found who could settle a case between two parties. The daysman would put his hands on both individuals to demonstrate his authority over the matter and his power to arbitrate between them. Now there is a title we hear a lot about today, arbitrator. It is an honorable profession and much needed in the conflicts we have today between clients, businesses, and individuals. There are arbitrations going on between employers and employees, baseball players and management. **Umpires are no longer only needed behind the plate!** So what was Job saying in his interesting comment about a "daysman?" Job was suggesting that there was no man on par with Job and his friends that could settle the case, but we know there was.

We Christians have an arbitrator, an umpire, a daysman, yes, a judge. In the New Testament the word is "mediator:" *"For there is one God, and one mediator between God and man, the man Christ Jesus."* (I Timothy 2:5) In her book Today's Good Word Ethel B. Sutton writes: "Over a deep gorge in Arizona lies a great tree, forming a natural bridge. It fell there ages ago, apparently a failure; yet it has now become a piece of solid agate, and is of enormous value and of noble use because many have crossed the great chasm on it. So, too, when Christ was crucified and rejected by men. He seemed a failure-yet through His resurrection and ascension He has now become the 'bridge' between heaven and earth over which our feet may pass to our Heavenly Home." Truly, we can see that between our souls and the safety of heaven there needed to be someone to stand between us and the judgment of God. It is in this word, this name we have, that "bridge," our mediator the Lord Jesus Christ, someone to stand upon, to bridge the gap.

For me that is what a mediator does. He bridges the gap between us and God. Truly sin has eroded a huge canyon between us and God. It started with Adam and Eve, but continued down through time for *"all have sinned"* (Romans 3:23). Like the great Colorado River and the years it has flowed through the Grand Canyon, each year it digs deeper and the valley becomes deeper and wider. So in the case of Christ, the gap was wide between us and His Farther. Even the New Testament word translated "mediator" means "peace-maker or arbitrator." That reminds me of a story that comes out of the life of the great evangelist D. L. Moody that goes like this:

> To an 11-year old boy, D. L. Moody's visit to his house seemed like a visit from God. So, when Mr. Moody mentioned that he had left his umbrella in a neighbor's house, the boy was thrilled to run over and get it for him. On his return, while playing along the way, he stumbled and broke the umbrella. Guilt and fear swept over him. Then he thought, "I'll tell my dad and he can tell Mr. Moody." Rushing home, the youngster poured out

his heart to his father. So his father went to Mr. Moody and told him the story. Mr. Moody called the boy to his side. "When you broke my umbrella," he said, "You became afraid. Then you thought, if I tell my father, he can go between me and Mr. Moody and fix things up. Now that your father has done this, you can come to me." The boy's eyes brightened. Moody continued, "My boy, that is the way it is with all of us. We are sinners, afraid of God. But he has provided a mediator to go between us and Him-and it is Jesus!"

Someone has said: **"That Jesus Christ is our Mediator, and He has never lost a case!"** That is what the mediator does; he is the judge between two groups on opposite sides of an issue. In our very judicial system of government, a mediator is brought in to settle a dispute so that the major leagues, a business, or an individual can go on with their lives. Reconcilable disputes can only be final when a final judgment is made that will satisfy both parties. So it was with the first rift between the Creator and His creation. When Adam and Eve fell into temptation and yielded to the trickery of Satan, an irreconcilable difference, division, was created between mankind and the Almighty. Not until the Christ was willing to stand in that gap and then made a bridge across that gap with his death on Calvary, was the rift resolved. Thank God he was willing to sacrifice His Son to pay the price of redemption, but the good news is that whenever there is any rift between God and man, the mediator, our Judge (II Timothy 4:1) will stand in for us!

Jesus is the one that stands between us and our opponents and judges us fairly. I think we come to the wrong conclusion as Job did when he thought that God was both an accuser and an arbitrator. Let us not forget that our prosecutor is not God, never has been God, but is Lucifer: *"For the accuser of our brethren is cast down, which accused them before our God day and night."* (Revelation 12:10) If you read the first two chapters of Job, you will see that it was Satan that accused, and it was God who stood up for his servant Job. Only Christ can lay His hands on Satan and us and settle the accusations. Despite the fact that we are nearly always guilty, we still have an advocate (I John 2:1) and an arbitrator (I Timothy 2:5) to defend us; not because we are guiltless, but because Jesus paid our guilt with a price (I Corinthians 6:20). (Remember, Satan's accusations against Job were false, as were the accusations of Job's wife [Job 2:9] and Job's friends]Job 3–38.]) Despite our swings and our strikes, our Umpire goes to bat for us at the throne of grace, and when you realize our lawyer is Christ and His Father is the judge, how can we lose? I like what Herbert Gabhart once wrote about this: **"Christ is our efficient daysman. He officiates without bias and prejudice, so the game of life can be played according to divine rules."**

What about your game of life today? Do you need an umpire in your life? What about your losses? Do you need an arbitrator? What about a mediator? You have one in Jesus.

Hebrews 12:24: *"And to Jesus the mediator of the new covenant, and to the blood sprinkled that speaketh better things than that of Abel."*

78.

ELKANAH: GOD IS POSSESSING

I Chronicles 12:6: "***ELKANAH**, and Jesiah, and Azareel, and Joezer, and Jashobeam, the Korhites.*"

IT IS TIME TO once again provoke Paul's classic precept of Romans 14:5: *"Let every man be fully persuaded in his own mind."* I believe in our study of David's "mighty men" that we have come to another major division of these amazing warriors. First, David listed his famous soldiers individually in II Samuel 23 of which there were 37 clearly described (II Samuel 23:39). Second, David repeats the first list and adds an additional number of names into the list in I Chronicles 11 of which there were 52 clearly described. There were more than 52 because David failed to name "the sons of Hashem." Were there two or five? We don't know (I Chronicles 11:34). When we combine the two separate lists and subtract the duplicates, we are able to come up with a total of 61 "mighty men" as the total number in the combined lists. Third, starting in I Chronicles 12, David begins to add to his list of "mighty men" by groups. In the first record David lists 16 "mighty men" from the tribe of Benjamin that joined him in Ziklag (I Chronicles 12:1–5). At the same time a group of five Korhites joined David's Band (I Chronicles 12:6). I believe that this group was a separate group from the Benjamin Battalion, and it will be this group that we will focus our attention on over the next few devotionals.

The Korhite Group were the descendants of Korah (Exodus 6:24 and Numbers 26:58). Korah was the grandson of Kohath, the son of Levi (I Chronicles 6:22). This family was known as the sacred musicians of the tribe of Levi, the tribe designated by God to be the priests of the

ELKANAH: GOD IS POSSESSING

nation of Israel. The Korhites are ascribed eleven of the Psalms in the greatest song book ever complied (Psalm 42, 44, 45, 46, 47, 48, 49, 84, 85, 87, and 88). This family was also famous for being the doorkeepers of the tabernacle and eventually the Temple (I Chronicles 9:19). Can musicians and doorkeepers become warriors? David himself was a famous musician before he became an even more famous soldier! I believe these men fit right in, and David probably found it a wonderful addition to his Band and "band." I can hear the music around the campfire now, can't you? Music has always been a part of military history so it is not hard for me to believe in this group being part of David's growing army. How many Korhites joined David's army we don't know, but what we do know is that five of them made David's list of "mighty men." I also believe that this group was probably the nucleus of the musical ministry David would eventually set up in his kingdom (II Chronicles 7:6): a military band?

The first name on this list is a man by the name of Elkanah. As with so many of the others, all we have is a name, but as with the others we have been able to find meaning and inspiration from those names. Elkanah means "God is possessing." When I discovered the meaning of Elkanah's name I thought of this verse in Isaiah 61:1: *"The Spirit of the Lord is upon me; because the Lord hath anointed me to preach good tidings unto the meek; He hath sent me to bind up the brokenhearted, to proclaim liberty to the captives, and the opening of the prison to them that are bound."* Jesus would read these very words in the synagogue in Nazareth (Luke 4:18) and proclaim that this possessing of the Spirit was upon Him. I yield on this term for the Christ to the master English devotional writer F. B. Meyer, (his book **Great Verses Through The Bible** as helped me a lot through this project) a man I have yielded to before, because his insightful explanation of this connection to Elkanah and Jesus:

> We can never disassociate those words from that memorable scene at the Jordan, when, after the Lord's baptism, the heaven's opened, and the Spirit, like a dove, rested upon Him, possessed Him! (Matthew 3:16) Forty days of fierce temptation could not deprive Him of that holy anointing; and He came to Galilee, stood up in the synagogue of Nazareth, and announced the anointing He had received. The Spirit was given Him without measure, as the power in which He was to cast out devils, preach the Gospel, and glorify His Father by His human life and ministry. What that scene was in the Life of the Lord, Pentecost was for the Church. Then she was anointed for her divine mission among men; the unction of the Holy One rested upon

(possessed) her (Acts 2:3), to be continued and renewed as the centuries slowly passed. What happened for the Church should take place in the history of each member of it. If the Master needed it, how much more do we. If He did not attempt to bind up the brokenhearted, proclaimed liberty to the captives, or the opening of the prison to the bound; if He would not preach, or comfort, or communicate joy, until that memorable unction had been imparted-how absurd it is for us to attempt similar works without this anointing! What a marvelous forecast is here of the mission of Christ through His Church to the world during the present age. She is sent to take up and pass on this blessed ministry. What a true forecast also of the needs of mankind! It is as though the Holy Spirit desired to reveal the salient characteristics of the great sad world, that it would be full of the broken-hearted, of captives, prisoners, and mourners, needing divine assistance and ministration. Man is a fallen and helpless that he needs the entire Trinity: the Lord God, the Father; Jesus, the Son; and the Spirit, the Holy Ghost. When Jesus quoted these words He stopped at the comma in the second verse (Isaiah 61:1–2), which stood therefore for at least nineteen hundred years which intervene between the proclamation of the year of mercy and the day of vengeance. The time for repentance is lengthening out, since God desires not the sinner's death, but that he should turn and live.

Whether Christ, whether the Church, or whether the Christian, the concept that "God is possessing" is applicable. Elkanah's name is a great reminder for every one of us that whether man or musician, pastor or parishioner, male or female, we need to be possessed by the Almighty by way of His Son and through His Spirit. As F. B. Meyer so fitly put it in the article you have just read, **"If Christ needed this possessing, so do we!"** Since my arrival in the Church of the Living God, I have noticed that the indwelling of the Holy Spirit isn't as important a doctrine as it used to be. It seems that after nearly two thousand years, the Church has come to the conclusion that it knows what to do, how to do it, and why is there any need of the Spirit? We give Him lip service, but rely little on Him. Is that the reason the Church is so weak today? Is that why the Church doesn't seem to be affecting the world as in ages past? I am on a five-year teaching program of Church History. One aspect that I have noticed in the study for that course is that the Church was at its best when the Holy Spirit was clearly seen working. It seems that when the Church thinks it has it all figured out, a decline begins, and only when the Church reaches rock bottom does someone or some group realize what is missing is the power of the Holy Spirit. The presence has been and always will be with the Church, but after years of "quenching" (I Thessalonians 5:19) and "grieving" (Ephesians 4:30), the Spirit seems to be missing. Is there time enough left for our generation to see this fault?

Could I ask in closing if the Spirit of the Lord is upon you, possessed you yet?

Luke 4:18: *"The Spirit of the Lord is upon me, because He hath anointed me to…*

79.

JESIAH: JEHOVAH EXISTS

I Chronicles 12:6: *"Elkanah, and **JESIAH,** and Azareel, and Joezer, and Jashobeam, the Korhites."*

JESIAH WAS THE SECOND Korhite to join David at Ziklag and to be named on the King's "mighty men" list. Jesiah is also a great name for a man from whom the priestly tribe of Levi, Jehovah exists. In a time like ours when the very existence of God is often questioned, we need names like Jesiah to remind us of the existence of the Almighty.

It was in the myriad of names given by the Hebrew prophet Isaiah that we first understand the connection between Jehovah and Jesus, the focus of our devotionals throughout this series of explorations into the "mighty men" that helped David gain the throne of Israel: *"For unto us a child is born, unto us a son is given; and the government shall be upon His shoulders: and His name shall be called Wonderful, Counsellor, The Mighty God, The Everlasting Father, The Prince of Peace."* (Isaiah 9:6) Just about every "mighty man" so far in these chapters has within the meaning of their names a title or a term that we have been able to link with the Christ, and we have been able to connect the titles of the Father with the Son, Jesus Christ. In Jesiah's name we can invoke I believe another marvelous title, "the ancient of days," because Jehovah is the existing One: *"Until the Ancient of Days came, and judgment was given to the saints of the Most High, and the time came that the saints possessed the kingdom."* (Daniel 7:22) In verses nine and thirteen of Daniel chapter seven, the title of "the Ancient of Days" is contributed to the Father. In this there is no doubt in my mind, but for me in verse twenty-two I believe this title is given to the Son because the Father is never portrayed in the Scriptures as coming. It is only the Son that would come (first coming of Christ as baby and eventually Savior) and come again (second coming of Christ as conqueror and eventually King). This verse in Daniel seems to me as speaking of Christ coming *"...with ten thousands of His saints..."* (Jude 14) to rule and to reign over all the earth (I Corinthians 6:2 and Revelation 1:6). To me this is the context, but why the title of "the Ancient of Days?" What does this have to do with the term "Jehovah exists?"

To understand the use of this title one must understand what Daniel was seeing in this prophecy. Daniel had just witnessed through his vision a review of human history still to unfold, specifically the four great, successive world powers that would dominate the Middle East (Babylon, Persia, Greece, and Rome). These nations would eventually control all aspects of the ancient world. Each seemed to be stable and secure (Daniel 7:1–8), but when compared to "the Ancient of Days," they would be just passing empires on the timeline of the Almighty. "The Ancient of Days" existed before these nations and would be around long after these empires were just a memory on the mind. As we know from reading history, these nations did rise and fall just like Daniel saw, and for "the Ancient of Days" He has been there all the time watching history unfold in time, unchanging, unmoving, and unconquered! Empires and emperors may come and go as they have, kingdoms and kings might rise and fall as they have, but "the Ancient of days" will remain forever. Jesus Christ through power given to Him by the Father is the real ruler of the world to this day. His control of the universe has not diminished one fraction or one day throughout history. Unlike other rulers, He is not only "ancient," but ageless and has and always will be in existence.

"The Ancient of Days" has moved unhindered through the ages as one at home in all times. Unlike Nebuchadnezzar or Nasser, Pharaoh or Philip, Cyrus or Castro, the Christ was and is *"...the same yesterday, today, and forever..."* (Hebrews 13:8) because He is the "ancient" One. That makes Him capable of living in the past, or the present, or the future without problem because He is comfortable in all times and ages, millennium, and "now." How wise it would be for us to follow Him rather than the temporary leaders of the "now." I write this as I have just been given my 13th president. I have only actual voted for four of them, and this last one (Trump) I didn't even vote because in my opinion there was no choice so I waited on the Lord to make that decision for me. As I have noticed in my life, not only do times change but presidents change, governors change, senators change, but I have stacked all that I believe in this concept of the Psalmist: *"Before the mountains were brought forth or ever thou hast formed the earth and the world, even from everlasting to everlasting, thou art God!"* (Psalm 90:2) So why wouldn't you follow the everlasting One, the always existing One, "the Ancient of Days?"

We stand today at the portal of a new day, a new time, a time we have never passed through, yet there is One who has. If we know not the way, wouldn't it be wise to put our trust into the hands of One who does? Let us step into the unknown singing these classic lines from the pen of the great English hymnologist Isaac Watts:

> O God, our help in ages past,
> Our hope for years to come.
> Our shelter from the stormy blast,
> And our eternal home.
> Before the hills in order stood,
> Or earth received her frame;
> From everlasting thou art God,
> To endless years the same.

It is in another name given to Christ that we have a great example of the existence of God: Emmanuel, God with us (Matthew 1:23). Jesus would tell His disciples just before He left them for the glory of Heaven: *"Lo, I am with you always, even unto the end of the world."* (Matthew 28:20) Only an always existing One can be with all people through all generations, and it was another great English hymnologist, Charles Wesley, who gave us these immortal lines: "Veiled in flesh the Godhead see, hail the incarnate deity, pleased as man with men to dwell, Jesus, our Emmanuel." God with us because Jehovah exists.

But why did Jesus come to dwell (John 1:14) with us? Was it a selfish move on His part? Never! When God does something, I find in the Bible that He always has an eternal reason. Perhaps, the little school boy from England said it best in an award- winning essay: "I believe," he wrote, "so many twins are born into the world today because little children are frightened of entering the world alone." His facts might stand on shaky ground with a faulty conclusion, but his theology is right on. Since the beginning God taught the world: *"It is not good that the man should be alone."* (Genesis 2:18) Many feel that this relationship was only revealed in the need of Adam for an Eve, but I don't believe so. For me the second aspect of this is shared in the story that even Adam and Eve were not left alone because Moses tells us: *"And they heard the voice of the Lord God walking in the garden in the cool of the day."* (Genesis 3:8) Why did the Almighty God visit His two primary creations? Why was God visiting them, and the suggestion is, every day? God knew that Adam and Eve needed each other, but He also knew that they needed Him. They needed to know that He existed. Do you know "the existing One?"

Isaiah 8:8: *"And He shall pass through Judah: He shall overflow and go over, He shall reach even to the neck; and the stretching out of His wings shall fill the breadth of Thy land, O, Emmanuel."*

80.

AZAREEL: GOD IS HELPER

I Chronicles 12:6: *"Elkanah, and Jesiah, and **AZAREEL**, and Joezer, and Jashobeam, the Korhites."*

JESUS HAD JUST RETURNED from the Mount of Transfiguration where for a few moments His divine glory (Colossians 2:9) broke through His earthly vessel (Philippians 2:7). At the base of the hill, He found "a great multitude" gathered around "a dad and his lad." Upon further investigation He discovered that this father had brought his son to the nine disciples that had remained behind at the foot of the mountain so that they might cast out the demon spirit that had haunted, hounded, harassed, and harmed the boy ever since he had been a child (Mark 9:21). Unable to do anything for "the dad and his lad" (Mark 9:20), the disciples waited the return of Christ from the summit. Upon hearing the story, the Lord became annoyed with His disciples faithlessness (Mark 9:19). Jesus had given all His disciples the power to cast out demons just as the father had requested: *"And when He called unto Him His disciples He gave them power against unclean spirits, to cast them out..."* (Matthew 10:1). After healing the boy and returning the lad back to his father cured, Jesus took the disciples aside and explain to them that they had failed to generate the power to cast out the devil because such force was only unleashed by *"...prayer and fasting..."* (Mark 9:29). You might ask what does this story out of the Life of Christ have to do with a "mighty man" named Azareel. As with our other devotions on David's Mighty Men, I have found a connection in the meaning of Azareel's name that helps us understand why Jesus helped the man with a troubled lad.

Now that we have the basic facts connected to this miraculous healing of this boy, let us focus our attention on the understanding this teaches us from the name Azareel, "God is Helper." Any man who has a troubled son needs this truth. I lived nearly twenty years with a troubled son. Is there anything that grieves a parent more than having an afflicted son or daughter? Sicknesses can come in so many forms, not just physical. The agony that is created when after doing all that one can for such a child is only frustrated more when nothing helps. It might be a physical aliment, or a mental disorder, or an emotional trauma, or a social stigma, or just an ordinary personal sickness. The more I read about this lad and his dad I remembered back to the days of Abraham and the situation that developed between the Father of the faithful and his first son, Ishmael, not Isaac. When Abraham learned through the messenger of God what kind of son his firstborn son would become, it grieved him terribly: *"And he will be a wild man, his hand will be against every man, and every man's hand against him."* (Genesis 16:12) A rebellious, violent spirit has been the curse to many a man's son. But what was Abraham going to do about it? Did he say, "There is nothing I can do about it; God has spoken?" Did Abraham throw up his hand in despair and ignore it? Did he just let the prophecy of the angel of God work itself out? No! Abraham did what the unnamed father in the story of Jesus did. Abraham did what all fathers should do. These fathers sought help from the Lord, the God of help. Fathers must set aside the fatherly pride that comes that we can do it all our selves. We must set aside manly honor and ask for help. Manliness stands in the way of so many fathers getting real help for their sons. It is a common practice for fathers to hide problems in their sons because of the implication of failure, rationalize the problem away thinking it will work itself out, or, as most men, they let their wife handle the situation. So many today simple say, "It's not my problem!" But that is part of the problem! If he is your son, then he is your responsibility.

That is why I love the actions of Abraham and "the dad with his lad." This Dad came to Jesus and simply asked, **"Help us!"** (Mark 9:22) Abraham went to God in prayer and simple asked: *"O that Ishmael might live before thee."* (Genesis 17:18) Interestingly, Abraham made this request at the same time that God revealed to Abraham that Sarah would be giving birth to the son of Promise. Some would ignore the first son, but not Abraham. He felt a responsibility despite the way Ishmael came into the world. Instead of giving up on Ishmael and starting afresh with Isaac, Abraham persevered with his petition about Ishmael until God answered his prayer. *"And as for Ishmael, I have heard thee, behold, I have blessed him, and will make him fruitful, and will multiply him exceedingly, twelve princes shall he beget and I will make him a great nation."* (Genesis 17:20) The very same thing happened to the father with the possessed lad. He persevered until he found help at the feet of Jesus. And in the end God helped my son!

Have you ever thought of praying for a change in your son? The answer to your troubled lad may be as simple as that: *"And all things whatsoever ye shall ask in prayer believing ye shall receive."* (Matthew 21:22) What did Jesus say to the father while his son was rolling on the ground in convulsions? (Mark 9:20) *"If thou canst believe, all things are possible to him that believeth."* (Mark 9:23) Most fathers with a troubled son, an addicted son, a prodigal son, say: "Nothing can help," or "he will never change, it has gone too long," instead of saying what the father said to Jesus: *"Lord, I believe help thou mine unbelief."* (Mark 9:24) For a second time the father cried out the word that most men find hard to utter, **"Help!"** This father, at the end of his rope, cornered, desperate, when seemingly all else had failed, broke down and asked for help from "the Stranger of Galilee," and what do you know he found Azareel!

There are three great lessons we can learn from this "dad and his lad." First, that this father had a real charity for his son. He could have sent him off to an asylum or a mental hospital somewhere, but he didn't. He kept him home until he could find a cure. Godly love is so lacking in so many homes today. Unless love is found, Jesus will never be found. Second, that this father had a real concern for his boy's condition. Like Abraham, he wanted something better for his boy, his boy's life, his boy's future. What parent doesn't want that? I am afraid over the years I have come across too many parents that had become content with their child's condition, attitude, and actions. Unless a parent constantly looks for something better for their child, the child never will. Lastly, that this father had a real conviction that Jesus was the answer for his son's condition. Jesus wasn't there so he tried the disciples, but he waited for Jesus to return. The disciples of Jesus couldn't help, but he ultimately believed that Jesus would be his helper. Let us never forget that no matter what is wrong with our child, Azareel is the Answer.

Let us, fathers and mothers, settle this right now. The soul of your child is too precious to be fooled around with. We need, as quickly as possible, to get them to Jesus before it is eternally too late. Even if your son or daughter doesn't have a demon or a disease, they are still eternally lost, dying in sin. Salvation in Christ will go a long way in solving any behavioral problem that is growing in the life of your lad. Azareel is a good name to give a child because it is the only name that can ultimate help a child. And for just a postscript it took cancer to bring my son back to the Lord, and when you pray you can't fight against what God will use to bring the result. Six months after my prayer was answered my son died, but now I have the hope of seeing him again. Amen and Amen!

Hebrews 13:6: *"So that we may boldly say, The Lord is my helper…"*

81.

JOEZER: JEHOVAH IS HELP

I Chronicles 12:6: *"Elkanah, and Jesiah, and Azareel, and **JOEZER**, and Jashobeam, the Korhites."*

JOEZER WAS THE FOURTH Korhite to join David's band at Ziklag, and the second Korhite whose name speaks of our "helping God." In our last chapter we dealt with the "mighty man" Azareel and the meaning of his name: God is Helper. In actuality, I have discovered at least four "mighty men" who in their names this wonderful attribute of God is revealed: Abiezer, Ahiezer, Azareel, and Joezer. So what else can we find in the Holy Writ that helps us understand the helpfulness of the Almighty?

One of the least known and promoted "spiritual gifts" is the underreported **"helps"** (I Corinthians 12:28). While the Church of the 21st century is striving again to acquire the sensational gifts (speaking in tongues, miracles) and the sign gifts (healings, interpretation of tongues), I think the Church ought to take seriously applying the greatest service gift of them all, **"helps"** (I Corinthians 12:31). Don't get me wrong, I believe love is what Paul wants us to have above all other attributes of God, and it is important in the practical sense of love that we demonstrate love with **"helps."** Despite my position as pastor/teacher in the body of Christ, I don't believe I have the spiritual gift of "ruler" (Romans 12:8). In my early years in the ministry I sought all the gifts, but found in time I only had been given a couple. One would think it strange in a leadership position God would not give me the gift of "administration" or sometimes called "governments" (I Corinthians 12:28), but I have learned over time the best support gift in a pastor/teacher is **"helps."** I have realized I might not know much or have the ability in much, but I can help just about anybody in their spiritual gift. Long before I got into the Lord's work I was shown that I was more of a helper than a leader; a follower more than an out-front kind of a guy. Oh, I am out front a lot in the pastorate, but my greatest gift is behind the scene helping others be the best they can be in the Body of Christ. I learned early I wasn't a farmer (Dad tried to pass the family farm on to me in 1969), but you ask anyone that I worked with on the family homestead and they will tell you I was a good farm hand. I am not a project starter, but I can help anyone finish their project. I am not a visionary, but once the vision is seen I can see that vision to the end. My experiment of starting a local church failed, but my three pastorates thereafter have shown my true calling.

I believe the Good Lord in His wise providence has given to me an excellent helping hand. I am no carpenter, or electrician, but I have helped many a carpenter and electrician over the years with an extra hand. Paul wrote of *"...Priscilla and Aquilla, my helpers..."* (Romans 16:3). Paul also wrote of *"...Urbane, our helper in Christ..."* (Romans 16:9). I believe these three saints had the spiritual gift of **"helps."** I bet one day even the Apostle Paul will confess that he would have never finished his course (II Timothy 4:7) without the help of Priscilla, Aquilla, and Urbane. The Body of Christ would be functionless if not for the individuals the Lord gifted with the necessary gift of **"helps."** But what we must realize is that before we can be of any help, we need help from Jehovah the greatest helper of them all because He is help, the very core of whom He is and what He is. So, if the Good Lord has given you this special gift, just remember before it was in you it was in Him. There is no better quality of God in you than the ability to help others as they journey through this old world.

One of my favorite helper stories of the Bible is the one that starts: *"The Amalekites came and attacked the Israelites at Rephidim."* (Exodus 17:8 NIV) This Bedouin war-loving tribe was a descendant from Esau (Genesis 36:12) and from this day on Israel's hated enemy. These desert raiders were always on the move in the Negev and Sinai (Numbers 13:29) and in the region of Kadesh (the country of the Amalekites-Genesis 14:7). Though not mentioned in the Exodus account, Moses does tell the next generation just how the Battle of Rephidim got started: *"Remember, what the Amalekites did to you along the way when you came out of Egypt. When you were weary and worn out, they met you on your journey and cut of all who were lagging behind, they had no fear of God."* (Deuteronomy 25:17–18 NIV) The Amalekites surprised the Israelites at Rephidim, but not by attacking the strong, but by attacking the stragglers. Though Israel hadn't had much time to prepare for war (the very reason that God had led the Israelites to Canaan another way-Exodus 13:17–18), the attack by the Amalekites couldn't be ignored so Moses called on Joshua to raise an army, and Moses' strategy was this: *"And Moses said unto Joshua, Choose us out men, and go out, fight with Amalek; tomorrow I will stand on the top of the hill with the Rod of God in my hand."* (Exodus 17:9) Note the word "us;" this would be a battle in which Joshua would fight, but Moses would help. Emily Dickinson once wrote: **"They might not need me, but they might, I'll let my head be just in sight!"** How important to understand the lesson of Rephidim. Most times we don't even make ourselves available to help. Granted, there are times, most of the time, when our family and friends don't need our help, or maybe, want our help. But do we like Moses at least position ourselves to help? Dickinson would write on: "If I can stop one heart from breaking, I shall not live in vain. If I can ease one life the aching, or cool one pain, or help one fainting robin unto his nest again, I shall not have lived in vain."

How many battles have been lost because of a shortage of helpers, not soldiers? At the Battle of Rephidim there was plenty of both (Exodus 17:13), and, if you remember, the story clearly tells that even the helper needed helpers (Exodus 17:12). As Moses' arms got tired raising the Rod of God, Aaron and Hur came along to hold up his hands. Remember, it was in the height of the rod that the battle was won (Exodus 17:11). But it is here I must underline to all helpers the reality that happens most of the time for helpers. Read carefully and you will notice that at the end of the Battle of Rephidim the helpers got no credit at all in the text. Even in the Scriptural text few helpers get much notice. I have come to believe the gift of **"helps"** is an out-of-sight gift that will only be recognized at the Bema-Seat Judgment (II Corinthians 5:10). Maybe that is the reason most don't want the gift; no credit, no recognition, no praise, because the glory is on the battlefield, not the hilltop or in the balcony! Despite this reality, the **"helps"** gift is essential (I Corinthians 12:22–24) so if you have it, use it, lest the soldiers on the frontline stumble and fall, defeated for lack of help. Could this be why the Church has lost so many battles lately?

Many years after this famous Biblical battle Moses was instructed to bring the 70 elders of Israel before the Lord to hear this: *"I will come down and speak with you there, and I will take of that Spirit that is on you and put the Spirit on them. They will help to carry the burden of the people so that you will not have to carry it alone."* (Numbers 11:7 NIV) This has always been the practice of God from the beginning when God created Eve for a *"...help meet for him."* (Genesis 2:18) God is help, and we are to help as well.

> I Chronicles 12:1: *"...these are they that came to David...mighty men, helpers of the war."*

82.

JASHOBEAM: TO WHOM THE PEOPLE TURN

I Chronicles 12:6 *"Elkanah, and Jesiah, and Azareel, and Joezer, and* **JASHOBEAM**, *the Korhites."*

AFTER DAVID NAMES 16 Benjaminites that turned to him at Ziklag, he then numbers five Korhites who chose him over King Saul. The last of that group is a warrior named Jashobeam, not to be confused with the Jashobeam of I Chronicles 11:11 better known as Adino (II Samuel 23:8), the second soldier on David's "mighty men" list. As with Jashobeam's fellow Korhites, Jashobeam's name once again turns our attention toward God and God's anointed king, "to whom the people turn." As Jashobeam and his fellow "mighty men" turned to David to be their captain, so, too, must we turn to Jesus to be *"...the captain of our salvation..."* (Hebrews 2:10). One of my favorite choruses contains these words: **"Turn your eyes upon Jesus, look full into His wonderful face; and the things of earth will grow strangely dim, in the light of His glory and grace."** In the Jewish army captain was the highest rank attainable. Before the days of generals and presidents the captain was the Commander-in-Chief of the armed services. Therefore, the captain was in charge, in control, and in constant contact with those under his authority. He determined the course of the army, led the way at the head of the army, and was there when the army's mission was accomplished. All these aspects of "the captain" can be seen in the Person of Christ. Using the concept of Jashobeam's name, let us see that Jesus is the one we must turn to for our salvation and everything else!

JASHOBEAM: TO WHOM THE PEOPLE TURN

In Hebrews Paul uses the term "captain" in speaking of Christ as the founder, or originator, of our salvation. Someone had to be in charge of it so in eternity past God the Father put His Son in the position of returning mankind back to the place they were before the fall of Adam and Eve in the Garden of Eden. Jesus believed that man was redeemable, worth whatever it would take to bring them back to the Father's good graces. Christ didn't go into this mission without a clear understanding of the heart of man or what He would have to endure (Hebrews 12:2). Christ *"…knew what was in man…"* (John 2:25), and He had *"…no confidence in the flesh…"* (Philippians 3:3), yet He still came to be "the captain of our salvation" with the knowledge that at least a few would turn to Him. He championed our cause, He took our case, and in the end He was willing to become like us to save us from ourselves. Jesus took on flesh to win us back to Himself, but He left the choice up to us "to whom the people turn." When Jesus came to this planet, it was like a great general going forth to war because there were an array of foes against Him, mortal and immortal enemies, that would resist His advances, his assaults, and His attacks again sin, self, and Satan himself!

So how did Jesus become known as "the captain of our salvation?" **"Through Suffering!"** (Hebrews 2:10) Unlike the captains of this day and age that stay and stand far back from the battlefield, Jesus was like David of old that led his forces from the front. It is one of the reasons I believe the "mighty men" followed David. David would suffer with them, David would eat what they ate, and sleep where they slept. That is why II Samuel 11:1 is a strange verse in the life of David. It was the first time it speaks that he didn't go to war. Only two other times do I recall in David's long military life does that happen. Just before the Battle of the Ephraim Woods (II Samuel 18) in the war against his son Absalom, he wanted to go into battle, but the people wouldn't let him (II Samuel 18:3), and after the Battle with the Giant Ishbibenob (II Samuel 15–16), where he almost died, the people did not allow him into battle again (II Samuel 23:17). As with David, so with the Christ, He faced all the trials and tests and temptations in the heat of everyday battle, and He suffered much, even before Calvary to win our salvation. From day one in Bethlehem, Jesus was under assault (Herod tried to kill him) and only when He died on the Battlefield of Golgotha was the war won. In His death He won while most see death as a loss! Austin Phelps has written: "Suffering is a wonderful fertilizer to the roots of character. The great object of this life is character. This is the only thing we can carry with us into eternity…To gain the most of it and the best of it is the object of probation." That is why the Scriptures keep telling us: *"But rejoice, inasmuch as ye are partakers of the Christ's sufferings; that, when His glory shall be revealed, ye may be glad also with exceeding joy"* (I Peter 4:13); as Jashobeam did when David became king!

To me, the greatest suffering Christ endured had to have been in that moment when he **"...became sin for us, who knew no sin..."** (II Corinthians 5:21). Our "Captain" had really become like us: *"...for all have sinned..."* (Romans 3:23), and even in Christ's greatest struggle in the Garden of Gethsemane, our Captain didn't turn His back on us and flee the torment and agony that was before Him. Christ was willing to make the supreme sacrifice as any true captain will make for his soldiers, and that is giving up his life for them (John 15:13). After such an act of self-sacrifice, why wouldn't those who believe in Him be willing to follow Him, take His orders, and live a life like His? Jesus proved Himself just "better" than any other, just like David proved to his men that he was a better king than Saul. I have come to the belief that to understand the book of Hebrews, you must trace the word **"better."** It occurs 13 times in 13 chapters (1:4, 6:9, 7:7, 7:22, 8:6, 9:23, 10:34, 11:16, 11:35, 11:40, and 12:24). You will note if you check these verses that more often than not the **"better"** is referring to Jesus. In my study I made this chart:

1. Christ is BETTER than a prophet because He is the Prophet (Deut. 18:15).
2. Christ is BETTER than a word because He is the Word (John 1:1).
3. Christ is BETTER than a son because He is the Son (Matthew 16:16).
4. Christ is BETTER than the creation because He is the Creator (John 1:3).
5. Christ is BETTER than a man because He is the Son of Man (Luke 9:58).
6. Christ is BETTER than a sacrifice because He is the Sacrifice (Hebrews 9:23).
7. Christ is BETTER than an angel because He is God (Hebrews 1:1–4).

Make your own chart, your own comparison, and I do believe that you will say as Matthew records **"...*a greater than___is here...*"** (Matthew

12:41–42), and, if a "better" One is here and a "greater" One is here, why wouldn't you turn to Him? Just like Jashobeam and his comrades the Korhites turned to David to be their captain and eventually their king, so, too, we must turn to Jesus, first as "the captain of our salvation" and one day our "King of kings!" (I Timothy 6:15) Try other leaders like Saul, but after all your experimentation and examination, you will come to the same conclusion that mankind has come to over twenty centuries--the best is found in the **"better"** Jesus, the "greater" Christ. Just like David was a better choice than Saul, so Jesus is a better choice than any other. "Turn your eyes upon Jesus, look full into His wonderful face............"

Hebrews 7:22: *"By so much was Jesus made a surety of a better testament."*

83.

JOELAH: GOD IS SNATCHING

I Chronicles 12:7-And **JOELAH**, and Zebadiah,
the sons of Jeroham of Gedor.

IT IS MY OPINION (Romans 14:5) that we have come to another group of men that join David in the Philistine town of Ziklag. These are the "mighty men" that became a part of the core of David's experienced army, an army in which he was their Captain and the one that hired this mercenary unit out to Philistia to protect their southern border against the desert raiders of the Negev. The three groups so far are the sixteen men from the tribe of Benjamin (I Chronicles 12:3–6); the five Korhites (I Chronicles 12:6) and now the two brothers, sons of Jeroham from Gedor (I Chronicles 12:7). The first of the brothers was the "mighty man" Joelah, and this is all we know about him: Zebadiah was his brother, and they joined David's band together; his father was Jeroham, which means "loved;" Joelah's hometown was a place called Gedor, a city in the mountainous region of Judah, a few miles north of Hebron (Joshua 15:58), and his name means "God is snatching!"

I must admit I had to do a bit of research to come up with what doctrine I was dealing with in the meaning of Joelah's name. When I have trouble understanding Greek words, I usually go to a great help book in "an Expository Dictionary of New Testament Words" by W. H. Vine. The word for "snatch" is *harpazo* or "to catch away." This word is found in five New Testament verses, and a reading of them will reveal to you the grand meaning of this attribute of God:

> *"And when they were come up out of the water, the Spirit of the Lord **caught away** Philip, that the eunuch saw him no more: and he went on his way rejoicing."* (Acts 8:39)
>
> *"I knew a man in Christ about fourteen years ago, (whether in the body, I cannot tell; or whether out of the body, I cannot tell: God knoweth;) such an one **caught up** to the third heaven...How that he was **caught up** into paradise, and heard unspeakable words, which it is not lawful for a man to utter."* (II Corinthians 12:2, 4)
>
> *"Then we which are alive and remain shall be **caught up** together with them in the clouds, to meet the Lord in the air: and so shall we ever be with the Lord."*
> (I Thessalonians 4:17)
>
> *"And she brought forth a man child, who was to rule all nations with a rod of iron: and her child was **caught up** unto God, and to his throne."* (Revelation 12:5)

This is the concept of "snatching," and with a simple read through the Bible, you will find that our God is the great snatcher.

Let me remind you of a few stories before we look into the greatest snatching event yet to take place. Enoch was "snatched away" (*"...and he was not, for God took him."* Genesis 5:24). Paul uses another word in Hebrews 11:5, but the concept is the same: *"By faith Enoch was translated that he should not see death; and was not found, because God had translated him: for before his translation he had this testimony, that he pleased God."* Translated and translation can only take place if there is a "snatching away," and Enoch became the prototype of all that would follow him when the Almighty decided to "snatch." And then there was Elijah: *"And it came to pass, as they still went on, and talked, that, behold, there appeared a chariot of fire, and horses of fire, and parted them both asunder; and Elijah **went up by** a whirlwind into heaven."* (II Kings 2:11) Enoch and Elijah were both snatched away from this world to another world without seeing death like everyone before and after them. This could only take place by the snatching power of the Almighty, and there is a day coming when God will do this to a grand multitude!

For this devotional, I would have us focus on the coming of Christ and the snatching away of His Church. Described in I Thessalonians 4:15–18, this snatching away will happen at a time picked out by God the Father Himself (Matthew 24:36). For me, this is one of those terms associated with our Savior that we have overlooked. The Lord will come again just like He promised (John 14:3) at the Passover Supper and as He promised His disciples again at His ascension (Acts 1:11) through the angels. Even the Psalmist spoke of *"Our God shall come!"* (Psalm 50:3) The promise of the second coming of Christ is a surety we can take to the bank in these last days (II Timothy 3:1), these dark days at the end of time as we know it (I Timothy 4:1). One of my favorite devotional authors, F. B. Meyer, gives us these thoughts on this up and coming "snatching away" of the saints:

> The years pass as snowflakes on the river: and as each drops into the mighty past, it cries, God will come! Each Advent season, with its cluster of services, heralded-voices, reminiscences and anticipations, lifts the message clear above the turmoil and tumult of mankind, God will come! The disappointments of our fairest hopes, the overcasting of our surprises, the failures of our politicians, statesmen, and counselors, to effect a permanent, and radical improvement of man's nature, all take up the word, our God shall come! Surely He cometh, and a thousand voices call to the saints and to the deaf and dumb; surely He cometh, and the earth rejoices, glad in His coming, who hath sworn, I come! Dear heart, get thee often to thine oriel window, and look out for the breaking of the day. Did not the Master assure us that He would soon return? Hearken; He saith again today, surely I come quickly. The little while will soon be over, and He will come first to receive His saints to Himself, and afterwards to come with them to the earth. Why are we disconsolate and dismayed? The perplexities of the eastern problem, the gradual return of the Jews to Palestine, the despair and lawlessness of men, the unrest of nations, the preparedness on the part of the Church-like so many minute guns at night-keep the heart awake. O, let your eyes flash with the glow of thanksgiving! Be glad and strong, confident and calm. Let your loins be girded, and your lamps burning. Through heaven's spaces you shall detect the Advent of your God; and when He comes He will break the silence of the ages with words of majesty and might!

And could I but add, He will then snatch us away to be with Him for all eternity!

Coming is the word of "snatching;" coming again the avenue the Almighty will use to snatch us away. He is coming to call us home, to take us home through His mighty snatching ability. How He will sort us all out I know not, and how He will gather the dust from the ground that contains the saint's old bodies to give them new bodies, my mind can barely understand it. But this one thing I believe, and that is, if God could do it for Enoch and Elijah, He can do it for me. Snatch me in a moment, in the midst of where I am and what I am doing, and catch me away to Gloryland. In a moment, in the twinkling of an eye (I Corinthians 15:52), it will happen--the greatest snatching of them all.

John 14:3: *"...I will come again, and receive you unto Myself; that where I am, there ye may be also."*

84.

ZEBADIAH: JEHOVAH IS ENDOWER

I Chronicles 12:7: *"And Joelah, and **ZEBADIAH**, the sons of Jeroham of Gedor."*

WE ARE ENDING TODAY in our quest to discover the names of David's "mighty men" in Scriptures another group or listing. We first looked at the names mentioned in II Samuel 23:8–39. We went on to highlight the names listed in I Chronicles 11:4–47 being careful to take out the duplicates from the first list. We finish in this chapter the names of the men that joined David at Ziklag (I Chronicles 12:1–7). This ends the first section of this chapter which seems to underline David's listing of his "mighty men" in groups (I Chronicles 12:2, 8, 19, 24, 25, 30, 32, 33, 34, 35, 36, 37). Note, David had "mighty men" from all of the twelve tribes of Israel. However, before we start listing the Gadites (I Chronicles 12:8) that were numbered among David's "mighty men," we have one more son of Jeroham of Gedor to consider. As I mentioned last time, I feel that these two brothers were probably from David's tribe of Judah because Gedor was a city just north of Hebron. There is, however, some evidence that there was also a town of Gedor in the allotment of Benjamin because of an ancestor of King Saul by that name (I Chronicles 8:31 and 9:37). This is not unusual because there is also a village of Gedor located in the territory of Simeon (I Chronicles 4:39). I see only three interpretations for these differences: (1) That all these men were from the tribe of Benjamin which would bring our total to twenty-three; (2) That as I suggested in our last article that we have 16 Benjamites, five Korhites, and two sons of Jeroham of Judah; or 3) that there were 18 Benjamites and five Korhites. The answer to this simple mystery lies in heaven (Romans 14:5).

Our focus again will be on what we know, and what we know is that Zebadiah's name means: Jehovah is Endower or God is a Rewarder. Paul wrote this about the Almighty God: *"But without faith it is impossible to please Him: for he that cometh to God must believe that He is and that He is the rewarder of them that diligently seek Him."* (Hebrews 11:6) In an article under the title of The Dispenser of Reward W. Glyn Evans in his devotional book "Daily With the King" makes these helpful observations concerning the Christ as a Rewarder or an Endower:

> I must not have a mistaken understanding about rewards. Normally, Christians make two mistakes about them: all rewards are spiritual, and all rewards are future. Not so, in both cases. God has promised many rewards that are to be claimed in this life, and some of them are material. When the disciples asked what their rewards would be, Jesus replied that no one who had forsaken all for Him would be overlooked. *"He shall receive a hundredfold now in this time…and in the age to come eternal life."* (Mark 10:28–30 ASV) Some of the material rewards to be received in this life are things such as houses and land. That puzzles me, Lord; yet I see what you mean. You do not want me to confuse my goals with my rewards. I am not to seek houses, properties, and money as a goal; my goal must always be to do God's will, regardless of the consequences. Yet, doing God's will bring its rewards, both spiritual and material, for the present time as well as in the age to come. The Israelites were encouraged to obey God and walk in His ways in order that they would live and multiply and prosper in the land that God gave them. (Deuteronomy 30:15–16) As a disciple, however, I must have a slightly different attitude. I must maintain a conscience indifference to material rewards; and, if they come, I must be humbly grateful for them and use them only for the future glory of God, not for selfish ends and aims. Lord, let me look to You as the Dispenser of both my needs and my rewards; I am encouraged to learn that You reward those who "…diligently seek…" You. But if reward is delayed, may I still glorify You with a thankful heart and a flowing word of praise!

I would have you underline and highlight Evan's conclusion. We must note that in our key verse (Hebrews 11:6), the Rewarder bases His rewards on those *"…that diligently seek Him."* Faithful and honorable service is more than a privilege; it is a solemn obligation demanding persistence and diligence. Shall we wait until we feel like serving the Almighty? Certainly not! It is easy to convince ourselves that it is hypocrisy to get on with service when we do not have the heart for service; but this would be a great mistake. Take for an example the prophet Jonah and his commission to preach repentance to the city of Nineveh (Jonah 1). You talk about a reluctant evangelist! Even when the Good Lord brought His disobedient servant back from his self-imposed vacation (Jonah 2), Jonah was never your enthusiastic preacher (Jonah 3). Despite the half-hearted attempt to warn the Ninevehites of impending doom, the city repented from the king to the pauper. Jonah was visibly unset (Jonah 4), yet the Lord rewarded Jonah's preaching with one of the great revivals of the ancient world. Sometimes, the reward is not deserved because it was of God, and we were only the instrument of God, but God's will will be fulfilled and each shall receive a reward according to their part. Paul wrote of this concept in I Corinthians 3:8: *"Now he that planteth and he that watereth are one: and every man shall receive his own reward according to his own labour."* Some would question whether or not Jonah got any reward from his actions, and in that we have another important precept: *"Look to yourselves, that we lose not those things which we have wrought, but that we receive a full reward."* (II John 8)

Dr. Thomas M. Carter, an ex-convict, tells this thrilling story of his mother who always prayed for him:

> On one occasion while I was in prison, she received a telegram stating that I was dead and asked what she wanted done with my body. Stunned by the news, she opened her Bible and laid the message before it. "Oh, God," she said, "I have steadfastly believed that you are the rewarder of them who diligently seek you. I felt sure that I would live to see Tom saved and preaching the Gospel; and now this wire says he is dead. Lord, which is true, this telegram or your promises to me?" When she arose from her knees, having won the victory, she sent this note to the prison: "You must be wrong. My boy is not dead!" And there had been a mistake-I was alive. I was later converted and I am alive today preaching the Gospel!"

When was the last time you had such a reward from God or maybe only a little reward from God? Could it be that you haven't been fulfilling the key requirement "diligence" for any reward? Remember that it doesn't have to be as dramatic as Tom's mother's reward because even the small things done for God will reap a reward. How about these words:

"And whosoever shall give unto one of these little ones a cup of cold water, only in the name of a disciple, verily I say unto you, he shall in no wise lose his reward." (Matthew 10:42)

Revelation 22:12: *"And, behold, I come quickly, and my reward is with me…"*

85.

EZER: HELP

I Chronicles 12:9: *"**EZER** the first, Obadiah the second, Eliab the third."*

AS WITH THE BENJAMITES before them, David gives us this general description of the Gadites before he starts to list the ones that he would classify as "mighty men:"

> *"And of the Gadites there separated themselves unto David into the hold to the wilderness them of might, and men of war fit for battle, that could handle shield and buckler, whose faces were like the faces of lions, and were swift as the roses upon the mountains."* (I Chronicles 12:8)

And David would also add this footnote to these eleven men (I Chronicles 12:9-13):

> *"These were the sons of Gad, captains of the host: one of the least was over a hundred, and the greatest over a thousand. These are they that went over Jordan in the first month, when it had overflowed all his banks; and they put to flight all them of the valley, both toward the east, and toward the west."* (I Chronicles 12:14-15)

What a testimonial to the Gadites, but what does this prelude and postlude mean? I like what Matthew Henry, the famous British commentator, says about the Gadites:

> Some of the tribe of Gad, though seated on the other side of Jordan, had such a conviction of David's title to, and fitness for, the government, that they separated themselves from their

brethren [a laudable separation it was] to go to David, though he was in the hold in the wilderness [either Adullam-I Samuel 22:1, or Engedi-I Samuel 24:1]. They were but a few, eleven in all, here named, but they added such to David's strength. Those that had hitherto come in to his assistance, were most of them men of broken fortune, distress, discontented, and soldiers of fortune, that came to him rather for protection, than to do him any service (I Samuel 22:2). But these Gadites were brave men, men of war, and fit for battle. They were able-bodied men, men of incredible swiftness, not to fly from, but to fly upon, the enemy, and to pursue the scattered forces; in this they were as swift as the roes [deer] upon the mountains, so that no man could run from them; and yet they had faces like the faces of lions, so that no man could out-fight them. They were disciplined men, trained up to military exercise; they could handle the shield and buckler, used both offensive and defensive weapons. They were officers of the militia in their own tribe, so that though they did not bring soldiers with them, they had them at command, hundreds, thousands. They were daring men, that could break through the greatest difficulties. Upon some expedition or other, perhaps this to David, they swam over the Jordan, when it overflowed all its banks. Those are fit to be employed in the cause of God, that venture this in a dependence upon divine aid. They were men that would go through with the business they engaged in. What enemies they were that they met with in the vallies, when they had passed over Jordan, does not appear; but they put them to flight with their lion-like faces, and pursued them with matchless fury both toward the east, and toward the west; which way soever they turned, they followed the blow, and did not do their work by halves."

I would only add these observations to Henry's take on the men from Gad, and that being their skills with the shield (larger defensive weapon) and buckler (usually a smaller round shield either held in the hand or worn on the arm). Remember the Benjamites were known for their ability to throw stones and shooting arrows (I Chronicles 12:2) skills that left them exposed to the enemy whereby requiring others to defend them, the Gadites! And as for their lion-like faces, Matthew suggests furiousness, but I thought of these men and their beards like a lion's mane.

The first (note, only group David literally numbered) was a warrior by the name of Ezer (I think, perhaps, the leader of the group, like

Ahiezer) (I Chronicles 12:3). Ezer means "help," a meaning we have seen often in this study of David's "mighty men," and, remember, like the Benjamites (I Chronicles 12:1), the Gadites were also "...helpers of the war..." It is only fitting in my opinion that the first name in the listing of the Gadites that Ezer would mean and no doubt has the characteristic of helpfulness. This concept reminded me how the Boy Scout movement came about. My Grandfather Roy Barton was one of the early leaders in this organization as it moved into Northern Maine. One of my favorite pictures of Gramp Barton was taken in 1937 standing with the famous radio announcer Lowell Thomas in Washington D. C. My Grandfather had been selected to be Jamboree Scoutmaster of Troop One of the Katahdin Council. In July of that year, he was in attendance to the first ever national jamboree. More than 27,000 Scouts and their leaders camped at the foot of the Washington Monument. Besides Lowell Thomas my Grandfather met Ban Beard, one of the founders of Boy Scouts of America. Scouting came to the United States because of a simple act of helping, and this is that story:

> William D. Boyne, a Chicago publisher, became lost one night in a London fog. A boy touched him and asked, "Can I help you, sir?" He escorted the publisher to his hotel, and upon arrival refused pay for his services. "I am a Boy Scout," he explained. "We do not accept pay for rendering a service to anyone in need." Boyne was impressed. He called on Sir Robert Baden-Powell, founder of British scouting, to learn more about the movement. Returning to America, he became one of the leaders in establishing Boy Scouting in this country!

Julius Rosenwald once said, **"All the other pleasures of life seem to wear out, but the pleasure of helping others in distress never does."**

The Bible is filled with the examples of helpfulness. The early Church showed this admirable quality of helpfulness in the city of Jerusalem (Acts 4:35). Jesus' famous parable of the "Good Samaritan," that unknown and unnamed traveler who showed an extraordinary form of helpfulness to the robbery and assault victim (Luke 10:33–35) is to this day told and retold. The great prophet Elisha was helped by the Shunammite woman (II Kings 4:13), and in turn Elisha helped her. Ponder for a few moments just how many Gospel stories deal with helpfulness and then take a look at Acts and the history of the Church, but these qualities first show up in the Old Testament with men like Ezer the Gadite. Oh, that we might look around our world and see who needs help, who could use a bit of help to bring them to their appointed place, just like Ezer did for David.

I Corinthians 12:28: *"And God hath set some in the Church…helps…"*

86.

OBADIAH: SERVANT OF GOD

EPI]I Chronicles 12:9: *"Ezer the first,* ***OBADIAH*** *the second, Eliab the third."*

    I have just spent a wonderful and insightful seven months in a portion of the Bible most Christians completely ignore, the five one-chapter books of the Scriptures, Obadiah, Philemon, II John, III John, and Jude. I had the special privilege of teaching and preaching every Monday evening from October through April these unique five books. I titled the series of lectures <u>Small Books With Big Blessings</u>, but, as I neared the end of the series, I thought of a better title: <u>Little Letters With Large Lessons</u>. They certainly were a blessing to me, and it was my wish and prayer that they will become an even greater blessing to my students. This group of evenings was spent at the Washington Street Baptist Church in Eastport, Maine, actually an island off the downeast coast of my home state. It was here I continued a long term ministry I call "Winter in the Word" that I had started in the 1970s when I was in-between churches. It was my way to have an outlet for the Biblical topics I was studying. As I write this article I have just finished another winter, a shortened winter because of the sickness (lung cancer that would take him in six months) of my son, but another part of what I have become as a pastor/teacher.

    The author of the first one-chapter books of the Bible was a man by the name of Obadiah, the same, interestingly, as one of David's "mighty men," by the same name. As we have seen from our first chapter on the men from Gad, this man was second to Ezer. What I found enlightening in my study of the Book of Obadiah was the fact that this famous prophet only appears once in Scripture, but his name appears thirteen times; yes,

13 Obadiah's of Holy Writ. Despite the fact that each Obadiah seems to be small and insignificant, yet, in the name is the lesson we all need to learn. God didn't repeat the Obadiah's, like David's soldier, he did repeat the name enough so that we would get the meaning of Obadiah, servant of God, and for me therein lies the lesson! It makes no difference how big the man, how important the man, or how famous the man when "Thus saith the Lord…" is connected to that man, he or she is important. I have preached for years on the truth that Heaven will be the big equalizer; that in Heaven there will not be the major and minor prophets, or of James the major and James the minor.

We all can't be Isaiah or Jeremiah in the literary world, or Joab and Benaiah in the military world either. Obadiah the prophet and Obadiah the warrior teaches us very clearly: *"All scripture is given by inspiration of God, and is profitable for doctrine, for reproof, for correction, for instruction in righteousness, that the man of God may be perfect, thoroughly furnished unto all good works."* (II Timothy 3:16–17) This, like Heaven, is the great equalizer on earth for me whether you are dealing with authors or "mighty men." The Book of Obadiah despite its shortness is just as important as the lengthy Book of Isaiah, and Obadiah was just as an important soldier in David's army as his more famous troopers. The little book of Obadiah is just as useful in our spiritual development as Genesis, just like Philemon is just as important an instructional Book as Romans; that Jude can be as helpful as the Ephesians, and the tiny epistles of John as valuable as his important Books of John and Revelation. Moses and David might be better known, and they might contain more of God's Word, but Obadiah doesn't contain less (II Peter 1:21) of God's Word. So it is true of our soldier Obadiah, the servant of God. The category of "servant of God" doesn't make a distinction between major and minor servants; they are all "holy men of God," "mighty men of God." Obadiah might have only written one short account about Edom and Israel, and Obadiah's name might have only been found in one listing of David's "mighty men," and just because he is "Obadiah the second" doesn't mean he was secondary behind any of the servants of God.

How we have missed out on this precept because "big is beautiful," "big is better," is the name of the game today. Little has become less, and tiny is a loser in the eyes of most, but we will miss some great blessings if we ignore certain sections of God's Word, if we bypass names like Obadiah tucked away in an obscure list of names in an isolated chapter in the Book of I Chronicles. Whether it is the one-chapter of the Bible or the last of David's "mighty men" (we only have twenty left), we miss a lot when we overlook or bypass the simple, the little. You haven't got all that you need if you fail to read and meditate on "all" the Bible. Your lamp (Psalm 119:105) might be a bit dim because you have not taken advantage of "all scripture." There are certain Biblical facts and certain Scriptural concepts you will never learn if you don't read and study the Obadiah's of the Bible. There are messages from God that He wants you to hear and learn that He hid within the little known section of His inspired Word, and, as a servant of God, we need to know these things.

Only in the book of Jude will you read of Lucifer's fight with the archangel Michael over the body of Moses (Jude 9). Only in the third epistle of John will you ever meet the super-saint Demetrius, one of the shining saints of the first century Church (III John 12). Only in the Book of Philemon will you hear the testimony of Onesimus, a real-life prodigal (Philemon 10). Only in II John will you learn about the only woman a Book of the Bible was addressed to (II John 1), and only in the Book of I Chronicles will you know of "Obadiah the second." There are teaching and truths that can only be found, only heard and heeded to, if you read these simple texts.

For me Obadiah is the classic illustration of the promise given to Abraham about *"...and curse him that curseth thee."* (Genesis 12:3) This is a warning we need today as anti-Semitic feeling is on the rise in this world. Obadiah reminds us of that curse, and I would challenge you to find an Edomite in the world today. Obadiah wrote of the doom of this race because of their assault on Israel, and Obadiah's warning is to all nations that will turn their hand against God's chosen people. The Book of Obadiah ought to be required reading at the United Nations because Obadiah highlights and underlines the precept: *"...ye shall reap what ye sow."* (Galatians 6:7) As seen in Obadiah 15 and again in verses 12 and 13, God always gives anyone or any nation a chance to see the error and repent, but Edom failed to heed the warning, fell upon Israel when they were down, and enslaved their refugees. Sound familiar? I like what a man by the name of Whittier once wrote: **"The tissue of the life to be weaved with colors all our own, and the field of destiny we reap as we have sown!"** I believe God has not given us the choice whether or not we read and study the Bible; I believe it is a command. Whether you like it or not, you will be judged on the Bible, the eternal quizzes will be on the Word, and your final exam will be from this text, and, just maybe, you will be asked about "Obadiah the second." What will you know about him? It might just be the proof that you are a servant of God!

Luke 1:70: *"As he spake by the mouth of the holy prophets, which have been since the world began."* (He also can speak to us through the mouth of the holy warrior!)

87.

ELIAB: GOD IS FATHER

I Chronicles 12:9: *"Ezer the first, Obadiah the second, **ELIAB** the third."*

THE THIRD GADITE TO join David's band of warriors and would become one of his "mighty men" was Eliab. We don't know which Israeli town he was from, we don't know any of his relatives, and we don't know any of his military exploits that brought him to David's attention, but we know the meaning of his name: God is Father. Another of David's "mighty men" had a name with a similar meaning: Abiel (I Chronicles 11:32). We wrote on "my Father is God" in a former chapter, but we will focus in this devotional on the Biblical truth as Christ *"...the everlasting Father..."* (Isaiah 9:6). In this chapter I would like to point you to this truth as Paul described it in Hebrews 1:5: *"For unto which of the angels said He at any time, Thou art my Son, this day have I begotten thee? And again, I will be to Him a Father, and he shall be to me a Son?"* This is not an easy theology because it deals with the unity of the Triune God. What is said of one is said of the others, and in One (Deuteronomy 6:4) is the Father, Son, and Holy Spirit; they are three Persons, but they are One!

As John was writing about the deity in his Gospel, he proclaimed this marvelous truth: *"And the Word became flesh, and dwelt among us, (and we beheld His glory, the glory of the only begotten of the Father), full of grace and truth."* (John 1:14) I have read a number of books written on the topic of the titles and terms connected to the Christ, but one of the best was Herbert C. Gabhart's classic, <u>The Name Above Every Name</u>. He made this comment on the term "begotten:"

ELIAB: GOD IS FATHER

When John referred to Jesus as the "begotten" of the Father, he was not trying to establish His Sonship necessarily. But he was saying that the only "begotten" son of God could act as God acted, talk as God talked, and love as God loved. In other words, Jesus bore the weight of the glory of God. As the only "begotten" of God, Christ was full of grace and truth. Grace reveals God's love; truth reveals God's light. These features were a part of Him from the beginning, but through His actions they became transparent. He was so full, so charted [today we might say "so overflowing"] that the glory which shone from Him gave the apostles the conception that it was that of the only "begotten" Son because who else could he be? (Acts 4:13)

For me, this doctrine is made perfectly clear when you consider this conversation between Jesus and Philip: *"Philip saith unto Him, Lord shew us the Father, and it sufficeth us. Jesus saith unto him, Have I been so long with you, and yet hast thou not known me, Philip? He that hath seen me hath seen the Father. Believeth thou not that I am in the Father, and the Father in me? The words that I speak unto you I speak not of myself; but the Father that dwelleth in me, He doth the works. Believeth me that I am in the Father and the Father in me..."* (John 14:8–11). That should make the name of Eliab very clear in Christ.

The great preacher of the nineteenth century, Charles Haddon Spurgeon, continues our thoughts on the union of the Father and the Son when he wrote this:

> Believer, you can bear your testimony that Christ is the only "begotten" of the Father, as well as the first "begotten" from the dead. You can say, "He is divine to me, if he be human to all the world beside." He has done that for me which none but a God could do. He has subdued my stubborn will, melted a heart of adamant, opened gates of brass, and snapped bars of iron. He hath turned for me my mourning into laughter, and my desolation into joy; he hath led my captivity captive, and made my heart rejoice with joy unspeakable and full of glory. Let others think as they will of Him, to me He must be the only "begotten" of the Father: blessed be His name! In life He is my life, and in death he shall be the death of death; in poverty Christ is my riches; in sickness He makes my bed; in darkness he is my star, and in brightness he is my sun; he is the manna of the camp of the wilderness, and He shall be the new corn of the host when they come to Canaan. Jesus is to me all grace and no wrath, all truth and no falsehood: and of truth and grace he is full,

infinitely full. My soul, this night, bless with all thy might, the only "begotten!"

Spurgeon seems to agree with Gabhart, and I agree with both of them of the unbreakable link between the Father and the Son. This is a cornerstone of our faith in the theology of the Eternal Trinity, and I know that there are a lot of people even within the Christian community that don't agree. How else will we have this wonderful truth in our heart?

And as He was the "begotten" of God, so should we. John the Apostle exhorts in his first epistle: *"We know that whosoever is born of God sinneth not, but he that is **begotten** of God keepeth himself, and that wicked one toucheth him not."* (I John 5:18) I will turn to one more trusted authority on this doctrine, a man I have read and studied with for years, the great commentator Matthew Henry. These are his thoughts on the last verse I quoted:

> A recapitulation of the privileges and advantages of the sound Christian believers: (1) They are secured against sin, against the fullness of it dominion, or the fullness of its guilt; we know that whosoever is born of God [and the believer in Christ is born of God, verse one] sinneth not; [verse 18] sinneth not with that fullness of heart and spirit that the unregenerate do, [as was said, chapter 3, 6, 9] and consequently not with that fullness of guilt that attends the sins of others; and so be is secured against that sin that is unavoidably unto death, or that infallibly binds the sinner over unto the wages of eternal death; the new nature, and the inhabitation of the divine Spirit thereby, prevent the admission of such unpardonable sin. (2) They are fortified against the devil's destructive attempts; He that is begotten of God, keepeth himself, that is, is enabled to guard himself, and the wicked one toucheth him not [verse 18] that is, the wicked one may not touch him, to death. It seems not to be barely a narration of the duty or the practice of the regenerate; but an indication of their power by virtue of their regeneration; they are thereby prepared and principled against the fatal touches, the sting, of the wicked one; he touches not their souls, to infuse that venom there that he does to others, or to expel that regenerative principles that is an antidote to his poison!

I know there was some deep theological reasoning in that explanation, but the point for me is made that will link us to the great theology that we have been adopted into this heavenly family (Galatians 4:4–7)!

God is not only Father to Christ and the Christian, but in saying God and in Paul's teaching that in Christ dwelt all the fullness of the Godhead bodily (Colossians 2:9), we have now become a part of the household of God (Ephesians 2:19). So today, we can both rejoice in the "begotten" (John 3:16) and what He did for us, but we can also rejoice in the truth that we are of the "begotten" as well. John would write this in the first chapter of his gospel: *"But as many as receive him, to them gave he power to become the sons of God, even to them that believe on His name."* (John 1:12) It is this doctrine that helps us understand the "born again" theology of Jesus. His conversation with Nicodemus (John 3) was the first insight into the relationship the Father and the Son had that would eventually deal with the fellowship us as Christians now have with them.

I John 1:3: *"...and truly our fellowship is with the Father, and with His Son Jesus Christ."*

88.

MISHMANNAH: FATNESS

I Chronicles 12:10: *"**MISHMANNAH** the fourth, Jeremiah the fifth."*

A MAN THAT WILL switch sides in the midst of a conflict, a war, or a national struggle is often called a traitor (like Benedict Arnold during our Revolutionary War), a turn coat, or a deserter. No doubt those were some of the terms used to describe men like Mishmannah after he joined David's small band of mercenaries in the Philistia town of Ziklag (I Chronicles 12:1). Mishmannah had changed sides, switched loyalties, and jumped ship, all in favor of following the fugitive David. Note Mishmannah wasn't the first to join David's group (the Benjamites -I Chronicles 12:2-were the first mentioned), and Mishmannah wasn't even the first Gadite to join (I Chronicles 12:8); in actuality he was the fourth. We are never given the reason for the switch, and, like so many, we don't know his hometown or his family because all we have is a name, a name of a "mighty man." As I have highlighted so often in this series of devotionals, I believe Mishmannah was motivated by the charisma of David, the clarity of purpose of David (I Chronicles 11:10), and the downfall of a very oppressing kingship in Saul versus the anointed future king of Israel. Maybe, Mishmannah had followed the tale of David since as a boy he became a national military hero with the killing of the Philistine giant Goliath. I see in the changing of sides in the case of Mishmannah and David a wonderful picture that takes place in the switching of side in the spiritual struggle that happens in the heart of those once loyal to sin, Satan, and self to a love affair with Jesus Christ.

MISHMANNAH: FATNESS

So it is for those of us who have followed Satan, our father (John 8:44), for years; followed the examples of sinners for decades, and followed our own selfish ambitions for a lifetime. We were once loyal soldiers in Satan's army of sinful endeavors. Satan seemed to satisfy all our earthly desires and worldly needs and pleasures, and we thought we were happy, enjoying a wonderful life. We were well adapted and admired the ways of Satan and our free living lifestyle was fulfilling, but in time the reaping of such license began to take a toll. We began to hear about another whose life and living and lifestyle was different, and of another kind of kingdom and another kind of king. Eventually, we became in debt to Satan, in debt to sin, and in distress. Discontentment filled our heart and soul, and we looked for a way out. Were these not the practical reasons given for those that abandoned King Saul for the refugee David? *"And every one that was in distress, and every one that was in debt, and every one that was discontented, gathered themselves unto him* [David]; *and he became a captain over them; and there were with him* [David] *about four hundred."* (I Samuel 22:1) Did Mishmannah settle under the flag of David for the same reasons? Like these men, we no longer wanted Satan to be our leader. We began to hate Satan's leadership and sin's license. Self now was a liability, not an asset. It was then we began to look for another, listen to another voice, a sweet voice that was calling us away from that old life to a new life with Christ.

It all started when someone dropped the name of Jesus. Once we heard it, it became the sweetest name we ever heard. We wanted to know more about this man from Bethlehem (interestingly). Then it happened one day. We met this "mighty man" on the battlefield of life, and we in a moment decided to switch sides. I tell people, just read the story of the other Saul (Paul) in Acts 9:1–16, and you will understand what happened to you and me! What drew us to our captain (Hebrews 2:10) was His love (Satan never spoke of love) and His forgiveness; Satan only led us into more transgressions and iniquities. Instantly, our old commander attacked us, took hold of us to draw us back, but our new Commander held us tight and would not let us go (Philippians 1:6). Granted, we had to leave our old comrades, but a few came with us (Mishmannah's friends) and we found in our new army better friends, supporting friends, and loving friends. Oh, day by day we had to face the rage of our old captain (I Peter 5:8), but also with each passing day we came to understand why we switched sides, changed allegiances, and jumped ship. Our future was different, our direction was changed, and we were on the winning side.

Ours was a new "fatness" (the meaning of Mishmannah's name), a new fullness!

When the patriarch Jacob was lying on his death bed, he predicted a few future characteristics of his son's descendants, men like Mishmannah. This is what he said about Mishmannah's forefather Gad: *"Gad, a troop shall overcome him, but he shall overcome at last."* (Genesis 49:19). Many years after this prophecy, Moses also foretold a few qualities of the Gadites when he wrote: *"And of Gad he said, Blessed be he that enlargeth Gad: he dwelleth as a lion, and teareth the arm with the crown of his head."* (Deuteronomy 33:20) Reading into these prophecies in the light of the story of Mishmannah, I see that these things happened to him. Mishmannah was first overcome by King Saul, but when he switched sides and followed David, he would eventually be an overcomer (I John 5:4). And by enlarging his course with David, Mishmannah would dwell with a lion, the symbol of Judah, the tribe of David (Genesis 49:8–12). Even the Lord Jesus Christ is likened to a lion in the Bible: *"And one of the elders saith unto me, Weep not: behold, the Lion of the tribe of Judah, the root of David, hath prevailed to open the book, and to lose the seven seals thereof."* (Revelation 5:5) And as Jesus was an overcomer (John 16:33) so would Mishmannah and so can we (I John 5:5). Despite the fact that Mishmannah was not from the tribe of Judah, his connection and choice of David brought him into the privileges and the blessings that come with being on David's side; just like we are entitled to all the blessings of Christ (Ephesians 1:3). Amen!

I have often likened men like Mishmannah to the Confederate General Robert E. Lee switching sides in the second day of the Battle of Gettysburg, the high water mark of the American Civil War. Bob didn't, but men like Mishmannah and Paul did! In the earliest days of the great struggle between the Sanhedrin and the Church there emerged a young man as the point of the spear in the attack that the Jewish organization hoped would destroy this upstart faith (Acts 7:58). Saul was there at that stoning of Stephen, and his fervor and fire soon spread through Judah and Samaria to distant cities where the early Church was scattered. I love the terminology Luke used in his description of this assault: *"...made havoc of the Church, entering into every house, and haling men and women committed them to prison...and Saul, yet breathing out threatenings and slaughter against the disciples of the Lord, went unto the High Priest, and desired of him letters to Damascus to the synagogues, that if he found any of the way, whether they were men or women, he might bring them bound to Jerusalem."* (Acts 8:3, 9:1) The first major persecution of the Church was at its height when the Church's chief antagonist switched sides. It would forever change the course of the church and for a time weaken the assault of Satan. Oh, the impact men like Mishmannah have is only fully known in heaven!

> Ephesians 2:2: *"Wherein in time past ye walked according to the course of this world, according to the prince of the power of the air, the spirit that now worketh…"*

89.

JEREMIAH: THE LORD IS EXALTED

I Chronicles 12:10: *"Mishmannah the fourth, **JEREMIAH** the fifth."*

WE HAVE COME TO the third man in David's "mighty men" that was named Jeremiah (I Chronicles 12:4, 10, 13). The best known Jeremiah in the Bible is the famous "weeping prophet" of Israel (Jeremiah 1:1), but what I will focus this devotional on is the connection this name has with Jesus Christ: *"And they said, some say that thou art John the Baptist; some, Elias* [Elijah]*; and other Jeremias* [Jeremiah]*, or one of the prophets."* (Matthew 16:14) In our last article on a mighty man named Jeremiah we concentrated on the meaning of the name, the Lord is exalted or Jehovah is high, but this time I would have you consider the reason Jesus was considered a Jeremiah.

In perhaps one of the first public opinion polls ever taken in history, the question proposed was who is Jesus? Jesus Himself asked for the poll according to Matthew 16:13: *"When Jesus came into the coasts of Caesarea Philippi, he asked his disciples, saying, Whom do men say that I the Son of Man am?"* In May of 2010, I, with my daughter Marnie and a score of Dallas Theological students, stopped in Caesarea Philippi for an afternoon of discovery. It was one of the more meaningful stops on our tour because of the Matthew account of Jesus' stopover. I had known the story and Jesus' question since I was a child, but to actually consider it in the very place it was purposed was inspiring. Caesarea Philippi is nothing but an archeological dig now, a tourist spot at best, but the ancient ruins and the stream that still runs through it helped me understand

JEREMIAH: THE LORD IS EXALTED

what Jesus was asking His disciples. Granted, we could focus on the other names suggested by the disciples: John the Baptist (even Herod the King thought that John had been resurrected in Jesus-Matthew 14:2), Elijah was always on the lips of the people in light of the prophecy (Malachi 4:5), and even to the end they thought that Elijah might come and help Jesus (Matthew 27:47), but then there was the mention of Jeremiah.

I will first yield to the thoughts of Herbert C. Gabhart and his opinions about this name recorded in his excellent book, <u>The Name Above Every Name</u>:

> Jeremiah was venerated by the Jews at the time of Jesus. The Jews fondly hoped that Jeremiah might return and restore the ark, the tabernacle, and the altar of incense. In the book "The Apocrypha," a compilation of fourteen books which were revered by the Jews, one of the books, II Maccabees 2:1–8, states that records tell of Jeremiah taking the ark to a cave for safety. The doctrine of metempsychosis, transmigration, or the passing of the soul from one body into another was accepted among the Jews, and therefore it seemed logical to them that the soul of Jeremiah might be reincarnated in Christ. Jeremiah was known as "the weeping prophet." He wept over the sins of the people. Jesus wept over Jerusalem: "When he came near, he beheld the city, and wept over it." (Luke 19:41) Jesus also wept in Bethany over the death of Lazarus (John 11:35); as Israel was God's instrument in Jeremiah's day, so spiritual Israel is God's instrument today. Jeremiah was a prophet of individualism which is one of Christianity's chief cornerstones, so the similarities could go on and on. Indeed, Jeremiah was not a bad guess. It was an advance in thinking to liken Christ to one of the spiritual, teaching prophets. However, the question still is: "Whom do you say that I am?"

I am not saying I agree with all that Gabhart wrote, but it does cause us to consider again just why Jeremiah was named in the poll.

As Gabhart leaves his comments with Jesus question, so, too, must we return to the personal question of Matthew 16:15. It will not do you any good in your day of judgment to know what other people thought because the verdict on your life will be only what you thought of Jesus, the Christ. Remember, that is exactly how Jesus dealt with Peter. It was good that Peter knew the different opinions, but what did Peter think? Unlike the others, Peter had thought it through, and his opinion was that Jesus was neither John, nor Jeremiah, but: **"Thou art the Christ, the Son** *of the Living God!"* (Matthew 16:16) I still remember the day when I was just a little boy that I was confronted with the question and was challenged to give my own answer, not the opinions of others. The day I made Peter's confession was the day I began to live for Christ. In over 67 years I have never changed my mind about Christ, sought another from the Christ, nor desired the multitude that sees the Christ as only a teacher, or a rebel, or a martyr, or a preacher, or a healer. For me, Jesus of Nazareth is still *"the Christ, the Son of the Living God!"*

Perhaps the most mournful book ever written is Jeremiah's classic work simply called The Lamentations of Jeremiah. Tradition from the old Jewish Septuagint begins with these lines: "And it came to pass that, after Israel was taken captive and Jerusalem was made desolate, Jeremiah sat weeping and lamented with this lamentation and said…" In a generation where it is not manly to weep, Jeremiah would stick out like a sour thumb, yet I am convinced that this is exactly what is needed today. We need a Jeremiah, like Jesus did, to tell us the truth about our age and the future. Jeremiah, like Jesus, wouldn't stick his head in the sand and ignore the signs of the time. We have become, like those of Jeremiah's Judah, only desirous of the good news (and I am not talking about the Good News). It is time for God's people to weep over their sins, the state of the world, and the downfall of our nation, just the way Jeremiah did in his age.

I have come to believe the reason that Jeremiah wept was his understanding revealed to him that his people in the end would not repent; that the destruction of his beloved Jerusalem was inevitable and the Levitical worship system and the Temple of God with the coveted Ark of the Covenant would inevitably be destroyed. The tears of Lamentation were the result of long years pleading and begging a stiffed necked people who would never listen to his warning and appeals. Jeremiah had been commissioned before his birth (Jeremiah 1:5) to proclaim God's message in the full understanding that he would never be heard. I am convinced that both Jeremiah and Noah had plenty to talk to Jesus about in Glory because all three had similar ministries in light of the people they preached to. Noah preached 120 years (II Peter 2:5) and only saw seven respond. Noah couldn't stop the flood waters, and Jeremiah couldn't stop the Babylonian surge, and neither can we stop the fire that will one day destroy our world (II Peter 3:16). Our job is not to stop the judgment of God, but simply to warn the world about the coming Judgment, whether or not they listen!

Weep and witness is our commission, and we should take heart through the testimony of men like Jeremiah that no matter the rejection, the stiff necks, and the closed ears, "the Lord will be exalted!" Maybe, it is your lot to be the weeper in your family because there seems to be those of each generation whose heart is broken enough to speak "the truth in tears." Jeremiah was the man of his generation like Noah before him and Jesus after him. Was Jeremiah David's weeping warrior?

Luke 9:20: *"He said...But whom say ye that I am? Peter answering said, The Christ of God!"*

90.

ATTAI: TIMELY

I Chronicles 12:11: *"**ATTAI** the sixth, Eliel the seventh."*

THE FABLE IS TOLD about a group of animals complaining about what humans take from them. The cow griped about losing her milk, the hen her eggs, and the pig her bacon. Others voiced their complaints until the snail said, "I have something these humans wish they could take from me and that something is time!" I smiled at this tale the first time because of my 21-month old grandson Judah Alan. For some reason Judah has a fascination with these slimy, slow creatures. For some reason he calls them "nees," his word, not ours, and he spends his mornings in his California backyard looking for them. Because of the recent rains, there is an abundance of snails so he is a pretty happy boy. He collects their shells and has been known to bring a living one into the house, something his mother tries to avoid. The other thing that drew my attention to this story was the truth of the fable: that time is precious, valuable, and wise is the individual that uses it wisely. The truth about the matter is the only one that does use time wisely is God. Interestingly, the sixth Gadite to join David's "mighty man" list was Attai and his name means "timely," and that is all we know about him, but what a name! Before we get through this study of David's top 105 "mighty men," I am going to introduce you to a group of Issacharites that were also a part of David's amazing army that had as their primary characteristic: **"...which were men that had understanding of the times, to know what Israel ought to do..."** (I Chronicles 12:32). Timing at times is a God thing!

It was not hard for me to make a connection between the meaning of Attai's name and what Paul wrote of the first coming of our Lord and Savior Jesus Christ: *"But when the fullness of time was come, God sent forth His Son, made of a woman, made under the law."* (Galatians 4:4) As I have done often in this series of devotionals, I have used a man's name to highlight and underline some aspect of the Christ. In this chapter I would like to connect the times and time of Jesus with his timeliness, starting from his birth to His departure. I hope my reader can accept the truth of John 1:14: *"...the Word became flesh, and dwelt among us..."* Paul takes this truth one step back to reveal that Christ's coming was timely. Granted, we don't know the exact date (No, December 25th was not the date), but we do know that it happened at a divinely set time: *"...in the fullness of time..."* I like what Richard DeHaan wrote on this thought:

> Looking again at the record. The account of Jesus' birth includes the details that any informed individual would recognize as reliable. The swaddling clothes, the inn, the shepherds' visit all support the conclusion that the Son of God did indeed enter this space-time world. There is no question about it. He did come. He did live a perfect life. He did die a sacrificial death. He did rise from the dead. These things are undeniable, and any open-minded person will acknowledge them as true. Remember, the exact date when our Lord was born is really quite incidental, but the fact that Jesus came to dwell on this planet means everything.

Timely isn't just about a day, an hour, and the minute something took place. To this day I don't remember the exact day I actually accepted Jesus as my Savior. I know the year (1958), I know the place (Perham Baptist Church), I know the occasion (Junior Church), and I know the lady that lead me to Christ (Lily Harris), but I was seven, and I didn't write down the date and seemingly no one else did, but that doesn't negate the truth that I gave my heart and my sins to Jesus to take care of. One of the things I have been trying to do in this series is to make a practical application to the theme of my devotional. I would like to do the same here. Jesus was sent to earth in a timely manner and so, too, shall we be sent. Jesus said to His disciples on the night of the resurrection: *"...* **As my Father hath sent me, even so send I you..."** (John 20:21. Like with our salvation, so, too, with our service; timing is everything!

Oswald Chambers, another favorite devotional writer, once wrote this:

A missionary is one sent by Jesus Christ as He was sent by God. The great dominant note is not the needs of men, but the command of Jesus. The source of our inspiration in work for God is behind, not before. The tendency today is to put the inspiration ahead, to sweep everything in front of us and bring it all out to our conception of success. In the New Testament the inspiration is put behind us, the Lord Jesus. The idea is to be true to Him, to carry out His enterprises.

It seems today that the eternal enterprises have been taken over by mankind. Jesus said, *"I came forth from God."* (John 8:42); we must say: "We have come forth from God!" God first gave Jesus (II Corinthians 9:15) to the world, and then Jesus gave His disciples to the world (Acts 1:8). One of my favorite Church hymns was written by E. Margret Clarkson, So Send I You. The history of the birth of that song goes something like this. As a 23-year-old school teacher in a gold-mining camp in northern Ontario, Canada, Margret Clarkson became very lonely. One evening, however, as she meditated on John 20:21, the Lord spoke to her through the phrase: "So Send I You." She was immediately released from her loneliness by the fact that this was the place the Lord had sent her to minister to Him, and that the Lord's timing was perfect; that the gold mining town was her mission field and her students and the town's people were her mission. Her desire was always to go to some foreign field of service, but because of a physical disability she was unable to leave Canada. She never did get to go but to a mining town in Canada, but her song went around the world! Let me remind you of some of her stirring words:

> So send I you to labour unrewarded,
> To serve unpaid, unloved, unsought, unknown;
> To bear rebuke, to suffer scorn and scoffing,
> So send I you, to toil for me alone.
> So send I you to bind the bruised and broken,
> Over wandering souls to work, to weep, to wake;
> To bear the burdens of a world a weary,
> So send I you, to suffer for my sake.
> So send I you to loneliness and longing,
> With heart a-hungering for the loved and known,
> Forsaking home and kindred, friend and dear one,
> So send I you, to know my love alone.
> So send I you to leave your life's ambition,
> To die to dear desire, self-will resign,

To labour alone and love where men revile you,
So send I you to lose your life in Mine.

So send I you to hearts made hard by hatred,
To eyes made blind because they will not see,
To spend though it be blood, to spend and spare not,
So send I you, to taste of Calvary.
As the Father hath sent me, so send I you!

And that sending is very timely. Remember the story of Philip and the Ethiopian eunuch in Acts 8 and the timing necessary for those two to get together. What about Jesus and the Samaritan woman at Jacobs well in John 4. The Bible is filled with timely stories that could have only happened if the God, who is not limited to time, is the governor of the timely events of our lives. I have often thought I would have loved to have been living in the great revival time of the Church towards the end of the nineteenth century, but I have come to realize that this is my time and times, and God has always had perfect timing in my life, from when I was born, to when I got saved, and to my service time.

Esther 4:14: *"Who knoweth whether thou art come to the kingdom for such a time as this?"*

91.

ELIEL: MY GOD IS GOD

I Chronicles 12:11: *"Attai the sixth,* **ELIEL** *the seventh."*

WE HAVE COME TO the third "Eliel" listed in David's "mighty men." Before this Gadite there was Eliel the Mahavite (I Chronicles 11:46) and Eliel the Mesobaite (I Chronicles 11:47). We have covered the deep meaning of this name: "My God is God" in previous devotionals so I thought I would focus my attention on the only difference between these three "mighty men" and that being this Eliel was called "the seventh."

According to J. Edwin Hartill in his book <u>Principles of Biblical Hermeneutics</u>, the number seven is "the number of divine fullness, perfection, and completeness." It is one of the perfect numbers and comes from a Hebrew word meaning "to be complete," "to be full," "to be satisfied," or "to be enough." The first illustration to this that comes to my mind is my Uncle Paul's (my father's only brother) obsession with this number. When he inherited his parent's home on the Blackstone homestead in 2003, he approached my brother and cousin (who owned the farm at the time) if they might consider selling him a few more acres around his house. At the time, he owned less than an acre. Jay and Gary agreed and hired another cousin (Dale), a surveyor, to mark out what he wanted. When asked, he said: "Exactly enough to make seven acres." He believed in the number that much. Hartill in his book gives these Biblical examples of the importance of this number to God:

> (1)There were seven men who lived over 900 years of age, Adam, Seth, Enos, Cainan, Jared, and Methuselah with Noah the seventh and perfect man (Genesis 6:9). Lamech, the father

of Noah, is recorded to have lived 777 years. (2) The phrase, "a new song," occurs seven times in the Old Testament, and is always given in connection with the Second Coming of our Lord. (3) The Greek word "agape," which means love, occurs seven times in John's Gospel. (4) In the seventh chapter of Isaiah in the second verse, there is a seven-fold description of the Holy Spirit resting upon the Lord. (5) There are seven "walks" in Ephesians. (6) Naaman was told to dip seven times in the Jordan. (7) Seven miracles are recorded in John's Gospel.

No doubt Hartill could have gone on and on, and though I believe that the numbers of the Bible are as much inspired as the words (II Timothy 3:16), I feel we need to be careful with putting too much stock in their importance, especially when all we do is try to see through and in the numbers.

For me, the meaning of seven is best seen in the Person of Jesus Christ because if seven is the perfect number, the complete number, the full number, then we ought to consider these verses: *"For in Him [Jesus] dwelleth all the 'fullness' of the Godhead bodily."* (Colossians 2:9); *"And ye are 'complete' in Him [Jesus], which is the Head of all principality and power."* (Colossians 2:10); *"For it became Him [Jesus], for whom are all things, and by whom all things, in bringing many souls unto glory, to make the captain of their salvation 'perfect' through suffering."* (Hebrews 2:10) We might ask ourselves, how someone like Jesus who was already "perfect" as the Son of God be made any more "perfect?" In the world if someone or something is considered exceptional, they are given the number "ten;" she is a ten or they get a perfect ten in their performance, but I believe this term and number seven in the Bible speaks of the matchless Person of Christ.

As we share a few thoughts on this aspect of Jesus, I first turn this page over to Gabhart, the man I have quoted often in this book, a man who wrote an excellent devotional on the titles and terms given to Jesus in the Bible:

> Jesus as a perfect man was faultless. After much questioning, Pilate said that he could find no fault in Him. Jesus did not have an Achilles' heel-a vulnerable spot. He was flawless. Many times, items for sale are reduced in price due to a tiny, almost unobservable flaw. But not so with Christ. The most powerful magnifying glass could not find a flaw. There were no flaws in His character. All the spiritual elements were properly woven

into His life. There were no weak spots, no broken threads. He was fadeless. He never lost His freshness of appearance, color, or brilliance. Priceless pictures painted years ago still maintain some of their brilliance although most of them have faded somewhat, but His brilliance has brightened with years!

I believe in the "faultlessness," "flawlessness," and "fadelessness" of our Lord and Savior Jesus Christ. Do you?

If all that Gabhart says about Jesus is true and all that Hartill says about seven is true, and I believe they are true, then what could Paul have been writing about in Hebrews 2:10 when he spoke of Jesus *"perfection through suffering?"* In a precious article on "perfection" from Luke 13:32 we learned that this word doesn't say that Christ was once imperfect and then became perfect. The idea remains that this speaks of Christ's completed work, not His character. He became the Captain of our salvation by completing the sacrificial work for sin through His suffering for our sin first in **Gethsemane** (the garden of suffering-Matthew 26:36), then at **Gabbatha** (Pilate's judgment hall of suffering-John 19:13), and finally at **Golgotha** (the final place of suffering on a cross-John 19:17). It was at these three places that we can understand the term of perfection applied to the Son of God.

Though perfection is not an attainable goal for us in this life because of the sinful flesh we still live in, it must remain a goal, a challenge, an attainment we work towards and reach for. As I have done in most of these chapters on David's "mighty men," I have tried to glean something from each topic that can be practical and applicable to us. Paul in Hebrews 11:40 writes of *"…they without us should not be made perfect…"* I like F. B. Meyer on this:

> This chapter [Hebrews 11] proves that the saints of all ages are essentially one. There is a link which unites them; a thrill which passed from hand to hand around a circle. One theme for many voices; one attitude for many faces; one inspiration for many hearts. The saints that lived before the Advent and those that have lived since are the ones in their faith in the living God, making the unseen visible, the distant near, and seeing the eternal through the transient and ephemeral. And now heaven waits. Its joys are not complete, its rapture not full. The blessed are blessed; but there is yet a margin between what they are and what they will be-between what they enjoy, and what they may enjoy. The choir is not full, and the anthem cannot be fully rendered till our voices blend in it. There is a pause, a halt,

expectancy, incompleteness, till we come. Your dear ones want you to be there. They have not gone far into the heart of God's bliss, but are lingering near the gate till you have joined them. From Switzerland your friends write to say it is perfectly beautiful, but "it will be better when you join us; we are reserving the best excursions till you arrive; we are incomplete without you; make haste." It is thus that the blessed await us!

This writing encouraged me today just three days after I buried my father and my son side by side in the family plot in Perham, Maine. Dad died of old age (92), but Scott died of cancer at 39 just two months apart. I can't wait until I reunite with them in that perfect place, and one day we all will be "a seven."

Psalm 18:30: *"As for God, His way is perfect…"*

92.

JOHANAN: JEHOVAH IS GRACIOUS

I Chronicles 12:12: "**JOHANAN** the eighth, Elzabad the ninth."

WE HAVE COME TO a reoccurring theme in the meaning of the names listed in David's "mighty men:" grace. Interestingly, Elhanan, the eighth man listed in II Samuel 23:24, means "God is Gracious." In this chapter the man of our attention is Johanan, the eighth man listed, and his name means: "Jehovah is Gracious." After our last chapter could we conclude that "eight" is the number of grace? In a recent article we looked at another Johanan (I Chronicles 12:4), a Benjaminite. This Johanan is a Gadite. Despite previous chapters on this topic, I believe we can never write enough about our gracious God!

Vance Havner once wrote: **"The grace of God transcends all our feeble efforts to describe it. It cannot be poured into any of our mental receptacles without running over!"** The great devotional writer Oswald Chambers has written: **"Never trust anything but the grace of God in yourself or in anyone else!"** Many years ago I was reading Chamber's classic devotional, <u>My Upmost for His Highest</u>, when I came across these comments by Oswald on Paul's challenging statement of: ***"We…beseech you that ye receive not the grace of God in vain."*** (II Corinthians 6:1) Chambers wrote this:

> The grace you had yesterday will not do for today. Grace is the overflowing favour of God; you can always reckon it is there to draw upon. "In much patience, in afflictions, in necessities, in distresses" that is where the test for patience comes. Are you

failing the grace of God there? It is not a question of praying and asking God to help you; it is taking the grace of God now. We make prayer the preparation for work. It is never that in the Bible. Prayer is the exercise of drawing on the grace of God. Don't say-I will endure this until I can get away to pray. Pray now; draw on the grace of God the moment of need. Prayer is the most practical thing. It is not the reflex action of devotion. Prayer is the last thing in which we lean to draw on God's grace. "In strips, in imprisonments, in tumults, in labors, in all these things manifest a drawing upon the grace of God that will make you a marvel to yourself and to others. Draw now, not presently. The one word in the spiritual vocabulary is "now!" Let circumstance bring you where they will, keep drawing on the grace of God in every conceivable condition you may be in. One of the greatest proofs that you are drawing on the grace of God is that you can be humiliated without manifesting the slightest trace of anything but His grace!

Annie Johnson Flint's hymn He Giveth More Grace comes to mind here: "He giveth more grace when the burden grows greater…His grace has no measure…He giveth, and giveth, and giveth again!" To which I can only add that if we do believe that we serve a gracious God, then why don't we rely on Him for the measure of grace we need in every situation and circumstance we face? Why don't we go to Him and trust in Him that He will measure out to us exactly the amount of grace we will need to face our challenge or overcome our obstacle or press through that barrier that is keeping us from going on with God? I have recently had to go again and again to God's well of grace and drink from that wonderful virtue to sustain me through six terrible months of watching my 39-year- old son pass away. Scott got an aggressive lung cancer last fall (2016) and died this spring (2017). (I have written of that six-month struggle in a book I called "Beyond the Bend"-published by Wipf and Stock in 2021.) It was a day by day grace, a measured grace because of the ups and downs of taking care of Scott that sustained my wife and I as we watched this healthy soldier (11 years in the regular army and army reserves) be overcome to the point he was no longer recognizable to most who knew him. That is when you need daily, moment by moment grace, a grace that will ease the trauma and help with the agony.

Another great devotional writer, F. B. Meyer, once challenged me with this straightforward, thought-provoking question and comment:

Doest thou need grace? He is full of it. His grace is sufficient. With both hands He will give and give and give again; only practice the habit of taking. Grace is the bud of which Glory is the flower. If He has given this, He will not without that. If thou knewest the gift of God, thou wouldst be sure that Glory in germ is within thee, waiting only the summer of Eternity to develop the perfect beauty. We have had out access by faith into this grace wherein we stand, and we rejoice in hope of Glory of God.

I think all my readers would believe with me that we all need grace at times, but what the world doesn't understand and what often Christians fail to adapt is the ever presence of a specialized grace for each and every one of us. What I need in light of my situation might not be what you need. That is why Peter calls it *"the manifold grace of God"* (I Peter 4:10). In my personal study of the Bible I have come up with different categories of grace that we might need at different times in our lives. I am not saying that I know them all or have experienced them all, but let this list get you going on your own search.

1. Saving grace (Ephesians 2:8-9); the container of salvation is grace (Titus 2:11).
2. Growing grace (II Peter 3:18); the course to maturity is grace (I Peter 2:2).
3. Teaching grace (Titus 2:11-12); the champion of righteousness is grace.
4. Sustaining grace (II Corinthians 12:9); the conductor of strength is grace.
5. Witnessing grace (Acts 4:33); the conduit of our testimony is grace (Acts 1:8).
6. Working grace (Acts 14:260; the culvert of service is grace (Ephesians 4:7-13).
7. Disciplining grace (Romans 6:14); the controller of any sin is grace (Romans 6:15).
8. Helping grace (Hebrews 4:16); the channel of prayer is grace (Philippians 4:6).
9. Departing grace (Revelation 22:21); the conclusion of life is by grace (II Timothy 4:6-7).

It was this last kind of grace that got my son through the last six months of his life.

Whether in a name like Johanan or in the Word of God, we must realize that we believe in a gracious God. Whether in nature or in a word, the Bible speaks about this wonderful attribute of God even in the listing of simple name, the names of the unknown. As this subject keeps coming up in David's "mighty men," it verifies this verse in Isaiah's classic prophecy: *"Therefore will the Lord wait, that He be gracious unto you."* (Isaiah 30:18) How long the Lord has waited as I week by week (I have been writing one chapter a week since I started this book project; I am nearing two years now.) have studied the "mighty men;" all this time for God to step by step teach me of his "amazing grace." How many times have I waited in my life for God's grace thinking I have to pray for it, wait for it, when in reality it had been there all the time and all I had to do was apply it. I didn't wait in my son's situation, but just day by day lived in God's grace. I had struggled in days past instead of grasping onto the rope of God's grace. I have knocked on other doors instead of knocking on God's door of grace. When will we realize that grace is not just a word, but a constant and continual working of God in our lives?

Exodus 22:27: *"…and it shall come to pass, when He crieth unto me, that I will hear; for I am gracious.*

93.

ELZABAD: GOD HAS GIVEN

I Chronicles 12:12: *"Johanan the eighth,* **ELZABAD** *the ninth."*

WE HEAR A LOT about the "vengeance of God" (Romans 12:19-*Dearly beloved, avenge not yourselves, but rather give place unto wrath: for it is written, Vengeance is mine; I will repay, saith the Lord.*), but when was the last time you heard a message on the "recompense of God?" I believe that all that God has to give in the form of recompense is through His Son Jesus Christ. It was the meaning of the name Elzabad, God has given, which set my mind on this course. This Gadite opens up a wonderful doctrine for our exploration and examination into the divine and eternal workings of the Almighty.

Recompense is a reward: *"...He is a rewarder of them that diligently seek Him."* (Hebrews 11:6) We know of the negative reward of God to the evil doer, but what of the positive reward to them that "walk by faith?" Jesus taught us: *"He that receiveth a prophet in the name of the prophet shall receive a prophet's reward; and he that receiveth a righteous man in the name of a righteous man shall receive a righteous man's reward. And whosoever shall give a drink unto one of these little ones, a cup of cold water only in the name of a disciple; verily I say unto you, he shall in no wise lose his reward."* (Matthew 10:41–42) So as Elzabad's name suggests and the rest of the Bible teaches, we serve a giving God, a rewarding Savior!

H. L. Gee tells the story of a cobbler who wanted to go into the ministry, but because of a lack of funds wasn't able to have a formal or traditional ministerial education. Although he was disappointed, he still studied on his own and eventually became a deeply spiritual man. One day this cobbler took a liking to a young man who was also interested in the pastorate. Despite his meager funds, he helped the boy through Bible School. Later, just before the young man entered into the Lord's work, the cobbler gave the boy a pair of shoes with these words: "Please wear these when you preach the Gospel. It will help me think that you are standing in my shoes and performing the task I always wanted to do!" As I ponder this simple story, I realize I, too, have many people whose shoes I am standing in, and I believe that these will share in any reward I might receive because of my Gospel ministries. I, too, after returning from India in 2006 started to help certain young people out that I had met that could have never finished Bible school on their own. Today there are those walking in my shoes in places in India that I will never be able to tread. A cup of cold water or a pair of shoes given in the name of the Lord will receive a just recompense. Remember what Paul wrote to the Corinthians: *"Now he that planteth and he that watereth are one: and every man shall receive his own reward according to his own labor."* (I Corinthians 3:8) Some make the shoes and some wear the shoes, but each will receive his own recompense. It isn't the size of the gift or the action, it is what is given or done in the name of the Lord that counts because it is the motivation and sacrifice behind the gift and the doing that will be rewarded. In the great day of reward (II Corinthians 5:10) we will realize the wonderful recompense our giving God will bestow.

    I found this story in an Our Daily Bread, and I think you will see clearly the application to our theme in this devotional: "Many years ago the Queen of England visited Canada. A gallant young man, seeing a muddy place in the pathway where the royal guest was to tread, removed his raincoat in the tradition of Sir Walter Raleigh and spread it over the puddle. The Queen gave him a grateful smile of recognition but took a slight detour to avoid the spot he had so graciously covered. The press, taking note of this moment, blazoned the young man's name across the front page of many newspapers around the world. You see, it was not the greatness of the deed, but the one for whom it was performed that made it noteworthy!" Someone has rightfully written: "**A small deed done in Jesus' name is no small deed!**"

    We have before us today another great name in Elzabad that can be associated with the Christ because God has given Him to the world. Without doubt, Jesus Christ is our rewarder and reconciler, reconciling us back to God, yet Paul makes it clear that reconciliation doesn't stop there: *"And all things are of God who hath reconciled unto Himself by Jesus*

Christ, and hath given us the ministry of reconciliation." (II Corinthians 5:18) If we have been the recipient of reconciliation, then we are the ones who know best of its blessings, its rewards. Therefore, we ought to be proclaiming its wonderful truth to a world that knows not of its rewards. Christ did a work for us that we might do a work for him. Recompense and reconciliation go hand in hand in the work. Someone else has written: **"If your Christianity is worth having, it is worth sharing!"**

I turn again to the wonderful devotional source the <u>Our Daily Bread</u>, but this time to the pen of Dave Egner for this illustration of reconciliation and the ministry that we are supposed to be involved in:

> In the mid-50s, the world was shocked when five missionaries were killed by some Auca Indians in South America. They were trying to reach these primitive people with the Gospel. Later, the tribe welcomed into their community the wife of one of the martyred missionaries and the sister of another, and translation work on a New Testament in their language began. Veteran missionary pilot Bob Griffin tells about the difficulty the translators had putting the word "reconciliation" into the Auca language. They searched for an equivalent but found none. Then one day a translator was traveling through the jungle with some of the Aucas. They came to a narrow, deep ravine, and the missionary thought they could go no further. The Aucas, however, took out their machetes and cut down a large tree so that it fell over the ravine, permitting them all to cross safely. The translator, listening intently to the Aucas, discovered that they had a word for "tree across the ravine." This seemed to be the best way to express the meaning of the word "reconciled." The deep "ravine" between sinful man and a holy God was bridged by Jesus Christ. He became a man, lived a sinless life, and died for us. He reconciled us to God. He is our "tree across the ravine."

God has given us the work of reconciliation, and He will reward us, recompense us, according to the work that we do, no matter the part we play in reconciliation.

God has given His Son to reconcile the world unto Himself, and now we are to bridge the gap between our family and friends so that the work of reconciliation can happen. Some of us will simply be involved in the prayer part of this ministry. Others of us might support others through our finances to see that they can go and tell. But for most of us, we will be able to play a direct part by sharing our faith with them. We, like the Aucas in the <u>Our Daily Bread</u> story, have the privilege and the right to bring our lost friend or family member to the "ravine" of sin and show them the "tree" (Calvary's tree) that crosses (Calvary's cross) the great divide between us and God. In the name of Elzabad we have revealed two great teachings of our Faith, recompense and reconciliation.

Romans 11:15: *"For if the casting away of them be reconciling of the world, what shall the receiving of them be, but life from the dead?"*

94.

JEREMIAH: THE LORD ESTABLISHES

I Chronicles 12:13: *"**JEREMIAH** the tenth, Machbanai the eleventh."*

WE HAVE COME TO the third Jeremiah in David's "mighty men" list (I Chronicles 12:4, 10, 13). He is also the tenth Gadite in this special listing of David's "mighty men" from the various tribes of Israel. We have seen in some of the other devotionals a general description of this group of eleven (I Chronicles 12:13) and in our other chapters on Jeremiah the general meaning of the name, so what else is there to write about a named warrior, but an unknown soldier? As I have in other chapters, I am going to highlight and underline the meaning of his position, tenth, and also a thought on how we can connect this warrior with the captain of our salvation, the Lord Jesus Christ.

Those who have done an in-depth study of the numbers of the Bible have come up with the understanding (II Peter 1:20) that ten in the Word is the number of responsibility. They suggest that the commandments summarized in "ten" tell of man's responsibility God-ward and man-ward (Exodus 20). Each man has been given ten fingers and ten toes for doing the divine work of God and for walking in the divine way of God. That man is responsible for giving back to God a tenth of all he has (Exodus 30:13). Now, whether or not you believe this, as with other numbers of the Bible, it is interesting to me that this number, like other numbers, does routinely show up in such situations, and, like with the #3 and the #7 before, there does seem to be a deliberate pattern in the use of "ten." Let me suggest a few: (1) God's dealing with Egypt was through **"ten"** plagues and the Egyptians rejection of God's command to *"let my people go"* (Exodus 7–12). (2) Israel's failure to listen and obey God during the wilderness journey was demonstrated through **"ten"** temptations (Numbers 14:22). (3) Noah was the **"tenth"** antediluvian patriarch (Genesis 5). (4) There are **"ten"** words describing the Word of God in the 119th Psalm; which are: way, precept, commandment, testimony, law, saying, statute, judgment, righteousness, and word. (5) Paul gives a **"ten"**-fold security of the believer in Romans 8:38–39. (Check them out!) And then there was Jeremiah the **"tenth."** As you read through your Bible the next time, make a note of when the number **"ten"** comes up and see if there is not some connection to responsibility or obedience. So, I have come to believe that this Jeremiah showed himself to be faithful and obedient to his commander David.

Going back to the original meaning of Jeremiah, the Lord establishes, I believe that the Almighty established the Lord Jesus as our *"high tower"* (Psalm 18:2) and the many more that we have seen in this exposition of the Scriptures. I feel this term and title for Jesus is established in the understanding that a "high tower" was a place of safety and security. The Psalmist speaks of "my high tower," our established "high tower," and to finish this devotional I would like to take these three words and illustrate just what this means to me. We must start with the word "my." I would have you consider the personal use of this pronoun in connection to so many aspects of what our Lord is to us: *"my"* song, salvation, strength, rock, fortress, God, and buckler, (Psalm 18:1–2) to name a few. I like the way that F. B. Meyer underlines this truth:

> Notice that repeated "my." David had learnt that nothing can take the place of personal dealing with God. Surely he had realized the fulfillment of his own thoughts about dwelling in the House of the Lord all the days of his life, and beholding His beauty. There is a great fear lest many of God's most earnest and devoted children may be losing sight of Jesus in these active days. We allow our work for Christ, our doctrines about Him, and our rules for becoming like Him, to intercept our view of Him. Too seldom do we get so near Him as to be able to talk to Him face to face; or pile word on word in our ineffectual effort to tell Him what we think of Him. One who loved much sang: "Jesus, Jesus, dearest Jesus, forgive men if I say, for very love, Thy dearest name, a thousand times a day!" After all, it is not thought about Christ, but Christ Himself that we all need.

For me, it is all about the "my." I remember early on in my faith that my parents taught me of this need of a personal relationship; not my mother's relationship or my father's relationship with Jesus, but mine. They taught me this by one of the songs that went something like this: **"Now I belong to Jesus, Jesus belongs to me; not for the years of time alone, but for eternity!"**

Then there is the word "high." This adjective gives our title for Christ an even greater meaning. He is not just "my tower," but He is "my high tower." High suggests: "a towering tower;" one that stands above all others; one that is easily seen from afar, and one that directs us like a lighthouse on a shore, like a beacon in a fog, like a high water mark. Christ is a tall tower of blessing that reaches out to all, and like the brazen serpent lifted up high above the people in the midst of a terrible plague (John 3:14), Jesus, too, was high and lifted up on the hill called Calvary. For the Israelites it was for a physical healing after the snake bite, but for us it is for a spiritual healing from our sins. So with our Christ, He stands above all others; He can be seen by all who will look. Another old song goes: "Look and live, my brother, live, look to Jesus now and live; it's recorded in the Word, 'hallelujah,' it is only as you look and live!" Jesus said of Himself: **"And I, if I be lifted up from the earth, will draw all men unto me."** (John 12:32) Erastus Johnson put this concept into a wonderful hymn with these words: "Oh, sometimes the shadows are deep, and rough seems the path to the goal, and sorrows sometimes how they sweep like tempests down over the soul. Oh, then to the Rock let me fly, to the Rock that is higher than I." High, the highest, and higher than any other, "my high tower!"

Finally, the word "tower" must be added to our three-word phrase. In David's day, the context of our verse, a tower was built primary to provide a place for a lookout. It might be put on a city wall, or in a vineyard, or any place that might be threatened. A watchman was placed in the tower to be the eyes and ears of the community or farm against an enemy. Perhaps, Jeremiah played such a role in David's army. Visibility was so much better from a "high tower." So, whether in a fortress, and sometimes the fortress was the tower, or at a vital crossroad in the country, the tower was strategically placed to keep an eye out for a foe. This reminds me of the all-seeing God we serve. David wasn't trusting in a man-made tower to protect him against his adversaries, but he was putting his trust in God. David was placing his safety into the One that could see beyond hills and through great distance, and, as Jehovah was David's tower, Jesus is our tower. Jesus knows and sees what we can't; what lays in the future, the attack that is coming, and He becomes to us our "high tower." From our "high tower" we can gaze beyond to Beulah Land and like Abraham see the city not made by hands (Hebrews 11:10). From that tower we can see demons, devils, and detours that can detract and distract from the right path. No one walks blind if Jesus is his tower. By the way, how is your sight? How is your safety? Have you joined David's Band yet and found your "high tower?"

II Samuel 22:3: *"The God of my rock; in Him will I trust: He is my shield, and the horn of my salvation, my high tower, and my refuge, my saviour: thou savest me from violence."*

95.

MACHBANAI: CLAD WITH A CLOAK

I Chronicles 12:13: *"Jeremiah the tenth,* **MACHBANAI** *the eleventh."*

WITH OUR 95TH "MIGHTY man," we have come to the end of another major listing of David's famous warriors. This might be a good place to remind you where we have come from and how we got here in our search for a list of the "mighty men" that helped David gain the throne of Israel. Here are the four sets of names we have already uncovered: (1) our first list contained 37 names and we discovered them in II Samuel 23:8–39 and a number of them repeated in I Chronicles 11:4–47. (2) The next 24 names came from the group of warriors that were numbered in I Chronicles 11:4–47, but not found in II Samuel 23:8–39. (3) The third set of soldiers, numbering 23, came from I Chronicles 12:1–7. These men came from the tribe of Benjamin joining David at Ziklag. (4) Today, we finish the fourth set of names, numbering 11, which are named in I Chronicles 12:8–15. These warriors came from the tribe of Gad, and the final soldier in this listing is Machbanai, and I found that his name means "clad with a cloak." This might be the most interesting meaning we have come across in our search. I hope you will permit this spiritualization.

Having come to believe that these men's names were listed in these four areas for the meaning of their names and little else, I have used the meaning to focus our attention to an Old Testament connection to the New Testament, Christ. Most of the names before Machbanai have had some reference to God or Jehovah, but this one was a mystery to me until I remembered this verse from John's book, the Revelation of Jesus

Christ: *"And He was covered with a vesture dipped in blood: and His name is called The Word of God."* (Revelation 19:13) A vesture can be a cloak and this verse speaks of the Christ clad with a cloak. I feel the bloody vesture is symbolic of Christ's death for us on Calvary. Interestingly, when Christ comes again, will He be wearing the bloody garments they cast lots over at the foot of the cross? *"And they crucified Him, and parted His garments, casting lots: that it might be fulfilled which was spoken by the prophet: they parted my garments, and upon my vesture did they cast lots."* (Matthew 27:35) Maybe it is because I have for these nearly two years (I have been compiling these chapters one chapter a week) been thinking down this line that my mind automatically looks for a connection with the Life of Jesus. But for me, I see a wonderful challenge provoked by the meaning of Machbanai's name.

Perhaps, the most attacked doctrine and criticized theology in Christendom is the teaching concerning the blood of Christ: *"And to Jesus the mediator of the new covenant, and to the blood of sprinkling that speaketh better things than that of Abel."* (Hebrews 12:24) I still hold to the old belief that if it was not for the shed blood of Christ, I would still be in my sin, still Unforgiven, still looking at a Christless eternity. Since the beginning of sin in the Garden of Eden, the concept of blood has been the key ingredient in the eternal, redemptive plan of God: *"...for without shedding of blood is no remission..."* (Hebrews 9:22) of sin! From the very first slaying of the animals by God Himself to make coverings for Adam and Eve, there has been a scarlet line from Genesis to the Revelation. That is why we can't miss Jesus' blood-stained vesture when He rides back to this planet to conquer. Blood was the key element in the Levitical worship system, but as Paul tells us in his book of Hebrews: *"How much more shall the blood of Christ, who through the eternal Spirit offered Himself without spot to God, purge your conscience from dead works to serve the Living God?"* (Hebrews 9:14) In a look at the doctrine of blood we must first acknowledge that Christ's blood was better.

Paul Van Gorder of the Radio Bible Class staff gives us this exciting story and application which highlights and underlines the importance of the blood of Christ in an <u>Our Daily Bread</u> article. This is what he wrote:

> A church bulletin carried an interesting story about an American tourist in Paris who purchased an inexpensive amber necklace in a trinket shop. While clearing customs in New York, he had to pay quite a high duty on the item. This aroused his curiosity, so he had it appraised, hoping to sell it for whatever he

could get. After looking at the object under a powerful magnifying glass, the jeweler said: "I'll give you $25,000 for it." Greatly surprised, the man decided to have his newly discovered treasure examined by another expert. When he did, he was offered $10,000 more for it. "What do you see that's so valuable about this old necklace?" asked the astonished man. "Look through this glass," replied the jeweler. There before his eyes was an inscription that read: "From Napoleon Bonaparte to Josephine!" The necklace was extremely valuable because of its identification with this famous man. Christians are in union with One who is far more important than any human being. They are "in Christ" who purchased their redemption with His precious blood, and that puts unmeasured worth upon every child of God. The Father does not deal with them apart from the Person of His Son. Their relationship with Him makes it possible for underserving sinners to be accepted and loved by a holy God. Praise His name; we are valued by our association with Christ!

To which I would but add that in this world today there are countless treasures just like the amber necklace that can be found in the trinket shops and trash bins of the world. What the world sees as cheap God sees as valuable and the most valuable is the soul of the human being, old or young, rich or poor, purchased by the Blood of Jesus!

It was the legendary church hymnist, Fanny Crosby, who put it this way in one of her wonderful songs: **"Redeemed, how I love to proclaim it! Redeemed by the blood of the Lamb!"** The word "redeemed" carries with it the idea of a slave on an auction block when the auctioneer says, "Sold!" the price, the blood of Christ, being the highest bid. In unconditional love, the new owner gives the newly purchased slave his unconditional freedom, but the freed slave, out of love for the Master, offers himself back to the Master as a bond slave for the rest of his life. Only divine redemption, bought with such a price (I Corinthians 6:20), could result in such an eternal commitment of love and loyalty. It is time we once again make and recognize the shed blood of Christ as the most valuable liquid on this planet: *"Forasmuch as ye know that ye were not redeemed with corruptible things, as silver and gold, from your vain conversation received by tradition from your fathers; but with the precious blood of Christ, as of a lamb without blemish and without spot: who verily was foreordained before the foundation of the world, but was manifest in these times for you."* (I Peter 1:18-20) Jesus' blood is still the only substance that can take away the stain of sin as well as sin itself.

"Clad with a cloak;" are you clad with a cloak? Most would say, "Yes," but are you "clad with a cloak" that can take away your sins? There is only one blood-stained garment that can do that and that vesture belongs to Jesus Christ. When the world sees Jesus again, he will be wearing it, and then the whole world will know who He is (Revelation 1:7)!

> I John 1:7: *"But if we walk in the light, as He is in the light, we have fellowship one with the other and the blood of Jesus Christ His Son cleanseth us from all sin."*

96.

AMASAI: BURDEN-BEARER

I Chronicles 12:18: *"Then the Spirit came upon **AMASAI**, who was chief of the captains, and he said, Thine are we, David, and on thy side, thou son of Jesse: peace, peace be unto thee, and peace be to thine helpers; for thy God helpeth thee. Then David received them, and made them captains of the band."*

I CHRONICLES 12 IS the third great chapter in the Bible that lists for us the "mighty men" of David. II Samuel 23 contains 37 names in its list with I Chronicles 12 containing 52 names in its list with some repetitions. If you have been counting with me, we have arrived at the 35th name in I Chronicles 12. Unlike the first two chapters, I Chronicles 12 has been divided around tribes versus individuals: **Benjamin** (1–7, 16–18, 29), **Gad** (8–5), **Manasseh** (19–23, 31, 37), **Judah** (24), **Simeon** (25), **Levi** (26–28), **Ephraim** (30), **Issachar** (32, 40), **Zebulun** (33, 40), **Naphtali** (34, 40), **Dan** (35), **Asher** (36), and **Reuben** (37). All thirteen tribes (remember there were thirteen by the time of David because Joseph got the double blessing from his father Jacob when Israel adopted Joseph's two grandson, Ephraim and Manasseh, into his family) are named in this chapter and, while we don't have individuals names from each tribe, David was already bringing a unity into the national consciousness. After David lists the eleven men from the tribe of Gad, he stops for a moment to add a footnote to what he wrote about in verses one and two: *"**And there came of the children of Benjamin** [according to I Chronicles 12:29- 3000 of them and remember the other Benjamin's came to Ziklag-I Chronicles 12:1] **and Judah** [first reference to David's own tribe; according to

Chronicles 12:24–6800 of them] *to the hold* [probably referring to the Cave of Adullam-I Samuel 22:1–2] *unto David. And David went out to meet them, and answered and said unto them, If ye become peaceably unto me to help me, mine heart shall be knit unto you: but if ye be come to betray me to mine enemies, seeing there is no wrong in mine hands, the God of our fathers look thereon, and rebuke it."* (I Chronicles 12:16–17) It is then our next "mighty man" is introduced to us. For the first time in a long time, we have more than a name to consider in this chapter on David's Mighty Men.

    I have come to believe that David is developing another pattern in the telling of the stories of his "mighty men;" not only their names and some of their exploits, but also the places that these mercenaries came to join him. First, they came (about 400 of them according to I Samuel 22:2) to David when he was held up in the Cave of Adullam, what he calls "the hold" in I Chronicles 12:16. Second, they came to David in Ziklag according to I Chronicles 12:1–7 and 19–22 and, third, they came to David in Hebron according to I Chronicles 12:23–40. If I am right about the order of the places, then our "mighty man" Amasai might be considered the first "mighty man" instead of #96. If the story that David records in I Chronicles 12:16–18 is in actuality a part of the historical account of I Samuel 22:1–2, then we have a statement from the leader of that group of 400 who came to David in peace. As David approached them, he asked in what spirit they came, and it was then the Spirit of the Lord, in my opinion, came upon Amasai and he made one of the great declarations of the Bible, a declaration of peace, but also of helpfulness. It is here we can see that Amasai will live up to his name, burden-bearer. David had many burdens at this time, and he needed "burden-bearers," and Amasai was one of those men. I also believe that Amasai was also a type of Christ in relationship to burden-bearing.

    Remember what Jesus told us: *"Come unto me, all ye that labour and are heavy laden, and I will give you rest. Take my yoke upon you, and learn of me; for I am meek and lowly in heart: and ye shall find rest unto your souls. For my yoke is easy, and my burden is light."* (Matthew 11:28–30) What Amasai did for David, our Lord does for us. Could John M. Moore's classic Church hymn <u>Burdens are Lifted at Calvary</u> still be accurate in the light of these verses? Could John Bunyan be scripturally correct as he portrayed Christian's burdens falling from him when he came to the foot of the Cross? Christ seems to be still talking of burdens even when we come to Him. What could He be referring to? With the exception of Acts

27:10, burdens are used metaphorical. Matthew 11:30 is referring to the burdens that come with the discipleship of Christ. Burdens of sins are certainly lifted at Calvary and removed on Golgotha's Hill. The burdens of sins, transgressions, and iniquities are not only lifted, removed, but done away with as far as the east is from the west (Psalm 103:12)! The old burdens are taken, but a new burden is laid, but compared to the original burden, lighter. Let me illustrate what I am talking about with this simple story from the pen of G. Campbell Morgan:

> A lady said to me some years ago, "I'm tired of this worldly life. I'm going to give myself to Christ. I know what it means: I will have to do all the things I most dislike, but I am determined to be a real Christian." "When I returned to her town a year later," said Morgan, "she was one of the first to welcome me." "Do you recall," she inquired, "what I said to you when I rededicated my life?" I told her I certainly did. Then she looked at me and the light of God was on her face as she exclaimed, "But it's been so different, Dr. Morgan! I began to follow Christ feeling that I would have to do all the things that were contrary to my desires, but now I do what I want every day because God has made me pleased with the things that please Him!"

Now that is a light burden because Jesus is our burden-bearer.

Paul writes of such burdens when he told the Galatians: *"Bear ye one another's burdens, and so fulfill the law of Christ…For every man shall bear his own burdens."* (Galatians 6:2, 5) The burdens of discipleship are much more like the burdens of wings on a bird. Wings add weight, but it is with those wings the bird is able to soar. When we take the burden of Christ, we certainly add something to our lives, but that burden will allow us to fly above the cares of this world. Christ's burden is not a bondage like a sin, but a wonderful help and blessing, just like the men like Amasai who came to David at Adullam added to the burden of his leadership, but they in turn helped care for the load as "captains of the band." H. W. Re Qua put it best in this little poem:

> **Tell me not of heavy crosses,**
> **Nor of burdens hard to bear,**
> **For I've found this great salvation**
> **Makes each burden light appear.**
> **And I love to follow Jesus,**
> **Gladly counting all but dross,**
> **Worldly honors all forsaking,**

For the glory of the Cross! [Galatians 6:14]

Someone has spoken of Christ's burden this way: **"It is light because it is upheld by His power, and it is lined with the soft down of His grace."** Isn't that good? Isn't that something that you would like to carry? Isn't that the kind of burden that you would like to bear? Come to Jesus today and exchange your heavy burden for His light burden. Not only will He help you carry that burden, but He has also created His Church to have our fellow-believers help in the carrying of those burdens. The Christian is surrounded with "burden-bearers." I believe Amasai came to David in Adullam and found someone he could be a "burden-bearer," too.

Psalm 55:22: *"Cast thy burden upon the Lord, and He shall sustain thee…"*

97.

ADNAH: PLEASURE

I Chronicles 12:20: *"As he went to Ziklag, there fell to him of Manasseh, **ADNAH**, Jozabad, and Jediael, and Michael, and Jozabad, and Elihu, and Zilthai, captains of the thousands that were of Manasseh."*

IN OUR STUDY OF David's "mighty men" we have highlighted and underlined the warriors that came (*"...fell to him..."*) to David's defense and support in his long struggle against his archenemy, King Saul. We have studied the Benjaminites that came to David at Ziklag (I Chronicles 12:1–7); we have studied the Gadites that came to David at Adullam (I Chronicles 12:8–15); and we have taken a quick look at the men of Judah that also came to David at the Cave of Adullam (I Chronicles 12:16–19). It is time we look at the special soldiers from the tribe of Manasseh that came to help David in his struggle at Ziklag. This is how David describes the men we have listed above: **"And they helped David against the band of rovers: for they were all mighty men of valour, and were captains in the host. For in that time day by day there came to David to help him, until a great host, like the host of God."** (I Chronicles 12:21–22)

For a more complete history of this period of time, the time David was a mercenary for King Achish (the man that gave David the city of Ziklag-I Samuel 27:6), you must read I Samuel 27–31. A summary of these chapters tells the story of how David was called to fight against Saul in the infamous Battle of Gilboa, but was rejected by the other kings of the Philistines. The commanders of the armies of Philistia feared that at the height of the coming battle, David might switch sides. This was a legitimate fear for it has happened more often than you might think in

ADNAH: PLEASURE

history. David and his men, including, I believe, this list of Manassehites, was ordered back to Ziklag before the confrontation between the men of Saul and the Philistine army. Upon returning to Ziklag, the men of David discovered that while they were away *"a band of rovers"* (Amalekites-I Samuel 30:1) had burned their city and taken their families into captivity. I believe it is this event that David is recognizing the Manassehites for their help. David led his men in pursuit of this "band of rovers" and eventually found them, defeated them, and recovered their families. Did some of these men faint on the way (I Samuel 30:9–10) or were they the ones that persevered and won the day? We know not all the details, but in David's final accounting of these Manassehite warriors a group stands out and David records them as *"…all might men of valour…"* so they will go on our "mighty men" list.

The first name on this list is a man named Adnah. As I have shared numerous times in this lengthy list, the first for me is always a significant place. Of all the men David had and even in these groupings somebody had to come first. As David reviewed the men from the tribe of Manasseh that came to help him and support him, the first name that came to him was Adnah. Why? We know not the exploit for sure, but in my spiritual imagination I feel maybe it was Adnah that encouraged the others on as they chased the Amalekites. Adnah stood out enough to David as he wrote his memoirs that Adnah should be named first in this final listing of David's "mighty men." Our only sure truth about this warrior, like so many others, is the meaning of his name, pleasure. We know he must have been a pleasure to David, but for us we will, as we have so often, take this meaning and apply it to our Lord and Savior Jesus Christ. Is Jesus your pleasure? Nehemiah wrote: **"…for the joy of the Lord is your strength…"** (Nehemiah 8:10). David would write: **"…in thy presence is fullness of joy…"** (Psalm 16:11). Now we add Paul's declaration that one of the pieces of the fruit of the Spirit is **"…joy…"** (Galatians 5:22). I have come to believe that the greatest pleasure is joy. We can't separate Jesus from joy, and we can't separate Adnah from pleasure. I would like for us for a few minutes to ponder this link between pleasure and joy.

Joyfulness is one of the most natural expressions of Jesus in a person's life. Jesus brings such pleasure to our entire being. It speaks of the early disciples as having been *"…filled with joy…"* (Acts 13:52). I feel this is just another way to say that the earliest followers of Jesus were **"…filled with the Spirit…"** (Ephesians 5:19). Jesus told His disciples just before He left them for Calvary: **"These things have I spoken unto you, that my joy** *might remain in you, and that your joy might be full."* (John 15:11) The pleasure of the Lord is the fullness of joy that comes when Jesus comes into your heart. Jesus was leaving His disciples, but He would leave them His joy. What pleasure that is.

One of my favorite devotional writers is a pastor by the name of E. Gyln Evans. I have shared other thoughts by him in this book, Daily With the King. He once wrote this on the joy and pleasure we can have in Christ:

> Too often I have looked upon joy as one of God's special treats, one that delights me but also surprises me. I should not be surprised. I am commanded to be joyful: **"rejoice in the Lord always; and again I say rejoice."** (Philippians 4:4 NSRB) Bible commands are always God's enablements; if I am commanded to rejoice, I can rejoice, regardless of the circumstances. I must realize that I can control my feelings far more than I think I can. The little boy who said: "I'd druthers be mad" was admitting that he could control his emotions. Possibly with the exception of organic difficulties, our feelings are controllable if we put on the right dress of mind. In other words, God holds me responsible for the kind of thinking that enables me to rejoice. Jesus said: **"that my joy be in you, and that your joy may be made full."** (John 15:11 ASV) Jesus Christ was the most optimistic, confident, radiant person the world ever saw. Can we imagine Him now being worried, harried, or depressed? If He is released to be free in us, joy will always result, for Jesus is the personal expression of joy. It is impossible for me to think of all that Christ has done for me, all that He is to me, and all that he has promised to do for me without feeling joy. I am joyless only when I set my mind on myself and begin to pity myself. The opposite of that is to keep Jesus Christ alive in my mind. Billy Bray called his left foot "glory" and his right one "hallelujah," so that as he walked it was "glory" and "hallelujah!" I also will walk in joy if I keep Christ in the center of my heart and mind. *"Be glad in the Lord and rejoice you righteous ones, and shout for joy all you who are upright in heart."* (Psalm 32:11)

Can there be any greater pleasure than that?

The tragedy today is that many like David's wife Michal (II Samuel 6:16, 21) are raising objections to heart-felt, Christ-ordained joy and pleasure in Christianity and Christendom. If Christ is in us, and Christ is pure pleasure and eternal joy, how can't we help but rejoice in the joy of the Lord? How can we help but find pleasure in the things of the Lord?

ADNAH: PLEASURE

Adnah reminds us that there are great pleasures to be found in serving Christ, just like Adnah and his companions found get pleasure in helping David. Is your pleasure in the Lord or the things of this world? Is your joy found in the Person of Christ or in some pleasure of the world? Focus on Jesus and you will find life's greatest pleasure!

John 17:13: *"And now come I to thee: and these things I speak in the world, that they might have my joy fulfilled in themselves."*

98.

JOZABAD: JEHOVAH ENDOWS

I Chronicles 12:20: *"As he went to Ziklag, there fell to him of Manasseh, Adnah,* **JOZABAD**, *and Jediael, and Michael, and Jozabad, and Elihu, and Zilthai, captains of the thousands that were of Manasseh."*

THE SECOND "MIGHTY MAN" from the tribe of Manasseh that joined David in the fight for the kingdom in Ziklag was Jozabad. As with his other companions, all we know of Jozabad is what is written in I Chronicles 12:19–22. In summary, we know these six things about the warrior Jozabad:

(1) Jozabad was from the split tribe of Manasseh. This very large tribe of Israel (actually a grandson of Jacob and the son of his favorite son Joseph) had possessions on both the east bank and west bank of the Jordan River (I Chronicles 12:19). Which section of the territory of Manasseh these soldiers came from is not told.

(2) Jozabad joined David's mercenary band just before the famous Battle of Gilboa (I Chronicles 12:19) where King Saul and some of his sons were killed by the Philistines.

(3) Jozabad was given command of a regiment of a thousand men as were his other six comrades (I Chronicles 12:20). Since the days of Moses when the army of Israel was formed under the leadership of Joshua, it was a common practice to divide the army up in units of ten, one hundred, and a thousand (Exodus 18:21).

(4) Jozabad was instrumental in helping David get his family and their families back after the Amalekites had capture the village of Ziklag (I Chronicles 12:21). This seems to be the pivotal event that endeared Jozabad to David.

(5) Jozabad was seen in the eyes of David as one of David's "mighty men" (I Chronicles 12:21), and it is for this reason we have added Jozabad to these devotional chapters.

(6) Jozabad means **"Jehovah endows"** (I Chronicles 12:20), and it is around this meaning that we will develop this devotional.

The Hebrew word for "endow" is *mahar*, and it is only found once in the ancient Old Testament text: *"And if a man entice a maid that is not betrothed, and lie with her, he shall surely endow her to be his wife."* (Exodus 22:16) The word can also be used to mean "to purchase." If we put these two thoughts together, we can find a link to Jesus Christ as we have been able to do over this lengthy study of listing and naming the "mighty men" of David. Luke tells us this in Acts 20:28: **"Take heed therefore unto yourselves, and to all the flock, over the which the Holy Ghost hath made you overseers, to feed the Church of God, which He hath purchased with His own blood."** The Greek word here is *peripoieomai* or "to acquire." Though this word is used little in the Bible, the doctrine is discussed a lot in the Word of God.

Paul tells us in his letter to the Corinthian Church: *"For ye are bought with a price: therefore glorify God in your body, and in your spirit, which are God's."* (I Corinthians 6:20) Then Peter speaks of this in his first epistle: *"Forasmuch as ye know that ye were not redeemed with corruptible things as silver and gold from your vain conversation received by tradition from your fathers; but with the precious blood of Christ, as of a lamb without blemish and without spot."* (I Peter 1:18–19) And once more Paul shares this with the Christians at Colosse: *"In whom we have redemption through His blood, even forgiveness of sins."* (Colossians 1:14) What I love best about all these verses is the use of the past tense in the verbs. The acquisition has already taken place. The purchase is finished. The endowment has already happened. The price was high, but God's Son was willing to pay the price for our redemption, and that price was His own life on the Cross of Calvary. Amen and Amen!

Being a pastor for over 52 years now, I was moved by these words from a commentary by Jamieson, Fausset, and Brown (I have used this instruction book throughout my ministry), and I quote:

...which He purchased-made His own-acquired-with His own blood-His own is emphatic: that glorified Lord who from the right hand of power in the heavens gathering and ruling the Church, and by His Spirit, through human agency, hath set you over it, cannot be indifferent to its welfare in your hands, seeing He hath given for it His own most precious blood, thus making it His own by the dearest of all ties. The transcendent sacredness of the Church of Christ is thus made to rest on the dignity of its Lord and the consequent preciousness of that blood which he shed for it. And as the sacrificial atoning character of Christ's death is here plainly expressed, so His supreme dignity is implied as clearly by the second reading as it is expressed by the first. What a motive to pastoral fidelity is here finished!

One cannot be moved more by these words when you realize what a tremendous privilege we have to share this endowment with others. To think the Almighty God, the Jew's Jehovah, has endowed us with the right to spread abroad this Good News we call the Gospel to every creature (Mark 16:15) on this planet with the truth that the price has already been paid, the atonement has already been supplied, and the redemption has already been acquired by Jesus' blood!

Paul's message to the elders at Ephesus was a plea to watch carefully over these spiritual folks. He was afraid of *"...grievous wolves..."* (Acts 20:29). There should be no greater motivation to the protection of the flock than the price that was paid to purchase that flock. It cost Jesus his life and the value of that life is clearly seen in Ephesians 1:7: *"In whom, we have redemption through His blood, the forgiveness of sins, according to the riches of His grace."* Despite the loss of life, this was the greatest purchase in all of history. Recently, I watched a documentary on the Lewis and Clark Expedition across the width of the newly established United States. That famous exploration was motivated by the purchase of the Louisiana Purchase from France in 1803. The United States got 825,000 square miles for $15,000,000. What a bargain! Then in 1867 we did it again when we purchased from Russia what would become the State of Alaska, 586,400 square miles of territory for $7,200,000, an even better deal! Twice the size of Texas and nearly one-fifth the size of the continental United States, Alaska and the Louisiana Purchase have gone down in American history as the best purchases in our history since the great bargain we got when we purchased Manhattan from the Indians. But Jesus' purchase of the sins of the whole world (I John 2:2) is still the best bargain, still the best deal, on this planet! Have you taken advantage of it yet?

Jesus put the value of one human soul (there are over eight billion souls still alive on the earth, but what of the billions before?) in this classic question: *"For what shall it profit a man, if he shall gain the whole world, and lose his own soul?"* (Mark 8:36) How many Alaska's and Louisiana Purchases are there in the world? One soul is priceless, so what of all souls, and yet Jesus purchased them back on Calvary with His blood. God's endowment was a gift (Romans 6:23 and Ephesians 2:8), a purchased gift. Jozabad's name says a lot of what God endowed. He purchased our redemption without cost to us.

Ephesians 1:14: *"Which is the earnest of our inheritance until the redemption of the purchased possession, unto the praise of His glory?"*

99.

JEDIAEL: GOD KNOWS

I Chronicles 12:20: *"As he went to Ziklag, there fell to him of Manasseh, Adnah, Jozabad, and **JEDIAEL**, and Michael, and Jozabad, and Elihu, and Zilthai, captains of the thousands that were of Manasseh."*

THE THIRD MAN FROM the tribe of Manasseh that made David's "mighty men" list was Jediael. His name means "God knows." To remind you just how much God really does know, I draw your attention to this verse written about the twelve year old boy Jesus: **"And all that heard Him were astonished at His understanding and answers."** (Luke 2:47) In this article I will once again make a link between one of David's soldiers and our Savior. All we know about Jediael is the meaning of his name, but, like so many of his comrades, Jediael gives us more insight in the attributes of our Lord and Savior Jesus Christ. When will we realize, when will mankind realize, that "God knows?"

Isaiah predicted this attribute of the Messiah when he wrote this: *"...there shall come forth a rod out of the stem of Jesse, and a branch shall grow out of his roots: and the spirit of the Lord shall rest upon Him, **the spirit of wisdom and understanding**..."* (Isaiah 11:1–2). Understanding is the fruit of wisdom. A lot of people have a vast amount of knowledge, but can make no practical application to the facts and figures they possess. This is why, in my opinion, Jesus so astonished and fascinated the scribes in the Temple in Jerusalem. He possessed the understanding of the Scriptures as well as its information. It was the wise man Solomon that taught us: *"A wise man will hear, and will increase learning; and a man of understanding shall attain unto wise counsel."* (Proverbs 1:5) This is what amazed the men of Judah when the Christ-child first came into their midst. How could a kid like Jesus both know the things of God as well as understand completely the wisdom of God? They had studied all their lives and here is a youngster from Galilee full of both wisdom and understanding. He seemingly already knew everything. He did because He was God: God knows!

It isn't that the world hasn't known of amazing kids. Herbert Gabhart writes of four prodigies:

> George Frederick Handel, the composer of The Messiah, made his debut as a performer at the age of 12 in Berlin. Clara Barton, the founder of the Red Cross, began teaching school at fifteen. Ludwig Van Beethoven, the composer of nine outstanding symphonies, showed unusual ability at the age of four. When Beethoven was eleven, he could play the organ, piano, and violin; had a good understanding of harmony and was already composing. Wolfgang Mozart, famous composer of operas, was playing the clavier, an early piano, at the age of three and was writing music at the age of four. He went on his first concert tour at the age of six!

On the television today there is a popular program called <u>Little Big Shots</u> in which the talent of young kids is highlighted. I have watched the program a few times and was amazed at what some of the kids could do, but I am persuaded the Child Jesus outdid them all! Jesus excels them all, far beyond the abilities mentioned, because of this simple truth taught by Paul: **"For in Him dwelleth all the fullness of the Godhead bodily."** (Colossians 2:9) Yes, even at twelve!

We set back and stand amazed at such understanding and knowledge when we, too, could have such understanding and knowledge. Paul also taught us this *"…that ye might be filled with the knowledge of His will in all wisdom and spiritual understanding."* (Colossians 1:9) What good is the knowledge of God without the ability to make daily, practical application of it in our lives? Paul went on to teach the Church of Colosse: *"…that their hearts might be comforted, being knit together in love, and unto all riches of full assurance of understanding."* (Colossians 2:2) Paul was always concerned that what he wrote wouldn't be understood so he often added this simple prayer with his pen: *"Consider what I say; and the Lord give thee understanding in all things."* (II Timothy 2:7) How we need this prayer answered in our lives!

Knowledge doesn't just know facts and figures, but the ability to take those facts and figures and apply them to knowledge, to knowing. Jesus not only had understanding at twelve, he also had all the answers as well. Throughout Jesus' earthly life, He was a puzzle to those surrounding Him. Most stood aside in amazement at the answers He would give to the questions they would throw at Him. His most famous encounter with a question that was left unanswered was: *"And went again into the judgment all, and saith unto Jesus, Whence art thou? But Jesus gave him no answer."* (John 19:9) Solomon wrote in his "Ecclesiastes:" *"To everything there is a season, and a time to every purpose under heaven…a time to keep silence and a time to speak…"* (Ecclesiastes 3:1, 7). Was it because Jesus didn't have an answer to Pilate's question? Certainly not; Jesus often told from where He had come. On this occasion Jesus felt it was necessary to keep the answer hidden from Pilate, like the time when Jesus was asked: *"By what authority doest thou these things? Or, who is he that gave thee this authority? And He answered and saith unto them. I will also ask you one thing, and answer me: the baptism of John, was it from heaven, or of men."* (Luke 20:2–4) Because they wouldn't answer His question He would not answer their question, but it wasn't because he didn't know the answer. Jesus is teaching us that we must be wise in sharing our answers, our knowledge, or we might be guilty of: *"Give not that which is holy unto the dogs, neither cast ye your pearls before swine, lest they trample them under their feet, and turn again and rend you."* (Matthew 7:6) Like Christ, we must be wise in the use of our knowing.

Peter challenges us: *"But sanctify the Lord God in your hearts: and be ready always to give an answer to every man that asketh you a reason of the hope that is in you with meekness and fear."* (I Peter 3:15) Jesus was "the answer-man" of His generation; we are called on to be "the answer-men" of our time. Herb Vander Lugt makes this point when he wrote:

> Michael Green tells of his visit with a cancer specialist who was dying of leukemia while still in his forties. At the beginning of his illness, the man was an agnostic, but he read two books that brought him into a clear and joyful faith in the risen Christ. However, he said he felt some anger: "Why have I never had the evidence clearly put to me before?" Many of us try to keep informed about the Bible and how it applies to relevant topics like marriage, the family, abortion, and pornography. It's good when we talk intelligently about these subjects. But it is even more important that we be prepared to show why we believe in

the resurrection of Christ. People around us need to hear resurrection talk. After all, belief in the resurrection is a matter of life or death!

God knows and He wants us to know why He sent His Son Jesus, but that is also why He gave us the Bible, the answer book. The Devil fights hard to keep people away from this book because he knows if people really read the Words of God, they will find the answers to their questions.

Luke 20:26: *"And they could not take hold of His words before the people: and they marveled at His answer, and held their peace."*

100.

MICHAEL: WHO IS LIKE GOD?

I Chronicles 12:20: *"As he went to Ziklag, there fell to him of Manasseh, Adnah, Jozabad, and Jediael, and **MICHAEL**, and Jozabad, and Elihu, and Zilthai, captains of the thousands that were of Manasseh."*

MICHAEL HAS A GREAT meaning: **who is like God?** A question that has only one answer: Jesus. Paul taught us in his theology: *"for in Him [Jesus] dwelleth all the fullness of the Godhead bodily!"* (Colossians 2:9) In this devotional on David's "mighty man" we will highlight and underline this concept in the Person of Jesus Christ.

I read this in an Our Daily Bread (from the ministry of the Radio Bible Class and the DeHaan boys) article. I hope it will help you understand the direction we are taking with this doctrine about Christ:

> A preacher once met a cultist on the street who challenged his orthodox views. "You say that Jesus Christ is co-equal with the Eternal Father, but He cannot be, for no son is ever as old as the one who has begotten Him." The minister looked at the detractor for a moment and then gave this devastating reply: "You yourself have just called God the Eternal Father. Have you ever thought that statement through? Don't you realize that God can only be the Eternal Father if he has an Eternal Son? If you rethink your position in the light of Scripture, you'd see that Eternal Fatherhood of necessity demands Eternal Sonship!" The cultist was silenced.

Michael is another wonderful name for Jesus because what is true of the Father is true of the Son.

This is the power of this term associated with the Christ. The Greek word for "fullness" in our verse from Colossians means simply "that which is full." In the text of the verse it is speaking of the completeness of the Being we call the Christ, but in the context it is referring to Jesus of Nazareth. Charles Wesley put it this way in one of his grand hymns: "Veiled in flesh the Godhead see; hail the incarnate deity! Pleased as man with men to dwell, Jesus our Emmanuel." But like the cultist in the story we shared above, unless we make this term practical, and see its benefits to us, we probably won't believe it either. Someone has said: **"Christ's incarnation brought the infinite God within reach of finite man!"** We live at a time when this truth has been totally masked by the attempt to make Jesus just another popular religious leader of a new faith. The world is ready to recognize Jesus as a great teacher and founder, but few will acknowledge Him to be God.

Charles Haddon Spurgeon, the well-known British Pastor and Writer, makes this case in his belief in the doctrine of "the fullness of Christ" in the Eternal Godhead of God:

> All the attributes of Christ, as God and man, are at our disposal. All the fullness of the Godhead, whatever that marvelous term may comprehend, is ours to make us complete. He cannot endow us with the attributes of Deity; but He has done all that can be done, for He has made even His divine power and Godhead subservient to our salvation. His omnipotence, omniscience, omnipresence, immutability and infallibility, are all combined for our defense. Arise, believer, and behold the Lord Jesus yoking the whole of His divine Godhead to the chariot of salvation! How vast His grace, how firm His faithfulness, how unswerving His immutability, how infinite His power, how limitless his knowledge! All these are by the Lord Jesus made the pillars of the temple of salvation; and all, without diminution of their infinity, are covenanted to us as our perpetual inheritance. The fathomless love of the Saviour's heart is every drop of it ours; every sinew in the arm of might, every jewel in the crown of majesty, the immensity of divine knowledge, and the sternness of divine justice, all are ours, and shall be employed for us. The whole of Christ, in His adorable character as the Son of God, is by Himself made over to us most richly to enjoy. His wisdom is our direction, His knowledge our instruction, His power our protection, His justice our surety, His love our comfort, His mercy our solace, His immutability our trust. He makes no reserves, but opens the recesses of the Mount of God and bids us

dig in its mines for the hidden treasures. "All, all, all are yours," saith he. "Be ye satisfied with favour and be full of the goodness of the Lord." Oh! How sweet thus to behold Jesus, and to call upon Him with the certain confidence that in seeking the interposition of His love, we are but asking for that which He has already faithfully promised.

For me, it can't be stated any clearer than this. When Jesus came into our lives after our salvation, He didn't give the Spirit, a piece of Himself, but all of Himself. When will we understand this concept of "the fullness of Christ?" When will we take advantage of this "fullness" and realize that our Lord and Savior is completely, fully God and we are filled and completed in Him?

Spurgeon took a look at this doctrine over a century ago, but another favorite author, W. Glyn Evans, in his wonderful devotional <u>Daily With The King</u> makes this interesting application to the theme of this devotional when he writes:

> I must at all costs avoid the deadly delusion of self-fulfillment. I am hounded on all sides to be the person I was meant to be, to realize my full potential, and to explore the capabilities of the possible me. Even Christians have succumbed to this idea, and now I am told that in Christ I shall be able to fulfill myself as God intended; in contrast to being self-fulfilled by the world. The error in all this is that the Bible nowhere talks of self-fulfillment. The only fullness the Bible knows about is the fullness of Christ. He is the fullness of God (Colossians 1:19; 2:9); he is the fullness of the Church (Ephesians 1:22–23); and he is the fullness of everyone who draws fullness from Him. Self-fulfillment is only another form of pride, and hardly different from the ignominious sin of Lucifer (Isaiah 14:12). We progressive moderns, however, have so covered the term with attractive clothing that it no longer appears as sin, but as an inherit right of the personality. Self-fulfillment is expressing my full self, achieving my glory, and carving out my niche in life. Its ultimate goal is the coronation of self. Further, it is a fatal contradiction. How can everyone fulfill himself? The total exaltation of everyone would result in racial mania. The fulfillment of all my desires usually means the denial of someone else's!

So there you have it; the practical application to the need to understand that fulfillment can only be found in One, and His name is Jesus. I can go Satan's route and try, but I will fall flat on my face eventually and find self-fulfillment or satanic fulfillment to be empty at best. Only in Christ will we ever find complete fulfillment because only in Him will we find the fullness of God!

Perhaps Dennis DeHaan's little poem can sum it up best for us:

> Eternal with the Father, one,
> Is Jesus Christ, His own dear Son;
> In Him God's fullness we can see,
> For Jesus Christ is deity!

May we believe it and practice it, lest we lose out in the magnificent fullness of the Lord Jesus Christ on our lives. Are you willing to give Jesus a try? Are you willing to set aside your ambitions and aspirations to seek a divine fulfillment in the plan and purpose of God in your life? I still remember when I made that commitment. It was scary because of the unknown, but nearly sixty-eight years later I see that I made the right choice; that I could and would have never been fulfilled in the plans I had!

Colossians 1:19: *"For it pleased the Father that in Him* [Jesus] *should all fullness dwell."*

101.

JOZABAD: THE LORD HAS BESTOWED

I Chronicles 12:20: *"As he went to Ziklag, there fell to him of Manasseh, Adnah, Jozabad, and Jediael, and Michael, and **JOZABAD**, and Elihu, and Zilthai, captains of the thousands that were of Manasseh."*

THE FIFTH MAN FROM Manasseh that made David's "mighty men" list has a familiar name: Jozabad. This is actually the third warrior with the same name, and we have determined that the meaning of Jozabad is either "God endows" or "God bestows." In our other chapters on these soldiers with the same name we have highlighted both meanings so I have determined in this article on our third Jozabad to underline what the Good Lord has bestowed or endowed us with. Could I start by sharing three:

1. First, according to Isaiah 63:7 God bestows loving-kindness and goodness to us: *"I will mention the lovingkindness of the Lord, and the praise of the Lord, according to all that the Lord hath bestowed on us, and the great goodness toward the house of Israel, which he hath bestowed on them according to His mercies, and according to the multitude of His lovingkindness."* Here we have two of the greatest blessings that the Lord could endow us with.

2. Second, according to II Corinthians 8:1 God bestows grace upon us: *"Moreover, Brethren, we do you to wit of the grace of God bestowed on the Churches of Macedonia."* As the old hymn says: "Grace, grace, wonderful grace, sent down from the Father above, sweep over us forever I pray in fathomless billows of love." Undeserved,

unmerited, but yet the Almighty God still endows us, bestows us with the marvelous virtue of His divine love, grace.

3. Third, according to I John 2:1 God bestows His love: *"Behold, what manner of love the Father hath bestowed upon is, that we should be called the sons of God: therefore the world knoweth us not, because it knew Him not."* It will be on this last bestowment that I will focus our attention for the remainder of this article. In all the endowments of God, in all His bestowments, there can be nothing greater than the eternal attribute of love from on high.

Ever since I was a very small child I have had John 3:16 in my mind: *"For God so loved the world that He gave His only begotten Son that whosoever believeth in Him should not perish but have everlasting life."* What God really sent to earth was His love in the form of His Son Jesus Christ. As we learned in our last chapter, the fullness of the Godhead was in Jesus (Colossians 1:9, 2:9) and part of that "fullness" is love *"...for God is love..."* (I John 4:9). You have to have love to bestow love, and you have to be loved to endow love. I believe in Christ dwelt all the love of God so we can honestly write: *"...for Christ is Love..."* I am interestingly writing this devotional on the day that the world celebrates love, Valentine's Day, but the tragedy of this day is that the world knows little about true, genuine love. Oh, man has developed a fleshly love, a parental love, a martial love, but all three fall far short of Godly love, divine love. The world puts on a good show of love at times, but most of the time that love turns ugly as we have witnessed in home violence and spousal abuse. Only when God's love is bestowed through the Person of Jesus, will true love be endowed!

Paul taught that *"...Christ also loved the Church, and gave Himself for it..."* (Ephesians 5:25). Paul was only relaying what Christ Himself told the disciples when He said: *"Greater love hath no man than this that a man lay down his life for his friends."* (John 15:13) That is why we can love Him because He first loved us (I John 4:19). The great English pastor Charles Spurgeon once put it: **"Because of our dependence upon Christ's love we dare much, and because of our love for Christ we do much!"** Do we? I often think when I hear the congregation sing the classic Church hymn "Oh, How I Love Jesus, Oh, How I Love Jesus, Oh, How I Love Jesus because He first loved me," if they really mean it. Do I really mean it? Do we live up to what we sing?

Despite our ups and downs with our love of God, one thing is very clear in Scripture. God's love never changes; He has never withdrawn His love from us or from this world. This thought reminds me of a story I once read in a biography of Charles Haddon Spurgeon in which the great preacher was rebuked. The story was recorded like this:

> One day C. H. Spurgeon was walking through the English countryside with a friend. As they strolled along, the evangelist noticed a barn with a weather vane on its roof. At the top of the vane were these words: God is love! Spurgeon remarked to his companion that he thought this was a rather inappropriate place for such a message. "Weather vanes are changeable," he said, "but God's love is constant!" "I don't agree with you about those words, Charles," replied his friend. "You misunderstand the meaning. That sign is indicating a truth: regardless of the way the wind blows, God is love!"

What a grand thought. No matter my circumstance or my situation, God's love for me stays steady. One of my favorite verses on love that has taught me the most about God's love is: **"But God commendeth His love towards us, in that, while we were yet sinners, Christ died for us."** (Romans 5:8) It doesn't get any better than that!

On this day that the world loves itself, focuses its attention on itself, God's character of love will not change because God still loves the world even if the world doesn't love Him. Most of the love of the world is conditional, but God's love is always unconditional (Matthew 5:43–46). Paul Van Gorder once wrote this in an Our Daily Bread article I read a long, long time ago, but kept for such a time as this, and I quote:

> What a contrast between God's love and our love! Ours fluctuates like the wind as the whims of a fallen nature cause it to change with our moods vary with our circumstances. But God's love is constant and unchangeable. Even when we were sinners, when we were without strength, and when we were the enemies of God, He demonstrated His own love towards us (Romans 5:6–10), and the apostle John said, "In this is love, not that we loved God, but that he loved us." (I John 4:10) God's love is not conditioned by our response. He keeps on loving us no matter which way the wind blows!

Frederick M. Lehman writes in his beloved Church hymn The Love of God these lines:

> O love of God, how rich and pure!
> How measureless and strong!

> It shall forevermore endure-
> The saints and angel's song!

February 14th changes from year to year in its fades and focus, but God's love is not a once in the year love, one day in the month of February love, but an everyday love, an every hour love, an every minute love, an every second love!

Have you taken advantage yet of this bestowed love, this endowed charity from the Almighty? It is there, and it will remain there until you either accept it or reject it. You can reject love as we know, but to reject divine love will be eternally harmful to you. Take this love, receive this charity, and really know love for the very first time!

Galatians 2:20: *"And the life which I now live in the flesh, I live by the faith of the Son of God, who loved me, and gave Himself for me."*

102.

ELIHU: GOD HIMSELF

I Chronicles 12:20: *"As he went to Ziklag, there fell to him of Manasseh, Adnah, Jozabad, and Jediael, and Michael, and Jozabad, and **ELIHU**, and Zilthai, captains of the thousands that were of Manasseh."*

ANOTHER MAN OF THE tribe of Manasseh that made David's "mighty men" list was the soldier Elihu. As I write this article, I am nearing the end of a year and a half long study and teaching of the Book of Job. In that study there is a man named Elihu, the fourth friend of Job to visit him in his afflictions (Job 32–37). Elihu has one of the longest discourses in the Book of Job, and he more than the others, including Job, seemed to understand what was happening with Job. Elihu was the last to speak because he was the youngest of the group of men (Job 32:6). We know more about Job's friend than we know about David's warrior, but their name has this common meaning, God Himself. I believe we have another great definition in this name for Jesus of Nazareth. Remember, when the demons in the demonic man of the synagogue of Capernaum shouted out against Jesus, they called Jesus by two names. First, the evil spirits referred to the earthly name of Jesus: *"...Let us alone; what have we to do with Thee, thou Jesus of Nazareth..."* (Luke 4:34). Then they acknowledged who Jesus really was and that He was known of them when they said: *"...I know Who Thou art, the Holy One of God..."* (Luke 4:34). In the statement of the demons, they recognized the unity found in the God Head, and that Jesus was "God Himself."

Moses had taught Israel centuries before: *"Hear, O Israel: the Lord our God is one Lord."* (Deuteronomy 6:4) David spoke of the Holy One in his prophecy about the Christ's death (Psalm 16:10). Despite the confusion this concept has generated over the years, belief in this doctrine is a fundamental cornerstone in our Christian Faith. Dennis DeHaan writing in an <u>Our Daily Bread</u> article gives us these challenging words about this theology, and I quote:

> The idea of the One God in three Persons has long been baffling to the human mind. But to reject it has given rise to cults and many false teachings. The problem is not the doctrine itself but our inability to understand it. It is said that Saint Augustine, the famous early church theologian, was walking on the shore of the ocean one day pondering the mystery of the trinity. He came upon a little boy who was playing with a seashell. The youngster would scoop a hole in the sand, then go down to the waves and get his shell full of water and pour it into the hole he had made. Augustine said, "What are you doing, my little fellow?" The boy replied, "I am going to pour the sea into that hole." "Ah," said Augustine. "That is what I am trying to do. Standing at the ocean of infinity, I have attempted to grasp it with my finite mind." The trinity does not fit the framework of common logic, nor can it be fully analyzed by the microscope of man's intellect. But this is no reason to say it is the invention of theologians. To declare that the One and only God has made Himself known as Father, Son, and Holy Spirit, three distinct, not separate, persons, is simply an attempt to define what the Scriptures teach. (John 10:29–30 and Acts 5:3–4) But to commit our lives to this triune God is to begin to see with the eye of faith His greatness as our Creator, Redeemer, and Sustainer. And doesn't it make sense that the One we worship, and to whom we entrust our lives, should be vastly greater than our limited ability to understand Him? Father, Son, and Holy Spirit, O thou blessed trinity: One in essence yet three Persons, thou art God, and we worship Thee. The idea of a triune God staggers the mind, but to know Him satisfies the heart!

Remember what Jesus said according to John 10:20: *"I and my Father are One."* And then there is what Paul wrote to the young man Timothy: *"Now unto the King eternal, immortal, invisible, the only wise God, be honour and glory forever and ever, Amen!"* (I Timothy 1:17) My attention was drawn to this verse, seeing I learned this verse in a chorus when I was just a lad, because of the desire of some in this world to unite all the "gods" because a multitude of "gods" is so much better than the belief of a single, triune God. This isn't a new philosophy in the world, but this is certainly a new belief in the United States of America where Christianity has been the dominate faith since our beginning. Christian America is how I have always seen our land, but years ago on a visit to Washington D.C. I came face to face with the changing America. As I walked through the National Cathedral, I met a tour guide and asked: "What denomination is this church?" He replied, "Episcopal, but all faiths worship here, and all "gods" are honored here." I was shocked. I was surprised. I was stunned. I didn't know my nation had slipped into the worship of all and that no longer was One God a part of our national religion. As my family and I walked around Washington D.C., we saw churches, chapels, and cathedrals to all the known and unknown gods of many nations. By the time our tour was over I felt like climbing the steps to the Capital building and shout at the top of my lungs: "Hear, O America: the Lord our God is one Lord." That Jesus is God Himself, the only God, the only Saviour, it is Him that we should worship and serve!

Monos is the Greek word for "only." The context of the verse I have already shared speaks of the solitariness of God, that He alone is God. This word is as much a part of the attributes of God as the big three: omnipotent, omnipresent, and omniscient. Consider, if you will, these New Testament verses; ponder on them until "only" is a part of your vocabulary. Should it be so hard if the demons and devils believe? *"Thou believeth that there is one God; thou doest well: the devils also believe, and tremble."* (James 2:19)

1. John 5:44: *"How can ye believe, which receive honour one of another and seek not the honour that cometh from God **only**!"*
2. John 17:3: *"And this is life eternal, that they might know the **only** true God, and Jesus Christ whom Thou has sent!"*
3. Romans 16:27: *"To the **only** wise God, be glory through Jesus Christ forever! Amen."*
4. I Timothy 6:15: *"Which in His times He shall shew, who is the blessed and **Only** Potentate, the King of kings, and Lord of lords!"*

We stand in a day when we must hear again Jude's admonition: *"And exhort you that ye should earnestly contend for the faith which was once delivered unto the saints. For there are certain men crept in unawares who were before of old ordained to this condemnation, ungodly men, turning the grace of God into lasciviousness, and denying the **ONLY** Lord God, and our Lord Jesus Christ."* (Jude 3–4) Accommodation is running wild in Christian circles today under the disguise of unity and love, but this one thing we can't accommodate or compromise on, Jesus Christ is God Himself and God alone!

Jude 25: *"To the Only wise God our Saviour, be glory and majesty, dominion and power…"*

103.

ZILTHAI: SHADOW

I Chronicles 12:20: *"As he went to Ziklag, there fell to him of Manasseh, Adnah, Jozabad, and Jediael, and Michael, and Jozabad, and Elihu, and **ZILTHAI**, captains of the thousands that were of Manasseh."*

IT TOOK ONE HUNDRED and three names for David's "mighty men" to finally stump me. This last amazing soldier of the Manasseh Band presented me with a difficult task. In Young's Analytical Concordance to the Bible, where I have been getting my information for the meaning of these strange Hebrew names, I found that Young's gives no meaning for Zilthai. With no meaning I had no way of writing about this warrior because, as with most of his comrades, all we have is a name. I had come this far, and I wasn't going to leave out a name that David put on this list so I looked a bit deeper. It was then I discovered in the Revised Standard Version of the Bible a different spelling for Zilthai: Zillethai. In another book on the "Who's Who of the Bible," I learned that the second spelling means "shadow or protection." Immediately I recalled this verse in the Book of the Psalms: **"He that dwelleth in the secret place of the Most High shall abide under the 'shadow' of the Almighty."** (Psalm 91:1) And in Isaiah 32:2 I read: *"And a man shall be as a hiding place from the wind, and a convert from the tempest; as rivers of water in a dry place, as **the 'shadow' of a great rock in a weary land**."* According to the Apostle Paul, Christ was that Rock (I Corinthians 10:4), and, if so, then it is Jesus' shadow that overshadows us with protection.

The Psalmist writes: *"You are my hiding place; you will protect me from trouble and surround me with songs of deliverance."* (Psalm 32:7)

I believe another man that saw this symbol of the Christ was Vernon Charlesworth, an English pastor, and at one time the headmaster of the Charles Spurgeon Stockwell Orphanage. It was this man who gave to the Church this beloved hymn, <u>A Shelter in the Time of Storm</u>:

> The Lord's our Rock, in Him we hide;
> A shelter in the time of storm.
> Secure whatever ill betide;
> A shelter in the time of storm.
> A shade by day, defense by night;
> A shelter in the time of storm.
> No fears alarm, no foes affright;
> A shelter in the time of storm.
> The raging storms may round us beat:
> A shelter in the time of storm.
> We'll never leave our safe retreat;
> A shelter in the time of storm.
> O Rock divine, O refuge dear;
> A shelter in the time of storm.
> Be thou our helper ever near;
> A shelter in the time of storm.
> O, Jesus is a Rock in a weary land,
> A weary land, a weary land.
> O, Jesus is a Rock in a weary land,
> A shelter in the time of storm!

With Ira Sankey's music, this gospel hymn has been used around the world as a constant source of encouragement to countless millions; a comfort to the weary saint in the midst of a terrible storm, the believer looking for a shadow in a weary land, and for over a hundred years a song of hope to the Church.

Over the last six weeks my family and I have been entertaining a family of house finches. While away on vacation, the finch family decided that the best place to build their nest and raise their young was in my wife's hanging plant on our front porch. When we returned from a trip to visit my brother in Pennsylvania, we discovered a small nest tucked away in the stems of a red/white plant with four light blue eggs in it. Each day we would check their progress. Finally, the four eggs hatched, and yesterday the final two birds flew away leaving an empty nest. We will miss them. The constant flying in and out to warm and feed their young was exciting. The continual chirping of mother and father as they tried to talk their youngsters into flight was educational. Their crying calls to keep away was thrilling as they protected their babies, but day after day as I watched this miracle of nature unfold I was reminded of my God's protecting shadow. *"And my hand hath found a nest the riches of the people: and as one gathereth eggs that are left, have I gathered all the earth; and there was none that moved the wing, or opened the mouth, or peeped!"* (Isaiah 10:14), a simple lesson from nature that will help us understand God's divine hand of protection on His creation and on us.

Did you know God's law even protects a house finch? Moses commanded with God's approval: *"If a bird's nest chance to be before thee in the way, in any tree, or on the ground* [or in a hanging plant] *whether they be young ones, or eggs, thou shalt not take the dam with the young; but thou shalt in any wise let the dam go, and take the young to thee that it may be well with thee, and thou mayest prolong thy days."* (Deuteronomy 22:6–7) In the Book of Isaiah, the nest and the hand of God are talked about in the same way. This reminded me of the verses of John when he explained the protection of God's children this way: **"And I gave unto them eternal life; and they shall never perish, neither shall any man pluck them out of my hand. My Father, which gave them to me, is greater than all; and no man is able to pluck them out of my Father's hand."** (John 10:28–29) The hand of Jesus and the hand of God are the nest in which we need to nestle. It is in the shadow of the hands of God that we have what I love to call "double security" because can there be any greater protection in the universe than being in the hands of God? Jeremiah once wrote: *"O ye that dwell in Moab, leave the cities, and dwell in the Rock, and be like the dove that maketh her nest in the sides of the hole's mouth."* (Jeremiah 48:28) Christ is our Rock and not only does the Rock cast a shadow over us, it gives us a hole to nestle in and that hole is formed by the hands of God.

In 2010, I had the privilege to go to Israel. While I was there I learned a very valuable lesson when traveling through a sunny land and that lesson was this: any shade, any shadow is better than no shade or shadow. To get out from under the direct rays of the sun was needful. When we traveled through the deserts of southern Israel, we learned that the shadow of a single tree could bring relief to a whole group of weary and hot tourists. It was then I heard for the first time the meaning of the "cloud" that traveled with the children of Israel from Egypt to Canaan (Exodus 13:2–22). Then our guide reminded us of Psalm 121:5–6: *"The Lord is thy keeper; the Lord is thy shade upon thy right hand. The sun shall not smite thee by day, nor the moon by night."* People need all kinds of protection, and our God is ready to protect even with a shadow.

ZILTHAI: SHADOW

Are you today abiding under the protection of the shadow of God? Are you resting today in the protection of the nest formed by the hands of God? Are you building your life in the Rock and on the Rock? (I Corinthians 3:11) If you are a follower of Christ, than you can be assured that His long shadow is your constant covering, and in His hands is a nesting place for you to rest. Sometimes, when you can't find anything to write about, it is nice when you persevere until you discover something about your God you never knew about. We serve an awesome God whose ways are still being found out. In the simple concept of "a shadow of protection" we have discovered another wonderful attribute of our Lord and Savior Jesus Christ: He is our shade and shadow, our nest and rest, our Rock and Refuge, our protection from every ill and harm. Isn't it about time that you start living under His shadow of protection?

Job 29:18: *"Then I said, I shall die in my nest, and I shall multiply my days as the sand!"*

104.

JEHOIADA: THE LORD KNOWS

I Chronicles 12:27: *"And **JEHOIADA** was the leader of the Aaronites, and with him three thousand and seven hundred."*

WE HAVE COME TO the final division in I Chronicles 12. In the first twenty-two verses
42 of David's "mighty men" are named, but in the last eighteen verses David only names two. This section has more to do with numbers than members, and the place they came to him: *"And these are the numbers of bands that were ready armed to the war, and came to David to Hebron, to turn the kingdom of Saul to him, according to the Word of the Lord."* (I Chronicles 12:23) Of the tribe of Judah came 6,800 (I Chronicles 12:24), of the tribe of Simeon came 7,100 (I Chronicles 12:25), of the tribe of Levi came 4,600 (I Chronicles 12:26), of the tribe of Benjamin came 3,000 (I Chronicles 12:29), of the tribe of Ephraim came 20,800 (I Chronicles 12:30), of the half tribe of Manasseh came 18,000 (I Chronicles 12:31), of the tribe of Issachar came 200 leaders and troops (I Chronicles 12:32), of the tribe of Zebulun came 50,000 (I Chronicles 12:33), of the tribe of Naphtali came 38,000 (I Chronicles 12:34), of the tribe of Dan came 28,600 (I Chronicles 12:35), of the tribe of Asher came 40,000 (I Chronicles 12:36), and from the three tribes of Reuben, Gad, and Manasseh came 120,000 (I Chronicles 12:37). I believe in this way David was saying each of his soldiers was important to him, but he coveted the men that led the way. The final two men on David's "mighty men" list came from the tribe of Levi, but in particular from the house of Aaron, the first High Priest.

If you know your history of the sons of Jacob, his son Levi was his third son (Genesis 29:34), and it was out of that family the priests of Israel would come (Exodus 6:16). But out of those Levites, the high priests would come from the line of Aaron (Exodus 6:20). It was the family of Aaron himself that Jehoiada came and when he came, he brought 3,700 others with him, and he was their leader. The tribe of Levi wasn't known for its fighting ability, but I have come to believe that David had warrior-priests in his army who not only took care of the spiritual needs of the army, but fought as well. Today we might call these men, combat chaplains. These were the men that after David had established his first capital in Hebron (II Samuel 5), it was time to join David. The first "few" men that joined David were trying to establish David's claim to the throne of Israel and were eventually joined by the masses (see numbers above) and among them were the Levites and in particular the Aaronites and Jehoiada. Again, we only have his name, Jehoiada, but I believe in him being listed in this "mighty man" chapter, Jehoiada must be added to our complete list. As with so many others, it is the meaning of his name that makes me think of this connection to our "warrior-priest" (compare Hebrews 2:10 and Hebrews 3:1) and the truth of **"the Lord knows,"** or the only wise God.

It was the Apostle Paul who perhaps spoke of this concept best when writing to his young disciple Timothy these words: *"Now unto the king eternal, immortal, invisible, the only wise God, be honour and glory forever, and ever. Amen."* (I Timothy 1:17) Jude, the brother of Jesus, would also end his short epistle with the same thought: *"To the only wise God our Saviour, be glory and majesty, dominion and power, both now and ever. Amen."* (Jude 25) Highlighting and underlining the word "wise" in these two verses, we have the connection between the Almighty God and Jesus, our Jehoiada. What doesn't the Lord know and what didn't Jesus know when He came to earth? In Him dwelt the fullness of the Godhead bodily (Colossians 1:19, 2:9) and that included all wisdom and all knowledge. Jesus was talking of this aspect of His life when He said: **"The queen of the south shall rise up in judgment with this generation, and shall condemn it; for she came from the uttermost parts of the earth to hear the Wisdom of Solomon; and behold, a greater than Solomon is here!"** (Matthew 12:42) Remember, Jesus was saying this to a group of people who knew this about their great king Solomon: *"Behold, I have done according to thy words: lo, I have given thee a wise and an understanding heart; so that there was none like thee."* (I Kings 3:12) Not like any other normal human being, but nobody would ever be compared to the Christ because those around Jesus thought he was a mere man (Matthew 12:38). These were the scribes and Pharisees who had confronted Jesus as a boy in the Temple *"and all heard Him were astonished at His understanding and answers."* (Luke 2:47) Why were they surprised?

Paul defines this aspect of Christ's nature in these words: ***"...and of Christ; to whom are hid all the treasures of wisdom and knowledge..."*** (Colossians 2:2–3). Note the word "all;" nothing not known by Him, nor nothing not understood by Him. I like the way M. R. DeHaan, the founder of the Radio Bible Class and the original publisher of the Our Daily Bread, writes on this topic:

> There is a well-known proverb which, like most of this world's philosophies, is just not true. It is as follows: "where ignorance is bliss, tis folly to be wise!" What a lot of rubbish! It's a lie! Apply this silly reasoning to a man sleeping in a burning house, or a man suffering from cancer, or a sinner going to Hell because he is ignorant of God's way of salvation. Ignorance may give you a false sense of security, but see what one may lose. We hear the saying: "what a man doesn't know won't hurt him!" Is that true? Ask the fellow who sat down on a "yellow-jacket" nest (stinging insect) on the beach, or the victim in the hospital who didn't know the gun was loaded? How much people lose through ignorance? You have probably heard of the old lady who was crossing the ocean on a ticket her son had bought for her. She prepared a very large lunch to eat on the long journey. Toward the end of the voyage the milk was sour, the bread was dry, the butter was rancid, and the fruit was decayed. And then-to top it off, just before landing she found out that her ticket included all first-class meals at the captain's table! Due to ignorance she had starved herself!

The all-wise One is able to make us wise unto salvation. The all-wise One is able to warn us of the pitfalls in our pathway. The all-wise One is able to instruct us and teach us how to live. There is only one way to be wise and that is to know the only wise God. The wisdom of this world is foolishness compared to the wisdom of God (I Corinthians 1:19–21). The Good News is the "wisdom" of God (I Corinthians 1:30), and our Lord and Savior Jesus Christ came down from heaven to give us that wisdom (James 3:17–18). As we have worked our way through this lengthy list of "mighty men," we have come to a better understanding and knowledge of just who the Captain of our salvation really is, and we have added "wise" and "wisdom" to our list of wonderful characteristics and attributes. As we near the end of this exploration, we haven't come as yet to the depth of the wisdom of God, and to the One that brought that wisdom to us. So, we must ask again before our asking in this book is over. Do you know the wisdom of God? Are you seeking to understand His wisdom versus the false wisdom of the World? Only when you "know" Him will you "know" God!

Romans 16:27: *"To God only wise, be glory through Jesus Christ forever. Amen."*

105.

ZADOK: RIGHTEOUS

I Chronicles 12:28: *"And **ZADOK**, a young man mighty in valour, and of his father's house twenty-two captains."*

OFTEN BECAUSE THE BIBLE was never complied in chronological order, we miss some wonderful truths in Scripture. A case in point is the young warrior Zadok, the "mighty man" of our last devotional on David's "mighty men." We have come to the last, and, just like the first, I have come to believe the last is as significant, number one hundred and five and the last name given in David's final chapter on his "mighty men." And David ends with these simple words: **"...And Zadok, a young man mighty in valor..."**

In Biblical order, Zadok is first mentioned in II Samuel 8:17 as one of David's personal priests, a highly respected political and religious leader in David's newly established kingdom. But I have come to believe in my research on this young man that the roots of Zadok's rise to prominence goes back when David's capital was at Hebron (I Chronicles 12:23) and not in Jerusalem. According to II Samuel 5:4-5 David ruled in Hebron for seven and a half years and in Jerusalem for thirty-three years. We often forget that once King Saul was dead, it didn't mean that everything went well for David. He had to fight a bloody civil war (II Samuel 3:1) before he gained the trust of all Israel so during those years David used Hebron as his headquarters, and it was there that all of Israel finally rallied to him (I Chronicles 12:23-40). Once he had the tribe's support, David decided to establish a new capital in the middle of the country to unite the country, much like our forefathers did when the thirteen colonies made a new capital in Washington D. C. For David it was the Jebusite citadel of Jerusalem.

Put in the context of the tribe of Levi, we know that Zadok was from the priestly tribe, and though some think we are talking about two different Zadoks, I feel it is the same man, young in I Chronicles 12 and older in II Samuel 8. The Levites were not known for their fighting, but I feel the youthful Zadok rose to the occasion and joined David's Band and fought (a young man mighty in valor) to gain the kingdom for David. One of our better known presidents, Andrew Jackson, once said: **"Every good citizen makes his country's honor his own, and cherishes it not only as precious but as sacred. He is willing to risk his life in its defense and is conscious that he gains protection while he gives it."** With perhaps his mentor Jehoiada (I Chronicles 12:27), Zadok was the next generation of the "army chaplain," but when his war was over he, like so many after him, laid down the sword for the scroll!

Eventually, Zadok would jointly preside over David's sanctuary in Jerusalem with another priest, Abiathar, a man who joined David's "mighty men" even earlier. Abiathar came to David after the slaughter of his family in Nob (I Samuel 22:19–23). I have come to believe Abiathar was David's first personal priest and was the spiritual leader during the many years of wandering, exile, and a fugitive from King Saul. But it was Zadok who, during the Absalom rebellion, was ready to leave Jerusalem with the ark (II Samuel 15:24), but David sent him back to be an informant in the midst of the Absalom government (II Samuel 15:27–29). So the once faithful soldier that became a faithful servant of God was now a faithful spy for David. Each responsibility required Zadok to have great courage and loyalty of which the "righteous" Zadok seemed to have plenty of! I have come to believe that Zadok was one of those truly righteous men who rose to the occasion no matter what occasion and was found not only faithful to his king, but he was also found faithful and righteous before his eternal King.

How we need such courage in the Church of God today. Those who like Stephen of old gave a courageous testimony to a hostile Sanhedrin, the same Sanhedrin that had called for the death of Jesus, and despite the danger, proclaimed the Word of the Lord (Acts 6:15). How we need the courage of Obadiah, the overseer of the house of Ahab and Jezebel, who hid and fed the Lord's servants in a wicked and dangerous age, an age when the government was killing God's men (I Kings 18:4). Courage like Nehemiah had and displayed when he refused to flee to the Temple for refuge when threatened by his enemies, Sanballat, Tobiah, and Geshem (Nehemiah 6:11). What we need also is the courage of Christ's secret disciples, Joseph and Nicodemus, who came to get Jesus' body off the tree while the other disciples of Jesus hid. I like the way the Weymouth translation puts it: **"...the secret disciples summoned up courage..."** (Mark 15:43). To claim Jesus when He is least popular is true courage. It doesn't take much courage to be a follower of Christ when everybody is following Christ. Zadok showed himself courageous not only on the battlefield, but the home field as well. Through a variety of situations and circumstances, Zadok always seemed to have the bravery and loyalty, no matter the changing times. That is why I believe Zadok was named correctly, righteous, because he showed himself righteous in every Bible story he is found.

Zadok's last great accomplishment, called to Biblical fame, was in David final hours when a rivalry between two of David's sons threatened to split the nation in half. Zadok sided with Solomon, God's choice, while Abiathar sided with Adonijah, man's choice, because Adonijah was the oldest son, a tradition sometimes applied, but a rule God is not obligated to follow. God always chooses the best man, not the first man; and this was true in the case of Isaac over Ishmael, Jacob over Esau, and Judah over Reuben. Zadok helped Solomon gain the throne just like he helped his father David gain the throne. After the political struggle was over, Abiathar was forced to retire and Zadok alone became the top spiritual leader in the nation (I Kings 2:35). Loyalty is another wonderful attribute of the righteous that is sorely lacking in the Church of God today. How we need men like Shadrach, Meshach, and Abednego who were loyal enough to their God to be willing to lay down their lives rather than be disloyal and bow down to another god (Daniel 3:1-12). Daniel, the great Hebrew prophet of Babylon, was also willing to remain loyal to His God in the area of prayer even when the national law forbid such praying (Daniel 6:10). (Do we not have such a law in our land today when we say kids can't pray in school?) If there is an area in the Church where loyalty has been lost, it is in the area of the prayer meeting. How many go to the prayer meeting anymore? How many are loyal to Paul's instruction to **"...pray without ceasing..."** (I Thessalonians 5:17)? What has happened to the faithful, righteous prayer warriors?

We need more like Zadok and Joshua who challenged Israel: **"Choose you this day whom ye will serve!"** (Joshua 24:15) Where does our loyalty and courage lie? There is only one source for such courage and loyalty and that is from the righteousness of God. This is the connection I make in the life of Zadok and the life of our Lord and Savior Jesus Christ: ***"…the righteousness of God…"*** (I Corinthians 1:30). A man once said: "You can buy a man's time…but you cannot buy enthusiasm, loyalty, or devotion of heart, mind, or soul. You have to earn these things." I believe Zadok was one that earned these things.

Joshua 1:6: "…be strong and of a good courage…"

POSTLUDE

THE MIGHTY MEN OF THE MIGHTY MAN

So there you have it; one hundred and five portraits of David's top warriors, the characteristics mostly seen in the meaning of their names and the amazing parallels to the Captain of our Salvation (Hebrews 2:10), our Lord and Savior Jesus Christ. I started this exploration by taking a look at the broad characteristics of the man that called, inspired, and drew these "mighty men" to his side, David. I would like to end this Biblical project by giving you some general qualities of these men as a group, and I hope you will see that these ought to be the virtues of every soldier of Jesus Christ (II Timothy 2:3–4).

First, we must highlight once again their BOSS. David was the only common factor I could find in their mention in the Scriptural text. David was the glue that held them together, kept their ranks unified, in good times and bad times. So it must be with us as soldiers of Christ. Despite our different cultural backgrounds, our various racial differences, and our diverse national interests, we ought to be one in Christ, following one leader, our one head (Ephesians 1:22–23). David's "mighty men" came from different countries, different towns, and different circumstances and situations, but they found in David a common cause. They followed David to victory after victory as we can follow our Captain (I Corinthians 15:57 and II Corinthians 2:14) to the ultimate triumph.

Second, we must highlight their BEGINNING. As you know by now, I believe this amazing relationship between David and his "mighty men" all began with this verse in the Book of I Samuel: *"And every one that was in distress, and every one that was in debt, and every one that was discontented, gathered themselves unto him* [David]; *and he became*

DAVID'S MIGHTY MEN

a captain over them: and there were with him about four hundred men." (I Samuel 22:2) It was from this first group of followers that David would create and command an army of a million and more. Distressed, in debt, discontented, this doesn't sound like the right material to develop "mighty men." The key isn't the clay, but the hands of the master, and so it is with us and Christ. Did not we come to Christ in distress over our sins (Romans 3:23), in debt to the Almighty over our transgressions, and in discontent over our iniquities? We found in Christ a caring, compassionate (Matthew 9:36), and forgiving Captain. As David changed his "mighty men," so, too, did Christ change us (II Corinthians 5:17). No wonder these men followed David, and no wonder we follow Christ!

Third, we must highlight their BRAVERY. Was there ever a collection of soldiers, courageous warriors, assembled under one flag, uncommon valor from just common men? From taking on 800 enemy soldier's singlehandedly to fighting through an entrenched foe just to get a cup of water for their commander, the exploits of these men became legendary. Yet, when I read in the history of the history of the Church of men like Martin Luther and John Huss, I read of men with no less courage; valiant men fighting in some respects a more difficult battle (Ephesians 6:12). David Livingstone singlehandedly taking on the wickedness of an entire continent is now the folklore of our faith. The bravery of Jim Elliot and his brethren as they took the Auca arrows without firing or fighting back is a valor of the highest order in my opinion. Like David, Christ has been able to give to His men and women a brave heart! (II Timothy 1:7)

Fourth, we must highlight their BROTHERHOOD. I find very little internal fighting recorded between these "mighty men." I believe as they developed a love for their commander, they formed a love for each other. A battlefield bond is not unusual in a combat situation. Lifelong friendships and fellowships have been forged in the heat of battle. Back to back, outnumbered, surrounded, these "mighty men" learned to depend on each other and only such events created an unbreakable bond, a brotherhood unmatched. Their loyalty to each other, their charity for each other, and their unity can only be explained by a battle-tested brotherhood. When will the Church of God realize that not only did Christ unite us as a body (Ephesians 1), a bride (Ephesians 5), a building (Ephesians 2), but also as a brotherhood (I Peter 2:17)?

Lastly, we must underline their BATTALIONS. As you have noticed in this study, I ended with a chapter that few have added to their research. Certainly the "mighty men" are listed and numbered in II Samuel 23 and

POSTLUDE

I Chronicles 11, but I have in my opinion discovered the best of material in I Chronicles 12. Not only were we able to add to the list we gleaned from the other two chapters, but we now have a wealth of information about the various groups in I Chronicles 12. I will give credit where credit is due, and tell you, if it were not for a pastor friend of mine from Pennsylvania, Dave Natalie, I would probably have stopped my story of David's "mighty men" in I Chronicles 11. On a fishing trip together in the North Maine Woods, we were talking about spiritual things, and he asked if I had ever noticed the wonderful spiritual lessons found in I Chronicles 12. I had to confess that I hadn't, but when I got home from that trout fishing trip I took a careful look and found some amazing things about these soldiers of David. As we have revealed, few names are shared in this chapter, but their characteristics are underlined by some insightful phrases about them. My favorite is: *"…the mighty men, helpers of the war…"* (I Chronicles 12:1). As I have already shared one of the most neglected spiritual gifts is the gift of *"…helps…"* (I Corinthians 12:28). I would now like to finish this study by highlighting twelve fantastic virtues worthy of a "mighty man," whether in David's army or in the Lord's army:

1. They were AMBIDEXTROUS: **"…and could use both the right hand and the left…"** (I Chronicles 12:2). Great dexterity in shooting and slinging was a virtue of the "mighty men" from the battalion from the tribe of Benjamin. Could I ask? What has happened to balance in the believer today? It seems that we are either right or left. We live in a world that has no balance. Lukewarmness (Revelation 3:16–17) has swept over the Church, and we have forgotten just how valuable an ambidextrous soldier can be: *"Let your moderation be known unto all men. The Lord is at hand."* (Philippians 4:5) How one sided have you become?

2. They were AVAILABLE: **"…and men of war fit for the battle…"** (I Chronicles 12:8). I take this phrase to mean that these men were prepared, conditioned, ready, and available to fight at a moment's notice. We have forgotten in the modern Church that when we are not in the battle, we are preparing for the battle! (II Timothy 2:17, 3:17) Are you available? Are you ready and fit for any fight? Most Christian soldiers today can't even find their sword (Ephesians 6:17-the Word) let alone able to use it in a confrontation, in a spiritual battle.

3. They were AGILE: *"...whose faces were like the faces of lions, and were as swift as the roes upon the mountains..."* (I Chronicles 12:8). These men had a fierce, lion-like countenance (beards?) and a great agility in the pursuit of the enemy. They were quick on their feet, not to flee, but to fight. Part of being Christ-like is to be lion-like (Revelation 5:5); God would have us quick in the struggle, not sluggish in the battle. Remember how quick Jesus was to quote Scripture in his fight with the devil in the wilderness temptation as He quoted verse after verse to block Satan's attacks. We need this kind of agility with the Bible according to I Peter 3:15: *"...and be ready always to give an answer to every man that asketh you a reason of the hope that is in you with meekness and fear!"*

4. They were AUDACIOUS: *"...for they were all mighty men of valour..."* (I Chronicles 12:21). I have come to believe that there is a difference between being brave and being bold. These men were not only courageous, they were daring. They would take risks. I have a missionary friend, Doretta Dail, a mighty woman of valour in my opinion who literally rode her bike into the interior of Nigeria, West Africa, in the early 1950s, all alone! She went where most men feared to go and established the Benue Evangelical Mission. She has overcome numerous tropical diseases, cancer, and pneumonia several times to proclaim God's Love in the bush to people who had never heard. The Church needs brave soldiers, but it also needs bold soldier. Soldiers that are willing to take daring spiritual chances to spread the Gospel in dangerous places in the world (Hebrews 11:34). I have had the honor of meeting such people today, especially in India.

5. They were ARMED: *"...that were ready armed to the war..."* (I Chronicles 12:23). These "mighty men" were ready to fight because their weapons were ready to fight. This sounds like Paul's challenge to the Christians in Corinth (II Corinthians 10:4). We are given in Ephesians 6:10–18 a list of our weapons, both offensive and defensive, but these weapons are only useful if we arm ourselves every day with them (II Timothy 2:4). What good is the armor if is still in the armory? What good is the sword if it is still in the sheath?

6. They were AFFLUENT: *"...famous throughout the house of their fathers..."* (I Chronicles 12:30). Literally this phrase is saying "men of names." Proverbs 22:1 is still true today: *"A good name is rather*

to be chosen than great riches..." History is full of men and women who made a name for themselves who were also Christians. Famous kings and queens, famous generals and military men, famous businessmen, politicians, and scientists and educators. Just because I Corinthians 1:26 speaks of not many wise, mighty, or noble doesn't mean there wasn't any! It is not wrong to be a household name, if, when your name is mentioned, it makes people think of Jesus. Remember what Paul said in I Corinthians 11:1.

7. They were APPOINTED: **"...which were expressed by name, to come and make David king..."** (I Chronicles 12:31). Throughout our study we have referred back again and again to the truth that these were the men that helped David attain to the kingdom (I Chronicles 11:10). It was their calling, their appointment, and so it is for us to spread the news that one day the Lord Jesus will be Lord of lords and King of kings (I Timothy 6:15).

8. They were ACUTE: **"...which were men that had an understanding of the times..."** (I Chronicles 12:23). Jewish scholars suggest that the meaning of this phrase is that these men of Issachar were knowledgeable in astronomical truth and physical science. These were David's engineers, perhaps, David's meteorologists. Men who can read the skies and forecast the weather and build powerful instruments of war, like siege weapons, are valuable. And then there is the idea of the "times." A good soldier of Jesus Christ needs to be able to understand *"the signs of the times"* (Romans 13:11–13).

9. They were ASTUTE: **"...to know what Israel ought to do..."** (I Chronicles 12:32). And what Israel needed to do is make David king. I like this definition of them also: *"All these men of war, that keep rank, came with a perfect heart to Hebron, to make David king over all Israel: and all the rest also of Israel were of one heart to make David king."* (I Chronicles 12:38) One purpose, one plan, one accord, is a wonderful characteristic, and so should we be in Christ (Philippians 2:1–2). We are called to unity, but we are called to know what we ought to do in our life, living, and lifestyle (I Timothy 4:12). The Bible gives us the advantage simply to "know," but we have to act on that knowledge as well.

10. They were ABLE: **"...expert in war, with all instruments of war..."** (I Chronicles 12:33). Experts! Specialists! The modern military

term is "ace!" Literally, the old Hebrew reads: *"...to set the battle in array..."* These "mighty men" not only led the way, started the assault, but planned the strategy and set forth the techniques for the battlefield. *"Experts in war"* is also mentioned in I Chronicles 12:35, 36. To me, this speaks more of the ability of being out front, to lead the way. Paul boldly proclaimed: *"Be ye followers of me, even as I also am of Christ!"* (I Corinthians 11:1) Most of us like to follow, but "mighty men" have the ability and are able to lead from the front.

11. They were ARRANGED: *"...keep rank..."* (I Chronicles 12:33, 38). As I pondered the orderliness of these "mighty men," I thought of a couple of things that they were and we should be: disciplined (II Timothy 1:7) and orderly (I Corinthians 14:40). These were men who knew their place in the line as we should know our place in the body of Christ (I Corinthians 12:14–20). They were not privates that wanted to be generals, or generals who wanted to be privates. You might be surprised to know how many soldiers of Christ think they are lower in the ranks than they are, but none of us are surprised by those who think themselves higher in the ranks than they are.

12. They were AGREED: ***"...they were not of double heart..."*** (I Chronicles 12:33). As we have seen so often in this book, they were perfect in their hearts concerning their purpose. No double-minded men in this group of "mighty men" (James 1:8). The Bible is clear that we, too, must be agreeable and agree on the purpose and cause of Christ (Ephesians 4:4).

Could I close out this exploration of the characteristics of "mighty men" of God with these words from the great English preacher Charles Spurgeon:

> The Lord, He it is that doth go before thee; He will be with thee, He will not fail thee, neither forsake thee; fear not neither be dismayed. (Deuteronomy 31:8) In the presence of a great work or a great warfare, here is a text which should help us to buckle on our harness. If Jehovah Himself goes before us, it must be safe to follow. Who can obstruct our progress if the Lord Himself is in the van? Come, brother soldiers, let us make a prompt advance! Why do we hesitate to pass on to victory? Nor is the Lord before us only; He is with us. Above, beneath, around, within is the omnipotent, omnipresent One. In all time, even to eternity. He will be with us even as He has been. How this should nerve our arm! Dash at it boldly, ye soldiers of the Cross,

POSTLUDE

for the Lord of hosts is with us! Let us not fear nor be dismayed; for the Lord of hosts will go down to battle with us, will bear the blunt of the fight, and give us the victory!

Fight on O mighty man!
Barry Blackstone
August 22, 2025

www.ingramcontent.com/pod-product-compliance
Lightning Source LLC
Chambersburg PA
CBHW071225290426
44108CB00013B/1289